Studies of the Max Planck Institute Luxembourg for
International, European and Regulatory Procedural Law

edited by
Prof. Dr. Dres. h.c. Burkhard Hess
Prof. Dr. Hélène Ruiz Fabri

Volume 10

Burkhard Hess/Paul Oberhammer/Stefania Bariatti
Christian Koller/Björn Laukemann/Marta Requejo Isidro
Francesca Clara Villata (eds.)

# The Implementation of the New Insolvency Regulation

Improving Cooperation and Mutual Trust

**The Deutsche Nationalbibliothek** lists this publication in the
Deutsche Nationalbibliografie; detailed bibliographic data
are available on the Internet at http://dnb.d-nb.de

ISBN:   HB (Nomos)         978-3-8487-4448-0
        ePDF (Nomos)       978-3-8452-8697-6


**British Library Cataloguing-in-Publication Data**
A catalogue record for this book is available from the British Library.

ISBN:   HB (Hart)          978-1-5099-2131-7


**Library of Congress Cataloging-in-Publication Data**
Hess, Burkhard / Oberhammer, Paul / Bariatti, Stefania / Koller, Christian /
Laukemann, Björn / Requejo Isidro, Marta / Villata, Francesca Clara
The Implementation of the New Insolvency Regulation
Improving Cooperation and Mutual Trust
Burkhard Hess / Paul Oberhammer / Stefania Bariatti / Christian Koller /
Björn Laukemann/ Marta Requejo Isidro / Francesca Clara Villata (eds.)
320 p.
Includes bibliographic references.

ISBN    978-1-5099-2131-7     (hardcover Hart)


1st Edition 2017
© Nomos Verlagsgesellschaft, Baden-Baden, Germany 2017. Printed and bound in Germany.

# Preface

This book presents the results of a Study on 'The Implementation of the New Insolvency Regulation – Improving Cooperation and Mutual Trust'. Supported by the European Commission under the Specific Programme 'Civil Justice',[1] this Study is a follow-up research project to the Heidelberg-Luxembourg-Vienna Report.[2] It pursues a two-fold objective: first, to analyse the application of the Regulation's reformed – and sometimes innovative – rules in practice, and, second, to examine and implement the new procedures and changes to national insolvency law. This book constitutes a revised version of the final report that was sent to the Commission in January 2017.

Apart from the core Study, the book contains reports of distinguished insolvency academics and practitioners supporting the project teams as external experts. We therefore would like to express our gratitude to Professor *Reinhard Bork* (University of Hamburg), Avv. *Giorgio Corno* (Milan), Professor *Renato Mangano* (University of Palermo), Professor *Irit Mevorach* (University of Nottingham), Professor *Christoph Thole* (University of Cologne), and Professor em. *Bob Wessels* (University of Leiden).

We are equally grateful to Dr. *Reinhard Dammann* (Paris), *Daniel F. Fritz* (Frankfurt), *Robert van Galen* (Amsterdam), Professor *Maria Chiara Malaguti* (Università Cattolica del Sacro Cuore, Rome), *Adrián Thery Martí* (Madrid), Professor *Gabriel Moss*, QC (London) and Professor *Christoph G. Paulus* (Humboldt University of Berlin) for contributing as panelists to the successful outcome of the conferences.

Moreover, we have to thank *Sandra Becker* (MPI Luxembourg) and Mag. *Kevin Labner* (Vienna) who greatly assisted in preparing the publication of the Study. Our particular gratitude is owed to Dr. *Robert Arts* (MPI Luxembourg). This book would not have been published without his unreserved and excellent support.

It was an honour and privilege to conduct the present Study as part of the European Commission's scientific programme. We hope that its results

---

1  JUST/2013/JCIV/AG/4679.
2  *Hess/Oberhammer/Pfeiffer* (eds), European Insolvency Law – Heidelberg-Luxembourg-Vienna Report, Munich 2014.

provide a valuable contribution to the ongoing dialogue between academia and legal practice on the application of the new European Insolvency Regulation.

*Luxembourg/Milan/Vienna*                                        The editors

# Table of Contents

# List of Abbreviations

| | |
|---|---|
| ad ex. | ad extra |
| a.F. | alte Fassung (old version) |
| Affd. | affirmed |
| ALI | American Law Institute |
| Am. Bankr. Inst. J. | American Bankruptcy Institute Journal |
| Anm. | Anmerkung (comment) |
| arg e | argumentum e |
| Art(s) | Article(s) |
| | |
| BCC | British Company Law Cases (British legal journal) |
| BGH | Bundesgerichtshof (German Federal Court of Justice) |
| Brook.J.Corp.Fi.&Com.L. | Brooklyn Journal of Corporate, Financial & Commercial Law (American legal journal) |
| Brook. J. Int'l. L. | Brooklyn Journal of International Law (American legal journal) |
| Bull. Joly Sociétés | Bulletin Joly Sociétés (French legal journal) |
| Bus. L. Int'l | Business Law International |
| BT-Drs. | Bundestagsdrucksache (official document of the German Bundestag) |
| BV | Besloten vennootschap met beperkte aansprakelijkheid (Dutch private limited liability company) |
| | |
| Cass. Sez. Un. | Corte Suprema di Cassazione Sezioni Unite (Italian Supreme Court grand chamber) |
| cf | confer (compare) |
| ch | chapter |
| CJEU | Court of Justice of the European Union |
| CLLS | City of London Law Society |
| CLJ | Cambridge Law Journal |
| CLP | Current legal Problems |

| | |
|---|---|
| CNAJMJ | French Conseil National des Administrateurs Judiciaires et des Mandataires Judiciaires |
| CoCo (guidelines) | European Communication and Cooperation Guidelines for Cross-border Insolvency |
| Colum. J. Transnat´l L. | Columbia Journal of Transnational Law (American legal journal) |
| COMI | centre of the debtor´s main interests |
| dAktG | German Stock Corporation Act (deutsches Aktiengesetz) |
| DAV | Deutscher Anwaltsverein |
| DB | Der Betrieb (German legal journal) |
| DZWIR | Deutsche Zeitschrift für Wirtschafts- und Insolvenzrecht (German legal journal) |
| EBDJ | Emory Bankruptcy Developments Journal (American legal journal) |
| EBOR | European Business Organization Law Review |
| EC | European Council |
| ECFR | European Company and Financial Law Review (German legal journal) |
| ECGI | European Corporate Governance Institute |
| ECJ | European Court of Justice |
| ECL | European Company Law |
| ecolex | Fachzeitschrift für Wirtschaftsrecht (Austrian legal journal) |
| ed(s) | editor(s) |
| edn | edition |
| e.g. | exempli gratia (for example) |
| EGInsO | German Introductory Act to the Insolvency Act (Einführungsgesetz Insolvenzordnung) |
| EIR 2000 | European Insolvency Regulation (Council Regulation (EC) No 1346/2000 of 29 May 2000 on Insolvency Proceedings) |
| EIR | European Insolvency Regulation (Regulation (EU) 2015/848 of 20 May 2015 on Insolvency Proceedings) |
| EJ | The Economic Journal |

| | |
|---|---|
| Emory Bankr. Dev. J. | Emory Bankruptcy Developments Journal |
| ERA Forum | Journal of the Academy of European Law |
| et al. | et alii (and others) |
| etc. | et cetera (and so forth) |
| EU | European Union |
| EuInsVO | Europäische Insolvenzverordnung (European Insolvency Regulation) |
| EUJudgeCo | European Judge Cooperation |
| EuZW | Europäische Zeitschrift für Wirtschaftsrecht (German legal journal) |
| EWHC (Ch) | High Court of Justice (High Court of England and Wales), Chancery Division |
| EWiR | Entscheidungen zum Wirtschaftsrecht (German legal journal) |
| EWS | Europäisches Wirtschafts- und Steuerrecht (German legal journal) |
| | |
| f, ff | following |
| fn | footnote (external) |
| Foro it. | Il Foro italiano |
| FS | Festschrift (German for Liber Amicorum) |
| | |
| GmbHG | Gesetz betreffend die Gesellschaften mit beschränkter Haftung (German Law on Limited Liability Companies) |
| Giur.comm. | Giurisprudenza commerciale (Italian legal journal) |
| GPR | Zeitschrift für das Privatrecht der Europäischen Union (German legal journal) |
| | |
| Harv. Int'l L.J. | Harvard International Law Journal (American legal journal) |
| | |
| IBA | International Bar Association |
| ibid | ibidem (in the same place) |
| ICCLR | International Company and Commercial Law Review (British legal journal) |
| ICLQ | International and Comparative Law Quarterly |

19

| | |
|---|---|
| i.e. | id es (that is) |
| Il dir. fallim. | Il diritto fallimentare (Italian legal journal) |
| Il Fall. | Il Fallimento e le altre procedure concorsuali (Italian legal journal) |
| IILR | International Insolvency Law Review |
| IJLSR | International Journal of Legal Studies and Research |
| ILA | The Inception Impact Assessment |
| Inc. | incorporated |
| infra | see below |
| InsO | Insolvenzordnung (German Insolvency Code) |
| INSOL | International Association of Restructuring, Insolvency & Bankruptcy Professionals |
| Insolv. Int. | Insolvency Intelligence (British legal journal) |
| Int. Insolv. Rev. | International Insolvency Review |
| Int'l Lis | Corriere trimestrale della litigation internazionale (Italian legal journal) |
| insolvency practitioner(s) | Insolvency Practitioner(s) |
| IPRax | Praxis des Internationalen Privat- und Verfahrensrechts (German legal journal) |
| JCL | Journal of Cooperation Law (American legal journal) |
| JCLS | Journal of Corporate Law Studies |
| J. Int'l Bus. & L. | Journal of International Business and Law (American legal journal) |
| J Int'l L | Journal of International Law |
| JPE | Journal of Political Economy (American legal journal) |
| J.Priv.Int.L. | Journal of Private International Law |
| jurisPR-InsR | Juris Praxisreport Insolvenzrecht (German legal database) |
| JZ | Juristen Zeitung (German legal journal) |
| KSzW | Kölner Schrift zum Wirtschaftsrecht (German legal journal) |
| KTS | Zeitschrift für Insolvenzrecht (German legal journal) |
| LC | Ley Concursal (Spanish Insolvency Act) |

| | |
|---|---|
| lit. | litera |
| LMK | Lindenmaier-Möhring- Kommentierte BGH-Rechtsprechung (German legal journal) |
| LOPJ | Ley Orgánica del Poder Judicial |
| LS | Legal Studies (British legal journal) |
| Ltd | Limited Liability Company |
| | |
| MJ | Maastricht Journal of European and Comparative Law |
| MLR | The Modern Law Review |
| MS | Member State |
| MüKoInsO | Münchener Kommentar zur Insolvenzordnung (German commentary) |
| | |
| n/nn | footnote (internal) |
| NICh | High Court of Justice in Northern Ireland, Chancery Division |
| NILR | Netherlands International Law Review |
| no(s) | number(s) |
| Norton J. Bankr. L. & Prac. | Norton Journal of Bankruptcy Law and Practice |
| NV | Naamloze vennootschap (Dutch public limited liability company) |
| NVRII | Nederlandse Vereniging voor Rechtsvergelijkend en Internationaal Insolventierecht (Netherlands Association for Comparative and International Insolvency Law) |
| Nw. J. Int'l L. & Bus. | Northwestern Journal of International Law & Business |
| NZG | Neue Zeitschrift für Gesellschaftsrecht (German legal journal) |
| NZI | Neue Zeitschrift für Insolvenz- und Sanierungsrecht (German legal journal) |
| | |
| p | page(s) |
| para(s) | Paragraph(s) |
| passim | indicates that something is to be found at many places in the same book |
| pers | persons |

| | |
|---|---|
| Q | Question |
| | |
| RabelsZ | Rabels Zeitschrift für ausländisches und internationales Privatrecht (German legal journal) |
| REGSOL | Central Solvency Registrar (Digital Bankruptcy Platform for Belgian bankruptcies) |
| Rev. crit. DIP | Revue critique de droit international privé (French legal journal) |
| Rev. proc. coll. | Revue des procédures collectives (French legal journal) |
| Riv.dir.int.priv. e proc. | Rivista di diritto internazionale private e processuale (Italian legal journal) |
| RIW | Recht der internationalen Wirtschaft (German legal journal) |
| | |
| s. | sentence |
| sec | section |
| SA | Société anonyme/Sociedad Anónima |
| San Diego Int'l L.J. | San Diego International Law Journal (American legal journal) |
| SIA | Sabiedriba ar ierobezotu atbildibu (Latvian limited liability company) |
| SpA | Società per Azioni (Italian shared company) |
| Stan. J.L Bus. & Fin. | Stanford Journal of Law, Business and Finance |
| STS | Sentencia del Tribunal Supremo |
| subpara | subparagraph |
| supra | see above |
| | |
| Tex.Int'l L.J. | Texas International Law Journal (American legal journal) |
| TEU | Treaty on European Union |
| TFEU | Treaty on the Functioning of the European Union |
| The Geo. Wash. Int'l L. Rev. | The George Washington International Law Review (American legal journal) |
| | |
| UK | United Kingdom |
| UNCITRAL | United Nations Commission on International Trade Law |

| | |
|---|---|
| UNIDROIT | International Institute for the Unification of Private Law |
| U.S. | United States |
| | |
| v | versus |
| VO | Verordnung (Regulation) |
| | |
| WM | Zeitschrift für Wirtschafts- und Bankrecht (German legal journal) |
| | |
| Yale L.J. | The Yale Law Journal (American legal journal) |
| | |
| ZEuP | Zeitschrift für Europäisches Privatrecht (German legal journal) |
| ZGR | Zeitschrift für Unternehmens- und Gesellschaftsrecht (German legal journal) |
| ZIK | Zeitschrift für Insolvenzrecht und Kreditschutz (Austrian legal journal) |
| ZInsO | Zeitschrift für das gesamte Insolvenzrecht (German legal journal) |
| ZIP | Zeitschrift für Wirtschaftsrecht (German legal journal) |
| ZR | Zivilrechtssenat (Civil Panel) |
| ZVglRWiss | Zeitschrift für Vergleichende Rechtswissenschaft (German legal journal) |
| ZZP | Zeitschrift für Zivilprozeß (German legal journal) |

# Introduction

Insolvency law has changed considerably over the last decade. Legislative activity across the EU Member States mirrors a still ongoing shift from liquidation towards the reorganisation of companies, or, to put it differently, from a creditor based approach towards a more debtor oriented concept of insolvency.[1] This trend of rescue culture embedded in preventive out-of-court proceedings is complemented by the debt discharge of consumers and self-employed persons.[2] At the same time, complex cross-border cases raise the need for flexible regulatory instruments adjusting a company's debts right on the eve of insolvency – with the participation of only parts of the creditors deciding on the basis of a majority vote. From a legal perspective, these so-called pre-insolvency proceedings tend to blur the boundaries between insolvency law, general procedural law, company law and even contract law.[3] In addition, the opening of insolvency proceedings against members of a corporate group raises intricate questions in a cross-border setting.[4]

As a consequence, the EU legislator was held to evaluate the efficiency of the regulatory regime in place and to keep pace with these substantial developments of domestic law by reforming the European rules on cross-border insolvencies.

---

1 See, e.g., *Hess*, in: Festschrift Stürner (2013), p 1253; *Paulus*, RIW 2013, 577; *Thole*, JZ 2011, 765.

2 Cf *infra* Part 1, II. 1.2, regarding the Swedish debt relief proceeding, analyzed by the CJEU, 8 November 2012, Case C-461/11, *Radziejewski*, ECLI:EU:C:2012:704; see also the provisions on debt discharge in case of natural persons, consumers and self-employed persons (§§ 182 ff of the Austrian Insolvency Act, as lastly amended by the Insolvency Act Amendment Act 2017, Federal Law Gazette I 2017/122.

3 Cf *Jacoby*, ZGR 2010, 359; *Madaus*, KSzW 2015, 183, 184 ff; *Piekenbrock*, IILR 2014, 424.

4 Cf, for instance, *Oberhammer*, in: Hess/Oberhammer/Pfeiffer (eds), Heidelberg-Luxembourg-Vienna Report (2014), para 5.2.1.1; *Eble*, NZI 2016, 115; *Hirte*, ECFR 2008, 213.

## I. Genesis of the Study

After winning a European Commission tender, the MPI Luxembourg for Procedural Law together with the Universities of Heidelberg (Professor *Burkhard Hess* and Professor *Thomas Pfeiffer*) and Vienna (Professor *Paul Oberhammer*) in a first research project evaluated the functioning of the European Insolvency Regulation since its adoption in 2002. The main objective of this study was to analyse the Regulation's application in practice and examine and implement the new procedures and changes to national insolvency law. The legal analysis and empirical data carried out and collected in 26 EU Member States resulted in the so-called Heidelberg-Luxembourg-Vienna Report of December 2012 which drew up proposals for the amendment of the Regulation. A great number of these proposals, such as the recommendation to introduce pre-insolvency proceedings, to insert a new head of jurisdiction for insolvency-related actions as well as to improve the coordination of proceedings were adopted by the European Commission and are now incorporated in the binding text of the new Regulation taking effect from June 2017.

This reform gave rise to the present follow-up research project. Carried out by the MPI Luxembourg for Procedural Law (Professor *Burkhard Hess*), in cooperation with the University of Vienna (Professor *Paul Oberhammer*) and the University of Milano (Professor *Stefania Bariatti*), and supported by the European Commission under the Specific Programme 'Civil Justice',[5] this Study addresses the implementation and interpretation of the new Insolvency Regulation.

## II. Methodology, scope and objective of the Study

The two-year project, which ended in December 2016, aimed to formulate guidelines and recommendations to the EU Commission. Apart from desk-study and archival research, the final report relies upon responses to an online questionnaire[6] as well as upon contributions by renowned insolvency academics, practitioners and representatives of the German Ministry of

---

5  JUST/2013/JCIV/AG/4679, see Decision No 1149/2007/EC of the European Parliament and the Council from 25 September 2007, OJ L 257, 3.10.2007, p 16.

6  The Online Questionnaire is available at the Website of the Max Planck Institute Luxembourg for Procedural Law (http://insreg.mpi.lu/Guidelines.pdf).

Justice during conferences in Vienna, Milano and Luxembourg. The input given by those distinguished experts significantly enhanced the academic dialogue. It enabled the project teams to put their ideas and suggestions under scrutiny. In order to make parts of this academic dialogue available to a broader audience many of the expert contributions are published in the Annex of this book.

From a *practical* perspective, this follow-up project was (and is) dedicated to provide guidance for the interpretation of the new Regulation, even before its entry into force. It goes without saying that many aspects raised by the reform of the Insolvency Regulation, both legal and empirical, need clarification – by the Court of Justice and legal doctrine. From an *academic* viewpoint, the new legal instruments introduced by the Regulation as well as its adaptation to modern types of rescue proceedings have opened up new and innovative fields of research. At the same time, these regulatory developments require adjustments to domestic insolvency law – thereby constituting some sort of regulatory dialogue within the European Union's multilevel system. That being said, conducting the Study at this early stage was not only helpful to provide interpretative guidance from the outset but also to raise the national legislators' awareness of the potential need for regulatory action. In that regard, the participation of the German Ministry of Justice in the conferences of the project made it possible to contribute to the Member States' implementing regulation.

## III. Outline of the Study

The original version of the European Insolvency Regulation already provided a successful instrument capable of facilitating cross-border insolvency proceedings within the European Union. Consequently, the reform does not fundamentally change the basic structures of the Regulation. The regulatory approach underpinning the amendments can, essentially, be divided into three groups: the codification of the CJEU's case law, the implementation of tools developed in practice (e.g. synthetic proceedings), and the adoption of entirely new rules (e.g. group coordination proceedings).

The reform relates in essence to four issues: the scope of the EIR; provisions dealing with jurisdiction; the coordination of proceedings, in particular with regard to groups of companies; and the information for creditors and the lodging of claims. The present Study focuses on provisions of the new Regulation that raise particularly intricate questions of interpretation and (potentially) interact with domestic insolvency law. To that end, the three main parts of the Study address the following issues:

1. Widening the scope of the Regulation: opening up for rescue culture (Part 1)

The EU legislator decided to considerably widen the scope of the new Regulation to include debt discharge proceedings in relation to consumers and self-employed persons, but also pre-insolvency proceedings. These latter proceedings, such as the French *procédure de sauvegarde financière accélérée,*[7] address the adjustment and renegotiation of debts if a company in actual or imminent financial distress faces only a likelihood of insolvency, thus leaving the debtor fully or partially in control of his assets or affairs. The 'semi-collective' nature is characteristic of pre-insolvency proceedings, which means that they do not include the creditors as a whole, but only a significant part of them – typically financial creditors deciding by a majority vote.

Against this backdrop, the follow-up Study had to clearly answer the intricate question of under what conditions these pre-insolvency proceedings will be covered by the new Regulation, by establishing criteria for drawing the line between its scope, on the one hand, and the Brussels I regime, the Rome I Regulation and the autonomous rules of national procedural law, on the other.[8]

2. Coordination between main and secondary proceedings (Part 2)

Along with the recommendations of the first research project, the EU legislator was not only willing to reshape the conceptual balance between universalism and territoriality, but also strengthen procedural cooperation. In this context, new regulatory paths have been laid for cross-border proceedings. Three of them shall be singled out:

---

7  Cf *Piekenbrock,* KSzW 2015, 191, 192 f; *J. Schmidt,* in: Mankowski/Müller/ Schmidt, EuInsVO 2015 (2016), Art 1, para 14; *Degenhardt,* NZI 2013, 830.
8  Cf *infra,* Part 1, III. 1.2.

## 2.1 Judicial cooperation: from soft law to innovative hard law

The new Insolvency Regulation sets up a framework for enhanced cooperation – not only between insolvency practitioners, but also between courts. This approach tends to overcome classical means of cross-border mutual assistance, by providing for an increasingly refined mechanism of coordination, including cooperation and communication. Following existing soft law principles and guidelines from international organizations, the new Regulation introduces a legal duty of judges to properly cooperate and communicate with one another.[9]

In that regard, the Study recommends, *inter alia*, a practice guide to be established by the Commission raising awareness and explaining the new rules through technical advice, the compilation of best practices, case studies and links to other pertinent documents of soft law,[10] thereby helping to remove the well-known legal and factual obstacles to judicial cooperation.

## 2.2 Synthetic proceedings: from practice to regulation

The opening of parallel territorial proceedings against the same debtor may hamper the efficient administration of the insolvency estate as a whole and, therefore, the concept of universality. Following British restructuring culture, the new Regulation entitles a main practitioner to give a so-called undertaking to foreign local creditors with the aim of preventing the opening of territorial proceedings.[11] By approving such an undertaking, those creditors are treated with respect to distribution and priority rights as if territorial proceedings had been opened and local insolvency law (familiar to them) applied.[12] This contract-related instrument which is based on a conflict of laws mechanism well illustrates that once it becomes subject to regulation, the rule of law and, more precisely, procedural guarantees need to be strictly taken into account: such as the right of foreign creditors to be heard and to have access to the proceedings, their

---

9 See Art 42 (regarding secondary proceedings) and Art 57 (regarding groups of companies) EIR.
10 See *infra* Annex, VI. 6.
11 See Art 36 EIR.
12 Art 36(2) EIR.

right to challenge an undertaking, and also liability issues if the insolvency practitioner fails to comply with its provisions.[13] However, as demonstrated by the reform, this approach entails the risk of overregulation, undermining the attractiveness of an instrument which has proven to work in practice before being regulated.[14] For many Member States the concept of synthetic proceedings is entirely new and triggers the need to adopt specific rules on a domestic level that ensure effectiveness of the instrument. To that end, the Study highlights interfaces between the Regulation and domestic law that might require the Member States' attention.

3. Group of companies: contractual flexibility versus procedural overregulation (Part 3)

Finally, the Study had to consider the conflict between the need for clear and foreseeable rules, on the one hand, and the requirement to regulate cross-border insolvencies flexibly, on the other. When it comes to the insolvency of group of companies, we developed criteria for coordinating the proceedings of different group members: firstly, with regard to *jurisdiction* by proposing a stronger and more refined consideration of economic parameters which facilitate concentration of different proceedings under one jurisdiction and one insolvency statute;[15] and secondly, from a *contractual* perspective, by means of agreements and protocols concluded between the representatives of the different group members in order to facilitate and improve the administration of multiple insolvency proceedings in the best interest of the whole group of companies and its creditors.[16] The Study further stresses that issues of coordination between the respective group members' proceedings might appear in a number of scenarios subject to different coordination regimes. It provides guidelines for the interpretation of key provisions, such as Article 60 EIR dealing with the powers of an insolvency practitioner in proceedings concerning (other) group members.

The collapse of Lehman Brothers serves as a prime example, being the largest bankruptcy in history with over $600 billion in liabilities. In this case, a cross-border insolvency protocol has been reached, covering

---

13  See Art 36(3)-(10) EIR.
14  Cf *infra* Part 2, I. 2, 3.3 and Annex III. 2.
15  See *infra* Part 3, II.
16  See *infra* Part 3, III. 3.1.

Lehman entities all over the world, including sixteen different jurisdictions of both common law and civil law. The main objectives of this protocol were to encourage the sharing of information; to permit insolvency representatives to appear and be heard in meetings in other countries, but also to communicate among courts and creditor committees; to coordinate the realization of assets; and the way to deal with the extensive intercompany claims within the Lehman group.[17]

The underlying *academic* question is how to draft legal rules which are embedded in a highly economic environment. As to the coordination of cross-border insolvencies, the Study concludes that contractual flexibility should, as a matter of principle, prevail over the detailed codification of mandatory procedural rules. Only specific issues should be 'proceduralized', such as those entailing an institutional change to the architecture of European procedural law. The newly introduced duty of national judges to properly cooperate and communicate with one another serves as a good example. Indeed, this approach reflects a structural change of EU policy-making towards a horizontal model for cooperative justice and procedure in cross-border scenarios.

## IV. Distribution of responsibilities

The Study is the result of a fruitful cooperation between the project teams who exchanged views on all relevant issues. The responsibilities regarding the specific topics were subdivided between the teams as follows:

The team of the University of Milano (Professor *Stefania Bariatti*, Professor *Ilaria Viarengo*, Professor *Francesca Clara Villata*; *Fabio Vecchi*) addressed the scope of application (pre-insolvency and hybrid proceedings, Part 1); the team of the MPI Luxembourg for Procedural Law (Professor *Burkhard Hess*, Dr *Matteo Gargantini*, Dr *Björn Laukemann*, Professor *Marta Requejo Isidro*, Dr *Robert Arts*, *Georgia Koutsoukou*, LL.M.) focused on the cooperation between main and secondary proceedings (Part 2); and, finally, the team of the University of Vienna (Professor *Paul Oberhammer*, Professor *Christian Koller*, Mag. *Katharina Auernig*,

---

17 See, e.g., *Bufford*, IILR 2012, 341, 355; *Gropper*, IILR 2015, 364, 368 ff; the Lehman Group protocol is available at: https://www.lukb.ch/documents/10620/44536/LUKB_CrossBorderProtocol.pdf/26163479-98db-4c6f-91c2-2b223af9a85b.

Mag. *Lukas Planitzer*) dealt with insolvencies of groups of companies (Part 3).

*Luxembourg/Vienna*                                    *Christian Koller*
                                                       *Björn Laukemann*

# Part 1: Scope of application*

Università degli Studi di Milano

## I. The scope of the Regulation

Article 1(1) EIR

### 1. Legal framework

#### 1.1 A new European approach to business failure and insolvency

In *Eurofood IFSC*,[18] the CJEU stated that 'the wording of Article 1(1) of the Regulation shows that the insolvency proceedings to which it applies must have four characteristics. They must be collective proceedings, based on the debtor's insolvency, which entail at least partial divestment of that debtor and prompt the appointment of a liquidator'.

These four requirements delineate the traditional concept of insolvency proceedings, that is, proceedings which are exclusively aimed at the distribution of an insolvent debtor's assets among creditors, being the debtor perceived as incapable of overcoming its difficulties.[19] Since the EIR 2000 was based upon a convention signed in 1995,[20] it is no wonder that this

---

\* Prof. *Stefania Bariatti*; Prof. Dr. *Ilaria Viarengo*; Prof. Dr. *Francesca Clara Villata*; *Fabio Vecchi*, Università degli Studi di Milano. Part 1 of the Study is attributed to its authors in the following way: I.1.1.1 (Bariatti, Villata), I.1.1.2-1.1.3 (Vecchi), I.1.2-1.3 (Bariatti, Villata, Viarengo, Vecchi), II.1 (Vecchi), II.2-3 (Bariatti, Villata, Viarengo, Vecchi), III.1 (Vecchi), III.2-3 (Bariatti, Villata, Viarengo, Vecchi), IV.1 (Vecchi), IV.2-3 (Bariatti, Villata, Viarengo, Vecchi).

18 CJEU, 2 May 2006, Case C-341/04, *Eurofood IFSC*, ECLI:EU:C:2006:281, para 46.
19 *Wessels*, Insolv.Int. 2014, 4, stated that 'this one-sided approach to corporate distress is clearly reflected in the EU Insolvency Regulation, which, for instance, allows the opening of secondary proceedings, which must be winding-up proceedings. The one-sidedness of the aforementioned approach is also indicated by the chosen name for the responsible insolvency office holder in either main or secondary insolvency proceedings: 'liquidator''.
20 Convention on Insolvency Proceedings of 23 November 1995, available at: http://aei.pitt.edu/2840/.

concept sounded 'old' and outdated since the beginning:[21] at the moment the EIR 2000 was being adopted, some national legislations already provided proceedings which were not focused (or not only focused) on the liquidation of distressed businesses. It is not by chance that, even at the start, Annex A to the EIR 2000 included proceedings which did not satisfy *all* the conditions set out in Article 1(1);[22] or that proceedings which do not meet *all* those conditions were later added by amendment to Annex A.[23]

In the report on the application of the EIR 2000[24] of 12 December 2012, the Commission maintained that 'due to new trends and approaches in the Member States, the current scope of the Regulation no longer covers a wide range of national proceedings aiming at resolving the indebtedness of companies and individuals', and suggested to extend the scope of the Regulation to pre-insolvency and hybrid proceedings, defined respectively as 'quasi-collective proceedings under the supervision of a court or an administrative authority which give a debtor in financial difficulties the opportunity to restructure at a pre-insolvency stage and to avoid the commencement of insolvency proceedings in the traditional sense', and as 'proceedings in which the debtor retains some control over its assets and affairs albeit subject to the control or supervision by a court or an insolvency practitioner'.[25]

---

21  For this reason, since its enactment, there have been calls for reforms to the EIR 2000. Among the earlier works dealing with suggestions as to the amendment, see *Moss/Paulus*, Insolv.Int. 2006, 1; and *Omar*, Insolv.Int. 2007, 7.

22  As noted by *Moss*, in: Moss/Fletcher/Isaacs (eds), The EU Regulation on Insolvency Proceedings, 3rd edn (2016), para 8.472, Annex A included UK *administration proceedings*, 'which do not require proof of actual insolvency but only that the corporate debtor was likely to become insolvent'.

23  See the French *sauvegarde* proceeding, which, pursuant to Art L620-1 of *Code de Commerce*, can be opened by a debtor that, without being unable to pay, is unable to overcome its difficulties and is aimed at easing the reorganization of its business.

24  Report from the Commission to the European Parliament, the Council and the European Economic and Social Committee on the application of Council Regulation (EC) No 1346/2000 of 29 May 2000 on insolvency proceedings, COM(2012)0744 – C7-0413/2012 – 2012/0360(COD).

25  The Commission underlined that '15 Member States have pre-insolvency or hybrid proceedings which are currently not listed in Annex A of the Regulation', thus implicitly confirming that some pre-insolvency and hybrid proceedings were already listed in Annex A.

In 2014 the Commission adopted a recommendation,[26] with the objective to 'encourage Member States to put in place a framework that enables the efficient restructuring of viable enterprises in financial difficulty and give honest entrepreneurs a second chance'. In pursuit of this objective, 'the Recommendation provides for minimum standards on: *(a)* preventive restructuring frameworks; and *(b)* discharge of debts of bankrupt entrepreneurs' (hereafter, 'Recommendation'). It is noteworthy that among the core principles that Member States were urged to adhere to (by 12 months from the publication of the Recommendation) there were the 'pre-insolvency recourse' and the 'debtor-in-possession'.[27] According to the former principle, the Commission recommended that debtors be able to have access to restructuring proceedings 'at an early stage, as soon as it is apparent that there is a likelihood of insolvency';[28] according to the latter, consistently with the goal of ensuring business continuity while the restructuring is negotiated, the Commission recommended that the debtor 'keeps control over the day-to-day operation of its business' while the restructuring framework is used.[29]

---

26  Commission Recommendation of 12 March 2014 on a new approach to business failure and insolvency, C(2014) 1500/F1. In the *Impact Assessment* accompanying the Recommendation (Impact assessment accompanying the document Commission Recommendation on a New Approach to Business Failure and Insolvency), the Commission explained that the Recommendation was intended as complementary to the European Insolvency Regulation's proposal: restructuring procedures of the kind proposed in its Recommendation would – if introduced by Member States – have been eligible for inclusion within Annex A of the EIR. It is not by chance that the expression used in the Recommendation, No 1 ('the objective of this Recommendation is to encourage Member States to put in place a framework that enables the efficient restructuring of viable enterprises in financial difficulty and give honest entrepreneurs a second chance') is almost identical to that used in the recital 10, 1st s. EIR ('the scope of this Regulation should extend to proceedings which promote the rescue of economically viable but distressed businesses and which give a second chance to entrepreneurs').

27  For the identification of the (six) core principles of the Recommendation, see *Eidenmüller/Van Zwieten*, Restructuring the European Business Enterprise: The EU Commission Recommendation on a New Approach to Business Failure and Insolvency, European Corporate Governance Institute (ECGI) Law Working Paper No 301/2015, Oxford Legal Studies Research Paper No 52/2015, available at: papers.ssrn.com, 1, 12.

28  See Recommendation No 6(a).

29  See Recommendation No 6(b) and *Eidenmüller/Van Zwieten*, Restructuring the European Business Enterprise: The EU Commission Recommendation on a New

However, 'the Recommendation has been [only] partially taken up by some Member States';[30] for this reason, the Commission has recently proposed to adopt a directive with the purpose of harmonizing the topics covered by the Recommendation and some other areas where be equally worthwhile and achievable.[31] Among the topics that this directive has intention to address, there will be preventive restructuring procedures and discharge of debts for entrepreneurs.

Several Member States have already amended their national laws introducing new proceedings for reorganization and rescue in order to allow entrepreneurs to survive and to encourage them to take a second chance. Further amendments and updatings are on the way to be introduced, or are expected to be introduced (or – if a directive is adopted – will be required to be introduced), in the national insolvency legislations in accordance with the abovementioned inputs. Therefore, pre-insolvency and hybrid proceedings are likely to early take on the leading role in the insolvency framework (unless they have taken it yet).

The EIR Recast (Regulation [EU] 2015/848 of the European Parliament and of the Council of 20 May 2015 on insolvency proceedings [recast] – hereafter EIR) encompasses 'pre-insolvency' and 'hybrid' proceedings, as proposed by the Commission.

1.2  Pre-insolvency and hybrid proceedings

Commonly, proceedings are defined 'hybrid' which combine the characteristics of out-of-court settlements and judicial insolvency proceedings. They are based on an agreement between the debtor and his creditors, which has binding effect *vis à vis* minority creditors (preventing the debtor from the need of seeking the consent of all creditors) and is subject to an examination of a judicial authority (which can be an in-depth one, but usually consists in a verification as to whether the formal requirements of the

---

Approach to Business Failure and Insolvency, European Corporate Governance Institute (ECGI) Law Working Paper No 301/2015, Oxford Legal Studies Research Paper No 52/2015, available at: papers.ssrn.com, 13.

30  And 'even those Member States which have taken up the European Commission Insolvency Recommendation did so in a selective manner, meaning that differences remain': see *IIA*, adopted on 3 March 2016.

31  COM (2016) 723 final of 22 November 2016.

proceedings exist). In order to ease the agreement, a stay of enforcement actions is granted or can be granted. Often an insolvency practitioner is appointed, acting as a supervisor, and generally the debtor is not divested of its assets.[32]

Hybrid proceedings, as described, are pre-insolvency proceedings, since the court-approved arrangement is aimed at preventing the insolvency of the debtor. Not all pre-insolvency proceedings, however, are hybrid proceedings, since 'out-of-court' settlements and the so-called 'confidential procedures' are to be considered pre-insolvency proceedings as well. Out-of-court settlements consist in negotiations between the debtor and its creditors in order to modify the terms and the conditions of their contracts.[33] Being purely contractual transactions, they are based on the individual consent of all affected creditors: no creditor can judicially or legally be forced to change the content of his right against his will.[34] Similarly, confidential procedures are proceedings in which the debtor tries to reach an agreement with the creditors and the debtor has no means to force any creditors to accept a reduction or modification of their claims or a standstill period, they being not publicised, advertised or other persons except those directly involved made aware of them; however, an expert or insolvency practitioner is usually appointed to assist the debtor and these proceedings generally involve protection against applications for the opening of insolvency proceedings. Sometimes, confidential procedures can provide a stay of enforcement of certain debts or can order modification of debts such as postponement of their due date.[35]

---

32 For these remarks see *Garcimartín*, The review of the EU Insolvency Regulation: some proposals for amendment, NVRII Preadviezen/Reports 2011, 17, 28 ff; and *Hess*, in: Hess/Oberhammer/Pfeiffer (eds), Heidelberg-Luxembourg-Vienna Report (2014), para 3.3.2.
33 'These modifications may result, for example, in a rescheduling of payments, a reduction of their interest rates, a total or partial debt write-off or new loan facilities': see *Garcimartín*, The review of the EU Insolvency Regulation: some proposals for amendment, NVRII Preadviezen/Reports 2011, 17, 28 ff.
34 For this reason, they are governed – from a conflict-of-laws perspective – by the general conflict-of-laws rules on contractual obligations according to the Rome I Regulation (Regulation (EC) No 593/2008 of the European Parliament and of the Council of 17 June 2008 on the law applicable to contractual obligations). See *Garcimartín*, The review of the EU Insolvency Regulation: some proposals for amendment, NVRII Preadviezen/Reports 2011, 17, 29.
35 For a categorization of pre-insolvency proceedings in Member States, see INSOL Europe report 'Study on a new approach to business failure and insolvency –

Nonetheless, the term 'hybrid' does not always indicate the proceedings having the set of features seen above. Indeed, 'hybrid' may also refer to the more general concept of 'debtor in possession', that is, proceedings in which the debtor is not divested of the assets but administers them under supervision by a court or a court appointed supervisor. This is the meaning attached to 'hybrid' in the Commission's proposal to amend the EIR 2000 of 12 December 2012 (see *supra* para 1.1). Thus understood, 'hybrid proceedings' cover the whole area of pre-insolvency proceedings, insofar as the debtor is always left in possession in out-of-court settlements and confidential proceedings. Furthermore, also (traditional) insolvency proceedings can be 'hybrid proceedings', given that in some Member States the debtor may remain in possession also after the opening of 'full insolvency proceedings', i.e. 'insolvency proceedings which are not pre-insolvency proceedings' (since they are opened 'after the insolvency test has been carried out and the court has determined that the debtor is insolvent').[36]

Therefore, the relationship between 'pre-insolvency proceedings' and 'hybrid proceedings' varies depending on the meaning ascribed to the term 'hybrid'.

Although there is no provision in the EIR clearly providing for a definition of these two concepts, their inclusion in the scope of the EIR is implied by recital 10, according to which the EIR 'should (…) extend to *(i)* proceedings which provide for restructuring of a debtor at a stage where there is only likelihood of insolvency, and to *(ii)* proceedings which leave the debtor fully or partially in control of its assets and affairs' – provided that 'they take place under the control or supervision of a court', 'since such proceedings do not necessarily entail the appointment of an insolvency practitioner'. However, the EIR provides a definition of 'debtor in possession': pursuant to Article 2(3), debtor in possession proceedings are those which 'do not necessarily involve the appointment of an insolvency practitioner or the complete transfer of the rights and duties to administer the debtor's assets to an insolvency practitioner and where, therefore, the debtor remains totally or at least partially in control of its assets and affairs'. For this definition is very similar to the phrasing of the second part

---

Comparative legal analysis of the Member States' relevant provisions and practices' of 12 May 2014 ( JUST/2012/JCIV/CT/0194/A4).

36  See INSOL Europe report 'Study on a new approach to business failure and insolvency – Comparative legal analysis of the Member States' relevant provisions and practice' of 12 May 2014 (JUST/2012/JCIV/CT/0194/A4), 25.

of the abovementioned recital 10, it is likely that 'debtor in possession' corresponds, in the language of the EIR, to the 'hybrid proceedings' of the Commission's proposal: As a consequence, the EIR would enlarge its scope to *(i)* pre-insolvency proceedings, and *(ii)* debtor in possession proceedings (which indeed fall outside the scope of the EIR 2000[37]).

The essential elements of 'pre-insolvency' and 'hybrid' proceedings under the EIR are to be found in the definition laid down in Article 1(1) EIR.

### 1.2.1 Article 1(1) EIR[38]

Article 1(1) EIR is a provision far more detailed and complex than Article 1(1) EIR 2000. According to Article 1(1) EIR, proceedings fall within the scope of the EIR which:

*(i)*   are based on laws relating to insolvency for the purpose of rescue, adjustment of debt, reorganization or liquidation;
*(ii)*  are public (including interim proceedings);
*(iii)* are collective;
*(iv)*  entail certain limitations on the individual rights of the debtor and/or his creditors, that can be represented by: a) the total or partial divestment of debtor's assets and the appointment of an insolvency practitioner; b) a control or supervision over the assets and affairs of the

---

37  See *Moss*, in: Moss/Fletcher/Isaacs (eds), The EU Regulation on Insolvency Proceedings, 3rd edn (2016), para 8.514.
38  With regard to this Article, a preliminary remark is to be made: Art 1(1) EIR only deals with the so-called 'material scope' of the Regulation, whereas provides no guidance as to the 'personal scope' and 'territorial scope'. As for the personal scope, recital 9 is to be taken into consideration, which provides that 'this Regulation should apply to insolvency proceedings which meet the conditions set out in it, irrespective of whether the debtor is a natural or a legal person, a trader or an individual'. This recital almost literally mirrors recital 9 EIR 2000, which maintains that 'this Regulation should apply to insolvency proceedings, whether the debtor is a natural person or a legal person, a trader or an individual'. Thus, in theory the personal scopes of the two Regulations correspond. What in practice makes the personal scope of the EIR wider is the enlargement of the material scope: as expressed in recital 9, EIR 'should also extend to proceedings providing for a debt discharge or a debt adjustment in relation to consumers and self-employed persons, for example by reducing the amount to be paid by the debtor or by extending the payment period granted to the debtor'. For this reason, the relevance of personal scope issues may be limited.

debtor exercised by a court; c) a temporary stay of individual enforcement proceedings granted by a court or by operation of law in order to allow for negotiations between the debtor and his creditors.

### 1.2.2  Proceedings 'based on laws relating to insolvency for the purpose of rescue, adjustment of debt, reorganisation or liquidation'

Proceedings which meet the conditions set out in the EIR are defined 'insolvency proceedings',[39] pursuant to Article 2(4) EIR. However, debtor's insolvency is no longer a requirement for a proceeding to fall under the scope of the EIR. According to Article 1(1) EIR, proceedings are covered by the EIR which also 'may be commenced in situations where there is only a likelihood of insolvency'.

The EIR provides no definition of insolvency nor of likelihood of insolvency. As a consequence, it must be held that there is no test as to the existence of insolvency or likelihood of insolvency other than that demanded by the national legislation of the State in which proceedings are opened.[40] The insolvency test differs in the Member States: the most common criteria for initiating proceedings based on insolvency are the cessation of payments test, and the balance sheet test (which depends on it being established that the debtor's liabilities exceed the value of its assets). The judgment on the existence of a likelihood of insolvency differs too; and even the term expressing the concept of likelihood of insolvency varies from State to State *(*e.g. 'crisis', 'distress', 'imminent insolvency'). In general terms, proceedings based on a condition of likelihood of insolvency (or pre-insolvency) are those whose opening is conditional upon a certain level of difficulties but without any prior insolvency test.[41] For the EIR to apply, there is no need that such difficulties have a financial nature: accord-

---

39  Actually, Art 2(4) EIR defines 'insolvency proceedings' as 'the proceedings listed in Annex A'; and according to recital 10, proceedings are listed exhaustively in Annex A 'which meet the conditions set out in it'. Thus, it is possible to say that the term 'insolvency proceedings' refers to the proceedings which satisfy the conditions set out in Art 1(1) EIR.

40  This is the solution proposed under the EIR 2000 by the *Virgós-Schmit report*, Report on the Convention on Insolvency Proceedings (1996), para 49(b).

41  See INSOL Europe report 'Study on a new approach to business failure and insolvency – Comparative legal analysis of the Member States' relevant provisions and practices' of 12 May 2014 (JUST/2012/JCIV/CT/0194/A4).

ing to recital 17, 'proceedings which are triggered by situations in which the debtor faces non-financial difficulties' are covered by the EIR, 'provided that such difficulties give rise to a real and serious threat to the debtor's actual or future ability to pay'. Recital 17 further explains that the time horizon for the determination of such a threat 'may extend to a period of several months or even longer, in order to account for cases in which the debtor is faced with non-financial difficulties threatening the status of its business as a going concern and, in the medium term, its liquidity'; and that 'this may be the case (...) where the debtor has lost a contract of key importance to him'.

In order to encompass most proceedings based on the mere likelihood of insolvency (as well as proceedings which leave the debtor in possession), the EIR simply requires that the proceedings be 'based on laws relating to insolvency'. Proceedings are 'based on laws relating to insolvency' when:

– have 'the purpose of rescue, adjustment of debt, reorganisation or liquidation'. Under the EIR 2000, proceedings based on the debtor's insolvency and on its divestment may always entail the liquidation of the debtor's assets, but may also entail the reorganization of the business, when are main proceedings.[42] Under the EIR, proceedings are no longer aimed necessarily at the distribution of the debtor's assets or at the reorganization. In particular, proceedings cannot be aimed at the liquidation (nor at the reorganization, if meant as possible only in re-

---

42 *Virgós-Schmit report*, Report on the Convention on Insolvency Proceedings (1996), para 51, states that: '... Limiting the application of the Convention to winding-up proceedings would have had the advantage of simplifying the resulting rules. The disadvantage would have been that it would have excluded from European cooperation very important proceedings in bankruptcy practice in certain Contracting States .... For some Contracting States the exclusion of reorganization proceedings would therefore be unjustified. The outcome of the negotiations was a compromise to extend the Convention system to insolvency proceedings the main aim of which was not winding-up but reorganization. As part of this compromise, however, local territorial proceedings opened after the main proceedings may only be winding-up proceedings (see points 83 and 86). If opened before, local territorial proceedings are subject to conversion into winding-up proceedings if the liquidator of the main proceedings so requests. The complications of compatibility and coordination between secondary reorganization proceedings (of which there could be several, if the debtor was based in several different Contracting States) and the main proceedings have led to restriction'.

spect of an insolvent debtor) which may be commenced in situations where there is only a likelihood of insolvency (see Article 1(1), 2nd s. EIR);

– are based on insolvency law or on 'general company law (…) designed exclusively for insolvency situations' (see recital 16: with regard to this aspect, see *infra* Part 1 III, 2.1.1).

1.2.3 'Public'

Proceedings based on laws relating to insolvency aimed at the rescue, the adjustment of debt, the reorganization or the liquidation should be 'public'. According to recital 12 EIR, proceedings are 'public' if their opening is subject to publicity, 'in order to allow creditors to become aware of the proceedings and to lodge their claims, thereby ensuring the collective nature of the proceedings, and in order to give creditors the opportunity to challenge the jurisdiction of the court which has opened the proceedings'. Provisions as to the practical application of this condition are to be found in Article 24 ff EIR, which accommodate a detailed regime on insolvency registers.[43] According to these Articles, Member States are called to establish national insolvency registers, in which certain information concerning insolvency proceedings should be published ('as soon as possible after the opening of such proceedings') and made publicly available, including the date of the opening and the court having jurisdiction, the type of insolvency, whether it is a main, secondary or territorial proceeding, and the court and time limit within which a challenge as to jurisdiction may be brought.[44]

Pursuant to recital 13, 'insolvency proceedings which are confidential should be excluded from the scope of this Regulation'. As seen above,[45] confidential proceedings are those in which the debtor tries to reach an agreement with its creditors and which are not made public in order to prevent the adverse effect of the insolvency stigma on the negotiations. Recital 13 justifies the exclusion with the difficulties to provide for their recognition abroad, given that the confidential nature makes it impossible for creditors or courts in other Member States to know that such proceed-

---

43  See *Garcimartín*, ZEuP 2015, 694, 698.
44  For the information to be included in the registers, see Art 24(2) EIR.
45  See *supra* Part 1, I. 1.2..

ings have been opened. It has been remarked that confidential proceedings should be covered by the scope of the EIR as from the moment they become public.[46]

Article 1(1) and recital 15 EIR specify that proceedings which are 'conducted (…) on an interim or provisional basis' fall under the scope of the EIR as well. This clarification clearly codifies the decision rendered in the *Eurofood IFSC* case, where the CJEU held that the judgment appointing a provisional liquidator constituted a decision opening insolvency proceedings recognizable in other Member States, since it met all the requirements set out in Article 1 EIR.[47] Accordingly, recital 15 EIR states that 'such proceedings should meet all other requirements of this Regulation' in order to be included in the scope of the EIR. 'Interim' proceedings are those which usually are opened upon mere request of the debtor and entail the appointment of a provisional insolvency administrator for a limited period of time, until 'a court issues an order confirming the continuation of the proceedings on a non-interim basis'.[48]

## 1.2.4 'Collective'

Public proceedings based on laws relating to insolvency aimed at the rescue, the adjustment of debt, the reorganization or the liquidation should also be 'collective'. According to Article 2(1) EIR, collective proceedings are 'proceedings which include all or a significant part of a debtor's creditors, provided that, in the latter case, the proceedings do not affect the claims of creditors which are not involved in them'. Recital 14 explains that *(i)* the creditors involved in the proceedings must represent all or a substantial proportion of the debtor's outstanding debts; that *(ii)* proceedings which involve only the financial creditors of a debtor should also be covered; and, most importantly, that *(iii)* proceedings involving only part of the creditors should be aimed at rescuing the debtor; conversely, liquidation proceedings should include all the debtor's creditors. It has been noted that this last clarification is intended to prevent abuse of the process by excluding some creditors who would otherwise be left with extant

---

46 See *Garcimartin*, ZEuP 2015, 694, 699.
47 CJEU, 2 May 2006, Case C-341/04, *Eurofood IFSC*, ECLI:EU:C:2006:281, paras 45 ff.
48 See recital 15.

claims against the debtor but no assets against which to enforce them, sidestepping the statutory order of priorities and *pari passu* distribution rules in the relevant Member State.[49]

### 1.2.5 Which entail some kind of 'interference' upon the individual rights of the debtor and/or its creditors…[50]

Public collective proceedings based on laws relating to insolvency aimed at the rescue, the adjustment of debt, the reorganization or the liquidation should then entail some kind of interference upon the individual rights of the debtor and/or his creditors.

The first kind of interference consists in the total or partial divestment of the debtor and the appointment of an insolvency practitioner (see Article 1(1) lit. a) EIR).

The second kind of impairment consists in the control or supervision exerted by a court over the assets and affairs of a debtor.[51] According to Article 2(6) lit. i) EIR, the term 'court' means, in Article 1(1) lit. b) EIR, 'the judicial body of a Member State'. Pursuant to recital 10 EIR, 'control' include situations 'where the court only intervenes on appeal by a creditor or other interested parties'. The term 'appeal' seems to be a reference to cases where the court intervenes on application by a party.[52]

The third kind of interference consists in a temporary stay of individual enforcement actions granted by a court or by operation of law in order to allow for negotiations between the debtor and its creditors to reach an agreement on a restructuring plan.[53] In fact, pursuant to recital 10 EIR, in the absence of such 'moratoria' negotiations may be adversely affected and the prospects of restructuring hampered. Yet, 'moratoria' 'should not be detrimental to the general body of creditors': for this reason, proceedings in which such measure is granted should provide for suitable measures to protect creditors. Furthermore, 'moratoria' should be preliminary

---

49 These are the words used by *Bewick*, Int.Insolv.Rev. 2015, 172, 177.
50 These are the exact words used by *Garcimartín*, ZEuP 2015, 694, 701, to summarize the content of lit. a), b) and c) of Art 1(1) EIR.
51 Art 1(1) lit. b) EIR.
52 See *Moss*, in: Moss/Fletcher/Isaacs (eds), The EU Regulation on Insolvency Proceedings, 3rd edn (2016), para 8.492.
53 See Art 1(1) lit. c) and recital 11 EIR.

to one of the proceedings referred to in Article 1(1), lit. a) or b) EIR, if no agreement on a restructuring plan is reached. Being treated as autonomous proceedings, the jurisdiction to open such 'moratoria' is governed by Article 3 EIR, and their recognition by Articles 19 and 20 EIR. In accordance with these provisions, 'moratoria' may constitute main proceedings, and thus cover assets abroad (at least until a secondary proceeding is opened) and result in a stay on individual enforcement proceedings in other Member State.

1.2.6 ...and which may leave the debtor in possession

Although it is not stated in Article 1(1) EIR, proceedings which fulfil all the said requirements may leave the debtor in possession.

According to the report 'Study on a new approach to business failure and insolvency – Comparative legal analysis of the Member States' relevant provisions and practices' of 12 May 2014,[54] proceedings are defined in possession in which the debtor is not divested of the assets but administers his assets under supervision by a court or a court appointed supervisor. They being designed to avoid bankruptcy and facilitate restructuring, two main models can be followed, which may be alternative to one another: *(a)* a reorganization plan voted on by the creditors and confirmed by the court, sometimes accompanied by a short moratorium; *(b)* a moratorium ending with an agreement, that may be carried out under the supervision of the court and implies a stay of enforcement for claims covered by the agreement, which provides effects if the company complies with the collective agreement. If these scenarios fail, the proceedings may end up in reorganization through sales ordered by the court under a judicial administrator. The outcomes of the said study show that in some Member States proceedings do provide that the debtor may remain in possession also after

---

54 INSOL Europe report 'Study on a new approach to business failure and insolvency – Comparative legal analysis of the Member States' relevant provisions and practices' of 12 May 2014 (JUST/2012/JCIV/CT/0194/A4), commissioned by the Directorate-General Justice in the European Commission to INSOL Europe 'to provide information on restructuring mechanisms already available in all Member States, their main features, effective use, rate of success, cost to the debtor and length'.

the opening of full insolvency proceedings, and thus, also after the debtor having been declared insolvent.

Article 2(3) EIR provides for a definition of debtor in possession proceedings (see *supra* para 1.2). This definition seems to suggest that also proceedings under Article 1(1) lit. a) EIR may be in possession: in fact, debtor in possession proceedings do not require, but may provide for the appointment of, an insolvency practitioner, and are compatible with a partial divestment of the debtor. These proceedings may leave the debtor in possession when are not aimed at liquidating the debtor's assets among the creditors, but promote the reorganization of its business (in spite of the debtor's insolvency). The question arises whether proceedings that fall under Article 1(1) lit. c) EIR are in possession, or rather – since the debtor is never divested in 'moratoria' – whether those proceedings are in possession in the meaning of Article 2(3) EIR. Recital 10 EIR provides that 'since such proceedings (i.e. proceedings which leave the debtor fully or partially in control of its assets and affairs) do not necessarily entail the appointment of an insolvency practitioner, they should be covered by this Regulation if they take place under the control or supervision of a court'. Given that the expression used in this recital is the same used to describe proceedings under Article 1(1) lit. b) EIR, it is better to hold that proceedings under Article 1(1) lit. c) EIR may not be considered debtor-in-possession pursuant to Article 2(3) EIR. Obviously, proceedings under Article 1(1) lit. b) EIR are debtor-in-possession proceedings par excellence.

## 1.3 Territorial scope

According to Article 3 and recitals 25 and 33, the EIR applies only to proceedings in respect of a debtor whose COMI is located in the EU. However, it is not expressed in the text of the EIR whether that requirement suffice or other territorial requirements are to be met for the instrument to apply. In particular, it is not clear whether the EIR *(i)* apply to purely domestic matters and *(ii)* apply where the cross-border connection is between one Member State and a non-EU State.[55] The same questions arise with regard to the EIR 2000, and the CJEU answered to both in the nega-

---

55 *Bork*, in: Bork/Mangano (eds), European Cross-Border Insolvency Law (2016), para 2.71. See also CJEU, 8 June 2017, Case C-54/16, *Vinyls Italia SpA*, ECLI:EU:C:2017:433.

tive:[56] it must be assessed whether these answers are still up-to-date (see *infra* para 2.2.3).

## 2. Evaluation

### 2.1 Legal issues

#### 2.1.1 The title of the EIR: is it still up-to-date?

Notwithstanding also proceedings which may be opened in case of a mere likelihood of insolvency fall in the scope of the EIR, the title of the EIR is still to be considered up-to-date. In fact, the term 'insolvency' refers no longer to the financial or economic condition of a debtor unable to redress its business, but to the place (national insolvency law or national general company law – provided, in this last case, that proceedings ruled by such law are designed exclusively for 'insolvency situations': but see *infra* Part 1 III, 2.2.1) in which the rules concerning the proceedings covered by the EIR are to be found. Thus, 'on insolvency proceedings' must now be read as 'on proceedings based on laws relating to insolvency'.

#### 2.1.2 The notion of insolvency (recital 17 EIR)

The questions arise whether: *(i)* a uniform definition of insolvency is needed; *(ii)* in case of an affirmative answer, (whether) a liquidity test should be preferred. It is to be preliminarily underlined that these questions are relevant only in a *de iure condendo* perspective: as seen above (para 1.2.2), the EIR provides no definition of insolvency.

The first question has received a slight majority of affirmative answers from the stakeholders to whom the questionnaire prepared within this research project has been submitted. Respondents who have answered in the affirmative highlighted that a uniform definition should be desirable especially to avoid that the opening of territorial proceedings prior to the opening of main proceedings could be obtained only in some Member States.[57] According to the opposite view, the notion of insolvency should be contin-

---

56 CJEU, 16 January 2014, Case C-328/12, *Schmid*, ECLI:EU:C:2014:6.
57 According to Art 3(4) lit. a) EIR, territorial proceedings may be opened prior to the opening of main proceedings where 'insolvency proceedings under paragraph

ued to be determined according to the law of main or secondary proceedings. Indeed, this second interpretation seems to be endorsed by Article 34, 2nd s. EIR (newly introduced in the EIR), that is (also) aimed at preventing the risks implied by the different national definitions of insolvency: according to this provision, in fact, 'where the main insolvency proceedings required that the debtor be insolvent, the debtor's insolvency shall not be re-examined in the Member State in which secondary insolvency proceedings may be opened'.[58]

It is worth stressing that some respondents have held that a uniform definition of insolvency would be practical only within the framework of a harmonized substantive insolvency law; and that other respondents, symmetrically, have held that the conflict-of-law approach is the most appropriate as long as there are divergent national insolvency definitions. This opinion must be emphasized as the most persuasive: the notion of insolvency seems to be a topic that can better be addressed within an instrument designed to further harmonization of national insolvency laws than within an instrument based on a conflict-of-law approach. In fact, *(i)* if a definition of insolvency were included in the EIR with the aim to promote harmonization of the national definitions, such objective would hardly be achieved, since the EIR is not conceived to encourage harmonization, and in any case harmonization would be encouraged in a worse manner than a directive (and maybe also a recommendation) would; *(ii)* if a definition of insolvency were included in the EIR to be read as a material provision of private international law, then the relationship between that definition and the potential different definitions provided in each national legislation should be clarified: which one will apply?; in particular, which one will apply in cases in which proceedings involve only purely domestic matters (see *infra* para 2.2.3)?

Yet, two reasons that are more convincing have been raised against the necessity to amend the EIR providing a definition of insolvency. The first

---

l cannot be opened because of the conditions laid down by the law of the Member State within the territory of which the centre of the debtor's main interests is situated'. On the other hand, it must be underlined that, if the EIR provided a definition of insolvency, there would be less possibilities to open territorial proceedings, since insolvency could no longer be a reason which may prevent the opening of main proceedings.

58  On this point, see CJEU, 22 November 2012, Case C-116/11, *Bank Handlowy*, ECLI:EU:C:2012:739, paras 68 ff.

reason consists in the fact that, due to the enlargement of its scope to pre-insolvency proceedings, 'insolvency' is no longer the burden of inclusion/exclusion of proceedings within the EIR. The second (and main) reason consists in the fact that the adoption of a common definition would not prevent each Member State from interpreting that definition in its own manner, making use of different national criteria.[59]

In conclusion, it is not advisable to introduce a definition of insolvency in the EIR; if need be, a uniform definition of insolvency will have to be adopted in the national legislations, should the establishment of a framework of harmonized insolvency law be promoted also as to the definition of insolvency.

In the light of this, the second question takes second place. Nonetheless, it is to be underlined that a large majority of the stakeholders to whom the questionnaire has been submitted who maintained that an insolvency definition is needed held that a liquidity test should be preferred over a balance sheet test. This answer seems rational: proceedings based on insolvency are generally opened upon request of both the debtor and creditors;[60] and creditors who are not institutional (banks, insurance companies, etc.) usually rely on a liquidity test, since only the inability to pay debts as they fall due is perceptible by them. The EIR itself seems to show a preference for the liquidity test: according to recital 17 EIR (see *supra* para 1.2.2), non-financial difficulties are only relevant when they give rise to a real and serious threat to 'the debtor's actual or future ability to pay its debts as they fall due'.

As far as this recital is concerned, the question has been asked in the questionnaire submitted among stakeholders whether the possibility to open insolvency proceedings where the debtor faces non-financial difficulties raise any concerns (e.g. where 'the debtor has lost a contract which is of key importance to him'). A slight majority of the respondents has answered in the affirmative, highlighting two main issues raised by such a possibility. The first one consists in that the opening of insolvency proceedings in case of non-financial difficulties may prejudice the creditors' rights, which is unjustified at a very early stage of crisis (such a prejudice could only be accepted to the extent that enforcement proceedings by

---

59  But see *infra* para 2.2.2.
60  See INSOL Europe report 'Study on a new approach to business failure and insolvency – Comparative legal analysis of the Member States' relevant provisions and practices' of 12 May 2014 (JUST/2012/JCIV/CT/0194/A4), 29.

creditors are not precluded or interrupted). The second one – strictly connected with the former – is the risk of abuse: being 'non-financial difficulties' a broad and ultimately subjective concept, debtors could always rely on it in order to apply for insolvency proceeding; with the consequence that debtors could also file for the opening of insolvency proceedings with the aim either of preventing individual enforcement actions or of handling more easily with lay-offs and shareholder conflicts. Conversely, respondents who have held that recital 17 EIR does not raise any particular concerns have underlined, on the one hand, that the opening of proceedings at a stage in which there are only non-financial difficulties correspond to the current approach to distress and to the promotion of the 'rescue culture' endorsed, *inter alia*, in the Recommendation; on the other hand, that non-financial difficulties are only relevant to the extent that they give rise to a real and serious threat to the debtor's actual or future ability to pay its debts as they fall due: as a consequence, they should be deemed to fall under the general category of pre-insolvency.

The second position seems consistent with the letter of recital 17 EIR: while pre-insolvency (likelihood of insolvency) should be read as a real and serious threat to the debtor's actual or future ability to pay, i.e. serious *financial* difficulties or imminent insolvency; non-financial difficulties should be read as difficulties that, in the short term, threaten the status of the debtor's business as a going concern, but that are only relevant for the purposes of the EIR when are susceptible to evolve, in the medium term, in a real and serious threat to the debtor's actual or future ability to pay its debts as they fall due (that is, in serious financial difficulties or imminent insolvency). Since non-financial difficulties are relevant insofar as they are able to give rise to difficulty or inability to pay, it is clear that also proceedings triggered by a non-financial distress should fall under the category of pre-insolvency proceedings, and be subject to a test not far from that to which other pre-insolvency proceedings are subject. Obviously, the effectiveness of such a test depends on the party having power to commence proceedings under national legislation.

2.1.3  Scope of secondary proceedings

Since under the EIR 2000, secondary proceedings 'must be winding-up proceedings' (see Article 3(3) EIR) 'listed in Annex B' (see Article 27 EIR), to implement restructuring may be difficult, as the decision rendered in the *Bank Handlowy* case made evident. In this case, a French court held that the COMI of a subsidiary company incorporated in Poland was located in France, and opened a proceeding aimed at rescuing the whole group of companies (whose parent company was incorporated in France) according to French law. Nevertheless, creditors of the Polish subsidiary filed for a secondary proceeding in Poland, where the whole assets were situated. The CJEU was asked to establish whether Article 27 EIR 2000 must be interpreted as meaning that it allows for the opening of secondary insolvency proceedings in the Member State in which all of the debtor's assets are situated, where the main proceedings have a protective (rescue) purpose. The CJEU acknowledged that the opening of territorial proceedings 'risks running counter to the purpose served by main proceedings'; the only solution, however, was found in the principle of sincere cooperation laid down in Article 4(3) of the TFEU, which 'requires the court having jurisdiction to open secondary proceedings, in applying those provisions, to have regard to the objectives of the main proceedings'.[61] It was established, on the contrary, that no provision of the EIR 2000 prevents from opening secondary proceedings when main proceedings have rescue purposes: in fact, neither Article 3(3) nor Article 27 EIR distinguish according to the purposes of main proceedings.[62] Thus, the EIR 2000 does not effectively coordinate secondary and main proceedings.[63]

The provision that secondary proceedings should have winding-up purposes has not been recast in the EIR, and the list containing proceedings only aimed at the winding-up has been deleted: therefore, secondary proceedings can now aim at helping the main proceeding in restructuring a distressed business. For present purposes, it has to be underlined that now the *scope* of main proceedings and secondary proceedings is *coextended*, unlike in the EIR 2000.

### 2.1.4 The COMI presumption for pre-insolvency proceedings

The EIR has improved the way to ascertain where a debtor's COMI is located. According to Article 3 EIR, the place of the registered office (for

---

61  *Mucciarelli*, ECFR 2016, 1, 25.
62  CJEU, 22 November 2012, Case C-116/11, *Bank Handlowy*, ECLI:EU:C:2012:739, paras 55-57.
63  On this topic see *Leandro*, Riv.dir.int.priv. e proc. 2014, 317, 323 ff.

companies and legal persons), the principal place of business (for individuals exercising an independent business or a professional activity) and the habitual residence (for other individuals) shall be presumed to be the COMI, unless they have not been moved within the 3-month period (6-month for non-professional debtors) prior to the request for the opening of proceedings.[64] When the reform process was still on the way, a proposal had been made[65] to apply the presumptions laid down in Article 3 EIR only to insolvent debtors, and not to merely financially distressed debtors, on the assumption that the purposes pursued by the former and the latter by means of the COMI shift would be deeply different. In fact, while an insolvent debtor would be more likely to relocate the COMI in the *suspect period* in order to benefit from 'a more favourable legal position to the detriment of the general body of creditors' (as stated in recital 5 EIR), a debtor who suffers from a simple financial distress would be more likely to do the same 'in (…) search for a more favourable legislation (…) into the general freedom of movement (see Articles 49 and 54 TFEU), rather than necessarily into a suspicious scenario'.

Article 3 EIR does not distinguish at all between insolvency and pre-insolvency proceedings as to the application of the COMI presumption. There seems not to be the possibility to offer an interpretation of this article in the sense of that proposal, since it would be contrary to the clear letter of the EIR; nor it seems to be possible to assess on a case by case basis what the purposes for the COMI shift are, and to apply the presumptions only to relocations made with abusive purposes. In any case, debtors which relocate the COMI with the aim to a better 'restructuring environment' will have the possibility to rebut those presumptions.

## 2.2  Practical problems

### 2.2.1  Pre-insolvency and hybrid proceedings before a 'judgment opening insolvency proceedings' is rendered

Article 19 EIR provides that 'any judgment opening insolvency proceedings handed down by a court of a Member State which has jurisdiction

---

64  On this topic, see *Bariatti/Corno*, Centro degli interessi principali, available at: il-fallimentarista.it 2016.
65  It is the proposal made by *Latella*, ECFR 2015, 479.

pursuant to Article 3 shall be recognised in all other Member States from the moment that it becomes effective in the State of the opening of proceedings'. The CJEU, however, has established that the EIR 2000 applies even before a judgment opening insolvency proceedings has been delivered but the request has been lodged; furthermore, the EIR 2000 contains provisions concerning the conduct of the proceedings for the period between the request for their opening and the opening judgment (see Article 38 EIR 2000). Now, the EIR also considers the case of proceedings that have already commenced but have not been 'formally' opened: pursuant to Article 2(7) EIR, 'judgment opening insolvency proceedings' is not only the decision of any court to open insolvency proceedings or the decision of a court to appoint an insolvency practitioner, but also the decision of any court to confirm the opening of insolvency proceedings. This introduction was needed in view of the inclusion in the EIR of hybrid and pre-insolvency proceedings, that, as seen above, may be started by a debtor and by creditors, and may also entail the intervention of a court on appeal by creditors or other interested parties. In many cases, according to the national legislations, such proceedings are 'substantially' already opened at the moment a judgment pursuant to Article 2(7) lit. i) EIR is rendered, but the opening under national legislation, however, does not fit the (autonomous) definition of Article 2(7) lit. i) EIR.

The reference in Article 2(7) lit. i) EIR to the decision confirming the opening of proceedings may also hint at 'interim' proceedings, which, pursuant to recital 15, are opened and conducted for a certain period on an interim or provisional basis before a court issues an order 'confirming' the continuation of the proceedings on a non-interim basis. 'Interim' proceedings currently provided in national laws see the appointment of a provisional insolvency practitioner[66] included in Annex B: for this reason, they seem to be recognizable abroad since the decision to appoint the insolvency practitioner is taken (see Article 2(7) lit. ii) EIR). Should there be 'interim' proceedings not appointing an insolvency practitioner listed in Annex B (or should they be introduced), they should be recognizable abroad since the final decision confirming the opening is issued.

Difficulties may arise concerning the early phase in which a judgment confirming the opening of insolvency proceedings (pursuant to the defini-

---

66 This is the case when a German *vorläufiger Insolvenzverwalter* or an Irish *provisional liquidator* are appointed.

tion given at Article 2(7) lit. i) EIR) has not been rendered yet: in particular, there might be cases where the debtor is not protected against individual enforcement actions from the outset, but only after a court or authority intervenes confirming the opening of proceedings. Two instruments (both already available in the EIR 2000) are of some help to deal with this issue. The first one is the power for the court competent for the main insolvency proceedings to order in the application stage of such proceedings provisional and protective measures covering assets situated in other Member States (see recital 36, 4th s. EIR). Judgments relating to these measures are automatically recognized abroad, pursuant to Article 32(1), (3) EIR. The second one is the power for the temporary insolvency practitioner appointed in the main proceedings to request, in the application stage, any measure to secure and preserve any of the debtor's assets situated in another Member State, provided for under the law of that Member State (see Article 52 EIR).

Each of these tools suffers from shortcomings. The first one may prevent foreign creditors from enforcing payment claims, but not from applying for the opening of secondary proceedings. In fact, there is no rule for 'moratoria' imposed during the application stage similar to Article 38(3) EIR, which provides that the court may stay the opening of secondary proceedings at the request of the insolvency practitioner or the debtor where a temporary stay of individual enforcement has been granted in another Member State to allow for negotiations between the debtors and its creditors.[67] The consequence is that creditors may always resort to local insolvency proceedings in order to prevent foreign main proceedings from grabbing local assets. The second tool is available only in main proceedings in which a temporary insolvency practitioner has been appointed, not where the debtor remains in possession: a broad interpretation seems not to be allowed, since the EIR usually mentions the debtor in possession where it wants to treat the same to the insolvency practitioner.

---

67  The reason is why only the 'moratorium' under Art 1(1) lit. c) EIR (and not that provided in the application stage) is considered to constitute a main insolvency proceeding within the scope of the EIR 2000, with the power to preclude secondary proceedings: see *Bork*, Insolv.Int. 2016, 1, 4.

## 2.2.2 Article 34, 2nd s. EIR

According to Article 34, 2nd s. EIR (former Article 27 EIR 2000), 'where main insolvency proceedings required that the debtor be insolvent, the debtor's insolvency shall not be re-examined in the Member State in which secondary insolvency proceedings may be opened'. Annex A does not distinguish among proceedings based on insolvency, proceedings based on a mere likelihood of insolvency and proceedings that can be based both on insolvency and likelihood of insolvency: thus, it may be difficult for courts requested to open a secondary proceeding to know whether foreign main proceedings are based on insolvency or not. For the provision contained in Article 34 EIR to be effective, it is essential that Member States provide, pursuant to Article 86 EIR, a short description of their national legislation and procedures relating to insolvency, with a particular reference to the level of distress upon which the opening of each procedure[68] may be triggered.

However, this may not be sufficient, since there are procedures listed in Annex A which can be based on both insolvency and likelihood of insolvency. In these cases, there would not be other way to know whether main proceedings required debtor's insolvency but to analyze the circumstances which brought to their opening. It is obvious that such a check would barely be consistent with the principle of mutual recognition and would hinder the efficiency of the EIR. Two possible ways can be devised to face this shortcoming. The first one is to interpret Article 34, 2nd s. EIR, as it states that the debtor's insolvency should not be re-examined by the court opening a secondary proceeding not only 'where main insolvency proceedings required that the debtor be insolvent' but also where main insolvency proceedings *could* be based on debtor's insolvency. This first method, however, may be contrary to the intention underlying the EIR to limit the opening of secondary proceedings and to promote rescue: if foreign courts were relieved to check insolvency also in cases in which main proceedings can be based on both likelihood of insolvency and insolvency, in fact, there would be more possibilities that several secondary proceedings aimed at liquidation be opened in respect of a debtor subject to a

---

68  With regard to this problem, see *Csöke*, Eurofenix 2016, 29.

main proceeding aimed at its rescue.[69] The second method consists in encouraging the courts opening main proceedings to always specify in the
judgment opening such proceedings whether the debtor is insolvent.[70]
This second method seems not to raise concerns, and thus must be recommended.


### 2.2.3 The territorial scope

As seen above (para 1.3), doubts arise as to whether the EIR applies: *(i)* to
purely domestic matters; *(ii)* to proceedings whose sole cross-border connection is with a third state. The two issues must be separately examined.

*(i)* In the *Schmid* case, the CJEU, asked to determine 'whether, in order
for the Regulation to apply, there must in any event be cross-border elements in the sense that only situations involving connecting factors with
two or several Member States fall within the Regulation's scope', observed that 'a general and absolute condition of this kind does not result
from the wording of the Regulation's provisions',[71] and that 'the objectives pursued by the Regulation, as resulting in particular from the recitals
in its preamble, likewise do not support a narrow interpretation of the
Regulation's scope, requiring the presence of such an element'.[72] The
Court also noted that the COMI is to be determined at the time when the
request to open insolvency proceedings has been lodged (as it had been
decided in the *Staubitz-Schreiber* case[73]): 'at that early stage, the existence

---

69  This solution does not, then, seem consistent with the decision rendered in the
    *Bank Handlowy* case (CJEU, 22 November 2012, Case C-116/11, *Bank Handlowy*,
    ECLI:EU:C:2012:739), where the CJEU noted that 'when a court before which an
    application for secondary proceedings has been made draws conclusions from the
    finding of insolvency in the main proceedings, it must have regard to the objec-
    tives of the main proceedings and take account of the scheme of the Regulation as
    well as the principles on which it is based' (para 73).
70  In *Virgós-Schmit* Report, the authors observed that 'States which list proceedings
    which can be used for purposes other than insolvency, must provide sufficient
    means of identification of the proceedings to facilitate the application of the Con-
    vention. For instance, requiring their courts or competent bodies to specify clearly
    the grounds on which the decision to open proceedings is based, so that these can
    then be used as an identification "label"' (para 49).
71  CJEU, 16 January 2014, Case C-328/12, *Schmid*, ECLI:EU:C:2014:6, para 20.
72  CJEU, 16 January 2014, Case C-328/12, *Schmid*, ECLI:EU:C:2014:6, para 24.
73  CJEU, 17 January 2006, Case C-1/04, *Staubitz-Schreiber*, ECLI:EU:C:2006:39.

of any cross-border element may be unknown', and yet to postpone the determination of the court having jurisdiction until such time as the locations of various aspects of the proceedings (such as the residence of a potential defendant to an ancillary action) are known, 'would frustrate the objectives of improving the efficiency and effectiveness of insolvency proceedings having cross-border effects'.[74]

No provision or recital contained in the EIR expressly requires for the existence of a cross-border connection. Furthermore, the provisions and recitals on the grounds of which the CJEU founded its decision have been recast, without amendments or with trivial amendments. These elements may be sufficient to consider the *Schmid* judgment still up-to-date. However, further elements to support the view that a cross-border connection is not needed can be indirectly found in two provisions newly introduced in the EIR. The first (and main) provision is Article 4, 2nd s., according to which 'the judgment opening insolvency proceedings shall specify (...) whether jurisdiction is based on Article 3(1) or (2)'. As the CJEU pointed out in the *Schmid* judgment, at the moment the proceedings are opened the cross-border connection may be still unknown: this rule clarifies that courts, *whenever* open a procedure included in the Annex, must declare whether it is a main or a secondary proceeding, irrespective of there being such cross-border element, or it having been apparent yet. The second rule is Article 24 EIR, pursuant to which 'Member States shall establish and maintain in their territory one or several registers in which information

---

74 Arts 6, 14 and 44(3) lit. a) EIR 2000 have been recast in Arts 9, 17 and 85(3) lit. a) EIR; recitals 4, 8 and 12 EIR 2000 are now recitals 5,8 and 23 EIR. *Laukemann,* IILR 2014, 101, 103, summarizes the principles on which the decision is based as follows: 'neither Article 1(1) ... non Annex A thereto nor recital 14 appeared to limit the application of the Regulation to proceedings that involve any cross-border element (...). The same held true, apart from Articles 6 and 14 EIR, for the wording of Article 3(1) EIR confining the determination of the competent court to the centre of a debtor's main interests, adding no further condition such as an element involving two or more Member States (...). Instead, implementing such intra-EU element would lead to a significant legal uncertainty and delay at the outset of cross-border proceedings and therefore diminish their effectiveness and efficiency. This is because the determination of the competent court had to be made at the earliest possible stage, so that action may be taken to preserve the debtor's estate for the sake of the general body of creditors. This legislative approach reflected the principles of unity and universality of insolvency proceedings (...), militating in favor of a general applicability of the Regulation in case of a simple connection to third States'.

concerning insolvency proceedings is published ('insolvency registers'). That information shall be published as soon as possible after the opening of such proceedings'. For this provision to be effective, it has to be held that <u>all</u> national procedures listed in Annex A must be published.

In the light of this, the EIR should be deemed applicable also to purely domestic matters. It has been highlighted that, though the principle of effectiveness cited in the *Schmid* judgment (and now underpinned by Article 4) is reasonable, it would seem 'disproportionate to completely displace national rules on jurisdiction due to an unspecified risk of the insolvency at hand having cross-border effects, and this is certainly contrary to the pluralistic approach generally taken by the Regulation'.[75] The fewer issues will arise, the more similar the interpretation of the COMI criterion and the national jurisdiction criteria will be.

*(ii)* Once admitted that a Member State's jurisdiction should not depend on the existence of a cross-border link, the solution to the question whether the EIR applies also to proceedings whose sole cross-border connection is with a non-EU State (or with Denmark) is quite easy. On the one hand, if the EIR applies to proceedings which at the moment of their opening do not show any cross-border elements, it goes without saying that proceedings whose cross-border connection with a third state becomes apparent at a later stage should fall within the scope of the EIR. On the other hand, proceedings which at the moment of their opening show as sole cross-border connection an element involving a non-EU State should also be covered by the EIR, since further elements involving a Member State may become apparent at a later stage.[76]

Some major doubts may arise as to whether judgments directly deriving and closely linked to insolvency proceedings in which a defendant domiciled in a third state is sued fall in the scope of the EIR as well. Firstly, in 'insolvency-related' actions it is possible to know in advance whether the

---

75  *Bork*, in: Bork/Mangano (eds), European cross-border insolvency law (2016), para 2.75.

76  In the English case of *Re BRAC Rent-A-Car* (*Re BRAC Rent-A-Car International Inc.* [2003] EWHC 128 (Ch)) the EIR 2000 had already been deemed applicable to proceedings involving a third state, i.e. the insolvency of a company incorporated in the U.S. The English court said that the only limitation on territorial scope is the COMI concept, and that if only debtors incorporated in a Member State were to be affected, the EIR 2000 would have explicitly stated this. The *Schmid* goes beyond, since it establishes that the EIR 2000 applies regardless of any cross-border implication.

sole cross-border element involved is with a non-EU state, unlike in collective proceedings. Secondly, and most importantly, 'compared to collective proceedings, the defendant's protection guaranteed in civil procedure on the basis of the actor sequitur forum rei-principle enunciated in Article 2 Brussels I Regulation (Article 4 Brussels I[bis] – editor's note) is of paramount importance and can thus only be ousted by overarching jurisdictional, i.e. insolvency-specific interests in this context', especially for 'third-state defendants devoid of any sufficient connection to the state of the opening of insolvency proceedings within the European Union'.[77] Nevertheless, the *Schmid* judgment decided precisely this issue, establishing that the courts of the Member State 'within the territory of which insolvency proceedings have been opened have jurisdiction to hear and determine an action to set a transaction aside by virtue of insolvency that is brought against a person whose place of residence is not within the territory of a Member State'.[78] In accordance with this judgment, a large majority of the stakeholders to whom the questionnaire prepared within this research project has been submitted has argued that insolvency-related actions should fall within the scope of the EIR because they fulfil the only requirement provided, i.e. the debtor's COMI being in a Member State; and that this conclusion is consistent with new Article 6 EIR (dealing with the jurisdiction to open actions directly deriving and closely connected to the insolvency proceedings – see *infra* Part 1, IV. 1), which does not require that the defendant is resident within the EU for the EIR to apply.

In light of this (in particular considering that the reform does not deal with this topic), it seems logic to confirm the solution given in *Schmid*, both for collective and individual actions. To deem the EIR applicable to proceedings (both collective and individual) whose sole cross-border link is with a third state raises some concerns, both theoretical and practical. As for the theoretical issues,[79] it has been highlighted that such a solution, firstly, would violate the mutual trust requirement, since the EIR would apply to third states' assets, creditors, defendants etc., without those States having decided to adhere to any bilateral or multilateral agreement; sec-

---

77  *Laukemann*, IILR 2014, 101, 102.

78  See also CJEU, 4 December 2014, Case C-295/13, *H*, ECLI:EU:C:2014:2410, para 33.

79  For the following considerations, see *Paulus*, Insolv.Int. 2014, 70, 70 ff. They have been expressed with regard to the EIR 2000, but they seem valid also with regard to the EIR.

ondly, would disregard the *rationale* underlying the EIR, as emerging from Article 3( 2)-(4) EIR, which deals with territorial proceedings limited to the territory of a Member State. To the second consideration, it has been incisively replied that there is a fundamental difference between the universal scope of main proceedings and the strictly territorial scope of secondary or territorial proceedings, and that assets or other matters outside the EU are the concern solely of the main proceedings.[80] To the first point, it has been replied that only recognition (and not jurisdiction) is based on mutual trust: thus, 'the fact that non-EU countries may or may not recognize EU avoidance judgments should not of itself prevent the EU courts from taking jurisdiction over defendants resident outside the EU'.[81]

Albeit correct, this last remark confirms that including in the scope of the EIR proceedings involving only third states' implications may entail recognition and enforcement issues in those States[82] (and now we turn to the practical issues). On this point, the CJEU in the *Schmid* judgment noted that, if in a given case it is not possible to rely on the EIR 2000 itself for the recognition and enforcement of judgments, it is sometimes possible to obtain the recognition and enforcement of the judgment delivered by the court with jurisdiction under a bilateral convention, or – in case of insolvency-related actions – under Article 25 EIR 2000, in particular insofar as part of the defendant's assets are in the territory of other Member States.[83] Therefore, where a bilateral convention between the Member State taking jurisdiction and the third state lacks, and where Article 25 EIR 2000 (now Article 32 EIR) cannot apply, it is likely that proceedings will not be recognized and enforced in the third state. In this case, the risk exists that the proceeding remains useless, especially when most part of the assets (in collective proceedings) or the whole assets whose restitution is claimed (in insolvency-related actions) are located in the third state. For this reason, it has been proposed by some of the respondents to the questionnaire submitted within this research project that Member States should

---

80  *Moss*, Insolv.Int. 2015, 6.
81  *Moss*, Insolv.Int. 2015, 6.
82  Also part of those who deem that such an extension of the scope of the EIR is not excessive admits that it could raise recognition concerns.
83  'However, it is arguable that if the defendant did have assets in other Member States, the Regulation would apply anyway, since there is a cross-border situation as between two Member States': see *Bork*, in: Bork/Mangano (eds), European Cross-Border Insolvency Law (2016), para 2.80.

open proceedings involving a non-EU State connection only when these proceedings can find recognition and enforcement in that State; it has also been proposed to adopt an international convention on recognition, in order to avoid that such proceedings remain ineffectual.

In conclusion, it can be observed that the application of the EIR both to purely domestic proceedings and to proceedings involving a connection with non-EU states raises some issues;[84] nonetheless, such application is congruous with the text of the EIR, whose only test for jurisdiction refers to the COMI being located within a Member State.[85]

3. Theses and recommendations

In light of the above, the following recommendations should be issued.

3.1 The definition of 'debtor-in-possession' proceedings, provided in Article 2(3) EIR, should be considered equivalent to the concept of 'hybrid proceedings' laid down in the Commission's proposal of 12 December 2012.

3.2 It is recommended not to introduce a uniform definition of 'insolvency' in the EIR. 'Insolvency' is no longer the burden of inclusion/exclusion within the scope of the Regulation. Furthermore, a definition to be included in the EIR would require a specific amendment, would not prevent divergent interpretations and would only have the effect to (try to) further harmonize the substantive insolvency law of the different Member States.

If need be, it is advisable that a uniform definition be introduced directly in the national insolvency laws.

3.3 Pursuant to recital 17, the scope of the EIR should extend to proceedings which are triggered by situations in which the debtor faces non-financial difficulties (e.g. the loss of a contract of key importance to it).

---

84 In the contrary sense, see *Linna*, Int.Insolv.Rev. 2014, 20, 32, who observed (with concern to the Commission's proposal of 12 December 2012) that proceedings mentioned in Annex A should fall within the scope of the new Regulation only if 'the concrete case (...) [has] cross-border implications'. She added that 'there is no need for a specific definition in this respect in the EIR or in the amendment draft'.

85 For this reason, proceedings opened in respect of a debtor which has an establishment in a Member State and whose COMI is outside the EU do not fall within the scope of the EIR. See *Laukemann*, IILR 2014, 101.

The EIR does not provide specific rules for these proceedings. Since non-financial difficulties are significant insofar as 'give rise to a real and serious threat to the debtor's actual or future ability to pay its debts as they fall due', proceedings opened in these situations should fall under the general category of pre-insolvency proceedings.

Therefore, proceedings triggered by non-financial difficulties should be considered to raise the same issues as proceedings triggered by financial difficulties.

3.4 For the purposes of the EIR, proceedings based on the insolvency of the debtor are equated to proceedings which are based on a mere likelihood of insolvency (both fall under the general definition of 'insolvency proceedings'). As a matter of fact, the EIR does not provide specific rules on jurisdiction, recognition and applicable law concerning proceedings based on a mere likelihood of insolvency.

Consequently, the COMI presumption and the *suspect period* established in Article 3(1) EIR should also be applicable to proceedings based on a mere likelihood of insolvency.

3.5 The provision requiring that secondary proceedings have to be aimed at the winding-up has not been recast in the EIR. As a consequence, secondary proceedings may now also be aimed at the debtor's rescue or adjustment of debt, and may be coordinated with main insolvency proceedings in order to promote a debtor's restructuring.

Therefore, main insolvency proceedings and secondary insolvency proceedings have now coextended scopes.

3.6 Protection against actions from the outset might not be guaranteed in the early phase of proceedings which are formally opened only when a judgment confirming the opening is rendered, pursuant to Article 2(7) lit. i) EIR.

In these cases, debtors may resort to instruments provided in recital 36, 4th s. EIR ('provisional and protective measures covering assets situated in the territory of other Member States' ordered by the court competent for the main insolvency proceedings), and in Article 52 EIR ('any measures to secure and preserve any of the debtor's assets situated in another Member State, provided for under the law of that Member State', upon request of a temporary administrator).

However, the first tool does not prevent from the opening of secondary proceedings abroad: such opening may only be stayed when *moratoria* provided in Article 1(1) lit. c) EIR have been granted. The second tool is not available in proceedings in which the debtor is left in possession.

3.7 The provision has been recast according to which 'where the main insolvency proceedings required that the debtor be insolvent, the debtor's insolvency shall not be re-examined in the Member State in which secondary insolvency proceedings may be opened' (Article 34, 2nd s. EIR).

For this provision being effective, it is recommended that Member States, in the short description of their national legislation and procedures relating to insolvency to be provided pursuant to Article 86 EIR, specify what proceedings can be opened in a situation of insolvency, what in a situation of likelihood of insolvency and what in both situations.

With the same purpose, it is advisable that Members States' courts, in opening main proceedings that can be based both on insolvency and on a likelihood of insolvency, specify in the judgment whether the debtor is insolvent.

3.8 Pursuant to Article 3(1), the EIR applies to proceedings in respect of a debtor whose COMI is situated in a Member State. This is the only condition laid down as to the territorial scope of application of the EIR.

Accordingly, the EIR applies also to

- proceedings devoid of cross-border implications. This is suggested by Article 4 EIR, according to which every judgment opening insolvency proceedings listed in Annex A shall specify whether such proceedings are main or secondary ones (provided that the debtor's COMI is in the EU);
- proceedings whose sole cross-border implications involve a third state (i.e. a non-EU State or Denmark), irrespective of whether the judgment opening such proceedings and judgments concerning their course and closure shall be recognized in the third state.

## II. The relationship between Article 1(1) of the Regulation (EU) No 2015/848 and Annex A

Articles 1(1), (3), 2(4), recital 9, Annex A

### 1. Legal framework

#### 1.1 The framework under the EIR 2000

The EIR 2000 has three provisions concerning the relationship between the scope of the instrument – as laid down in Article 1(1) – and Annex A: Article 1(1) itself, Article 2 lit. a) and recital 9. Article 1(1) defines the framework of the EIR 2000, requiring for a set of cumulative conditions which national proceedings needed to meet. Article 2 lit. a) stated that 'insolvency proceedings', i.e. the collective proceedings referred to in Article 1(1), 'are listed in Annex A'; similarly, recital 9 provided that 'the insolvency proceedings to which this Regulation applies are listed in the Annexes'.

According to the *Virgós-Schmit* Report,[86] Article 1(1) and Article 2 lit. a) had to be interpreted in the sense that only those proceedings expressly entered in the list of the Annex should have been considered as 'insolvency proceedings' as covered by the Regulation and should have been able to benefit from its provisions. As the *Virgós-Schmit* Report seems to suggest, in the mind of the drafters of the EIR 2000 Article 1(1) and Annex A should not have shown any discrepancies. The relationship between Article 1(1) and Annex A had been envisaged as a very simple one: on the one hand, *only* the national procedures fulfilling the conditions of Article 1(1) should have been included in the Annex; on the other hand, *all* the national procedures fulfilling the conditions of Article 1(1) should have been included in the Annex.

However, in practice, discrepancies have become a widespread phenomenon. In particular, cases have arisen in which: *(i)* national procedures which did not satisfy all the requirements laid down in Article 1(1) were listed in Annex A, and *(ii)* national procedures which satisfied the requirements laid down in Article 1(1) were not listed in Annex A. This situation also depended on the procedure to amend Annex A, set forth in Article 45.

---

86 *Virgós-Schmit Report*, Report on the Convention on Insolvency Proceedings (1996), para 48.

Pursuant to this provision, the power of amending Annexes was vested in the Council, which acts by qualified majority on initiative of a Member State or the Commission. Since the Commission did not verify whether the proceedings notified by Member States fulfilled the requirements of Article 1(1), Member States, on one hand, had the power to promote at their discretion the inclusion in the Annex of whatever proceeding. This is what happened in practice: in fact, some Member States have listed in Annex A pre-insolvency proceedings, which were not 'insolvency proceedings' in the sense provided for by Article 1(1).[87] On the other hand, Member States were not under any obligation to notify new domestic proceedings.

Two CJEU's judgments dealt with such discrepancies. The *Bank Handlowy* case[88] addressed the issue of the recognition in other Member States of a French procedure (the *sauvegarde* established by the French Commercial Code) which had been included in Annex A although it did not comply with the scope of the Regulation (since it did not require the debtor's insolvency and aimed at its rescue). The CJEU decided that 'once proceedings are listed in Annex A to the Regulation, they must be regarded as coming within the scope of the Regulation'; and that 'inclusion in the list has the direct, binding effect attaching to the provisions of a regulation'.[89] The *Radziejewski* case[90] was perfectly in line with *Bank Handlowy*. Since the debt relief procedure at issue – the Swedish *skuldsanering* – was not listed in Annex A, the CJEU stated that it fell outside the scope of the EIR 2000. This procedure did not comply with all the requirements of Article 1(1) and thus probably it could not be included in Annex A. However, corollary of this decision is that the Regulation is not applicable to proceedings not included in Annex A even though they fit in its scope.

These judgments were not without consequences on the relationship between Article 1(1) and Annex A and their respective role. And indeed, *(i)* if the courts in other Member States were not to second-guess whether

---

87  See, e.g., French *procédure de sauveguarde* (as it will be seen below) and Italian *concordato preventivo*, which were included in Annex A to the EIR 2000 even if they do not fit the requirements set out in its Art 1(1).

88  CJEU, 22 November 2012, Case C-116/11, Bank Handlowy, ECLI:EU:C:2012:739.

89  CJEU, 22 November 2012, Case C-116/11, *Bank Handlowy*, ECLI:EU:C:2012:739, para 33.

90  CJEU, 8 November 2012, Case C-461/11, *Radziejewski*, ECLI:EU:C:2012:704.

proceedings listed in Annex are 'true' insolvency proceedings, but should apply the Regulation for the simple reason of their listing; and *(ii)* if nothing prevented from the Annex being 'over-inclusive', i.e. covering procedures that are not collective and did not entail the partial or total divestment of a debtor and the appointment of a liquidator; or 'under-inclusive', in that certain procedures in some Member States may satisfy the Article 1(1) conditions without being listed in the Annex;[91] then the application of the Regulation should have been entirely up to the discretion of the Member States and parties should have not been able to rely on the cross-border effect of insolvency proceedings not included in Annex A.

## 1.2 The proposals to amend the EIR 2000

In view of the described outcomes, proposals were put forward to amend the EIR 2000 and set up a different relationship between Article 1(1) and Annex A.[92] In particular, within the Heidelberg-Luxembourg-Vienna Report, it was suggested to regard the Annexes not as an integral part of the Regulation (having the same status), but as delegated acts (as provided for in Article 290 TFEU) or implementing provisions (as provided for in Article 291 TFEU), having nature of an exemplifying list. According to this option, *(i)* when proceedings were listed in the Annex, courts should have been bound to apply the Regulation; *(ii)* when proceedings were not listed in the Annex, parties could have in any case relied on the Regulation where those proceedings had to correspond to the definition of Article 1(1).[93]

Following this suggestion, the Commission proposed a new procedure for amending Annex A, as follows: 'in order to trigger an amendment of Annex A, Member States shall notify the Commission of their national rules on insolvency proceedings which they want to have included in Annex A, accompanied by a short description. The Commission shall examine whether the notified rules comply with the condition set out in Article 1 and, where this is the case, shall amend Annex A by way of delegated

---

91  *McCormack*, J.Priv.Int.L. 2014, 41, 45 ff.
92  See on this topic *Eidenmüller*, MJ 2013, 133, 139 ff.
93  *Hess*, in: Hess/Oberhammer/Pfeiffer (eds), Heidelberg-Luxembourg-Vienna Report (2014), para 3.4.2.

act'.[94] However, this proposal tackled the problem only partially, i.e. with regard to the inclusion in the Annex of proceedings not fitting in the scope of the Regulation; it left unresolved the issue of whether the Member States were obliged to notify all the proceedings which meet the conditions laid down by the new Regulation. Indeed, since the amending power was vested in the Commission at the Member States' request, Member States would have retained a 'negative' filter power and might have refrained from notifying proceedings if they did not want so.[95]

### 1.3 The framework under the EIR

### 1.3.1 As to the nature of Annex A...

The choice made in the EIR is very clear-cut. Like the EIR 2000, Article 1(1), (3) and Article 2(4) EIR prescribe that the proceedings fulfilling the requirements of the new Article 1(1) – i.e. the 'insolvency proceedings' in the meaning of the Regulation – are listed in Annex A. What makes the choice unambiguous are the statements contained in the new recital 9. On the one hand, insolvency proceedings which fulfil the conditions set out in the Regulation 'are listed exhaustively in Annex A' and the Regulation 'should apply [to them] without any further examination by the courts of another Member State'. On the other hand, 'national insolvency procedures not listed in Annex A should not be covered by this Regulation'. As it has been pointed out, the EIR has codified CJEU'S decisions rendered in the cases *Bank Handlowy* and *Radziejewski* on the binding force of Annex A.[96] Therefore, now it seems to be beyond dispute that the inclusion or exclusion of proceedings from Annex A acts as a definitive proof of whether it benefits from the provisions of the EIR: what is in the Annex, benefits from the Regulation; what is outside the Annex, does not.[97]

---

94 See Art 47(2) of the Proposal for a Regulation of the European Parliament and of the Council amending Council Regulation (EC) No 1346/2000 on insolvency proceedings, COM/2012/0744 final – 2012/0360 (COD).
95 *Mucciarelli*, ECFR 2016, 1, 12.
96 *Mucciarelli*, ECFR 2016, 1, 11.
97 See *Bariatti/Corno*, Il Regolamento (UE) 2015/848 del Parlamento Europeo e del Consiglio del 20 maggio 2015 relativo alle procedure di insolvenza (rifusione). Una prima lettura, available at: ilfallimentarista.it 2015, 1, 4; *Moss*, in: Moss/Fletcher/Isaacs (eds), The EU Regulation on Insolvency Proceedings, 3rd edn

### 1.3.2 ...and as to the amendment of Annex A

The provision for periodically revising the Annexes contained in Article 45 EIR 2000 has not been recast; nor the original Commission's proposal of a revised Article 45 has been retained in the EIR. Therefore, no provision in the EIR deals with the amendments of Annex A. Article 90(1) EIR, dealing with the periodical reports which the Commission is required to produce on the application of the Regulation, does not mention the revision of the Annexes.

## 2. Evaluation

### 2.1 Legal issues

#### 2.1.1 The underlying policy

The relation established in the EIR between Article 1 EIR and Annex A reflects a twofold policy.

The apparent policy is to have privileged legal certainty and predictability over a continuous check of Article 1(1) EIR requirements, which would have entailed an inevitable degree of uncertainty.[98] Indeed:

*(i)*  the EIR should not apply to proceedings not listed in Annex A: even if a national procedure (either brand-new or omitted on purpose from the Annex) were to fulfil all the requirements set out in Article 1(1), the EIR would not be applicable. The inclusion in the Annex is a necessary condition to apply the EIR;

*(ii)*  the application of the EIR to proceedings included in Annex A which do not fulfil the conditions set out in Article 1(1) EIR should not be disregarded: the EIR should be applied without any further examina-

---

(2016), para 8.475; *Bork*, in: Bork/Mangano (eds), European Cross-Border Insolvency law (2016), paras 2.50-2.51; *Wessels*, ECL 2016, 129; *Garcimartín*, ZEuP 2015, 694, 703; *Fletcher*, Insolv.Int. 2015, 97, 98; *McCormack*, MLR 2016, 121, 126 ff; *Van Calster*, COMIng, and here to stay. The Review of the European Insolvency Regulation, 2016, available at: papers.ssrn.com, 1, 6; *Bewick*, Int.Insolv.Rev. 2015, 172, 176 ff; *Weiss*, Int.Insolv.Rev. 2015, 192, 196 ff.

98  See *Garcimartín*, ZEuP 2015, 694, 703; and *Weiss*, Int.Insolv.Rev. 2015, 192, 197.

tion as to whether the conditions set out in Article 1(1) are met. The inclusion in the Annex is a sufficient condition to apply the EIR.[99]

The undercurrent policy is the Member States reluctance to deprive themselves of their power to determine which proceedings have to be included in the scope of the Regulation.[100] In the light of the foregoing, it is no wonder that the original Commission's proposal of a revised Article 45 EIR has been deleted. As it has been highlighted, according to that proposal the Commission would have acted 'as gatekeeper in relation to the addition of proceedings to Annex A': for this reason, it was not accepted by the Member States.[101] Under the EIR, Member States, on the one hand, (still) retain the exclusive power to include national procedures in the Annex; on the other hand, cannot be forced to stimulate an amendment of the Regulation in order to include new national procedures in Annex A.

### 2.1.2 The role of Article 1(1) EIR

In view of the established 'Annex approach', it is undisputable that Article 1(1) EIR has become partially redundant; nevertheless, it may still play a role, acting as a blueprint that should be taken into account when new pro-

---

99  With reference to the EIR 2000, *Panzani*, Scope of application of the Council Regulation 1346/2000, available at: iiiglobal.org, asserted that 'it follows from Art 1(1) EIR that proceedings listed in Annex A that serve purposes that are not confined to insolvency law, only fall within the scope of the Insolvency Regulation if they are based on the debtor's insolvency'. By reason of the amended material scope of the recast, it is now more unlikely that proceedings are listed in Annex A which are out of the scope of Art 1(1) EIR; nonetheless, the relation between Annex A and Art 1(1) EIR could not be that envisaged by the author: EIR should apply to proceeding not fulfilling the conditions provided for in Art 1(1) EIR.

100  See *Van Calster*, COMIng, and here to stay. The Review of the European Insolvency Regulation, 2016, available at: papers.ssrn.com, 1, 6, where the author observes that 'the Annex is the trigger and it is the Member States that pull it'; and *Panzani*, Scope of application of the Council Regulation 1346/2000, available at: iiiglobal.org.

101  See *Moss*, in: Moss/Fletcher/Isaacs (eds), The EU Regulation on Insolvency Proceedings, 3rd edn (2016), para 8.475 (fn 1), where it can be read that 'a Commission proposal to act as gatekeeper in relation to the addition of proceedings to Annex A was not accepted'.

ceedings are in the process of being included in Annex A.[102] It has been underlined that the EIR ensures better congruence between Annex A and Article 1(1) EIR.[103] Thus, ideally, Annex A and Article 1(1) EIR are still intended not to show any discrepancies, as it was envisaged under the EIR 2000 according to the *Virgós-Schmit* report: all the national procedures meeting the conditions under Article 1(1) EIR should – at least theoretically – be included in Annex A. Accordingly, Article 1(1) EIR should be regarded as a substantive provision.

### 2.1.3  Amendments to Annex A

In the absence of a provision, it has been stressed that the future amendments of Annex A will have to be adopted according to the ordinary legislative procedure set forth in Article 294 TFEU.[104] This viewpoint has found a prompt confirmation in practice. On 30 May 2016, the Commission issued the first 'proposal for a Regulation of the European Parliament and of the Council replacing the lists of insolvency proceedings and insolvency practitioners in Annexes A and B to Regulation (EU) 2015/848 on insolvency proceedings',[105] reacting to the initiative of Poland, which on 4 December 2015 notified the Commission of a substantial reform of its domestic law on restructuring, taking effect as of 1 January 2016, and requested to change the lists set out in Annexes A and B to the Regulation accordingly. In its proposal, the Commission has maintained that 'since the Annexes are intrinsic part of the Regulation, their modification can *only* be achieved via the legislative amendment of the Regulation' (emphasis added). By the same token, in the explanatory statement attached to the 'draft European Parliament legislative resolution' on the said Commission

---

102  *Mucciarelli*, ECFR 2016, 1, 11.

103  *Bork*, in: Bork/Mangano (eds), European Cross-Border Insolvency Law (2016), para 2.50.

104  *Bariatti/Corno*, Il Regolamento (UE) 2015/848 del Parlamento Europeo e del Consiglio del 20 maggio 2015 relativo alle procedure di insolvenza (rifusione). Una prima lettura, available at: ilfallimentarista.it 2015, 1, 4 ff; and *Mucciarelli*, ECFR 2016, 1, 12.

105  'Proposal for a Regulation of the European Parliament and of the Council replacing the lists of insolvency proceedings and insolvency practitioners in Annexes A and B to Regulation (EU) 2015/848 on insolvency proceedings', COM/2016/0317 final – 2016/0159 (COD).

proposal,[106] it has been underlined that 'the Annexes to the Regulation can be amended only by a regulation to be adopted following the ordinary legislative procedure under the legal base on which the original regulation was adopted, namely Article 81 TFEU'.

### 2.1.4 A tentative alternative interpretation

Some of the stakeholders have highlighted the drawbacks that may be brought about by the long and cumbersome procedure to make the EIR applicable to newly introduced national procedures. Hence, the (provocative) suggestion to consider the EIR applicable also to proceedings not listed in Annex A but which satisfy the conditions set out in Article 1 EIR.

Despite this interpretation is not an easy one, it can be noted that:

*(i)* the only definite statement as to the relationship between Article 1(1) and Annex A is contained in a recital (no 9). Articles 1(1), (3) and 2(4) EIR maintain that proceedings meeting the conditions set out in Article 1(1) are listed in Annex A EIR, but do not expressly state that proceedings outside the Annex are also outside the Regulation;[107] for this reason, they are not far from Article 2(1) lit. a) EIR 2000, which raised the doubts which were then solved in *Bank Handlowy* and *Radziejewski* judgments. As it is acknowledged, recitals are not binding provisions, but only general expressions of purpose; therefore, they should have no legal value;

*(ii)* the statement that 'in respect of the national procedures contained in Annex A, this Regulation should apply without any further examination', may be interpreted in the sense that only for procedures included in Annex A the EIR applies without any further examination, whereas

---

106 'Draft European Parliament legislative resolution on the proposal for a regulation of the European Parliament and of the Council replacing the lists of insolvency proceedings and insolvency practitioners in Annexes A and B to Regulation (EU) 2015/848 on insolvency proceedings', COM(2016)0317 – C8-0196/2016 – 2016/0159(COD).

107 *McCormack*, MLR 2016, 121, 127, noted, with regard to English schemes of arrangement (not included in Annex A, see *infra*), that the fact that proceedings not listed in the Annex are outside the EIR 'is stated with admirable clarity in recital 9 of the preamble but not in any substantive provision of the Regulation'.

for procedures not included in the Annex the EIR could apply after an examination having shown that they meet the conditions set out in the Regulation.

However, this tentative interpretation is destined to remain an end in itself, in view of the clear background seen above.[108]

## 2.2 Practical problems

### 2.2.1 The shortcomings of ordinary legislative procedure

The major problems will probably arise with regard to amendments to Annex A. Indeed, several Member States are working on the modernisation of their insolvency laws, also with the aim of implementing the Recommendation mentioned above. Since the ordinary legislative procedure is rather long (approximately two years), it is unlikely that the Council will be able to react promptly to the evolution of the Member States' legislations and thus there will always be a transitory period during which new national proceedings in line with the conditions set forth in Article 1(1) EIR will not be covered by the Regulation.[109] Furthermore, concerns have been raised that Member States could tend to be more reluctant to notify new national procedures due to the difficulty to amend the Annex. For these reasons, in general stakeholders agree that the procedure to amend Annex should be rendered more flexible.[110]

---

108  See *supra* Part 1, I.
109  See, in this sense, *Wessels*, ECL 2016, 129. He stated: 'the system of amending Annex A is not mirroring the vast changes taking place in the insolvency laws of many Member States. Contrary to what the Commission proposed (to change Annex A with the instrument of a delegated act) the system chosen is to amend the Regulation itself. Only looking at the tune that may cost (apart form political squabbling), it is the worst choice that could have been made'.
110  However, *Monsèrié-Bon*, in: Sautonie-Laguionie/Lisanti (eds), Règlement (UE) n °2015/848 du 20 mai 2015 relatif aux procédures d'insolvabilité, Commentaire article par article, 2015, Art 1, 35, stressed a value of the ordinary legislative procedure: it allows to establish a blocking minority in order to decide on the new procedures to be included in the Annex, so as to prevent from the introduction of proceeding not meeting the conditions of Art 1(1).

### 2.2.2 How to deal with the difficulty to amend Annex A

A proposal to face and, in a certain sense, to 'bypass', the difficulty to amend Annex A should be recommended, i.e. to qualify new national procedures as a sub-category of proceedings which are already listed in Annex A. This solution, however, is not always viable. Firstly, there are still Member States where no pre-insolvency proceedings exist yet, and thus no general category of such proceedings is listed in Annex A. Secondly, it is not granted that sub-categories of listed national proceedings are also included automatically (under the EIR 2000 it was uncertain whether it applies also to the French *sauvegarde financière accelerée* and the Italian *amministrazione straordinaria delle grandi imprese in crisi*, that are considered as sub-categories of *sauvegarde* and *amministrazione straordinaria*, respectively, that were listed in Annex A). Thirdly, this solution may lead to a systematic circumvention of the exhaustive nature of Annex A.[111]

### 2.2.3 Two problematic cases

Doubts have been raised concerning whether the EIR applies to *(i)* existing national procedures that qualify as *species* of proceedings included in Annex A, and to *(ii)* national procedures, included in Annex A, that should change their content yet maintaining their name.

As to the first issue, the example can be made of Italian *concordato preventivo con continuità aziendale, concordato in bianco, accordi di ristrutturazione with financial creditors* and *convenzione di* moratoria,[112] which are not expressly included in Annex A. These proceedings clearly meet the conditions set forth in Article 1 EIR, and clearly constitute sub-categories of general proceedings included in Annex A (*concordato preventivo and accordi di ristrutturazione dei debiti*): therefore, no reasonable Italian judge would put them outside the scope of the EIR. Issues may arise with reference to the recognition abroad since it cannot be excluded that

---

111   See, for these remarks, *Bariatti,* The Extension of the Scope of the EIR, in: 'EU Project 'Implementation of the New Insolvency Regulation'': Kick-off conference' (paper drafted for the conference which took place in Vienna on 17 April 2015), p 1, 6 ff.

112   Respectively regulated by Art 186[bis], 161(6), 182[septies] and 182[septies](5) of Italian Bankruptcy Act (*Regio decreto 16 March 1942, n. 267*).

foreign courts will refuse to recognize these proceedings because they are not expressly mentioned in the Annex. A solution seems to be provided by Article 4(1), 2^nd s. EIR, according to which 'the judgment opening insolvency proceedings shall specify the grounds on which the jurisdiction of the court is based and, in particular, whether jurisdiction is based on Article 3(1) or (2)'. Since Italian courts opening the said proceedings should specify whether they are opening a main or a secondary proceeding, foreign courts requested to recognize the judgments opening the proceedings could not but comply with the Italian judgments, and grant automatic recognition.

The solution to the second issue is more difficult. The inclusion of a certain proceeding in the Annex is always done with reference to the shape and the content it has at the moment in which the same has been notified; thus, the risk exists that Member States radically change the content of a proceeding without subsequently changing the name of the proceeding. Obviously, this change would have practical relevance only when the proceeding (as resulting after the make-up) should not fit the requirements of Article 1(1) EIR. The only way to avoid the EIR to be applied to a proceeding listed in Annex A but no longer satisfying the conditions set out in Article 1(1) EIR would be to allow the courts to verify the content of that proceeding. It must though be underlined that such a check, on the one side, would hinder the efficiency of the EIR, since it would compel courts to perform that 'further examination' which should be precluded under the new regime; on the other side, would raise the concern of the framework under which the judgment as to the meeting of the conditions of Article 1(1) EIR is conducted (whether it should be that of the Member State of opening or the Member State in which recognition is sought). For this reason, it seems to be advisable to *always* apply the EIR to the procedures listed in Annex A 'without any further examination'.

### 2.2.4 The 'duty' to notify new national procedures

Some of the stakeholders have underlined that Member States will be under the 'duty' to notify the Commission of proceedings newly introduced in their national legislations. However, it has been pointed out that a 'duty' would exist only if Member States could be forced to include a certain proceeding in the Annex. Since no rule can be found which provides such an obligation (or power to oblige), it seems improper to talk of 'duty' in the strict sense of the term.

Albeit not subject to a duty, it is nevertheless recommendable that Member States promote the amendment of Annex A as soon as new national procedures fulfilling the requirements of Article 1(1) EIR are introduced in the national legislation. It is also advisable that Member States delay the entry into force of the national provisions until the inclusion of the new proceedings in Annex A.

3.  Theses and recommendations

In light of the above, the following recommendations should be issued.

3.1 Pursuant to recital 9, proceedings covered by the EIR are listed exhaustively in Annex A.

Conversely, national insolvency proceedings not listed in Annex A should fall outside the scope of the EIR.

3.2 Courts requested to open proceedings included in Annex A should not be permitted to examine whether they comply with the EIR. At the same time, courts of Member States other than that in which those proceedings are opened should recognize and enforce judgments opening them without any further examination as to whether they meet the conditions set out in the EIR.

Consequently:

–   proceedings listed in Annex A automatically fall under the scope of the EIR;
–   proceedings listed in Annex A should be deemed to fall within the scope of the EIR even if they do not meet the conditions set out in Article 1(1) EIR.

3.3 Accordingly, courts of Member States other than that in which proceedings are opened should recognize and enforce without any further examination also:

–   judgments opening proceedings whose name cannot be found in Annex A, for they constitute sub-categories of proceedings listed in Annex A;
–   judgments opening proceedings whose contents have been so radically changed that they no longer meet the requirements laid down in Article 1(1) EIR.

3.4 Although Annex A is an exhaustive list, Article 1 EIR should be interpreted as a substantive provision.

In particular, it should function as a blueprint to be taken into account when deciding on the procedures to be included in Annex A.

3.5 Article 45 EIR 2000 ('Amendment of the Annexes') provided for a simplified procedure of amendment of Annex A.

This provision has not been recast in the EIR.

In the absence of a specific rule, the amendment of Annex A should follow the formal ordinary legislative procedure, set forth in Article 294 TFEU.

3.6 It is likely that the formal ordinary legislative procedure will be too long and cumbersome to react flexibly and promptly to the new national procedures which are envisaged to be introduced in the national legislations – especially with the aim of implementing the Commission Recommendation of 12 March 2014 on a new approach to business failure and insolvency.

In order to tackle that shortcoming, Member States should, where possible without it constituting a circumvention of the exhaustive nature of Annex A, qualify new proceedings that will be introduced in their national legislations as a sub-category of proceedings that are already listed in Annex A. Also in this case, courts should apply the EIR without any examination.

When it is not possible to update Annex A resorting to the said solution, the formal ordinary legislative procedure to amend the EIR should be adopted.

3.7 It is better to hold that Member States are not under any obligation to notify the Commission of new national proceedings fulfilling the requirements set out in Annex A.

Nonetheless, it is recommended that Member States should request to change their own list set out in Annex A as soon as a new procedure is introduced in the national legislation. Moreover, if possible, they should delay the entry into force of the national provisions until the inclusion has been reached.

3.8 Member States should request to change their own list set out in Annex A with reference only to national procedures which comply with the conditions set forth in Article 1(1) EIR.

## III. The boundary between the European Insolvency Regulation and the Brussels I^bis Regulation

Article 1(1), recitals 7, 16 EIR; Article 1(2) lit. b) Brussels Ibis

### 1. Legal framework

#### 1.1 Introduction

The demarcation between the Judgment Regulation (Brussels I and then Brussels Recast Regulation – hereafter Brussels I^bis) and the EIR 2000 has always been one of the most controversial problems related to cross-border insolvencies.[113]

Yet, according to CJEU's decisions (some of which are quite recent), the relationship between the two instruments is a very definite one: the Judgment Regulation and the Insolvency Regulation should 'dovetail' (i.e. to slot into one another leaving no spare space[114]). In one of the most recent judgments dealing with the question, in fact, one can read: '… the Court has already held that Regulations No 44/2001 and 1346/2000 must be interpreted in such a way as to avoid any overlap between the rules of law that those instruments lay down and any legal vacuum. Accordingly, actions excluded, under Article 1(2) lit. b) of Regulation No 44/2001, from the scope of that regulation in so far as they come under 'bankruptcy, proceedings relating to the winding-up of insolvent companies or other legal persons, judicial arrangements, compositions and analogous proceedings' fall within the scope of Regulation No 1346/2000. Correspondingly, actions which fall outside the scope of Article 3(1) of Regulation No 1346/2000 fall within the scope of Regulation No 44/2001...'.[115]

---

113 *Laukemann*, in: Hess/Oberhammer/Pfeiffer (eds), Heidelberg-Luxembourg-Vienna Report (2014), para 4.2.1.

114 *Van Calster*, COMIng, and here to stay. The Review of the European Insolvency Regulation, 2016, available at: papers.ssrn.com, 1, 7.

115 CJEU, 11 June 2015, Case C-649/13, *Comité d'entreprise de Nortel Networks and Others*, ECLI:EU:C:2015:384, para 21; but similar wording is used in *Nickel & Goeldner Spedition* judgment (CJEU, 4 September 2014, Case C-157/13, *Nickel*

However, a different view was taken by the CJEU in *German Graphics Graphische Maschinen* decision,[116] in which it was established that 'there are some judgments which will come within the scope of application neither of Regulation No 1346/2000 nor of Regulation No 44/2001'. The idea that the alignment between the two Regulations is far from being perfect emerges, by the way, also from the *Virgós-Schmit* Report.[117] Indeed, it could be said that the two Regulations perfectly dovetail only if 'bankruptcy, proceedings relating to the winding-up of insolvent companies or other legal persons, judicial arrangements, compositions and analogous proceedings' (that is, matters which are carved out from the scope of Brussels I and Brussels Ibis, pursuant to Article 1(2) lit. b)) coincided with the scope of the EIR 2000, and *vice versa*, if the scope of the EIR 2000 could exhaustively and entirely be defined by referring to that *formula*.

Practice has shown that such ideal relationship cannot (always) be established. In fact, dovetailing had to face with the three following circumstances: *(i)* the thriving in the national legislations of pre-insolvency and hybrid proceedings; *(ii)* the judicial assertion of the binding force of Annex A; and *(iii)* the judicial building of the notion of 'insolvency-related actions'.

---

& *Goeldner Spedition*, ECLI:EU:C:2014:2145). See also *F-Tex* judgment (CJEU, 19 April 2012, Case C-213/10, *F-Tex*, ECLI:EU:C:2012:215).

116 CJEU, 10 September 2009, Case C-292/08, *German Graphics Graphische Maschinen*, ECLI:EU:C:2009:544, para 17.

117 Albeit maintaining that insolvency-related actions 'should be considered subject to the Convention on insolvency proceedings and to its rules of jurisdiction' in order 'to avoid unjustifiable loopholes between the two Conventions' (para 77), it states that proceedings fall 'within the scope of the Convention [on insolvency proceedings, editor's note] only if [they are] based on the debtor's insolvency (where appropriate the 1968 Brussels Convention will be applied)' (para 49(b)). See also the 'Schlosser Report' ('Report on the Convention of 9 October 1978 on the Accession of the Kingdom of Denmark, Ireland and the United Kingdom of Great Britain and Northern Ireland to the Brussels Convention and to the Protocol on its interpretation by the Court of Justice'), which stated that 'the two Conventions were intended to dovetail almost completely with each other'.

## 1.2 Obstacles to the dovetailing

### 1.2.1 Pre-insolvency proceedings and hybrid proceedings

Most pre-insolvency and hybrid proceedings (those which are not listed in Annex A to the EIR 2000) are outside the scope of the EIR 2000, because they do not fulfil the requirements set out in Article 1(1).

According to an opinion, clearly inspired by the theory of the dovetailing, these proceedings fall in the scope of Brussels I, insofar as the renegotiation of private and commercial debts qualifies as a civil and commercial matter.[118] The jurisdiction for the intervention of a court approving the restructuring of debts must be determined by Articles 2-24 Brussels I (Articles 4-26 Brussels I[bis]): in particular Articles 2, 5(1), 6(1) and 22(2) (i.e. 4, 7(1), 8(1) and 24(2) of the recast Regulation) could be relevant. As far as recognition and enforcement are concerned, debt restructuring arrangements *(i)* where formally approved by a court decision, are to be considered 'judgments' in the sense of Brussels I and Brussels I[bis] and recognized according to Article 32 Brussels I (Article 34 Brussels I[bis]);[119] *(ii)* where not formally approved by a court, must be recognized as a settlement under Article 57 Brussels I (Article 58 Brussels I[bis]): in this case, however, the substantive effects of the arrangement on the regulated debts depend on the applicable conflict of law rules – to be determined according to the Rome I Regulation.[120]

---

118 See *Hess*, in: Hess/Oberhammer/Pfeiffer (eds), Heidelberg-Luxembourg-Vienna Report (2014), para 3.4.1, fn 231.

119 See Art 32 Brussels I (Art 32 lit. a) Brussels I[bis]: 'any judgment given by a court or tribunal of a Member State, whatever the judgment may be called, including a decree, order, decision or writ of execution, as well as a decision on the determination of costs or expenses by an officer of the court'.

120 See *Hess*, in: Hess/Oberhammer/Pfeiffer (eds), Heidelberg-Luxembourg-Vienna Report (2014), para 3.4.1. The option has been suggested to apply the Rome I Regulation to pre-insolvency and hybrid proceedings. Since these proceedings generally imply an amendment of the terms and conditions of a contract, in fact, there are grounds to argue that they are subject to *lex contractus*. It is true that they amount to a very peculiar way of amending contracts, but in the Rome I Regulation there are no carve-outs for cases where the amendments are made by means of collective consent sanctioned by a court and aimed at preventing the insolvency of the debtor. Based on this approach, it is possible to link procedural aspects to the applicable law: on the one hand, the rules to determine the competent court should derive from the law applicable to the amendments of creditors'

However, it has been observed that Brussels I does not offer appropriate and balanced solutions. Firstly, its terminology refers to ordinary civil claims, based on rules formulated in terms of contentious or adversary proceedings between a claimant and a defendant ('be sued', 'contracts', 'defendants').[121] Pre-insolvency and hybrid proceedings are of a different nature, as they are not based on the structure of claimant v defendant: the judge does not rule on a dispute existing between the parties, but intervenes to ensure that the shifting to the majority consent is not unreasonable. In other words, pre-insolvency and hybrid proceedings barely seemed to qualify as proceedings for the purpose of the application of Brussels I.[122] Secondly, the rules on jurisdiction of Brussels I do not appear to be suitable for these kinds of proceedings. Since Articles 2, 5(1) and 6(1) Brussels I (Articles 4, 7(1), 8(1) Brussels I[bis]) are based upon the notion of defendant and the proximity principle, i.e. the domicile of the defendant or the link with the subject matter of the litigation, they do not seem to fit in the special features of pre-insolvency and hybrid proceedings, where there is no defendant. By the same token, it is questionable whether Article 24(2) Brussels I[bis] which establishes exclusive jurisdiction of the courts of a Member State in proceedings having as their object 'the dissolution of companies' – is applicable, since the existence of a link between debt adjustment and dissolution of companies is questionable.[123] In line with this criticism, the CJEU, in *Radziejewski* judgment,[124] affirmed that a Swedish debt relief proceeding (which belongs to the category of

---

rights; on the other hand, recognition of such proceedings should be governed by conflict of law rules. For these remarks, see *Garcimartín*, IILR 2011, 321, 332, who underlines that this solution 'is not fitting from a policy – or *lege ferenda* – perspective'.

121  *Linna*, Int.Insolv.Rev. 2014, 20, 26.
122  *Garcimartín*, IILR 2011, 321, 329.
123  The Rome I Regulation proved even less suitable. Given that debt adjustment proceedings basically imply the amendment of a contract, it was suggested that they were subject to *lex contractus* (see, for instance, Art 12(1) of the Rome I Regulation, which states that 'the various ways of exstinguishing obligations' are governed by the *lex contractus*). Following this approach, it was also suggested to link procedural aspects, i.e. jurisdiction and recognition, to the applicable law. The shortcoming of this solution was that only creditors whose claims were governed by, e.g., English law, would have been subject to an English debt adjustment proceeding; as a result, foreign creditors would have always been able to uphold their claims and to jeopardize the proceeding.
124  CJEU, 8 November 2012, Case C-461/11, *Radziejewski*, ECLI:EU:C:2012:704.

pre-insolvency proceedings providing for a debt adjustment in relation to consumers and self-employed persons, and is not included in Annex A) did not fall within the scope of Brussels I, since the authority which adopted the debt relief decision at issue could not be classified as a 'court or tribunal' within the meaning of Article 32 of that instrument.

Even if it was possible to dispel these doubts, a major obstacle exists to consider pre-insolvency and hybrid proceedings covered by Brussels I: (many) pre-insolvency and hybrid proceedings can be considered '*judicial arrangements*', '*compositions*', or also forms of '*analogous proceedings*'; thus, they should fall within Article 1(2) lit. b) exemption. This is the proof that the formula '*bankruptcy, proceedings relating to the winding-up of insolvent companies or other legal persons, judicial arrangements, compositions and analogous proceedings*' provided in Article 1(2) lit. b) Brussels I and the definition contained in Article 1(1) EIR 2000 do not cover a coextended area (the former's is broader).

### 1.2.2 Annex A EIR

As seen above, in the *Bank Handlowy* and *Radziejewski* judgments the CJEU established that only proceedings which are listed in Annex A fall within the scope of the EIR 2000. Following these decisions, the scope of the EIR 2000 is no longer circumscribed by Article 1(1) definition, but 'corresponds' with the proceedings listed in Annex A. It has been pointed out that this way to define the scope of application has arguably upset any dovetailing that might have been intended: the 1968 Brussels Convention, in fact, would have not envisaged the Member States being in the definitional driver's seat of the EIR 2000.[125] Therefore, even if the formula 'bankruptcy, proceedings relating to the winding-up of insolvent companies or other legal persons, judicial arrangements, compositions and analogous proceedings' provided in Article 1(2) lit. b) Brussels I and the definition contained in Article 1(1) EIR 2000 covered a coextended area (but this is not the case), no dovetailing would be guaranteed anyway, since the EIR 2000 may include in its scope all the proceedings which Member States choose to notify, whatever their contents may be.

---

125 *Van Calster*, COMIng, and here to stay. The Review of the European Insolvency Regulation, 2016, available at: papers.ssrn.com, 1, 8.

### 1.2.3  The notion of 'insolvency-related' actions

'Insolvency-related' actions are the name with which actions 'in some measure' linked with insolvency proceedings (e.g. avoidance actions) are indicated. They are ordinary civil actions, in which a defendant is sued by a plaintiff before a court, and that according to the general rules should be brought before the courts of the State in which the former is domiciled; at the same time, they are so strictly intertwined with insolvency proceedings, that in national legislations they are often to be brought before the courts opening insolvency proceedings. No specific rule concerning international jurisdiction for these actions is provided in the EIR 2000: according to the idea of the dovetailing, they would *consequently* be subject to Brussels I. By contrast, Article 1(2) lit. b) Brussels I excludes from its scope not only 'bankruptcy, proceedings relating to the winding-up of insolvent companies or other legal persons, judicial arrangements, compositions', but also 'analogous proceedings'; furthermore, Article 25(2) EIR 2000 grants automatic recognition to 'judgments deriving directly from the insolvency proceedings and which are closely linked with them'.

In the light of this, uncertainties exist as to the *forum* having jurisdiction on these actions. Some national courts have applied their national provisions on jurisdiction.[126] Other national courts have deemed Brussels I applicable, insofar as the exemption of Article 1(2) lit. b) has been considered as covering only insolvency proceedings.[127] On the contrary, the CJEU has always stated that insolvency-related actions should be brought before the courts of the Member State in which insolvency proceedings have been opened. This principle was for the first time asserted in the

---

126  It has been noted that this thesis is not considered to be persuasive, because national laws differ from each other and because this diversity could determine conflicts of jurisdiction: see *Mangano*, in: Bork/Mangano (eds), European Cross-Border-Insolvency Law (2016), para 3.69; and *Carballo Piñeiro*, Revista para el Análisis del Derecho 2010, 1, 7.

127  'However, this position was considered to be inefficient, because detaching the so-called connected actions from the insolvency proceedings meant that there would be various for a: namely, one forum for the insolvency proceedings (the so-called *forum concursus*) and one or more for a provided by the Brussels I Regulation for the one or more related actions': thus, *verbatim*, *Mangano*, in: Bork/Mangano (eds), European Cross-Border-Insolvency Law (2016), para 3.69.

*Gourdain* decision,[128] whereby the CJEU established that 'if decisions relating to bankruptcy and winding-up are to be excluded from the scope of the [Brussels] Convention, [...] they must derive directly from the bankruptcy or winding-up and be closely connected with the proceedings for the 'liquidation des biens' or the 'règlement judiciaire',[129] thus, correlatively, it established that decisions not 'so closely' linked with insolvency proceedings should be included in the scope of Brussels Convention (then Brussels I). The *rationale* underpinning *Gourdain* was confirmed also with regard to the EIR 2000, for the first time in the *Seagon* case,[130] where the CJEU reproduced the definition of insolvency-related actions which had been adopted in the former;[131] however, soon the puzzling issue emerged as to how to interpret that definition. In *German Graphics Graphische Maschinen* case,[132] the CJEU suggested that Brussels I should be given as wide a reading as possible and that the EIR 2000 should be interpreted in a restrictive fashion.[133] In practice, however, often doubts have arisen as to whether a certain action falls legitimately within the ju-

---

128  This decision could be considered as a precedent *avant la lettre* because at the time this decision was rendered the EIR 2000's existence had only been envisaged: see *Mangano*, in: Bork/Mangano (eds), European Cross-Border-Insolvency Law (2016), para 3.70.

129  In this decision the CJEU ruled that the action brought by the liquidator of an insolvent company for the declaration of enforceability of a judgment concerning a kind of wrongful trading claim regulated by French law – *action en comblement du passif* – was directly deriving and closely linked with insolvency and must be brought before the courts of the Member State in which insolvency proceedings have been opened).

130  CJEU, 12 February 2009, Case C-339/07, *Seagon*, ECLI:EU:C:2009:83.

131  Recital 6 EIR 2000 explains that it applies also to 'judgments which are delivered directly on the basis of the insolvency proceedings and are closely connected with such proceedings'.

132  CJEU, 10 September 2009, Case C-292/08, *German Graphics Graphische Maschinen*, ECLI:EU:C:2009:544.

133  The recitals 7 and 15 in the preamble to Brussels I Regulation 'indicate the intention on the part of the Community legislature to provide for a broad definition of the concept of 'civil and commercial matters' referred to in Art 1(1) of [said] Regulation [...] and, consequently to provide that the Article should be broad in its scope'; such an interpretation was also supported 'by the first sentence of the sixth recital in the preamble to Regulation No 1346/2000, according to which that regulation should, in accordance with the principle of proportionality, be confined to provisions governing jurisdiction for opening insolvency proceedings and judgments which are delivered directly on the basis of the insolvency proceedings and are closely connected with such proceedings. Consequently, the

risdictional rules of EIR 2000, of Brussels I or of either Regulation. In *F-Tex* case, the CJEU was expressly asked to say whether the jurisdiction conferred by the EIR 2000 to hear and determine insolvency-related actions constitute exclusive jurisdiction, but it declined to answer, stating that this was not necessary for a decision in the case.[134] In conclusion, sometimes insolvency-related actions have been considered as falling in a gap between the EIR 2000 and Brussels I; more often, it has turned out difficult to distinguish when an action 'to some degree' connected with an insolvency proceeding constitutes an action directly deriving and closely linked to insolvency proceedings, thus falling within the scope of the EIR 2000; moreover, the question remains whether the EIR 2000 and Brussels I may overlap, i.e. whether (some) insolvency-related actions can be brought both before the courts of *forum concursus* and before the courts where the defendant is domiciled.

## 1.3 The EIR 2015

The relationship between Brussels I[bis] and the EIR should take into account the following elements:

*(i)* the material scope of Brussels I[bis] ('civil and commercial matters'); the definition of 'judgment' provided in its Article 2 lit. a) ('any judgment given by a court or tribunal of a Member State, whatever the judgment may be called, including a decree, order, decision or writ of execution, as well as a decision on the determination of costs or expenses by an officer of the court'); the rules on jurisdiction provided in Brussels I[bis] (in particular Articles 4, 7(1), 8(1) and 24(2)); the rules on recognition and enforcement, provided in chapter I;

*(ii)* Article 1(2) lit. b) Brussels I[bis], which – as said above – carves out from its scope 'bankruptcy, proceedings relating to the winding-up of insolvent companies or other legal persons, judicial arrangements, compositions and analogous proceedings';

*(iii)* Article 1(1) EIR, that has loosened its requirements in order to include within its scope pre-insolvency proceedings, hybrid proceed-

---

scope of application of Regulation No 1346/2000 should not be broadly interpreted' (paras 23-25).

134  CJEU, 19 April 2012, Case C-213/10, *F-Tex*, ECLI:EU:C:2012:215, para 50.

ings and proceedings providing for a debt discharge or a debt adjustment in relation to consumers and self-employed persons;

*(iv)* Annex A, Article 1(1), 1(2), Article 2(4) and recital 9 EIR, which clarify that all the proceedings to which the EIR is applicable are listed in Annex A, and that the EIR is applicable only to these proceedings;

*(v)* Article 6 EIR, which confers jurisdiction to hear and determine any action which derives directly from the insolvency proceedings and is closely linked with them to the courts of the Member State within the territory of which insolvency proceedings have been opened. Article 6(2) EIR states that such actions may be brought before the courts of the Member State within the territory of which the defendant (or one of the defendants) is domiciled when such actions are related to an action in civil and commercial matters (see also recital 35 EIR);

*(vi)* recital 7 EIR, that after having reproduced the exemption of Article 1(2) lit. b) Brussels I<sup>bis</sup> (to which 'actions related to such proceedings' have been added) and having established that proceedings covered by this exemption 'should be covered by this Regulation', states that 'the interpretation of this Regulation should as much as possible avoid regulatory loopholes between the two instruments. However, the mere fact that a national procedure is not listed in Annex A to this Regulation should not imply that it is covered by Regulation (EU) No 1215/2012';

*(vii)* recital 16 EIR, according to which this Regulation 'should apply to proceedings which are based on laws relating to insolvency'; 'however, proceedings that are based on general company law not designed exclusively for insolvency situations should not be considered to be based on laws relating to insolvency'.

## 2. Evaluation

### 2.1 Legal issues

#### 2.1.1 Setting-up the relationship between Brussels Ibis and the EIR

There are two possible ways to combine the elements listed in para 1.3:

*(i)* a first way acknowledges the binding role of Annex A, as well as the principles of the dovetailing between the two regulations and of the broad interpretation of the scope of Brussels I<sup>bis</sup>, as established in the

CJEU's judgments. Proceedings listed in Annex A are within the scope of the EIR; proceedings which meet the conditions laid down in Article 1(1) EIR but are not listed should fall in the scope of Brussels I[bis]. Per this interpretation, Brussels I[bis] and the EIR act as communicating vessels:[135] whatever is excluded from Annex A should fall within the scope of Brussels I[bis];

*(ii)* a second way to establish the relationship is based on the following assumptions: *a)* the scope of the EIR encompasses the proceedings included in Annex A, whereas it does not encompass the proceedings which fulfil the criteria set out in Article 1(1) EIR but are not included in the Annex; *b)* the exclusion of a national proceeding from Annex A does not automatically lead to its inclusion in the scope of Brussels I[bis] (see recital 7 EIR), since the area covered by Article 1(1) EIR and the area covered by the exemption provided for in Article 1(2) lit. b) Brussels I[bis] are not exactly the same and since proceedings outside Annex A do not *automatically* satisfy the requirements to fall within the scope of Brussels I[bis] (see *supra* para 1.2.1). These assumptions lead to a twofold outcome: firstly, proceedings should be deemed characterised as 'insolvency proceedings' if they fall in the material scope of the EIR: Annex A plays a role of 'positive integration', enabling States to benefit from a *safe niche* of automatic recognition and 'curing' possible deficiencies for the purposes of characterisation and the obligation by the other Member States to recognize their insolvency nature, but does not also play a role of negative integration, turning into non-insolvency everything is outside Annex A;[136] secondly (and consequently), whatever dovetailing might have been conceived, it seems not to be maintained in practice.

---

135  See *Kuipers*, J.Priv.Int.L. 2012, 225, 228.
136  *Carrasco Perera/Torralba Mendiola*, UK "schemes of arrangement" are "outside" the scope of the European Regulation on Insolvency Proceedings. What does "outside" actually mean?, available at: http://www.gomezacebo-pombo.com/media/k2/attachments/uk-schemes-of-arrangement-are-outside-the-scope-of-the-european-regulation-on-insolvency-proceedings-what-does-outside-actually-mean.pdf, 1, 2.

2.1.2 Loopholes

The second way is by far the most appropriate to describe the current relationship between the EIR and Brussels I[bis]: according to the vast majority of the stakeholders to whom the questionnaire prepared within this research project has been submitted, in fact, there are (still) regulatory loopholes between the EIR and Brussels I[bis]. In particular, two cases of possible loopholes may be envisaged:

*(i)* proceedings which are not listed in Annex A but meet the conditions set out in Article 1(1) EIR. On the one hand, these proceedings are 'insolvency proceedings', but fall outside the EIR because the corresponding Member State has opted not to include them in Annex A – or because the ordinary legislative procedure to amend Annex A is underway. On the other hand, they fall outside Brussels I[bis] because they are covered by the exemption of Article 1(2) lit. b). As a consequence, jurisdiction should be determined and recognition be sought (unless there is an applicable convention) according to the domestic rules of insolvency law or of private international law. This outcome may have adverse relevant impact. Firstly, when a rescue arrangement is confirmed by the court, it may not be recognizable or enforceable in other Member States. As a result, creditors might be able to 'free ride' and to recover full debt amounts in other Member States. Secondly, when no recognition or enforcement can be obtained in other Member States, it may not be possible to collect the scheduled payments by compulsory methods in those Member States; thus, the debtor might be able to avoid its liabilities merely by moving to another State. These shortcomings encourage the inclusion in Annex A of proceedings falling in this regulatory gap. Also from this point of view, Article 1(1) EIR should be considered a substantive provision: since the proceedings fulfilling the conditions set out in it (but not included in the Annex) must be deemed falling in an unpleasant regulatory loophole, it should also play a role in 'promoting' their inclusion in the most fitting regulatory environment, i.e. the EIR;

*(ii)* proceedings which are not listed in Annex A, are based on general company law and are not designed exclusively for insolvency situations, but meet the conditions set out in Article 1(1). This possible loophole has been deliberately created having in mind UK *schemes of arrangement*, whose regulation is contained in a corporate statute and

which can also be used for non-insolvency purpose (mainly to seek to transfer control of a company as an alternative to a takeover offer).[137] These proceedings have allowed restructuring huge foreign companies having a 'sufficiently close connection' with England and Wales, thus 'enhancing the reputation of the UK as a leading commercial centre';[138] therefore, if they had been included in the EIR, they would have necessarily been less attractive, since the COMI requirement would have been applicable. *Schemes* are not included in Annex A: this would have sufficed to exclude them from the scope of the EIR; however, the UK lobbied for (and succeeded in) having inserted recital 16 in order to emphasize such exclusion. By means of recital 16, *schemes* seem not even eligible for a future inclusion in the Annex.

The question arises whether *schemes* fall in a 'real' loophole or fall within the scope of Brussels I[bis]. In order to answer this question, it is necessary to establish whether *schemes* are insolvency proceedings *notwithstanding* recital 16:[139] in fact, if they are not insolvency proceedings, there would be room for arguing that they fall in the scope of Brussels I[bis]; by contrast,

---

137 Companies Act 2006, Part 26. According to Section 895, a *scheme* is 'a compromise or arrangement between a company and its creditors, or any class of them, or its members, or any class of them'. A *scheme* involves three stages: *(i)* an arrangement between the company and its members/creditors is proposed by the board of the company; *(ii)* a meeting of the members/creditors, summoned in order to seek approval of the *scheme*, in which members/creditors meet in classes to consider and vote on the *scheme*; *(iii)* the sanction of the *scheme* by the court, which requires that all of the relevant classes have approved it and a majority in number representing 75% in value has been gathered. For further information, see *Payne*, Oxford Legal Studies Research Paper No. 68/2013, 1, 2 ff.

138 See *City of London Law Society (CLLS)*, Response to Proposed changes to the European Insolvency Regulation: Call for Evidence, available at: https://www.gov.uk/government/uploads/system/uploads/attachment_data/file/279289/insolvency-lawyers-association-evidence.pdf, 25 February 2013.

139 We have assumed *a priori* that *schemes*, when proposed to effect a reorganization of the debt capital by a company in a situation of financial distress, meet the requirements of Art 1(1) EIR. As a matter of fact, in this situation *schemes* pursue the objective of rescue and adjustment of debt; make the assets and affairs of the debtor subject to control or supervision by a court; are collective for the purpose of the EIR, as – being aimed at rescuing – can involve also only a significant part of a debtor's creditors, especially financial ones (but see *McCormack*, J.Priv.Int.L. 2014, 41, 48 (fn 23), who states that *schemes* are not necessarily collective); finally, can be conducted as proceeding described in Art 1(1) lit. c) EIR.

if they are insolvency proceedings, they should be deemed as falling in a regulatory loophole. According to the prevailing opinion, recital 16 should not contribute to delineate the material scope of application of the EIR: if the requirement of 'exclusivity' were really an essential one, firstly, it should have been included in the body of the Articles;[140] secondly, it would be easy for Member States to escape the COMI requirement, by putting a proceeding in a corporate statute (see *infra* para 2.2.1). For these reasons, it is better to hold that *schemes of arrangements* proposed by debtors in financial difficulties to restructure their debts fit the definition of 'insolvency proceedings': consequently, they should be considered as falling in a regulatory loophole between the EIR and Brussels I^bis.[141] Accordingly, jurisdiction should be determined and recognition be sought (unless there is an applicable convention) according to the domestic rules of insolvency law or of private international law.

Besides, even if *schemes* were to be regarded as a 'civil and commercial matter',[142] many doubts would arise as to whether Brussels I^bis would fit for *schemes*. In fact, English courts have applied jurisdiction criteria in

---

A further element in the sense that *schemes* are insolvency proceedings is that they are capable of recognition in the U.S. under Chapter 15 of the U.S. Bankruptcy Code.

140  *Carrasco Perera/Torralba Mendiola*, UK "schemes of arrangement" are "outside" the scope of the European Regulation on Insolvency Proceedings. What does "outside" actually mean?, available at: http://www.gomezacebo-pombo.com/media/k2/attachments/uk-schemes-of-arrangement-are-outside-the-scope-of-the-european-regulation-on-insolvency-proceedings-what-does-outside-actually-mean.pdf, 4.

141  A similar approach had been adopted in the English case *DAP Holding NV* ([2005] EWHC 2092 (Ch): according to this decision, *schemes* can be regarded as 'judicial arrangements, compositions and analogous proceedings', and therefore they fall outside the scope of Brussels I^bis. It has been underlined that 'this approach would point to a lacuna in the law, such that schemes (both solvent and insolvent) fall outside both Regulations. In the event of a lacuna of this kind each Member State would then apply its own jurisdictional rules to this issue' (*Payne*, Oxford Legal Studies Research Paper No. 68/2013, 1, 17).

142  In the *Rodenstock* case ([2011] EWHC 1104 (Ch)), Briggs J took the view that the court's sanction of a *scheme* in relation to a solvent company fell within the scope of Brussels I; he left open the question whether *schemes* involving insolvent companies could fall within Brussels I as well. However, the approach adopted as to solvent companies (with reference to which he noted that the exemption of Art 1(2) lit. b) does not exclude from the scope of Brussels I matters which do not fall within the EIR 2000 or that are not connected with bankruptcy

a *sui generis* manner, arguing that Brussels I does not impact on their jurisdiction to convene and sanction *schemes*.[143] As for recognition, there has been some uncertainty as to whether a decision of a court sanctioning a *scheme* should be regarded as a judgment for the purposes of Brussels I, and as to whether such judgment should be considered as rendered by 'a judicial body of a Contracting State deciding on its own authority on the issues between the parties'; however, it must be underlined that the Bundesgerichtshof (BGH) determined, *obiter dicta*, that decision sanctioning a *scheme* should be recognized under Brussels I because they have potential adversarial nature and because the term 'judgment' has a broad meaning within that Regulation.[144]

As it has been pointed out with regard to proceedings falling in the first loophole, the application of domestic insolvency or private international law rules is liable to make more difficult the recognition abroad of *schemes* in respect of foreign companies. English courts have been reluctant to affirm jurisdiction on *schemes* concerning foreign companies in cases where the recognition abroad was uncertain:[145] if they are not legally effective in the relevant foreign countries, creditors could always pursue their contractual claims in foreign courts and hinder the fairness of the *scheme*, as well as initiate a separate insolvency or restructuring process abroad. In order to side step the difficulties associated with the recognition of *schemes* involving foreign companies, the practical solution has been proposed for companies seeking to make use of a *scheme* to require creditors wishing to take the benefit of it to sign an undertaking that they agree to be bound by the restructuring and by the *scheme*.[146]

In any case, the conundrum whether *schemes* fall in a regulatory gap or not may be soon nugatory. In fact, once the withdrawal of UK from the EU has occurred (if it occurs), in the absence of new instruments, provisions on jurisdiction and recognition contemplated in Brussels I[bis] will no

---

or insolvency) points to potentially different outcomes for *schemes* involving solvent and insolvent companies. See *Payne*, Oxford Legal Studies Research Paper No. 68/2013, 1, 18.

143  See *Rodenstock*, [2011] EWHC 1104 (Ch).

144  BGH, *Equitable Life*, judgment of 15 February 2012, IV ZR 194/09.

145  Hence, the practice of foreign applicants to deposit expert statements concerning the recognition of the *scheme* in the State where the company has its COMI: see *Vaccarella*, Int'l Lis, 2014, 52, 52 ff.

146  See *Payne*, Oxford Legal Studies Research Paper No. 68/2013, 1, 28.

longer be available, and *schemes* will necessarily have to be governed by the domestic law of each State.


### 2.1.3 Overlaps

The question arises whether overlaps between the EIR and Brussels I[bis] are possible: see *infra* Part 1, IV. 2.3.


## 2.2 Practical problems

### 2.2.1 Circumvention of the scope of the EIR by putting insolvency rules in general company law

It has been argued above that recital 16 should not contribute to identify the notion of 'insolvency proceedings': proceedings which meet the requirements laid down in Article 1(1) EIR should be deemed as falling within the material scope of the EIR also when are based on general company law and are not designed to tackle exclusively insolvency situations. This solution seems the most fitting in order to avoid the risk that Member States escape the COMI requirement in respect of new national proceedings. If the 'condition' provided in recital 16 were to be interpreted as a substantial requirement, a Member State which is interested in applying a national proceeding regardless of the COMI being in the State could include it in the *corpus* of corporate law, so as to not be under the duty (if any, see *supra* Part 1, II. 2.2.4) to notify it to the Commission for the inclusion in Annex A, and also with the aim that successive governments refrain from notifying. If recital 16 were to be interpreted as a substantial requirement, most importantly, national courts may be inclined to consider such proceedings covered by Brussels I[bis], on the basis of the concept of dovetailing, which would hardly tolerate proceedings systematically outside either Regulation. The effect would be that those proceedings might anyway benefit from automatic recognition abroad, regardless of the COMI requirement.

### 2.2.2 Recital 16 and insolvency-related actions

The question arises whether recital 16 concerns also insolvency-related actions: see *infra* Part 1, IV. 2.2.

### 3. Theses and recommendations

In light of the above, the following recommendations should be issued.

3.1 According to its Article 1(2) lit. b), Regulation (EU) No 1215/2012 on jurisdiction and the recognition and enforcement of judgments in civil and commercial matters shall not apply to bankruptcy, proceedings relating to the winding-up of insolvent companies or other legal persons, judicial arrangements, compositions and analogous proceedings.

Pursuant to recital 7 EIR, the EIR and Regulation (EU) No 1215/2012 should be interpreted so as to make the scope of the two instruments to dovetail.

Always according to recital 7 EIR, however, the mere fact that a national procedure is not listed in Annex A to the EIR should not imply that it is covered by Regulation (EU) No 1215/2012.

3.2 Two possible loopholes may be identified:

*(i)* proceedings which meet the conditions set out in Article 1(1) EIR but are not listed in Annex A;
*(ii)* proceedings based on general company law not designed exclusively for insolvency situations which meet the conditions set out in Article 1(1) EIR and are not listed in Annex A.

3.3 Albeit outside the scope of the EIR, proceedings under *(i)* should in any case be deemed 'insolvency proceedings' according to Article 1(1) EIR.

They should be considered to fall outside the scope of Regulation (EU) No 1215/2012, since they can be included in the Article 1(2) lit. b) exception ('bankruptcy, proceedings relating to the winding-up of insolvent companies or other legal persons, judicial arrangements, compositions and analogous proceedings').

Consequently, those proceedings would fall outside the scope of both the EIR and Regulation (EU) No 1215/2012.

Jurisdiction and recognition issues should be resolved according to the applicable domestic rules of insolvency law and private international law.

3.4 Proceedings under *(ii)* are English *schemes of arrangement*. Albeit outside the scope of the EIR, they should in any case be deemed 'insolvency proceedings' according to Article 1(1) EIR, when aimed at a debtor's restructuring.

In fact, if proceedings based on general company law not designed exclusively for insolvency situations were not to be deemed 'insolvency proceedings', Member States might always be able to circumvent the COMI requirement by putting insolvency proceedings in corporate statutes. Therefore, it is preferable to hold that proceedings based on general company law not designed exclusively for insolvency situations are 'insolvency proceedings' according to Article 1(1) EIR, when are aimed at a debtor's restructuring.

Those proceedings would fall outside the scope of both the EIR and Regulation (EU) No 1215/2012.

Jurisdiction and recognition issues should be resolved according to the applicable domestic rules of insolvency law and private international law.

IV. Insolvency-related proceedings

Article 6, recital 35 EIR; Article 1(2) lit. b) Brussels Ibis

1. Legal framework[147]

Article 6(1) EIR ('the courts of the Member State within the territory of which insolvency proceedings have been opened in accordance with Article 3 EIR shall have jurisdiction for any action which derives directly from the insolvency proceedings and is closely linked with them, such as avoidance actions') sets up the international *vis attractiva concursus* laid down in the *Seagon* decision.[148] The provision concerning recognition and enforcement 'with no further formalities' of judgments rendered on these actions (Article 32(1), (2) EIR) has exactly reproduced that contained in the EIR 2000 (Article 25(1), (2)). Now, it is made clear that these decisions enjoy automatic recognition all over the EU because they fall in the scope of the EIR.[149]

The jurisdiction established in Article 6(1) EIR is a form of accessory jurisdiction: the courts of the *forum concursus* only have to verify whether the conditions laid down in Article 6(1) EIR are satisfied, while a further examination by the seized court of the jurisdictional conditions set out in Article 3 EIR is precluded.[150] It is noteworthy that this *vis attractiva* is solely to be understood in the context of international jurisdiction: Article 6(1) EIR prescribes that actions connected with insolvency proceedings must be brought before the courts of the Member State in which insolvency proceedings have been opened; no annex jurisdiction of the court opening insolvency proceedings have been established.[151] Thus, jurisdiction

---

147  See *supra* Part 1, III. 1.2.3.
148  CJEU, 12 February 2009, Case C-339/07, *Seagon*, ECLI:EU:C:2009:83.
149  See *Carballo Piñeiro*, Revista para el Análisis del Derecho 2010, 1, 6 ff.
150  See *Mangano*, in: Bork/Mangano (eds), European Cross-Border Insolvency Law (2016), para 3.67; and *Laukemann*, in: Hess/Oberhammer/Pfeiffer (eds), Heidelberg-Luxembourg-Vienna Report (2014), para 4.2.1; *Castagnola*, Riv. dir. proc., 2010, 925, 928.
151  This finds confirmation in Art 32(1)(2), according to which insolvency-related actions are recognized without any further formalities 'even if they were handed down by another court', i.e. other than that opening the insolvency proceedings.

*ratione loci* as well as substantive jurisdiction are always to be determined according to national procedural law.[152]

Since Article 6(1) EIR does not distinguish between insolvency-related actions in which the insolvency practitioner (or the debtor in possession: *arg e* Article 6(2) EIR) acts as a plaintiff and insolvency-related actions in which the insolvency practitioner or the debtor in possession is sued as a defendant, it has to be held that both cases fall in the scope of the EIR. However, a rule has been introduced in Article 6(2) EIR only for actions commenced by the insolvency practitioner or the debtor in possession ('provided that national law allows [him] to bring actions on behalf of the insolvency estate').[153] According to this rule, in cases in which an insolvency-connected claim is 'related' to a claim based on general civil and commercial law (i.e. where actions 'are so closely connected that it is expedient to hear and determine them together to avoid the risk of irreconcilable judgments resulting from separate proceedings': see Article 6(3) EIR), the insolvency practitioner or the debtor in possession are entitled to bring such claims before the courts of the Member State within the territory of which the defendant is domiciled (or, where the defendants are more than one, before the courts of the Member State within the territory of which any of them is domiciled), provided that those courts have jurisdiction pursuant to Brussels I[bis]. This solution is available only if both actions are accumulated: therefore, it does not expressly permit an action to be brought before the courts of the defendant's domicile where the insolvency practitioner only exercises an insolvency-related action.[154] Recital 35 EIR provides an example of actions 'so closely connected': an action for director's liability based on insolvency law combined with an action based on company law or general tort law.

As far as the notion of 'insolvency-related' actions is concerned, the EIR has merely incorporated the '*Gourdain* formula', and provided two examples of actions that qualify as insolvency-related and one example of action that, on the contrary, does not qualify as insolvency-related. Avoidance actions and actions 'concerning obligations that arise in the course of

---

152 *Laukemann*, in: Hess/Oberhammer/Pfeiffer (eds), Heidelberg-Luxembourg-Vienna Report (2014), para 4.2.1, fn 494.
153 In accordance with the proposal formulated in the Heidelberg-Luxembourg-Vienna Report: see *Laukemann*, in: Hess/Oberhammer/Pfeiffer (eds), Heidelberg-Luxembourg-Vienna Report (2014), para 4.2.6.3.
154 *Garcimartín*, ZEuP 2015, 694, 715.

the insolvency proceedings, such as advance payment for costs of the proceedings' are highlighted as examples of the first category (however, only the former has been included in Article 6 EIR, while the latter is confined in recital 35 EIR). 'Actions for the performance of the obligations under a contract concluded by the debtor prior to the opening of proceedings' are brought as examples of the second category. The question arises whether the '*Gourdain* formula' and such examples provide appropriate guidance on what constitutes an insolvency-related action.

## 2. Evaluation: legal issues and practical problems

### 2.1 The notion of 'insolvency-related' actions

Most of the stakeholders to whom the questionnaire prepared within this research project has been submitted have held that the '*Gourdain* formula' provides appropriate guidance on what constitutes an insolvency-related action, that it should be broadly interpreted, in light of the relevant case law of the CJEU, and that the examples of insolvency-related actions provided by recital 35 are sufficient to shed light on possible borderline cases. By contrast, the minority of the respondents has found that recent case law failed to provide a better-suited criterion for the delineation between the realm of the EIR 2000 and of Brussels I (or Brussels I[bis]), and that the '*Gourdain* formula' gives no clear guidance as to what an insolvency-related action is.

Whatever may be the opinion, the choice adopted in the EIR seems clear: to leave to courts and practitioners the task of interpreting on a case-by-case basis the '*Gourdain* formula', in light of the (several) criteria individuated in CJEU's case law. What seems less clear is whether avoidance actions and actions 'concerning obligations that arise in the course of the insolvency proceedings, such as advance payment for costs of the proceedings' *always* align with the notion of 'insolvency-related' actions emerging by the case-law, and thus should *always* be considered as insolvency-related, or only *usually* align with such notion, and thus should be considered as insolvency-related only *on condition that* they align with the notion of 'insolvency-related' in the relevant case (*vice versa* for 'actions for the performance of the obligations under a contract concluded by the debtor prior to the opening of proceedings').

It is probably better to opt for the second alternative. As far as avoidance actions are concerned, the case law of the CJEU has provided sufficient legal certainty, and they are generally considered as insolvency-related by the national courts. However, two exceptions may be found (the second of which is dubious). The first one regards the case of an action for recovery of a sum of money on the basis of an assigned avoidance claim: in *F-Tex* case,[155] in fact, the CJEU decided that this kind of action is not closely linked to the insolvency proceedings, because the assignee can freely decide upon the exercise and the initiation of judicial proceedings over his right and acts in his own interest and not in the interest of the insolvency estate. The second one concerns the case in which the application of the *lex fori concursus* is excluded pursuant to Article 16 EIR, for the detrimental act being subject to the *lex causae* and this one not allowing any means of challenging that act: it has been underlined that it is uncertain whether an avoidance action fulfils the double criteria set out in the '*Gourdain* formula' even when an alliance between the jurisdiction and the applicable law has ceased.[156] By the same token, actions concerning obligations that arise in the course of insolvency proceedings are generally considered as directly deriving and closely connected to insolvency proceedings, in accordance with case-law; however, in the abovementioned *F-Tex* case, the CJEU has adjudicated that an action concerning an obligation arising in the course of insolvency proceedings (namely, a claw-back obligation) was not insolvency-related. As far as actions 'for the performance of the obligations under a contract concluded by the debtor prior to the opening of proceedings' are concerned, it has been underlined that, while they certainly are not insolvency-related when the debtor acts as plaintiff, they should be considered as insolvency-related when the debtor is sued as defendant and is entitled under the national insolvency law provisions to oppose the termination of the contract in the interest of the estate: it is unquestionable, in fact, that such power 'finds its source in the common rules of civil and commercial law or in the derogating rules specific to insolvency proceedings'.[157]

In light of this, it is advisable that courts and practitioners manage the examples of actions set out in Article 6(1) and recital 35 EIR as mere clues as to the existence (or non-existence) of an insolvency-related pur-

---

155  CJEU, 19 April 2012, Case C-213/10, *F-Tex*, ECLI:EU:C:2012:215.
156  *Linna*, J.Priv.Int.L. 2015, 568, 582 ff.
157  CJEU, 4 September 2014, Case C-157/13, *Nickel & Goeldner Spedition*, ECLI:EU:C:2014:2145, para 27.

pose, and always examine whether such actions are insolvency-related or not in the relevant case.

Notwithstanding in the CJEU's case-law several elements have been identified which contribute to characterize actions as insolvency-related, and notwithstanding such actions are developed rather diversely within the national legislations, it is possible to establish some general criteria in order to specify the broad '*Gourdain* formula' and to facilitate courts and practitioners to classify actions as included within the scope of either the EIR or Brussels I[bis]. The three following criteria have been suggested in the Heidelberg-Luxembourg-Vienna Report,[158] which should simultaneously be fulfilled:

*(i)*   whether the action at stake attains an insolvency-specific purpose which shapes or rather modifies its aim (e.g. the legal standing on behalf of and in the interest of the general body of creditors, or the binding effect of the decision upon persons other than the parties to the proceedings);

*(ii)*  whether the *effet utile* criterion encourages to bring the action before the courts of the Member State that opened the insolvency proceedings; i.e. whether the jurisdiction of these courts allows an efficient and cost-effective administration of the action;

*(iii)* whether common jurisdictional interests (above all, the *actor sequitur forum rei* rule laid down in Article 4 Brussels I[bis]) militate against the assumption of the *vis attractiva concursus*.

These criteria are still current, and thus their adoption should be recommended. Particular emphasis should be put on the first one, in view of the most recent CJEU's decisions, which have stressed that 'the decisive criterion (…) to identify the area within which an action falls is (…) the legal basis thereof', i.e. 'it must be determined whether the right or the obligation which respects the basis of the action finds its source in the common rules of civil and commercial law or in the derogating rules specific to insolvency proceedings'.[159]

---

158 See *Laukemann*, in: Hess/Oberhammer/Pfeiffer (eds), Heidelberg-Luxembourg-Vienna Report (2014), para 4.2.5.1 ff.

159 CJEU, 4 September 2014, Case C-157/13, *Nickel & Goeldner Spedition*, ECLI:EU:C:2014:2145, para 27; see also CJEU, 11 June 2015, Case C-649/13, *Comité d'entreprise de Nortel Networks and Others*, ECLI:EU:C:2015:384, para 28; CJEU, 4 December 2014, Case C-295/13, *H*, ECLI:EU:C:2014:2410, paras

## 2.2 Recital 16 EIR and insolvency-related actions[160]

The CJEU's decisions in the cases *H* and *Kornhaas*[161] dealt with the nature of actions brought pursuant to the first and second sentences of § 64 of the German Law on limited liability companies (GmbHG). According to this provision, the managing directors of a company are obliged to reimburse payments made after the company is declared insolvent or after it has been established that its liabilities exceed its assets. In the cases at hand, the actions had been brought by the insolvency practitioner in the interest of the estate; however, according to German Law, they can be brought not necessarily in the context of insolvency proceedings, but also outside that context. The CJEU held that in both cases the said actions were closely connected to and also stemming from insolvency proceedings: they were closely linked to insolvency proceedings because, in the relevant cases, had been brought in connection with insolvency proceedings; they were directly deriving from insolvency proceedings because they were based on a provision whose application, albeit not requiring insolvency proceedings to have formally been opened, requires the actual insolvency of the debtor, 'and thus (...) derogates from the common rules of civil and commercial law'.[162]

The principle established by the CJEU in these decisions may seem in contrast with recital 16 EIR:[163] hence, the question arises whether such principle has been superseded by this recital. The question has been answered in the negative by a large majority of the stakeholders to whom the questionnaire prepared within this research project has been submitted, according to whom actions based on general company not designed exclusively for insolvency situations may also be considered as falling within the scope of the EIR if they satisfy the double criteria set out in the '*Gour-*

---

23-24; and CJEU, 10 December 2015, Case C-594/14, *Kornhaas*, ECLI:EU:C:2015:806, para 16.

160 See *supra* Part 1, III. 2.2.1 and 2.2.2.

161 Respectively, CJEU, 4 December 2014, Case C-295/13, *H*, ECLI:EU:C:2014:2410; and CJEU, 10 December 2015, Case C-594/14, *Kornhaas*, ECLI:EU:C:2015:806.

162 CJEU, 4 December 2014, Case C-295/13, *H*, ECLI:EU:C:2014:2410, para 22.

163 'This Regulation should apply to proceedings which are based on laws relating to insolvency. However, proceedings that are based on general company law not designed exclusively for insolvency situations should not be considered to be based on laws relating to insolvency'.

*dain* formula'. The solution endorsed by most of the stakeholders seems largely preferable. Firstly, it is questionable that actions based on § 64 GmbHG are not designed exclusively for insolvency situations: even if they can be brought outside the context of insolvency proceedings, they require in any case the actual insolvency of the debtor, and thus, might be considered as encompassed by the expression 'insolvency situations', which has a broad meaning. Secondly, actions which lie at the intersection of company, insolvency and general civil law constitute an important part of claims that can be brought against/by an insolvency practitioner (or debtor in possession): if they were to be kept outside the scope of the EIR, the *vis attractiva concursus* established in Article 6 EIR would prove to be excessively weakened; furthermore, as stated by the CJEU,[164] an artificial and unacceptable distinction would arise between these actions and comparable actions, such as the actions to set transactions aside. Thirdly and most importantly, recital 16 seems to be tailored to collective proceedings, not to actions directly deriving and closely connected with them: in fact, the expression 'proceedings based on laws relating to insolvency' used in recital 16 is used in Article 1(1) EIR, which deals only with collective proceedings; moreover, 'insolvency-related' actions, in the text of the EIR, are always referred to as 'actions', not as 'proceedings'. Finally, it has been argued above[165] that the 'condition' laid down in recital 16 should not be interpreted as a substantial requirement even for collective proceedings: *a fortiori*, it should not be interpreted as such with regard to individual actions.

### 2.3 Overlaps between the EIR and Brussels Ibis

The question arises whether the *forum concursus* has exclusive jurisdiction on insolvency-related actions. The answer is easier now than under the EIR 2000. The *forum* provided in Article 6(2) EIR for insolvency-related actions connected to an action based on general civil and commercial law is elective. This results from the wording of Article 6(2) EIR, which lays down: 'where an action referred to in paragraph 1 is related to an action in civil and commercial matters against the same defendant, the insol-

---

164 CJEU, 4 December 2014, Case C-295/13, *H*, ECLI:EU:C:2014:2410, para 24.
165 See *supra* Part 1, III. 2.2.2.

vency practitioner may bring both actions'. In these cases, the debtor should be considered free to follow the rules on jurisdiction laid down by Article 6(1) EIR and by Brussels I$^{bis}$ and to bring the insolvency-related actions before the court opening the insolvency proceedings, and to bring the connected action to the court determined in accordance with Brussels I$^{bis}$. If a specific rule concerning an elective jurisdiction has been established, this would mean that the general rule for insolvency-related actions is that they *must* be brought before the courts opening insolvency proceedings. The exclusive nature of jurisdiction finds a confirmation in the phrasing of Article 6(1) EIR ('the courts of the Member State within the territory of which insolvency proceedings have been opened in accordance with Article 3 shall have jurisdiction'). Therefore, it has to be held that the EIR and Brussels I$^{bis}$ are not intended to overlap as to the jurisdiction on insolvency-related actions. The provision on the elective *forum*, however, is liable to relativize the classification of insolvency-related actions connected to actions in civil and commercial matters: as a consequence, frequent (but illusory) overlaps may arise in practice.

## 2.4 Insolvency-related actions and secondary proceedings

The CJEU, in *Comité d'entreprise de Nortel Networks and Others* judgment, has established that 'the rule on jurisdiction stated by the Court in the judgment in *Seagon*, based on *vis attractiva concursus*, can also apply in favour of the courts of the Member State in which secondary proceedings have been opened',[166] with reference to actions related to assets situated in the Member State of secondary proceedings. Since Article 6 does not lay down any limitation of the *vis attractiva concursus* to actions related to main proceedings, the solution adopted in *Comité d'entreprise de Nortel Networks and Others* has to be confirmed, and thus also courts of the Member States in which secondary proceedings have been opened have to be considered as having jurisdiction under the EIR to hear and determine insolvency-related actions. According to the abovementioned judgment, insolvency-related actions concerning assets located in the Member States of secondary proceedings are subject to a concurrent juris-

---

166 CJEU, 11 June 2015, Case C-649/13, *Comité d'entreprise de Nortel Networks and Others*, ECLI:EU:C:2015:384, para 32.

diction of the Member States' courts of both the secondary and the main proceedings.[167] Therefore, while the jurisdiction of the *forum concursus* is exclusive (in the sense that the courts of the State where the defendant is domiciled cannot have jurisdiction, except for actions falling under Article 6(2) EIR), concurrent jurisdiction may exist within the scope of the EIR among different *fora concursus*. In *Comité d'entreprise de Nortel Networks and Others*, the CJEU has showed awareness that, 'where there are concurrent fora, there is a risk of irreconcilable judgments', and has noted that 'as the law stands at present, only the mechanism for virtually automatic recognition provided for in Article 25(1) EIR 2000 would enable the risk of irreconcilable judgments to be avoided in cases of concurrent jurisdiction'. Since the EIR does not provide any different rules, the same Article 25 EIR 2000 (now Article 32 EIR) is applicable. This Article, however, provides a solution which is quite rudimentary, insofar as courts opening main proceedings and courts opening secondary proceedings will probably race to open the insolvency-related proceedings first.[168] The application of a rule similar to that laid down in Article 27 Brussels I, 'which, in the case of lis pendens, assigns jurisdiction to the court first seized', has been envisaged by the CJEU as a more efficient solution to the risk or irreconcilable judgments;[169] but the same CJEU has argued that 'it is not for the Court to incorporate such a rule into the scheme of the regulation by judicial decision'. In view of this decision, it seems not appropriate, at the moment, to recommend that national courts apply a solution based on rules along the lines of Article 29 Brussels I[bis]; thus, it is advisable that courts solve conflicts of jurisdiction which may arise by applying Article 32 EIR.

## 2.5 Insolvency-related actions against third state defendants

With reference to insolvency-related actions brought against defendants domiciled in a non-EU State (or in Denmark), see *supra* Part 1, I. 2.2.3.

---

167 CJEU, 11 June 2015, Case C-649/13, *Comité d'entreprise de Nortel Networks and Others*, ECLI:EU:C:2015:384, para 58.
168 *Mucciarelli*, Giur.comm. 2016, 13, 18; *Laukemann*, J.Priv.Int.L. 2016, 379, 386-387.
169 CJEU, 11 June 2015, Case C-649/13, *Comité d'entreprise de Nortel Networks and Others*, ECLI:EU:C:2015:384, para 60.

3. Theses and recommendations

In light of the above, the following recommendations should be issued.

3.1 Pursuant to Article 6(1) EIR, the courts of the Member State within the territory of which insolvency proceedings have been opened in accordance with Article 3 EIR shall have jurisdiction for any action which derives directly from the insolvency proceedings and is closely linked with them (i.e. that is 'insolvency-related').

3.2 According to Article 6(1) EIR, avoidance actions are an example of 'insolvency-related' actions. Similarly, according to recital 35, actions concerning obligations that arise in the course of the insolvency proceedings should be considered as 'insolvency-related'; on the contrary, actions for the performance of obligations under a contract concluded by the debtor prior to the opening of insolvency proceedings should not be considered as 'insolvency-related'.

Insofar as these categories of actions do not always satisfy the double criteria laid down in the '*Gourdain* formula', it is advisable that courts and practitioners manage the examples set out in Article 6(1) and in recital 35 EIR as mere clues as to the existence (or non-existence) of an insolvency-related purpose, and always examine whether such actions are 'insolvency-related' or not in the relevant case.

3.3 Therefore, the double criteria – 'directly deriving' and 'closely linked' – incorporated in Article 6(1) EIR should always be interpreted.

Both requirements must be simultaneously fulfilled.

3.4 Actions are closely linked to insolvency proceedings when they are brought in the context of insolvency proceedings.

3.5 Actions are directly deriving from insolvency proceedings when they find their source in a provision which derogates from the common rules of civil and commercial law and specific to insolvency proceedings.

Actions are directly deriving from insolvency proceedings even if they are based on a provision the application of which does not require insolvency proceedings to have formally been opened but does require the actual insolvency of the debtor, provided that they are brought in the context of insolvency proceedings.

In this respect, recital 16, which provides that proceedings based on general company law not designed exclusively for insolvency situations fall outside the scope of the EIR, should not be interpreted as applicable to 'insolvency-related' actions.

3.6 In order to specify the broad '*Gourdain* formula', courts and practitioners should assess whether:

(i)   actions serve an insolvency-specific purpose (i.e. actions aim at protecting the rights of the general body of creditors by adjusting rules and principles of general civil law or other areas of substantive law or by compensating insolvency-conditioned detriments);

(ii)  the international jurisdiction of the courts of the Member State in which insolvency proceedings were opened improves the efficiency and effectiveness of insolvency proceedings (*effet utile*);

(iii) the international jurisdiction of the courts of the Member State in which insolvency proceedings were opened does not infringe predominant general jurisdictional interest (e.g. the protection of the defendant, based upon the *actor sequitur forum rei* principle).

3.7 Actions should be deemed as 'insolvency-related', and consequently be brought before the courts of the Member State in which insolvency proceedings have been opened, which are brought by/against defendants who are not domiciled within the territory of a Member State.[170]

3.8 Article 6(1) EIR should be interpreted as meaning that it provides for the exclusive jurisdiction of the courts of the Member State in which insolvency proceedings are opened.

Pursuant to Article 6(2) EIR, insolvency practitioners should be allowed to derogate from the exclusive jurisdiction of the *forum concursus* and to bring the action before the courts of the Member State in which the defendant is domiciled only when actions referred to in Article 6(1) EIR are related to actions in civil and commercial matters against the same defendant (i.e., they are so closely connected that it is expedient to hear and determine them together to avoid the risk of irreconcilable judgments resulting from separate proceedings).

3.9 Also courts of the Member State in which secondary insolvency proceedings have been opened should be deemed as having jurisdiction to hear and determine 'insolvency-related actions'.

---

170  See *supra* Part 1, I. 2.2.3 and 3.8.

'Insolvency-related' actions concerning assets located in the Member States of secondary proceedings should be considered as subject to the concurrent jurisdiction of the Member States' courts of both the secondary and the main proceedings. For this reason, a concurrent jurisdiction may exist within the scope of the EIR among different *fora concursus*.

In order to solve possible conflicts of jurisdiction between the Member States' courts of main and secondary proceedings, it is advisable that the 'priority-rule' emerging from Article 32 EIR be applied.

# Part 2: Cooperation between main and secondary proceedings

Max Planck Institute Luxembourg

## I. Instruments to avoid or postpone secondary proceedings*

Articles 36 ff EIR

### 1. Legal framework

#### 1.1 Introduction

Contrary to the previous case law of the CJEU,[171] the recast of the Insolvency Regulation aims to reduce the opening of secondary proceedings which may hamper the efficient administration of the insolvency estate.[172] The main legislative motivation for this reduction is the detrimental effect secondary proceedings may have on carrying out the administration effectively: While organizational and procedural difficulties as well as potential disputes between the involved insolvency practitioners are both playing their part, the opening of parallel proceedings undoubtedly raises costs caused by the appointment of one or more additional insolvency practitioners and the involvement of another insolvency court, and may lead to delays.[173] In particular, the simultaneous application of different insolvency statutes is prone to increase complexity and aggravate the coordination of proceedings, especially when it comes to the realization of assets. According to data provided by the World Bank, the costs of insolvency pro-

---

\* Author: Dr. *Björn Laukemann*, Senior Research Fellow at the MPI Luxembourg; I would like to express my particular gratitude to Dr. *Robert Arts*, Research Fellow at the MPI Luxembourg, for his valuable thoughts and comments during the whole process of the Study.

171 According to the CJEU, 4 September 2014, Case C-327/13, *Burgo Group*, ECLI:EU:C:2014:2158, paras 20-7, 32-9, secondary proceedings may also be opened in the Member State in which the company's registered office is situated and in which it possesses legal personality.

172 Recital 41.

173 Cf *Dammann/Menjucq/Roussel Galle*, Rév. Procéd. Coll. 2015, n° 1, 1/2015, at para 28.

ceedings may substantially burden a debtor's estate.[174] Unilateral acts and uncoordinated splits of the estate might thus prove detrimental to the creditors as a whole. Experience has demonstrated that these structural conflicts arising between universal and local proceedings are exacerbated in corporate group insolvencies,[175] though it cannot be ruled out that the opening of secondary proceedings might, in specific situations, prove beneficial to carry on a debtor's business.[176]

Following practical experience gained from the English proceedings in *MG Rover*,[177] *Collins & Aikmann*,[178] or *Nortel Networks*,[179] the new regime empowers the court at the request of the main insolvency practitioner to postpone or even refuse the opening of secondary proceedings in specific situations (Articles 36 ff, recitals 42 ff EIR).

## 1.2 The undertaking ('synthetic proceedings')

### 1.2.1 Procedural function and conflict of laws mechanism

In contrast to the 'improvised nature' of so-called synthetic proceedings as implemented by the English courts under flexible national rules,[180] the new Insolvency Regulation provides for a detailed and complex procedural framework.[181] As an autonomous substantive provision enlarging the

---

174  In 2010, the cost of insolvency proceedings was about 6 percent of the estate in the United Kingdom, 8 percent of the estate in Germany, 9 percent in France and Sweden and as much as 15 percent in Spain and 22 percent in Italy, see *The World Bank*, Doing Business, Washington 2010, p 77 ff.

175  See CJEU, 22 November 2012, Case C-116/11, *Bank Handlowy and Adamiak*, ECLI:EU:C:2012:739, paras 53-63, with detailed analysis *Koller*, IPRax 2014, 490; *Laukemann*, ecolex 2013, 37.

176  *Undritz*, in: Festschrift Vallender (2015), p 745, 771; *Dammann/Rapp*, Recueil Dalloz 2015, 45.

177  *MG Rover Belux SA/NV* [2007] BCC 446.

178  *Collins & Aikman Europe SA* [2006] EWHC 1343 (Ch).

179  *Nortel Group* [2009] EWHC 206 (Ch); as to the decision of the CJEU, 11 June 2015, Case C-649/13, *Comite d'entreprise de Nortel Networks and Others*, ECLI:EU:C:2015:384, see *Laukemann*, J.Priv.Int.L. 2016, 379 ff.

180  For instance, in *MG Rover Belux SA/NV* [2007] BCC 446, the Court relied on para 65(3) Schedule B1 of the Insolvency Act 1986.

181  As to preliminary concepts see *Janger*, Colum. J. Transnat'l L. 2010, 401 ff; *Wessels*, Brook. J. Corp. Fin. & Com. L. 2014, 63, 80 ff; *Pottow*, Tex.Int'l L.J. 2011, 579. As to the European instrument see also: *Arts*, Norton J. Bankr. L. & Prac.

powers of the main practitioner, Article 36 EIR takes precedence over conflicting national insolvency law.[182] According to paragraph 1 of this Article, the main insolvency practitioner will be entitled to give an undertaking to local creditors which treats them with respect to distribution and priority rights as if secondary proceedings had been opened.[183] To this extent, the provision disaggregates the law applicable to the whole of the main proceedings beyond those issues that are already governed by specific rules on conflict of laws (Articles 8 ff EIR).[184] The objective of this instrument is to avoid the opening of secondary proceedings and its potentially adverse effects in order to expedite the proceedings and increase flexibility, efficiency and the overall return for *all* creditors (recital 41).[185] In tangible terms, the instrument helps to implement a concerted insolvency plan destined for selling the debtor company.[186] By applying the *lex fori concursus secundarii* to distribution and priority rights (alone), Article 36 EIR partially substitutes the legal effects of territorial proceedings. Additional legal safeguards of the *lex fori concursus secundarii* that local

---

2015, 436 ff; *Moss*, Brook. J. Int'l L. 2006/7, 1005, 1017 f; *McCormack*, MLR 2016, 121, 133 f; *Omar*, ICCLR 2012, 283, 288 ff.

182  At the same time, the power of a main insolvency practitioner to exercise – in the absence of secondary proceedings and preservation measures – all the powers conferred on him by the *lex fori concursus* in another Member State (Arts 7, 21(1) EIR), may not hamper the realization of an undertaking. In that regard, those latter provisions have to be interpreted in the light of Art 36 EIR. Insofar, Art 36(1) EIR does not encroach upon Art 21 EIR (= Art 18 EIR 2000). Differently: *Thole*, ZEuP 2014, 39, 65.

183  See also recital 42 EIR.

184  Likewise, the rules for approval of an undertaking are determined by the *lex fori concursus secundarii*, Art 36(5) EIR. Cf also the remedy under Art 36(9) EIR.

185  The decisive criterion for assessing the appropriateness and efficiency of synthetic proceedings is whether the giving of an undertaking is likely to assist the interests of the *creditors as a whole*, see *Laukemann*, in: Bornemann/Brinkmann/Dahl (eds), European Insolvency Regulation (to be published in 2017), Art 36, para 5; with a similar view regarding assurances under the English Insolvency Act 1986 see *MG Rover Belux SA/NV*, 30 March 2006, [2007] BCC 446 (J Norris), at paras 7, 9; *Collins & Aikman Europe SA*, 9 June 2006, [2006] EWHC 1343 (Ch), at para 49.

186  See *Dammann*, in: Festschrift Beck (2016), p 73, 81; cf also *Bewick*, Int. Insolv. Rev. 2015, 172, 182; *Alter/Lévy Morelle*, Forum Financier/Droit bancaire et financier 2015, 346, 348.

creditors could profit from may only be accorded by the opening of secondary proceedings (Article 35 EIR).[187]

The procedural function and effects of an undertaking are complemented by a conflict of laws mechanism.[188] According to Article 36(2) EIR, an approved undertaking *ipso iure* modifies the basic conflict of laws rule (Article 7 EIR) – and partly restricts Article 21(1) EIR – by making reference to particular substantive provisions of the *lex fori concursus secundarii*.[189] The deviation from Article 7 EIR shall, however, be confined to distribution and priority rights. Therefore, the realization of a debtor's assets located in the State of his establishment(s) will uniformly be governed by the *lex fori concursus*. Accordingly, assuming a sub-category of the insolvency estate (recital 43 EIR) will not lead to an additional procedure for the lodging of claims. Only the 'conclusion' of a binding undertaking by virtue of the practitioner's unilateral assurance, on the one hand, and the approval by the known local creditors,[190] on the other, approximates – although not equates to[191] – a contractual-related mechanism.[192]

---

187  Therefore, losing this added procedural value needs to be approved by the (known) local creditors in accordance with Art 36(5) EIR. It can be inferred from this that the function of an undertaking is neither to treat local creditors in any manner as if secondary proceedings had been opened by guaranteeing the same results, nor even to put them legally in a better position, see *Laukemann*, in: Bornemann/Brinkmann/Dahl (eds), European Insolvency Regulation (to be published in 2017), Art 36, para 4.

188  Also *Mangano*, in: Bork/van Zwieten (eds), Commentary on the European Insolvency Regulation (2016), Art 36, para 36.11.

189  In other words, the respective rules applicable to main proceedings are superseded, i.e. partially limited as to their territorial scope. Paragraph 2 thus constitutes a conflict of laws rule (*Sachnormverweisung*) rather than a substantive provision. As a consequence, Art 36(1) EIR does not simply mean to treat (local) creditors *from a practical result* as if the *lex fori concursus secundarii* applied, but rather to apply its respective provisions as if secondary proceedings were opened (Art 35 EIR), see detailed *Laukemann*, in: Bornemann/Brinkmann/Dahl (eds), European Insolvency Regulation (to be published in 2017), Art 36, para 7.

190  Art 36(5) EIR, in conjunction with Art 2(11) EIR.

191  See *Laukemann*, in: Bornemann/Brinkmann/Dahl (eds), European Insolvency Regulation (to be published in 2017), Art 36, paras 8 f.

192  However, advocating a contractual nature of an undertaking: *Mankowski*, NZI 2015, 961, 962; *Mankowski*, in: Mankowski/Müller/Schmidt, EuInsVO 2015 (2016), Art 36, para 4; *Henry*, Recueil Dalloz 2015, 979, 983, para 19 ('de type contractuel').

Indeed, this does not *per se* exclude additional assurances given on the basis of an undertaking. However, widening its scope should only be possible to a limited extent: first, in order to avoid excessive risks of liability that might hinder a practitioner in making use of the instrument; and second, given the preclusive effects under Article 38(2) EIR, in order to limit the risk of outvoting (a large number of) unknown local creditors by generously extending the scope of majority voting for the benefit of a small(er) number of institutional local creditors.[193] Whether the CJEU will in future develop an undertaking as a contractual or settlement-related instrument remains to be seen.

## 1.2.2 Scope

### 1.2.2.1 Local assets and liabilities (scope ratione materiae)

It is the objective of an undertaking to avoid and partly substitute for the opening of territorially-limited parallel proceedings. To this end, their scope will be confined to those assets of a debtor which are situated in the Member State(s) where secondary proceedings could be initiated (Article 36(1) EIR)[194] – in conformity with the Regulation's rules on the allocation of assets and rights.[195] Whether or not an individual local asset forms part of the sub-category of a debtor's estate is exclusively governed by the *lex*

---

193  *Laukemann*, in: Bornemann/Brinkmann/Dahl (eds), European Insolvency Regulation (to be published in 2017), Art 36, para 9. Considering also that an undertaking is not designed to (partly) substitute a (group-wide) restructuring plan adopted in accordance with the rules of the *lex fori concursus universalis*, the limited amount of autonomy Art 36 EIR provides for primarily aims at putting known local creditors in the position to opt for a reduced and (mainly) mandatory procedural alternative – in return for an equivalent but as to its scope limited legal standard, see *ibid*, para 9.

194  The relevant point in time for determining the local assets shall be the moment at which the undertaking is given, Art 36(2), 2nd s. EIR. This date coincides with the moment which is deemed to be authoritative for a practitioner's obligation to retransfer removed assets in case secondary proceedings have subsequently been opened, Art 36(6), 2nd s. EIR.

195  Art 2(9) EIR.

*fori concursus universalis*, and thus not by local law (*arg e* Article 36(2) EIR).[196]

At the same time, only *local* creditors, i.e. creditors whose claims against a debtor arose from or in connection with the operation of a foreign establishment,[197] will explicitly be addressed by an undertaking.[198] Still, this does not mean that local assets will be dedicated to local creditors only.[199] Instead, those assets situated in a Member State in which secondary proceedings could be opened (including the proceeds received from their realization) shall form a sub-category of the insolvency estate (cf recital 43 EIR). In view of a debtor's universal liability and the universal participation of his creditors as general principles underlying the Regulation,[200] those assets shall be held liable for *both* local and non-local creditors,[201] which otherwise would be entitled to lodge their claims in secondary proceedings according to Article 45 EIR.[202]

---

196 *Laukemann*, in: Bornemann/Brinkmann/Dahl (eds), European Insolvency Regulation (to be published in 2017), Art 36, para 14. The scope of a debtor's estate is determined by national rules (Art 7(2) lit. b) EIR), namely by exempting all non-seizable assets from the debtor's liability. However, the objective of an undertaking does not comprehend this internal debtor-creditor conflict on the liability of specific assets. When pointing to the *location* of assets in a Member State in which secondary insolvency proceedings could be opened, Art 36(1) EIR only refers to the *autonomous* rule on the allocation of a debtor's assets to partial insolvency estates (Art 2(9) EIR). Therefore, this latter provision only creates the possibility of allocating assets to one of the partial estates under the further conditions of national insolvency law.

197 Art 2(11) EIR. In this respect, the term 'local claims' proves more accurate.

198 Explicitly: recital 42 EIR (as well as Art 36(5), (10) EIR) against Art 36(1) EIR.

199 Moreover, the scope of an undertaking should not be limited to specific classes of local creditors benefitting from the commitment, thus exempting those local creditors whose legal position would deteriorate under the undertaking. Otherwise, this would unjustly privilege them compared to the legal status they would enjoy if secondary proceedings were initiated.

200 Arts 32, 39 EIR; cf more detailed *Laukemann*, J.Priv.Int.L. 2016, 379, 397.

201 In contrast, those assets which do not constitute a sub-category of the insolvency estate (non-local assets) are governed by the *lex concursus* uniformly applicable to *all* creditors. By the same token, although the definition of 'local creditors' as laid down in Art 2(11) EIR requires a creditor's claim to be connected with a debtor's foreign establishment, *all* the debtor's assets – wherever located – are principally liable for those 'local' claims (albeit governed by different distribution and priority regimes).

202 Only in this way will it be possible to avoid a privileged treatment of local creditors compared to their legal status under secondary proceedings. Consequently, a

### 1.2.2.2 Personal scope[203]

However, Article 36 EIR raises doubts as to the addressees of an undertaking, namely that of whether or not the distribution and priority rights under the law of a Member State where secondary proceedings could be initiated should apply to *all* creditors. Applying different regimes, i.e. both universal and territorial insolvency law to the *same* set of local assets would necessarily entail a conflict of laws, treating local and non-local creditors differently. If, under this scenario, the distributional and priority rules referred to in an undertaking deviate from the rules that would apply to all other creditors according to the *lex fori concursus universalis*, the former would necessarily have to prevail over the latter. This drawback, which is unknown to secondary proceedings, could be bypassed if the scope of an undertaking is considered to also embrace non-local creditors – along with the mechanism set out in Article 45 EIR.[204]

### 1.2.2.3 Law referred to by an undertaking and third parties' rights in rem[205]

By virtue of Article 36(2) EIR, the potential *lex fori concursus secundarii* applies to the distribution of proceeds from a realization of local assets, to the ranking of creditors' claims, and to the rights of creditors in relation to those assets.[206] Therefore, the exemption from Article 7 EIR and, consequently, the substituting procedural effect of an undertaking shall be con-

---

main insolvency practitioner has to take into account the interests of both local and all other creditors when realizing a debtor's assets subject to a (subsequent) undertaking, *Laukemann*, in: Bornemann/Brinkmann/Dahl (eds), European Insolvency Regulation (to be published in 2017), Art 36, para 17.

203 To this issue see *Laukemann*, in: Bornemann/Brinkmann/Dahl (eds), European Insolvency Regulation – Commentary (to be published in 2017), Art 36, para 18; see also *Bork*, in: Bork/Mangano (eds), European Cross-Border Insolvency Law (2016), at para 7.39 (fn 111).

204 Pointing in this direction the wording of Art 36(1) EIR ('comply with the (...) rights under national law that *creditors* would have (...)'). Furthermore, non-local creditors are likewise bound by a court's decision not to initiate secondary proceedings according to Arts 37(2), 38(2) EIR.

205 To this issue see *Laukemann*, in: Bornemann/Brinkmann/Dahl (eds), European Insolvency Regulation (to be published in 2017), Art 36, paras 19 ff.

206 Cf the similar scope of Art 7(2) lit. i) EIR.

fined to distribution and priority rights, while respecting the unity and singularity of the main proceedings as well as the competence of its procedural bodies. Accordingly, the realization of assets will – wherever located – uniformly be governed by the *lex fori concursus universalis*.[207] Finally, even though the lodging of claims and distribution of assets are subject to different insolvency laws, they are both placed under uniform judicial supervision.[208]

However, the term 'priority rights' should be understood in the broad sense of typically comprising provisions that determine the legal position of – unsecured or preferential – creditors, thereby necessarily influencing or interacting with that of other (classes) of creditors. As a matter of principle, this interpretation should also apply to debts incumbent on the estate as long as they arise in connection with a debtor's establishment.[209]

By contrast, provisions and instruments aiming to determine the scope of liable assets, or to protect the insolvency estate, or the interests of creditors as a whole (such as avoidance actions),[210] may not be covered by an undertaking, and fall instead within the ambit of Article 7 EIR.[211]

Moreover, the special rules on conflict of laws (Articles 8 ff EIR) should prevail over the instrument of an undertaking.[212] In that regard, Article 36 EIR has to be differentiated from the scope of Article 8 EIR, especially when considering this provision as a substantive rule rather than a

---

207  Though subject to Art 8 EIR. With the same result: *Skauradszun*, ZIP 2016, 1563, 1571.

208  Assuming a sub-category of the insolvency estate (recital 43 EIR) will not lead to an additional procedure for the lodging of claims.

209  More detailed see *Laukemann*, in: Bornemann/Brinkmann/Dahl (eds), European Insolvency Regulation – Commentary (to be published in 2017), Art 36, para 20.

210  Differently: *Reinhart*, in: Münchener Kommentar InsO, 3rd edn (2016), Art 36 EIR 2015, at para 15. However, should, according to national law, a local creditor's claim be re-established following an avoidance action (cf § 144(1) of the German Insolvency Act), this claim can be considered under the priority rules of the potential *lex fori concursus secundarii*.

211  At the same time, the power of a main insolvency practitioner to exercise – in the absence of secondary proceedings and preservation measures – all the powers conferred on him by the *lex fori concursus* in another Member State (Arts 7, 21(1) EIR), may not hamper the realization of the undertaking. In that regard, those latter provisions have to be interpreted in the light of Art 36 EIR. To this extent, Art 36(1) EIR does not encroach upon Art 21 EIR.

212  Also *Bork*, in: Bork/Mangano (eds), European Cross-Border Insolvency Law (2016), para 7.38.

rule on conflict of laws.[213] Note that under the latter assumption (substantive rule) assets encumbered with a right in rem may not be covered by local *insolvency* law (Article 35 EIR) when an undertaking is given to avoid the opening of secondary proceedings. As a consequence, individual enforcement measures are not prohibited. This interpretation, however, does confer a strong incentive for the opening of secondary proceedings to the detriment of an undertaking.[214] By contrast, Article 36 EIR may apply to a creditor with a right to separate satisfaction as long as his status as an insolvency creditor is concerned.[215]

### 1.2.3 Proposal and formal requirements

When giving an undertaking, i.e. a unilateral proposal, the insolvency practitioner has the duty to specify the factual assumptions underlying the undertaking[216] and meet the formal conditions as set out in Article 36(3)[217] and (4) EIR.[218] As can be deduced from Article 2(5) EIR, the provisional insolvency practitioner is equally entitled to give an undertaking based on Article 36 EIR.[219] This, however, is not the case with a debtor in possession (*arg e* Article 76 EIR).[220]

---

213  Cf CJEU, 16 April 2015, Case C-557/13, *Lutz*, ECLI:EU:C:2015:227, paras 39 f.
214  Cf *Dammann*, in: Festschrift Beck (2016), p 73, 76 f, alluding to the *Arkor* case.
215  This might be relevant when a secured creditor waives his right to separate satisfaction, or such separate satisfaction has (partly) failed, cf § 52 InsO under German law. Also *Wimmer*, in: Festschrift Beck (2016), p 587, 591 f.
216  Art 36(1), 2nd s. EIR, see *Laukemann*, in: Bornemann/Brinkmann/Dahl (eds), European Insolvency Regulation (to be published in 2017), Art 36, para 27.
217  An undertaking shall be made in the official language or one of the official languages of the Member State where secondary insolvency proceedings could have been opened, or, where there are several official languages in that Member State, the official language or one of the official languages of the place in which secondary insolvency proceedings could have been opened, Art 36(3) EIR.
218  According to Art 36(4), 1st s. EIR, the undertaking shall be made in writing and be subject to any other form requirements as to distributions, if the *lex fori concursus universalis* so requires.
219  Also *Wimmer*, in: Wimmer/Bornemann/Lienau (eds), Die Neufassung der EuInsVO (2016), para 423.
220  Similar *Mangano*, in: Bork/van Zwieten (eds), Commentary on the European Insolvency Regulation (2016), Art 36, para 36.10; *Reinhart*, in: Münchener Kommentar InsO, 3rd edn (2016), Art 36 EIR 2015, para 18.

### 1.2.4 Approval

In view of the preclusive effect of Article 38(2) EIR, the undertaking shall be approved (only) by the *known* local creditors,[221] being previously informed by the insolvency practitioner 'of the undertaking, of the rules and procedures for its approval, and of the approval or rejection of the undertaking'.[222] In that regard, the rules on qualified majorities and voting procedures that apply to the adoption of restructuring plans under local law shall apply – as appropriate[223] – to the approval of the undertaking.

In addition, an undertaking shall be subject to any other *approval* requirements as to distributions, if the *lex fori concursus universalis* so requires, Article 36(4) EIR.

### 1.2.5 Effects

#### 1.2.5.1 Direct effects of the undertaking as to the estate and the applicable law

An undertaking produces binding effects on the estate.[224] As a consequence of its approval, the distribution of proceeds from the realization of local assets, the ranking of creditors' claims, and the rights of creditors in relation to the local assets will not be governed by the *lex fori concursus universalis*, but rather by the law of the Member State in which secondary insolvency proceedings could have been opened 'local law'. In addition, (local) creditors may principally sue the practitioner for complying with these assurances. As described above, a debtor's local assets are also held liable for non-local creditors;[225] the local distribution and priority rights apply to *all* creditors, including local and non-local ones.[226]

---

221 Cf the legal definition of 'local creditors' in Art 2(11) as well as the specific provision in Art 36(11) EIR.

222 Art 36(5), 4th s. EIR.

223 Explicitly recital 44, 1st s. EIR, whereas missing in the operative text of the Regulation. This is exposed to criticism.

224 Art 36(6) EIR.

225 Differently *Mankowski*, in: Mankowski/Müller/Schmidt, EuInsVO 2015 (2016), Art 36, para 42; *Prager/Keller*, WM 2015, 805, 808.

226 See *supra* Part 2, I. 1.2.2.

### 1.2.5.2 Effects on the opening of secondary proceedings

As can be deduced from Articles 37(2), 38(2) EIR, local creditors do not legally waive their right to request the opening of secondary proceedings by approving the undertaking.[227] It is important to stress that, in the context of an undertaking, a request for initiating secondary proceedings may, subject to national law, only be rejected if *(i)* that request has been lodged later than 30 days after receiving notice of the *approved* undertaking,[228] or *(ii)* if it has been lodged within that time limit but the court seized is satisfied that the *approved* undertaking adequately protects the general interests of local creditors.[229] If neither of these conditions are met the court will not be hindered to open secondary proceedings, provided the legal conditions set forth by national law are met.

### 1.2.5.3 Removal of local assets[230]

When obliging a main practitioner – once secondary proceedings are opened – to transfer assets which were removed from the territory of a Member State after an undertaking had been given but before secondary proceedings were initiated, Article 36(6), 2nd s. EIR aims to mitigate a depletion of assets subject to the secondary proceedings. This provision has to be read in conjunction with Article 21(1) EIR. Accordingly, the obligation to remove local assets already applies before preservation measures have been taken further to a request for the opening of secondary proceedings in order to prevent the transfer of those assets. At the same time, such an obligation may arise only if secondary proceedings are opened and the previous transfer of assets has taken place *after* the undertaking was given.[231]

---

227 However, it might be argued that creditors explicitly approving an undertaking may lose their legitimate interest in subsequently requesting the opening of secondary proceedings, unless the insolvency practitioner has neglected his duty to inform the creditors correctly and comprehensively.
228 Art 37(2) EIR.
229 Art 38(2) EIR.
230 To this issue see *Laukemann*, in: Bornemann/Brinkmann/Dahl (eds), European Insolvency Regulation (to be published in 2017), Art 36, para 49.
231 Art 36(6), 2nd s. EIR.

From a practitioner's perspective, this mechanism enhances flexibility when implementing a (group-wide) restructuring strategy along with the purpose of the main proceedings, but also potential for abuse.[232] According to recital 46 EIR, however, a main insolvency practitioner is not allowed to relocate assets situated in the Member State of a debtor's establishment in an *abusive* manner, even prior to giving an undertaking. Recital 46 EIR thus mirrors the purpose of the Regulation to ensure effective protection of local interests also in the context of an undertaking. Should local creditors consider the removal of local assets to be abusive or at least detrimental, they may refuse their consent under Article 36(5) EIR, bring an action to establish the practitioner's liability according to paragraph 10,[233] and/or envisage a request for the opening of secondary proceedings.[234] And finally, when applying Article 38(3) EIR equally to flank the giving of an undertaking, the local court may order protective measures aiming to prevent a removal of local assets during a stay.[235]

### 1.2.6 Procedural safeguards

#### 1.2.6.1 Remedies

According to Article 36(7), (8) and (9) EIR, local creditors are entitled to challenge the distribution of assets[236] and proceedings not complying with the undertaking, or to request suitable measures necessary to implement its terms.[237] Both actions should be classified as annex actions in the sense of the new Article 6(1) EIR. Moreover, *local* creditors may require the local

---

232 Cf also *Wimmer*, juris-PR InsR 7/2015 Anm. 1 sub II 7b; *Mankowski*, in: Mankowski/Müller/Schmidt, EuInsVO 2015 (2016), Art 36, para 23.

233 However, remedies under Art 36(8) and (9) EIR are not yet applicable *ratione temporis*.

234 In this respect, an *abusive* removal of local assets should also be taken into account by a local court when assessing the capacity of an approved undertaking to adequately protect the general interests of local creditors, Art 38(2) EIR.

235 Art 38(3), subpara 2 EIR. However, these protective measures do not exclusively cover local assets removed in an *abusive* manner, whereas at the same time excluding those that have been relocated in the ordinary course of business.

236 Art 36(7), 2nd s. EIR presupposes that the practitioner's information about the intended distributions does not comply with the terms of an undertaking or the applicable law, cf *Weiss*, Int. Insolv. Rev. 2015, 192, 205 f.

237 Art 36(8), (9) EIR.

courts in the State of potential secondary proceedings to take provisional or protective measures to ensure compliance by the insolvency practitioner with the terms of the undertaking.[238]

The remedies set forth in Article 36(8) and (9) EIR have the following grounds in common:[239] As expressed in (nearly) parallel terms by paragraphs 8 and 9, local creditors may bring an action to ensure an insolvency practitioner complies with the terms of an undertaking and – one should add – with the law applicable according to Article 36(2) EIR.[240] Both claims are admissible regardless of whether a main practitioner inaccurately performs, or even refuses to perform the terms of an undertaking.[241] In conformity with Article 36(7), 2nd s. EIR, local as well as non-local creditors should have legal standing to file a complaint under paragraphs 8 and 9.

As a matter of principle, Article 36 EIR provides for a concurrent jurisdiction[242] of both the courts in the Member State of the main proceedings (paragraph 8) and the courts of the Member State in which secondary proceedings could have been opened (paragraph 9).[243] However, exclusive jurisdiction is vested in the courts seized under paragraph 8 when granting *final* judicial protection.[244] As can be deduced from Article 2(6) lit. i) EIR, the term 'court' referred to in both paragraphs must be interpreted as encompassing *any* judicial body of a Member State, thus not necessarily insolvency courts. In this respect, national legislators have the task of specifying rules on local and operational jurisdiction.[245]

The legitimate interest of (local) creditors in obtaining satisfaction of their claims may typically be jeopardized under the following circum-

---

238 Art 36(9) EIR.
239 See *Laukemann*, in: Bornemann/Brinkmann/Dahl (eds), European Insolvency Regulation (to be published in 2017), Art 36, paras 56 ff.
240 Therefore, the objective of both remedies is not to ensure direct performance of an undertaking's terms towards the respective creditor, also *Mankowski*, in: Mankowski/Müller/Schmidt, EuInsVO 2015 (2016), Art 36, para 65.
241 Unlike Art 36(7), 2nd s. EIR, the remedies under paragraphs 8 and 9 are neither vested with suspensive effect nor subject to time limits.
242 *Mankowski*, in: Mankowski/Müller/Schmidt, EuInsVO 2015 (2016), Art 36, para 66.
243 In specific cases, measures under paragraphs 8 and 9 may also be taken in parallel as long as they do not coincide as to their cause and subject-matter.
244 Also *Pluta/Keller*, in: Festschrift Vallender (2015), p 437, 450.
245 Cf Art 102c § 21(1), (2) EGInsO (German Introductory Act to the Insolvency Act).

stances: *(i)* non-compliance by a practitioner with the local distribution and priority rights; *(ii)* non-compliance with further assurances forming part of an undertaking; *(iii)* depletion of local assets and proceeds subject to distribution under local law:

*(i)*    As to the first group of cases, paragraphs 8 and 9 aim to ensure local law is applied, which is expected by (the known local) creditors to be beneficial for the satisfaction of their claims as compared to the respective rules of the *lex fori concursus universalis*. Therefore, failing to comply with these rules constitutes a sufficient reason for granting provisional measures under Article 36(8) and (9) EIR if there is a serious risk of a (local) creditor's financial situation deteriorating when awaiting the decision on the substance of his claim.[246]

*(ii)*   As regards the second group of cases, it should be recalled that an undertaking is principally designed to apply foreign local rules on distribution and priority rights within the main insolvency proceedings.[247] As a consequence, a practitioner is not obliged to give *additional* assurances on the basis of an undertaking. If he nevertheless decides to do so, for instance as to the (non-)realization of specific local assets,[248] creditors may, as a general rule and subject to reservations, sue the practitioner for complying with these assurances. However, deviating from assurances that exceed the legal content of an undertaking as delimited by Article 36(2) EIR cannot give reasonable ground for granting (provisional or protective) measures under paragraphs 8 and 9 – nor provide a basis for liability under paragraph 10 – as long as the objective of the *main* proceedings and (group-wide) restructuring strategy so requires without deteriorating a (local) creditor's financial situation as compared to a full respect of these assurances. Otherwise, the flexibility of the new instrument as well as a main practitioner's willingness to make use of it in the interest of the creditors *as a whole* would severely be restricted.

*(iii)*  In view of a practitioner's powers under Article 21(1) EIR and considering that realizing local assets is (subject to Article 8 EIR) gov-

---

246  Thus describing, under German law, a sufficient ground for authorizing a seizure order (under § 917 ZPO) or interim injunctions according to § 935 ZPO. To both aspects see *Skauradszun*, KTS 2016, 419, 434 ff.

247  Cf Art 36(1) and (2) EIR.

248  Cf *Skauradszun*, KTS 2016, 419, 431.

erned by the *lex fori concursus universalis* also in the context of an undertaking, the remedies under paragraphs 8 and 9 cannot be intended to deny a main practitioner access to local assets *as such*, especially when following a group-wide strategy in conformity with the objective of the *main* proceedings.[249] In this respect, claims under paragraphs 8 and 9 should be brought only to prevent any *abusive* removal of local assets and proceeds in terms of recital 46, or other forms of abusive depletion subsequent to the giving of an undertaking. This may in particular be the case when the question of whether or not specific (group of) assets are to be allocated to the local part of a debtor's estate is subject to legal uncertainty.

### 1.2.6.2 Liability of an insolvency practitioner under Article 36(10) EIR

According to Article 36(10) EIR, an insolvency practitioner who is obliged to ensure compliance with the terms of an undertaking shall be liable for any damage caused to local creditors in that respect. The wording of Article 36(10) EIR proves ambiguous as to whom this claim is attributed, and whether it shall cover the individual loss of single local creditors or rather the total loss sustained by the sub-category of the insolvency estate.[250] Given the extended personal scope of an undertaking (see *supra*), non-local creditors should be addressed by Article 36(10) EIR as well.

As a provision of Union law, paragraph 10 has principally to be interpreted autonomously,[251] that is to say in conformity with the concept of undertakings as set out in Article 36 EIR.[252] To this end, courts have to balance out the interest of (local) creditors in their claims being effectively

---

249 Similar to what occurred in *Emtec*, proceeds from the sale of local assets may be hold on fiduciary accounts also in the State of the main proceedings, provided that they will be subject to distribution according to the local rules on distribution and priority rights as set out in Art 36(2) EIR.

250 In that latter sense: Art 102c § 14 EGInsO (German Introductory Act to the Insolvency Act).

251 *Mangano*, however, advocates the application of the *lex fori concursus secundarii*, in: Bork/van Zwieten (eds), Commentary on the European Insolvency Regulation (2016), Art 36, para 36.25.

252 To this and the following issues see *Laukemann*, in: Bornemann/Brinkmann/Dahl (eds), European Insolvency Regulation (to be published in 2017), Art 36, paras 65 ff.

protected, on the one hand, with a legitimate concern, on the other, to avoid disproportionate liability risks of practitioners that would impede any reasonable use of the new instrument on behalf of the creditors as a whole. Accordingly, an insolvency practitioner should not be held responsible for *omitting* to give an undertaking.[253] By the same token, claiming compensation for false or omitted assumptions vis-à-vis an undertaking[254] should be considered under exceptional circumstances only.

### 1.2.6.3 Information of creditors and publication

The process of approval necessitates that comprehensive information is given by the administrator pursuing an undertaking, notably the rules and procedures of approval.[255] The equivalent duty applies, for instance, in the aftermath of the approval process, with regard to the intended distributions.[256]

### 1.3 The stay of proceedings

Apart from an undertaking, the court seized to initiate secondary proceedings will, at the request of the main practitioner or a debtor in possession, be empowered to stay their opening for a period not exceeding three months.[257] This instrument, however, may only apply if, firstly, a temporary stay of individual enforcement proceedings has been granted to allow negotiations between the debtor and his creditors, and, secondly, if suitable measures are adopted to protect the interests of local creditors.[258]

---

253 Whether or not an undertaking is given, falls under a practitioner's discretion. Moreover, (local) creditors are capable of putting pressure on a practitioner by the mere threat of requesting the opening of secondary proceedings. Differently, however, *Mankowski*, in: Mankowski/Müller/Schmidt, EuInsVO 2015 (2016), Art 36, para 21, though referring to the *lex fori concursus universalis*.

254 Art 36(1), 2nd s. EIR.

255 Art 36(5), 4th s. EIR.

256 Art 36(7), 1st s. EIR.

257 Art 38(3) EIR. This period is perceived as being too tight, cf *Brinkmann*, KTS 2014, 381, 400.

258 As to the combination of Art 38(3) EIR with the French *procédure de sauvegarde (financière) accélérée*, see *Dammann/Rapp*, Recueil Dalloz 2015, 45.

## 2. Evaluation

The objective of the recast to repel those secondary proceedings which might hamper an efficient administration of the insolvency estate is to be welcomed. For some aspects, however, the implementation of undertakings seems inconsistent and insufficient. First practical experiences will demonstrate under what conditions local creditors may be inclined to abstain from the opening of secondary proceedings, especially in terms of procedural costs, the volume of local assets, the number of (secured) local creditors and value of their claims, and, not least, their reliance on local law and domestic procedural bodies. So far, the new regulatory scheme is, to a large extent, conceived as complex, formalistic and cumbersome.[259] Whether or not the concept of 'synthetic proceedings' will prove to be a useful and attractive instrument in cross-border insolvencies to balance out (universal) efficiency with local protection remains to be seen – particularly in the context of corporate group insolvencies where the debtor's COMI is deemed to be different from its registered office, and with a view to the EIR's new approach to permit the opening of secondary proceeding with an objective different from liquidation.[260]

---

259 Cf *Garcimartin*, ZEuP 2015, 694, 727; *Thole/Swierczok*, ZIP 2013, 550, 555; *Wessels*, European Company Law (2016), 129, 133; *Eidenmüller* even suspects negative economic effects, thereby criticizing the general approach of 'modified universalism' in favor of a 'straightforward universalism', see MJ 2013, 133, 147, 150; as to the potential costs incurred by an undertaking: *Mendiola*, 'Synthetic' insolvency proceedings (11/2015), 2; less critical: *Bewick*, Int. Insolv. Rev. 2015, 172, 182; *Piekenbrock*, KSzW 2015, 191, 196; *Wimmer*, in: Festschrift Beck (2016), p 587, 590. Giving a differentiated estimation: *Madaus*, in: Festschrift Pannen (2017), p 223, 240, 241, describing virtual secondary proceedings according to Art 36 EIR, on the one hand, as 'remaining (…) an important instrument with respect to the insolvency of groups of companies', while, on the other, as 'not being capable of competing with the English insolvency venue').

260 Cf Art 47(1) EIR. See also Art 38(4) EIR allowing to align the restructuring objectives in main and secondary proceedings.

## 2.1 Legal issues

### 2.1.1 Article 36 EIR as a non-mandatory rule?[261]

The recast does not provide a clear picture on the (non-)mandatory character of Article 36 EIR. This question is particularly relevant – and only partly relativized by the alleged consequences of the Brexit – for ensuring whether an insolvency practitioner remains entitled to give an undertaking on the basis of national law. In that regard, the European legislator does not explicitly forbid the giving of an undertaking if the *lex fori concursus universalis* so permits.[262] Simultaneously, the new Regulation has implemented an instrument that has been practiced so far on a purely national level and enlarged its application to procedural structures comprising, *inter alia*, information duties, remedies and a liability regime. In order to prevent a circumvention of these legal guarantees and ensure their application to be ascertainable, especially for local creditors, the insolvency practitioner should clearly indicate whether an undertaking is given on the basis of Article 36 EIR or rather under a specific provision of national law. However, once the insolvency practitioner opts for the European instrument, Article 36 EIR fully applies, thus becoming binding as to its prerequisites and legal (especially preclusive) effects and taking precedence over conflicting national insolvency law. By generally increasing the bargaining position of local creditors, this latter aspect may, in the individual case, tip the scales in favour of the European mechanism.[263] In providing a clear perspective for all participants as to the (limited) conditions under which territorial proceedings can still be launched subsequent to an approved undertaking, this instrument might conceivably preserve its practical relevance also under the European regime. Legal uncertainty as to

---

261 To this issue see *Laukemann*, in: Bornemann/Brinkmann/Dahl (eds), European Insolvency Regulation (to be published in 2017), Art 36, para 11.

262 Also *Madaus*, in: Festschrift Pannen (2017), p 223, 236 ff. However, pleading for a mandatory nature of Art 36 EIR excluding the giving of an undertaking under national law: *Mankowski*, in: Mankowski/Müller/Schmidt, EuInsVO 2015 (2016), Art 36, para 8.

263 If an undertaking under national law disregards the *pari passu* principle, discriminated creditors may seek relief under the *lex fori concursus universalis* or request for the opening of secondary proceedings.

whether an undertaking under national law may be subject to recognition underpins the previous conclusion.[264]


### 2.1.2 Deferred and concerted secondary proceedings as an alternative option[265]

For group structures, secondary proceedings which are opened in a coordinated way after a concerted realization of group-wide assets might, in individual cases, turn out to be an alternative to giving an undertaking under Article 36 EIR.[266] As demonstrated in *Emtec*,[267] this approach proves particularly appropriate (albeit more expensive) for a complex structure or unclear allocation of the group assets, which require territorial proceedings to be administered and supervised by independent procedural bodies (court, insolvency practitioner) presumably instilling more confidence in local creditors than could be expected of a foreign practitioner appointed in the main proceedings.[268]

---

264 As a matter of principle, it is not an undertaking itself but only a court decision confirming an undertaking that has been given approval under national law which may *per se* be subject to recognition under Art 32(1), subpara 2 EIR. However, recognizing a national undertaking under the Regulation appears debatable, less as to the legal requirements of Art 32 EIR than to the consequence of impeding the right under Art 37 EIR to request the opening of secondary proceedings, especially with regard to unknown local creditors that have not taken part in the approval of the undertaking. If at all admissible, national law needs, first, to provide the same minimum procedural standards as laid down in Art 36 EIR. And second, the legal consequences arising from a recognised undertaking given and approved under national law may not reach further than those of an autonomous undertaking as set out in Art 38(2) EIR.

265 To this issue see *Laukemann*, in: Bornemann/Brinkmann/Dahl (eds), European Insolvency Regulation (to be published in 2017), Art 36, para 12.

266 In this respect, the recast definition of 'establishment' comes into play, Art 2(10) EIR.

267 Cf *Tribunal de commerce de Nanterre* (3ᵉ ch.), 15 February 2006, *SPA Emtec Consumer Media Italia*, Recueil Dalloz 2006, 793; approving: *Menjucq*, ECFR 2008, 135, 145; *Wautelet*, Insolvabilité européenne et procédures secondaires (June 8, 2015), available at SSRN: http://dx.doi.org/10.2139/ssrn.2687625.

268 This insight is owed to Dr. *Reinhart Dammann* given in the context of the Study. See also *Dammann*, in: Festschrift Beck (2016), p 73, 77 f.

### 2.1.3  Approval of an undertaking

### 2.1.3.1  Approval by the known local creditors

When referring to the *lex fori concursus secundarii*, Article 36(5) EIR re-mains silent on which voting rules designed under national law for the ap-proval of restructuring plans may be regarded as (in-)appropriate in terms of recital 44 to be (dis-)applied to the different instrument of an undertak-ing.[269] If those rules were comprehensively relevant, this would also acti-vate a number of provisions which would or could be inconsistent with the function of an undertaking as set out in Article 36 EIR.[270] Evidently, this does not preclude national (implementing) law providing for voting rules on the basis of body representation, e.g. by a (preliminary) creditors' com-mittee.[271] In contrast, it would run counter to the very purpose and word-ing of Article 36(1) and (5), 1st s. EIR if an undertaking were subject to a debtor's consent[272] or to a mandatory approval of a local court (*arg e* Arti-

---

269  Moreover, it is still unclear which voting mechanism shall apply if the rules on qualified majority referred to in Art 36(5) EIR do not exist under national law. According to *Mangano*, the undertaking should be approved unanimously ac-cording to the local law of contract if there is no procedure (in: Bork/van Zwieten (eds), Commentary on the European Insolvency Regulation (2016), Art 36, para 36.18).

270  This, for instance, would rather be the case with § 251 InsO (German Insolvency Act) dealing with the request of individual creditors that pretend to be placed at a disadvantage by the plan compared with their situation without a plan. This stan-dard, however, proves inappropriate for an undertaking: Being an advantageous instrument compared with the opening of secondary proceedings is not only diffi-cult to predict, but – due to the compromise nature of Art 36 EIR – not a formal legal (albeit an often practical) prerequisite for giving an undertaking. Now also Art 102c § 17(1), 1st s. EGInsO (German Introductory Act to the Insolvency Act), see Beschlussempfehlung und Bericht des Ausschusses für Recht und Verbrauch-erschutz (6. Ausschuss) zu dem Gesetzentwurf der Bundesregierung zur Durchführung der Verordnung (EU) 2015/848 über Insolvenzverfahren, BT-Drs. 18/12154, p 32. Still differently the Government draft from 11 January 2017 on the German Introductory Act to the Insolvency Act (Art 102c §§ 17(1), 19 RegE EGInsO, BT-Drs. 18/10823).

271  See *MG Rover Belux SA/NV* [2007] BCC 446, 451, at para 9 (approval by the Belgian creditors' committee); *Collins & Aikman Europe SA* [2006] EWHC 1343 (Ch), at para 46; cf also *Mankowski*, in: Mankowski/Müller/Schmidt, EuInsVO 2015 (2016), Art 36, para 46 with reference to French law.

272  Cf § 247 InsO (German Insolvency Act); likewise: *Pluta/Keller*, in: Festschrift Vallender (2015), p 437, 445.

cle 38(2) EIR).[273] As a matter of principle, the voting process is conducted by the insolvency practitioner appointed in the main proceedings.[274] In order to keep the instrument flexible and unfettered by (additional) formalism and legal uncertainty, the involvement of local courts should only be envisaged on an exceptional or, at least, reduced basis to supervise, for instance, a voting procedure under paragraph 5, to decide on the obstructive voting of individual creditor groups ('class cram-down'),[275] or on the voting rights of creditors with disputed claims.[276]

### 2.1.3.2 Voidability and replacement of an approved undertaking[277]

Article 36 EIR remains silent on whether an approved undertaking may be subject to review, voidability or adjustment if, for instance, the underlying assumptions of an insolvency practitioner prove inaccurate. At first, this question should not be governed by the *lex fori concursus secundarii*,[278] but rather be answered in conformity with the purpose and concept of an undertaking designed as an autonomous instrument. In addition, giving an undertaking at an early stage of the proceedings is exposed to a factual basis which typically proves uncertain, incomplete and prone to change. As a general rule, creditors should trust in the validity and legal effects of procedural agreements such as an undertaking which are entered into to modify the course of the proceedings as well as the applicable law.[279] In this light, the principle of legal certainty calls for an appropriate caution in

---

273  Cf § 248 InsO (German Insolvency Act); in the same sense: *Fritz*, DB 2015, 1882, 1888, against *Wimmer*, jurisPR-InsR 7/2015 Anm. 1, II 7 b.

274  Cf Art 102c § 17(1), 1st s. EGInsO (German Introductory Act to the Insolvency Act); *Wimmer*, jurisPR-InsR 11/2017 Anm. 1.

275  Cf § 245 InsO (German Insolvency Act), also Art 102c § 17(1) EGInsO (German Introductory Act to the Insolvency Act); differently *Madaus*, NZI 2017, 203, 205; *ibid.*, in: Festschrift Pannen (2017), p 223, 236.

276  Cf § 237(1) in conjunction with § 77 InsO (German Insolvency Act): Art 102c § 18 EGInsO (German Introductory Act to the Insolvency Act).

277  To this issue see *Laukemann*, in: Bornemann/Brinkmann/Dahl (eds), European Insolvency Regulation (to be published in 2017), Art 36, paras 36 f.

278  In this regard, however, *Mankowski*, in: Mankwoski/Müller/Schmidt, EuInsVO 2015 (2016), Art 36, para 20.

279  This is particularly relevant for the preclusive effect of an approved undertaking. By the same token, payments might have already been effected on the basis of the undertaking.

challenging a procedural agreement, excluding, at least, a unilateral right of the practitioner to avoid or terminate an approved undertaking.[280]

However, two remaining options might be considered: *(i)* local creditors will review the approved undertaking under Article 38(2) EIR within the 30-day time limit pursuant to Article 37(2) EIR; *(ii)* after that deadline and premised on adjusted assumptions, an insolvency practitioner will give a revised undertaking subject to renewed voting, thus replacing the first one through (dis-)approval[281] by the local creditors.[282] Nonetheless, both approaches may only be envisaged and successfully taken if, firstly, the factional assumptions underlying the initial undertaking prove incorrect to a *significant extent* and, secondly, the revised assumptions have the potential to change the local creditors' view on the appropriateness of an undertaking compared to the opening of secondary proceedings, by taking into account the (advanced) stage of proceedings.[283] Such adjustments may, for instance, be related to the range of local assets,[284] but also to local assets encumbered with a right in rem. Under these circumstances, the insolvency practitioner shall even be obliged to give notice of his revised assumptions, thereby enabling local creditors to rectify their initial decision.

---

280 Similarly, as to procedural acts under German procedural law: *Rosenberg/ Schwab/Gottwald*, Zivilprozessrecht, 17th edn (2010), § 65, para 46.

281 In the event of approval, the 30-day time-limit under Art 37(2) EIR starts to run again.

282 Whether the *clausula rebus sic stantibus* is the appropriate mechanism in this respect (cf *Mankowski*, in: Mankowski/Müller/Schmidt, EuInsVO 2015 (2016), Art 36, para 20), seems at least questionable given that the legal consequence of Art 36(2) EIR, which is to apply the *lex fori concursus secundarii* with respect to distribution and priority rights, equally applies to an initial and a revised undertaking and their underlying assumptions.

283 For instance, if an insolvency practitioner should have overvalued real estate property of a debtor located in the Member State of his establishment, this aspect alone will usually not provide incentives for the opening of secondary proceedings in which the realization of those assets were to be based upon the same real value.

284 If the number or value of local assets proves significantly higher than initially assumed, this might, in an individual case, provide incentives for the opening of secondary proceedings. The converse situation, however, will typically confirm the appropriateness of an undertaking.

### 2.1.3.3 Approval by the creditors of the main proceedings?

According to Article 36(4) EIR, an undertaking shall be subject to any other approval requirements as to distributions, if the *lex fori concursus universalis* so requires. However, establishing a dual approval of an undertaking both by the known local creditors and, commonly, by the (both local and non-local) creditors of the main proceedings raises doubts: In particular, conferring on the latter a right to approve an undertaking, conceived as a partial substitution of secondary proceedings, might not only give rise to delay, obstruction and legal uncertainty,[285] but would also contradict the general principle according to which (non-local) creditors cannot avoid the opening of subsequent territorial proceedings through disapproval.[286] Otherwise, the creditors of the main proceedings would have the power to overrule the approval of the known local creditors whose interests an undertaking aims to protect.

---

285  According to Art 102c § 11(1) EGInsO (German Introductory Act to the Insolvency Act), an undertaking given in German main insolvency proceedings shall be subject to approval by a (provisional) creditors' committee (if appointed), thereby following the *ratio legis* of § 187(3), 2nd s. InsO (German Insolvency Act), see Beschlussempfehlung und Bericht des Ausschusses für Recht und Verbraucherschutz (6. Ausschuss) zu dem Gesetzentwurf der Bundesregierung zur Durchführung der Verordnung (EU) 2015/848 über Insolvenzverfahren, BT-Drs. 18/12154, p 31; *Madaus*, NZI 2017, 203, 206. The provision predicates a distribution on the consent of a creditors' committee. In doing so, the rule aims to leave to the discretion of that committee whether or not to defer a distribution of proceeds in the interest of all creditors, see *Füchsl/Weishäupl/Kebekus/Schwarzer*, in: Münchener Kommentar InsO, 3rd edn (2013), § 187, para 12. This rationale, however, objects to the function and concept of Art 36 EIR. By the same token, applying § 160 InsO will give rise to legal uncertainty, especially if a creditor's vote is subject to the condition that the local assets are of minor importance; in that sense, though, the preliminary version of Art 102c § 12 RegE EGInsO (Government draft from 11 January 2017 on the German Introductory Act to the Insolvency Act, BT-Drs. 18/10823); also *Wimmer*, in: Wimmer/Bornemann/Lienau (eds), Die Neufassung der EuInsVO (2016), para 435.

286  As a consequence, it may occur that local creditors participating in the main proceedings vote on both sides of an undertaking.

### 2.1.3.4 Approval of an undertaking after the opening of secondary proceedings

Apart from Article 36 EIR, the new Regulation empowers a court at the request of a main insolvency practitioner to postpone the opening of secondary proceedings.[287] Principally, both mechanisms – i.e. synthetic proceedings and a stay of proceedings according to Article 38(3) EIR – may not come into play once secondary proceedings are opened.[288] This shortcoming considerably undermines the general policy approach of the recast: *Before* an undertaking becomes binding through approval, a court is permitted to initiate secondary proceedings even if the process of approving an undertaking is underway, without examining whether local interests are adequately protected. This bears the risk that local creditors might be tempted to pressure the administrator to grant privileges that exceed those gained by 'regular' secondary proceedings, or even outright subvert an undertaking by previously requesting the opening of secondary proceedings. This is exacerbated by the fact that a main practitioner will lack power to request the closing of secondary proceedings following an intermediate approval of the undertaking.[289] The wording of Article 38(3) EIR does not address that issue either.[290]

### 2.1.4 Undertaking and secondary proceedings

### 2.1.4.1 The start of time limit to request the opening of secondary proceedings

One of the most relevant practical issues is the start of the time limit to request the opening of secondary proceedings. According to Article 37(2) EIR, this request shall be lodged within 30 days of having received notice of the approval of the undertaking. A specific practical problem arises

---

287  Art 38(3) EIR.
288  Detailed to this problem: *Brinkmann*, KTS 2014, 381, 397.
289  Although challengeable under Art 39 EIR as well as under national law, a court decision which opens secondary proceedings contrary to Arts 37(2), 38(2) EIR, would nonetheless be subject to recognition.
290  It remains unclear under Art 38(3), subpara 3 EIR whether and under what conditions the court shall be entitled to refuse the opening of secondary proceedings if an agreement in the sense of subpara 1 has been concluded in the meantime.

from the unclear wording as to the addressee receiving notice of the approved undertaking. The provision excludes neither a uniform nor an individual start of the time limit. For reasons of legal certainty, this time limit should be determined collectively/uniformly rather than individually by referring to the respective date of an individual creditor's reception of that notice. Evidently, the insolvency practitioner may fulfil his obligation under Article 36(5), 4th s. EIR to inform the known local creditors about the approval or rejection of the undertaking individually.[291] However, the insolvency practitioner should additionally ensure a collective and reliable reception of notification under Article 37(2) EIR, also vis-à-vis unknown local creditors and even non-local creditors, whose (unimpeded) right to request the opening of secondary proceedings requires that they are given information regarding the deadline which is relevant for all creditors.[292] To that end, creditors should be informed through national insolvency registers both in the Member State of the main proceedings and in the Member State subject to the respective undertaking. In order to achieve a uniform start of that time limit, the register entry should indicate this specific date as well as possible rules under the *lex fori concurus secundarii* determining the time of publication and, thus, the start of the time limit under Article 37(2) EIR.[293]

---

291 In that regard, Art 102c § 19 in conjunction with § 12, 2nd s. EGInsO (German Introductory Act to the Insolvency Act) provides for a notification of the known local creditors through individual service. The same mechanism applies to the giving of an undertaking according to § 12, 2nd s. EGInsO.

292 Differently *Reinhart*, in: Münchener Kommentar InsO, 3rd edn (2016), Art 37 EIR 2015, para 4, advocating that Art 37(2) EIR is not binding upon non-local creditors. This, however, would mean conferring on those creditors – within the limits of Art 38(2) EIR – the power to deprive a binding undertaking from its effects at any time after the expiry of the time limit, thus causing legal uncertainty. Equally in favour of an individual start of time limit: *Legrand*, Petites affiches 2015, n° 16, 8, 11.

293 One could image, for instance, a national implementation rule similar to § 9(1), 2nd s. InsO (German Insolvency Act) according to which publication shall be deemed to have been effected when two additional days following the day of publication have expired.

## 2.1.4.2 The court's criterion to reject the opening of secondary proceedings, Article 38(2) EIR

According to Article 38(2) EIR, a court shall, at the request of the insolvency practitioner, not open secondary insolvency proceedings if it is satisfied that the undertaking adequately protects the general interests of local creditors. In that regard, however, the court shall, when assessing the interests of local creditors take into account that the undertaking has been approved by a qualified majority of local creditors.[294] Thus, even though the wording of Article 38(2) EIR states that the court should examine the protection provided by the undertaking only if and when the main administrator files a corresponding request, we suggest that the court should *(i)* examine *ex officio* if an undertaking has been given and whether or not it meets the criteria under Article 38(2) EIR whenever the opening of secondary proceedings is requested and *(ii)* treat an approved undertaking as an assumption that the interests of local creditors are being protected. This assumption should furthermore include those local creditors, who did not participate in the approval procedure, if they are bound to the outcome according to the domestic voting rules, and as long as they are given the realistic chance to become aware of the undertaking (e.g. via the publication in a register). It would thus fall *(iii)* to the local creditors to reverse this presumption by providing evidence that their interests are being endangered. In this regard, the mere fact that local creditors will suffer additional effort and costs by participating and lodging their claims in (foreign) main proceedings governed by foreign insolvency law may, by itself, not suffice to deny an adequate protection of local creditors' general interests. Equally, the fact that the secondary proceeding might provide other rules, which exceed the general scope of an undertaking, should not be considered a sufficient limitation of the local creditors' general interests.[295]

That being said, there remains an undeniable danger that judges in the Member State of potential secondary proceedings may, for reasons of protectionism, be inclined to conclude that an undertaking will *not* adequately protect the general interests of local creditors (Article 38(2) EIR).

---

294  Recital 42, 4th s. EIR.
295  Equally advocating a narrow interpretation of Art 38(2) EIR: *Jault-Seseke/ Robine*, Rev. crit. DIP 2016, p 21, at para 54 ('utilisé avec la plus grande parcimonie').

### 2.1.5 Undertaking and corporate group insolvencies

Finally, the mechanism of synthetic proceedings lacks adequate adjustment with the concentration of insolvency proceedings for several group companies in one single jurisdiction. Under the scenario of a 'group COMI', recital 24 EIR explicitly mentions the possibility of instituting secondary proceedings in the Member State(s) of a debtor's registered office(s), without, however, providing guidance as to whether the respective insolvency practitioners remain entitled to give an undertaking according to Article 36 EIR. In our view, this question should clearly be answered in the affirmative.

## 2.2 Practical problems

### 2.2.1 Criteria to be taken into account by an insolvency practitioner when giving an undertaking

It goes without saying that the decision of an insolvency practitioner to give an undertaking can only be reached by reference to the individual circumstances of each case. And, of course, the relevant aspects can be identified in a more conducive and fine-grained manner when this new mechanism will be applied under the new regime.

Nonetheless, we gathered non-exhaustive aspects that may play a role in the decision-making process of the insolvency practitioner (see *infra*, 3.2).

### 2.2.2 Identification and information of local creditors / publication

Another and even more important issue as to the practical implementation of Article 36 EIR is the identification and information of local creditors. Apart from the opening of main proceedings, creditors should generally be informed of *(i)* the intention of an insolvency practitioner to give an undertaking and the factual assumptions underlying that undertaking;[296] *(ii)* the undertaking being subject to approval (or disapproval), including the

---

296 Art 36(1), 2nd s. EIR.

respective legal consequences therefrom, in particular as to the start of the time limit for requesting secondary proceedings (Article 37(2) EIR);[297] *(iii)* the time of reception of the notice that the undertaking has been approved (Article 37(2) EIR); and *(iv)* legal remedies set forth in Article 36 EIR.

In so far as means of information are concerned, we ask whether or not (local) creditors can or should be reliably informed: *(i)* either through *non-individual* notification, such as national insolvency registers or nationwide daily newspapers in the Member State where secondary proceedings could be opened; or through a website specifically created by the insolvency practitioner; *(ii)* or rather through *decentralized individual* notification? In this respect, national insolvency registers appear to be best suited to guarantee reliable information to all creditors, combined with an individual notification of an undertaking's (dis-)approval vis-à-vis the known local creditors.[298] It is of utmost importance, however, to ensure a uniform and ascertainable start of the time limit under Article 37(2) EIR.[299] To that end, the insolvency register in the Member State in relation to which an undertaking has been given should be considered as the exclusively relevant medium for determining the start of that time limit. Given that the Regulation requires only a *minimum* amount of information to be published in the insolvency registers, Member States should not be precluded (and indeed be encouraged) from including additional information, cf recital 77, Article 24(3) EIR.[300]

As regards the addressee of information, the wording of Article 36(5), 4th s. EIR is confined to local creditors. As long as the duty to notify shall guarantee an informed consent under Article 36(5) EIR, this limitation in scope is not exposed to criticism. However, as far as the approval/disapproval of an undertaking is concerned, all – including non-local – creditors should be informed on this aspect, considering the right of *all* creditors to

---

297  Art 36(5), 4th s. EIR.
298  The individual notification shall be given in the language(s) referred to in paragraph 3. Cf also Art 102c § 19 in conjunction with § 12, 2nd s. EGInsO (German Introductory Act to the Insolvency Act) providing for a notification to the known local creditors through individual service. The same mechanism applies to the giving of an undertaking according to § 12, 2nd s. EGInsO.
299  See *supra* Part 2, I. 2.1.4.1.
300  Information on certain aspects of insolvency proceedings is essential for creditors, such as time limits for lodging claims or challenging decisions, recital 78 EIR.

request the opening of secondary proceedings. In this respect, the CJEU may, for the sake of coherency, overcome the limited wording of Article 36(5), 4th s. EIR by interpreting the provision in conformity with the purpose of Article 37(1) lit. b) EIR.[301]

## 3. Theses and recommendations

### 3.1 Scope of undertakings

3.1.1 Those assets situated in the Member State in which secondary proceedings could be opened (including the proceeds received from their realization) shall form a sub-category of the insolvency estate (cf recital 43 EIR) liable for both local and other creditors, which otherwise would be entitled to lodge their claims in secondary proceedings according to Article 45 EIR.

3.1.2 The scope of an undertaking, i.e. the distribution and priority rights under the law of the Member State where secondary proceedings could be initiated, should apply to all creditors, including non-local creditors.

3.1.3 The special rules on conflict of laws (Articles 8 ff EIR) should prevail over the instrument of an undertaking. In this respect, Article 36 EIR has to be differentiated from the scope of Article 8 EIR, especially when considering this provision as a substantive rule rather than a rule on conflict of laws.

### 3.2 Giving of an undertaking

In view of the non-mandatory nature of Article 36 EIR, an insolvency practitioner remains entitled to give an undertaking on the basis of national law. However, in order to prevent a circumvention of its procedural guarantees and ensure their application to be ascertainable especially for local creditors, the insolvency practitioner should clearly indicate whether an undertaking is given on the basis of Article 36 EIR or rather under a specific provision of national law. Once an insolvency practitioner opts for

---

301 See *Laukemann*, in: Bornemann/Brinkmann/Dahl (eds), European Insolvency Regulation (to be published in 2017), Art 36, para 42.

the European instrument, Article 36 EIR fully applies and becomes binding as to its prerequisites and legal effects.

## 3.3 Assessing the adequacy and efficacy of Article 36 EIR

The decision of an insolvency practitioner to give an undertaking according to Article 36 EIR can only be reached by reference to the individual circumstances of each case. Nonetheless, we recommend the following aspects to be taken into account:

– a certain likelihood that secondary proceedings legally can and factually will be opened;[302]
– possible adverse effects to be expected from the opening of secondary proceedings for an efficient administration of the main proceedings that could be avoided or mitigated by giving an undertaking;
– reasons for local creditors to disapprove an undertaking and, instead, to request the opening of secondary proceedings, especially due to a large number of local creditors;[303] the complexity of determining or applying different insolvency laws as to distribution and priority rights; beneficial rules on the realization of assets under local insolvency law; a complex structure or (unclear) allocation of the debtor's (local) assets; greater confidence in independent local procedural bodies (court/insolvency practitioner) to pay due regard to their local interests (e.g. as to local assets or the lodging of claims); particularities of a corporate group structure;
– and finally, the role of national judges when requested to open secondary proceedings who might be inclined to conclude that an undertaking will not adequately protect the general interests of local creditors in the sense of Article 38(2) EIR.

---

302  Cf *Nortel Group*, 27 August 2015, [2009] EWHC 2506 (Ch), at para 31.
303  Cf *MG Rover Belux SA/NV*, 30 March 2006, [2007] BCC 446, 450 (J Norris), at para 8.

## 3.4 Identifying and informing (local) creditors

The identification and information of (local) creditors is of vital importance when giving an undertaking. In that regard, the following aspects have to be kept in mind:

### 3.4.1 Creditors should be informed of…

- the opening of main insolvency proceedings (Article 28 EIR);
- the intention of an insolvency practitioner to give an undertaking and the factual assumptions underlying that undertaking;
- the undertaking being subject to approval (or disapproval), including the respective legal consequences therefrom, in particular as to the start of the time limit for requesting secondary proceedings (Article 37(2) EIR);
- the time of reception of the notice that an undertaking has been approved (Article 37(2) EIR);
- legal remedies set forth in Article 36 EIR.

### 3.4.2 Means of communication

In our view, national insolvency registers in combination with an individual notification of an undertaking's approval vis-à-vis the known local creditors are best suited to guarantee reliable information of all creditors. In that regard, the insolvency register in the Member State subject to the respective undertaking seems to be the most appropriate instrument for giving notice of an undertaking's (dis-)approval in order to ensure a uniform and ascertainable start of the time limit under Article 37(2) EIR.[304]

### 3.4.3 Creditors' information on the (dis-)approval of the undertaking

In light of the right of all creditors to request the opening of secondary proceedings (Article 37(1) lit. b) EIR) all – including non-local – creditors should be informed as to the approval/disapproval of an undertaking.

---

304 See *supra* Part 2, I. 2.1.4.1.

3.5  The start of time limit to request the opening of secondary
     proceedings (Article 37(2) EIR)

3.5.1 The starting point of the 30-day time limit to request the opening of secondary proceedings according to Article 37(2) EIR should, for reasons of legal certainty, be determined collectively/uniformly rather than individually.

3.5.2 The insolvency practitioner should ensure a collective and reliable reception of notification under Article 37(2) EIR, also vis-à-vis unknown local creditors (and non-local creditors), see also 3.4.2.

3.6  Temporary stay of the opening of secondary proceedings

3.6.1 The instrument of Article 38(3) subpara 1 EIR – so as to be more in line with the proposal's key objective to avoid detrimental secondary proceedings – should be extended to situations where the main insolvency practitioner has given or envisages giving an undertaking in the sense of Article 36 EIR, which, however, has not been approved yet.

3.6.2 This instrument should include the judicial power to close secondary proceedings at the request of the main practitioner once an undertaking, meeting the conditions under Article 38(2) EIR, has been approved according to Article 36 EIR.

3.7  Implementing Regulation

Article 36 EIR gives rise to national implementing regulation, especially with regard to the relevant domestic rules referred to in paragraph 5 on the approval of undertakings. As a general principle, national norms implementing EU regulations may not contravene the wording and objectives of the European legal act and its provisions. Consequently, the implementing legislator should, in the context of Article 36 EIR, generally avoid rules promoting formalism, legal uncertainty and increased complexity which makes the instrument of an undertaking less flexible or, at worst, practically irrelevant.[305] This is particularly true for two aspects:

- National voting rules on the adoption of restructuring plans should fit in with the purpose of an undertaking as set out in Article 36 EIR. In that respect, a provision under national law would prove inappropriate to undertakings in the sense of recital 44 if it provides, for instance, for a debtor's consent or mandatory approval of the local court (see *supra* 2.1.3.1).
- Given the partly substituting effect of undertakings vis-à-vis the opening of secondary proceedings, national implementing rules should not contradict this structural element by introducing provisions that might hamper, or even inhibit the approval and performance of an undertaking. Accordingly, domestic rules implementing a creditor's approval in the *main* proceedings would clearly infringe Article 36 EIR.

By contrast, the following issues should be subject to implementing regulation while respecting the limitations set by Article 36 EIR:

- Provisions obliging an insolvency practitioner to indicate whether he is giving an undertaking under Article 36 EIR or rather on the basis of national law;
- provisions concretizing the information to be given under Article 36(1), 2nd s. EIR;
- rules specifying those provisions on the adoption of restructuring plans that are appropriate to apply to the approval of undertakings according to Article 36(5), 2nd s. EIR;[306]
- rules on proofing the status of local creditors in the voting process, including the justification and amount of their claim;[307]
- rules specifying local jurisdiction in relation to the remedies provided for by Article 36(7), 2nd s., (8) and (9) EIR, potential time limits and whether or not the respective court decision is subject to appeal;[308]
- provisions concretizing the liability regime under Article 36(10) EIR.[309]

---

305  Pointing in the same direction: *Fritz*, DB 2015, 1882, 1887.
306  Cf Art 102c § 17(1) EGInsO (German Introductory Act to the Insolvency Act).
307  Cf Art 102c § 18(1) EGInsO (German Introductory Act to the Insolvency Act).
308  Cf Art 102c § 21 EGInsO (German Introductory Act to the Insolvency Act).
309  Cf Art 102c § 14 EGInsO (German Introductory Act to the Insolvency Act).

## II. Cooperation, Communication, Coordination*

Articles 41-44 EIR (single debtor)

### 1. Introduction

According to Article 31 EIR 2000 liquidators in the main proceedings and liquidators in the secondary proceedings shall be duty bound to communicate information to each other. Although the provision only refers to insolvency practitioners (insolvency practitioner), some interpretations extended it to encompass cooperation between courts, and also between courts and IPs. Case law applying this understanding of the text is to be found in the form of communication between courts to decide on the COMI – thus on jurisdiction –, or on the type of proceeding to be opened. Well-known examples of the working together of courts in cross-border insolvency settings are the BenQ and the PIN Group[310] cases. However, examples pointing to the opposite direction also exist,[311] and actually the prevailing opin-

---

* Prof. Dr. *Marta Requejo Isidro*, Senior Research Fellow MPI Luxembourg; Professor at the University of Santiago de Compostela.

310 *District Court of Amsterdam*, 27 February 2007. BenQ Holding BV had a permanent location in the Netherlands and a subsidiary in Munich. Employees were working in Munich and also in the Netherlands. All the activities were taking place in Munich. There were two managing directors, one in Amsterdam and one 'travelling part-time manager'. For all his decisions, the second director needed the consent of the other director. The director residing in the Netherlands had the power to make decisions on his own. In December 2006 the Dutch company filed a petition for a moratorium ('surseance van betaling'). The Amsterdam Court granted an immediate, but preliminary order. A couple of days later the German part of the company filed for bankruptcy in Munich. The judge granted the opening of insolvency proceedings, but did not yet decide on the type of proceedings. The story goes that the German judge phoned the judge in Amsterdam in order to decide what type of proceedings should be opened. The result was that on January 31, 2007 the Amsterdam Court opened main proceedings and a few days later secondary proceedings were opened in Munich. The communication between the courts (judges) prevented main insolvency proceedings from being opened in both the Netherlands and in Germany.

311 *Amtsgericht Köln*, 19 February 2008, NZI 2008, 257. The PIN group was a German enterprise with most of the operating companies having their registered office in Germany. The holding company had its registered office and its COMI in Luxembourg for financial reasons. A COMI shift to Germany occurred on the eve of insolvency; the *Amtsgericht Köln* held that the shift's purpose was to facilitate the restructuring of the group by coordinating the proceedings over all of the

139

ion on Article 31 EIR 2000 qualifies it as insufficient. As the Commission's Report on the application of the EIR 2000 stated:

'The duties to cooperate and communicate information under Article 31 of the Regulation are rather vague. The Regulation does not provide for cooperation duties between courts or liquidators and courts. There are examples where courts or liquidators did not sufficiently act in a cooperative manner. These findings are confirmed by the results of the public consultation where 48% of the respondents were dissatisfied with the coordination between main and secondary proceedings.'[312]

The reasons underlying the lack of cooperation between liquidators, which seem to be also pertinent regarding court-to-court and court-insolvency practitioner cooperation, are both legal and practical. The most relevant among the former are the lack of an explicit authorization or a mandate addressed to the actors involved; the lack of specific instructions or guidelines on how to proceed to actually implement the cooperation; the complexity of the legal framework, i.e. the plurality of procedural and substantive insolvency laws throughout Europe; the differing policies underlying national insolvency systems. Additional legal difficulties such as divergent national standards on data protection may also concur.

Typical practical difficulties are the lack of command of a foreign language; the fear (the actual risk) of losing time and increasing costs while organizing the cooperation, and in case it fails; depending on the jurisdiction, the (mediocre) quality and insufficient specialization of judges; the (poor) court' infrastructure and available means; the lack of detailed knowledge of the Insolvency Regulation; the limited experience in dealing with international insolvency cases; the absence of a real awareness of the

---

group's subsidiary companies, therefore it was not abusive. The German court requested information to the Luxembourg court by fax on the opening of main proceedings there and got an immediate answer, also by fax, on the same day.

312 As exemplified by the national proceedings underlying the preliminary question to the ECJ in case CJEU, 22 November 2012, Case C-116/11, *Bank Handlowy and Adamiak*, ECLI:EU:C:2012:739. Following the approval of a rescue plan (procédure de sauvegarde) by the French court in Meaux, the Polish court asked the Tribunal de commerce de Meaux whether the insolvency proceedings in France, which were main proceedings for the purposes of the Regulation, were still pending. The answer given by the French court did not provide the necessary clarification; the referring court then consulted an expert.

impact of insolvency and local proceedings in international business; and the unwillingness to cooperate, based on the absence of real mutual trust. [313]

## 2. Legal framework

Under the new Regulation, Articles 41 to 44 set up a framework for enhanced cooperation between insolvency practitioner, courts, and insolvency practitioner and courts involved in main and secondary/territorial proceedings concerning the same debtor.[314]

Article 41 EIR instructs the insolvency practitioners to communicate and cooperate among them in order to facilitate the coordination of main and territorial or secondary insolvency proceedings concerning the same debtor.[315] Cooperation is subject to the requirement that it does not run against the rules applicable to the proceedings; additional caveats are added in the case of insolvency of group of companies. Within the framework of those restrictions cooperation may take any form, including the conclusion of agreements or protocols, and some specific actions are proposed to the IPs.

An additional rule – Article 42 EIR establishes the duty to cooperate and communicate regarding the courts involved in proceedings concerning the same debtor. Once again, cooperation is subject to the conditions that it does not run against the rules applicable to the proceedings. Some examples of means of cooperation are included.[316]

Article 43 EIR introduces a duty for the insolvency practitioner in insolvency proceedings to cooperate and communicate with a court before which a request to open another insolvency proceedings is pending, or which has already opened such proceedings, in order to facilitate the coordination of main, territorial and secondary insolvency proceedings affecting the same debtor.

---

313 *Wessels*, Insolv. Int. 2014, 100-105.
314 For the case of insolvency proceedings relating to two or more members of a group of companies see Art 56 ff, and *infra* Part 3.
315 According to Art 41(3), the rule also applies in cases where the debtor remains in possession of its assets.
316 Indirect cooperation via the appointment of an independent person or body acting on the court's instructions (Art 42(1) EIR); direct communication (Art 42(2) EIR). Courts may agree on the insolvency practitioner; share information; coordinate the administration and supervision of the debtor's assets and affairs; coordinate the conduct of hearings and the approval of protocols.

Article 44 instructs on the allocation of the costs of cooperation and communication.

According to recital 48 EIR, in their cooperation insolvency practitioner and courts should take into account best practices set out in principles and guidelines adopted by European and international organizations active in the area of insolvency law and in particular those prepared by UNCITRAL. Recital 49 EIR adds the possibility of entering into agreements and protocols.

## 3. Recommendations

Articles 40-44 of the new regulation create a framework of duties[317] where some of the previous obstacles to cross-border cooperation disappear – such as the lack of a specific provision addressed to the courts; others remain and new ones come up. [318] In the absence or while waiting for answers from the European institutions (the CJEU included) the hurdles will have to be handled with by the Member States. Some obstacles are likely to be surmountable through an object-oriented interpretation of already in-force rules by the authorities in charge of applying the law. For others, some legislative activity is required, either to purge obstacles, or to facilitate compliance with the duties or the exercise of the faculties set up by the new regulation. It is to be hoped as well that future practice will be eased by the resource to the soft law instruments as advised by the EU lawmaker in recital 48 EIR.

It is here submitted that number of soft law principles and guidelines already existing to support insolvency practitioners and courts in their cooperative endeavours would make a new effort in the same lines from our side pointless. The research conducted to date under the present project[319] has led to the belief that the genuine problem lies with the lack of awareness and knowledge of the available soft law instruments and/or their con-

---

317 Both to provide the means and to engage in the efforts to cooperate.

318 For instance, whether the insolvency court has to, or is allowed to, adopt soft law instruments related to cooperation. Should the answer be 'yes', whether it has to be made in a particular form – which kind of decision; whether motivation is needed; whether the decision is subject to appeal. Other questions relate to the quality of the information provided by the foreign insolvency practitioner or court (is it an evidence?). How to qualify foreign insolvency practitioners (are they parties or third parties to the proceedings?) is also a source of debate.

319 See *supra*, Introduction, under I.

tents, together with the mistrust towards by the new rules, Articles 41 to 44 EIR. Therefore, our recommendations (actions to be undertaken by the European Commission, the national lawmaker, the courts or other authorities applying the law and the academia) are the following.[320]

### 3.1 To the European Commission

*Explaining the rules. Raising awareness of the instruments to comply therewith.* Once the regulation is in force and applicable, the European Commission's role is to a large extent a pedagogic one, focused in explaining the rules and raising awareness of the instruments and tools facilitating compliance therewith. In the current scenario a practice guide of the European Commission for practitioners (courts and insolvency practitioners) may prove to be a valuable document.[321] In general, practice guides include technical advice, recollections of best practices, case studies, and links to other pertinent documents. They have neither a binding effect nor an enhanced interpretative value, but they illustrate the applicable law and help understanding it. In the field of cross-border communication and cooperation in insolvency cases a practice guide should introduce to and explain the new rules:[322] (1) It should also raise awareness of the available

---

320 For the purposes of illustration we focus on Spain and the Spanish Ley Concursal, *Ley 22/2003, de 9 de julio, Concursal* (LC, Insolvency Act), still unamended in spite of the Regulation being already applicable. Some examples are also provided by German law as amended in June 5, 2017, by the Gesetz zur Durchführung der Verordnung (EU) 2015/848, BGBl. I 34 (EGInsO [German Introductory Act to the Insolvency Act], cf supra n 252), where some specific rules on cooperation entailing communication have been included, see Art 102c § 3(3) EGInsO: 'Vor der Einstellung nach § 2 Absatz 1 Satz 2 hat das Insolvenzgericht das Gericht des anderen Mitgliedstaats der Europäischen Union, bei dem das Verfahren anhängig ist, und den Insolvenzverwalter, der in dem anderen Mitgliedstaat bestellt wurde, über die bevorstehende Einstellung zu unterrichten'. Other provisions focus on cooperation in the framework of the insolvency of groups of companies. We would like to thank *Sandra Becker*, Research Fellow of the MPI, for her help in identifying the German examples.
321 Formally, the appropriate instrument should be a recommendation according to *Wessels* (ed), EU Cross-Border Insolvency Court-to-Court Cooperation Principles, 2015, at 39. The same proposal had been made for the Co-Co guidelines 2007, see *Wessels*, Insolv. Int. 2011, 65-73.
322 Although the final word lies with the Member States' courts and finally with the CJEU.

soft law instruments (2) as well as of the relevant national and CJEU case law (3).

Examples:

### 3.1.1 Introducing and explaining the rules

*In their systematic relation.* Ad ex., doubts have arisen on what's the relationship between Articles 40-43 EIR and other rules setting up specific forms of cross-border cooperation: do they share a common purpose? Are Articles 40-43 EIR residual or subsidiary rules on cooperation? Could it be claimed that specific rules – such as Article 38(1) EIR;[323] Article 46 EIR[324] – imposing direct obligations are dependent upon their compatibility with the procedural national rules (i.e., the caveat foreseen in Articles 41-43 EIR)? Could an insolvency practitioner complying with Articles 28, 29 EIR[325] be considered as acquitted of his obligations under Articles 41 and 43 EIR if the objective of the latter is reached in relation to the persons/bodies targeted by those provisions, i.e., the insolvency practitioner/court in the parallel proceeding?

*In their individual wording.* Ad ex., Article 31 EIR 2000 prompted a debate on whether courts – and not only insolvency practitioners – were duty bound to collaborate between them. Whereas in the new regulation this doubt has been sorted out further problems remain, such as what's the meaning of 'court': is 'court' to be understood as encompassing as well agents of the court or other bodies to whom the national legal rules entrust with duties to communicate, such as the Spanish *secretario judicial*,[326] the *mediador concursal*,[327] or even the registrar at the public insolvency reg-

---

323  A court seized of a request to open secondary insolvency proceedings shall immediately give notice to the insolvency practitioner in the main insolvency proceedings and accord him an opportunity to be heard on the request.

324  Stay the process of realization of assets in whole or in part on receipt of a request from the insolvency practitioner in the main insolvency proceedings.

325  Publication in another Member State; registration in public registers of another Member State.

326  See for instance Art 178[bis] 4 LC.

327  See Título X LC.

istry?[328] In the same lines, what about the German senior judicial officer, in the light of the tasks assigned by Section 3.2, lit. e) and g) of the Act on Senior Judicial Officers?[329] To some extent the definitions in Article 2(6) EIR may help, especially lit. ii) where the bodies empowered 'to take *decisions* in the course of such [insolvency] proceedings',[330] are mentioned; but it could still be discussed whether the 'decisions' alluded to encompass those taken by the above mentioned professionals.

*In their application in practice.* The above mentioned practice guide should include a non-exhaustive list of occasions for communication and cooperation, thus opening the eyes of practitioners and courts to envision chances to make it.[331]

### 3.1.2 Raising awareness and promoting the use of soft law instruments

Soft law instruments are meant to support cooperation and communication among the main actors in cross border insolvency proceedings. However, they are not always easy to handle: they are admittedly not well known by their intended public; their growing number makes it more difficult.[332]

---

328  According to Art 178^bis, 3.5 v) LC he is the one to decide on whether the applicant requesting access to a specific section of the Register – thus the information contained therein – is entitled to it. See also Art 27 Regulation.

329  Of 5 November 1969, as most recently amended by Art 5 para 2 of the Act of 10 October 2013, Federal Law Gazette [BGBl.] Part I 3799.

330  Italics added.

331  Such as the appointment of a common insolvency practitioner; allocation of tasks between insolvency practitioners in the concurrent proceedings; administration and supervision of debtor's assets and affairs; conduct of hearings (joint hearings; invitation to other court to attend the hearings before the concurrent court); approval of protocols; stay or moratorium of litigation pending relating to the debtor's assets: postponement of decision opening secondary proceedings; identification of the debtor's assets in the respective countries; debtor's assets realization; distribution of product; drafting of a reorganization plan.

332  To mention just some:
   –  UNCITRAL Model Law on Cross-border Insolvency 1997;
   –  American Law Institute Principles of Cooperation among the North American Free Trade Association (USA, Canada, Mexico) 2000 ('ALI NAFTA Principles');
   –  American Law Institute Guidelines Applicable to Court-to-Court Communications in Cross-Border Cases 2000 ('ALI NAFTA Guidelines');

They are usually accompanied by commentaries which, while providing for a better understanding,[333] make of them too lengthy documents.

A European Commission practice guide addressed to the insolvency practitioner and courts could compile and link to the existing bodies of soft law,[334] and briefly explain some of their main characteristics and how they could be used under the recast regulation, especially where they have drawn inspiration on the common-law world. *A priori* no soft law instrument is to be given precedence over the rest. It could be submitted that the UNCITRAL principles have some priority or better authority, as they are explicitly mentioned in recital 48. Actually, other instruments may be considered more appropriate because specifically conceived for the EU: the CoCo guidelines 2007, the EUJudgeCo principles and guidelines 2015. The correspondence with the regulation is however not always ensured: while some of the principles' rationale can be found in the CJEU case law,[335] not all the proposals are clearly in line with the regulation. By way of example: the commentary to principle 11, 'modification of recognition'

---

- European Bank of Reconstruction and Development Core Principles for an Insolvency Law Regime 2004;
- American Law Institute/UNIDROIT Principles of Transnational Civil Procedure 2004;
- UNCITRAL Legislative Guide on Insolvency Law Recommendations 2004, in 2009 supplemented with a Part Three: 'Treatment of enterprise groups in insolvency';
- European Bank of Reconstruction and Development Office Holders Principles 2007;
- European Communication & Cooperation Guidelines for Cross-border Insolvency 2007;
- UNCITRAL Practice Guide on Cross-Border Insolvency Cooperation 2009 (the 'Practice Guide');
- Guidelines for Coordination Multi-National Enterprise Group Insolvencies (July 2010 Draft);
- Prospective Model International Cross-border Insolvency Protocol.

333  See for instance in the EUjudgeCo principles the use of different verbal tenses: 'may', 'should', sometimes even 'shall' in spite of their self-declared non-binding nature.

334  Or other interesting documents, such as the glossary of terms and descriptions included as Appendix to the 2012 ALI Global Principles Report.

335  Ad ex., Principle 22, Assistance to reorganization, is allegedly based on case CJEU, 22 November 2012, Case C-116/11; *Bank Handlowy and Adamiak*, ECLI:EU:C:2012:739 as a consequence correspondence with the EU objectives is guaranteed, see *Wessels* (ed), EU Cross-Border Insolvency Court-to-Court Co-operation Principles (2015), at 92.

where it is submitted that in case of clear evidence to support the allegation of fraud in the opening of the main proceedings 'the appropriate form of modification could be revocation', gives raise to some doubts.[336]

### 3.1.3 Spreading the knowledge about case law

Article 40 EIR is not completely new for the EU Member States; Articles 42-43 are. Courts and insolvency practitioners are likely to be puzzled by them, and to face in many occasions the lack of provisions, or even of ideas, showing them how to proceed in order to achieve the cooperation aimed. To date the European – continental – practice on communication and cooperation involving insolvency practitioner and/or courts is scarce. A European Commission's practice guide should highlight the experiences where insolvency practitioners and courts of Member States have been involved, recollecting the practical and legal problems they faced, offering them as examples of ways-out for their colleagues.[337] The decisions on interpretation delivered by the CJEU should be included in such compilation. The instrument should be dynamic, i.e., be continuously updated.

### 3.2 To the national lawmaker

*Taking stock: Removing obstacles, paving and showing the way.* As all European regulations the new one on cross-border insolvency is of direct application in the Member States; therefore, it could be thought that no further elaboration on the part of the Member States is needed for the EU provisions to be applied. Of course, this does not hold true. Self-explaining, self-executing and exhaustive EU obligations are rare; the legal systems of the Member States are usually called upon to support them; sometimes an active intervention of the national lawmaker is required.[338] To as-

---

336 Revocation may be allowed under national law (see Art 220.5 LC), but it is impossible under the EU rules.

337 National cases such as *Sendo, Emtec, PIN Group II, BenQ, Nortel*. As for preliminary rulings, see affd CJEU, 22 November 2012, Case C-116/11, *Bank Handlowy and Adamiak*, ECLI:EU:C:2012:739 and affd CJEU, 4 September 2014, Case C-327/13, *Burgo Group*, ECLI:EU:C:2014:2158.

338 When interpretation of the existing materials is not enough to reach the desired outcome: see *infra*.

sess whether intervention is needed a task of assessment of the existing legal framework in each Member State must be performed to determine where the system stands, and to what extent it already allows for a swift implementation of the regulation – or, conversely, it hinders it (1). In the light of the outcome of the exam the next step may be a regulatory one, entailing the abrogation or amendment of the existing rules, and/or the adoption of new ones (2). Besides, the national lawmaker may also be willing to undertake a pedagogic or advisory role similar to the one we recommended above to the Commission (3).

Examples:

3.2.1  Taking stock

– Under Article 31 EIR 2000 some EU Member States already prescribed some specific forms of cooperation. In Spain the duty of international cooperation among insolvency practitioners, involving to some extent the courts,[339] had been formalized in some detail in Article 227 LC. German law also provides good examples: see the duty (*shall*) of the foreign insolvency administrator to inform the tribunal of essential changes in foreign proceedings, section 347 Insolvency Statute;[340] on the duty (*shall*) of cooperation between insolvency administrators, see section 357 Insolvency Statute; extending the possibility (*may*) to cooperate with a foreign court to the national ones, see section 348 Insolvency Statute.

– The analysis of the legal system in force in a Member State for the purposes of the assessment mentioned above should not be restrained to insolvency laws: an appropriate framework may be provided for by general rules. In Spain, the Ley 29/2015, de 31 de julio de 2015, de cooperación jurídica internacional, is *a priori* not applicable to cross-border insolvency by virtue of the *lex specialis* principle;[341] however,

---

339  See Art 227. 2.3 LC on the approval of protocols: 'La cooperación [of insolvency practitioners] podrá consistir, en particular, en: (...) La aprobación y aplicación por los tribunales o autoridades competentes de acuerdos relativos a la coordinación de los procedimientos'.

340  Insolvency Statute of 5 October 1994, last amended by Act of 5 June 2017 (BGBl. I S. 1476) (Federal Law Gazette I p 2854).

341  See Preamble, under no I.

where the Insolvency Act does not provide for a solution (especially if the gap is due to the fact that the law was adopted before the solution was felt as needed), it may be resorted to as 'common' law for cooperation in cross border civil matters. Interestingly, the *Ley 29/2015* allows for direct communication among courts in Article 4.[342]

3.2.2 Removing obstacles, paving the way

The regulation will be (generally) applicable from 26 June 2017; therefore, where the need for new rules is felt as unavoidable for a swift implementation of the Regulation, the national lawmaker should profit from the closest opportunity to introduce them. A current example can be found in Spain in relation to the appointment of the insolvency practitioner. Recital 50 EIR contemplates the choosing of a single insolvency practitioner for several insolvency proceedings concerning the same debtor or for different members of a group of companies, provided that this is compatible with the rules applicable to each of the proceedings, in particular with any requirements concerning the qualification and licensing of the insolvency practitioner.[343] In this regard it is worth recalling that the requirements to be met by insolvency practitioners are under debate in Spain since 2014. Article 27 LC on the 'Condiciones subjetivas para el nombramiento de administradores concursales', awaits further development by a 'reglamento'.[344] To the best of our knowledge[345] no agreement has been reached so far in spite of the several attempts made to date. Therefore, the opportunity remains to introduce a provision clarifying under which conditions a foreign insolvency practitioner may also be designated insolvency practitioner for the proceeding in Spain. A specific provision would be useful in the context of a regime such as the Spanish one, moving towards limiting

---

342  By contrast direct communication is regarded in the JudgeCo Guidelines as a last resort mechanism. *Wessels* (ed), EU Cross-Border Insolvency Court-to-Court Cooperation Principles (2015), p 104-106 (Commentary to Guideline 1).

343  And provided independence is ensured. Recital 50 does not allude to this requirement, neither does it appear as such in the dispositive parts of the EIR.

344  Disposición Transitoria n° 2 Ley 17/2014, de 30 de septiembre, por la que se adoptan medidas urgentes en materia de refinanciación y reestructuración de deuda empresarial.

345  Last checked: September 2017.

the judge's margin of manoeuvre in the choice of the insolvency practitioner.[346]

A common obstacle to communication between courts lies with language: not only with the lack of command of a foreign language – a *de facto* problem –, but also with the legal rules on the language of the proceedings.[347] Very little is said in the Spanish LC in this regard, thus the general rule of Article 231 LO 6/1985, de 1 de julio, Ley Orgánica del Poder Judicial, should apply. This entails that only Spanish official languages (Castilian or the official language of a Comunidad Autónoma) are accepted. Article 219 LC foresees the translation to French and English of the terms 'Convocatoria para la presentación de créditos. Plazos aplicables' when the Spanish insolvency proceeding is part of a larger, cross-border setting; however, the information included under such heading will still be drafted in one of the Spanish official languages. Besides, foreign creditors shall communicate their claims in Spanish; insolvency practitioners are empowered to ask them for a translation.[348] It is disputable to what extent the activities in which cooperation materialize pertain to the proceedings (and therefore are subjected to strict language requirements);[349]

---

346 The current system (Art 27 LC) imposes the sequential order of a pre-drafted list of potential insolvency practitioners. Some leeway is of course permitted in complex cases, but complexity is defined by the size of the insolvency – that it is a cross-border one does not have *per se* any particular weight. The retribution of the insolvency practitioner is also fixed by reference to rigid rules; it may nevertheless exceed the limits imposed according to Art 34 LC, but what 'complexity' means here is unclear.

347 The Regulation itself is not particularly intrusive in this regard, with the exception of Art 73, para 2 (*infra*, n 352): see Art 22, on the proof of the insolvency practitioner's appointment, para 2 (a translation into the official language or one of the official languages of the Member State within the territory of which it intends to act may be required). Regarding the duty to inform creditors according to Art 54, it is for the Member State to declare whether and which non-official languages they accept to communicate the opening of proceedings. For the lodging of claims, see Art 55, para 5: Claims may be lodged in any official language of the institutions of the Union, but the court, the insolvency practitioner or the debtor in possession may require the creditor to provide a translation in the official language of the State of the opening of proceedings. See also Art 36, on the language of the undertaking in order to avoid secondary insolvency proceedings.

348 Art 33.1.g.9 LC, Art 219 LC.

349 What exactly is comprised within the 'perimeter' of the proceeding may be discussed.

at any rate, for the sake of efficiency their language regimen should be as flexible as possible.[350]

### 3.2.3 Valuable clarifications; pro-cooperation orientations

According to Article 42(1) EIR, 'the courts may, where appropriate, appoint an independent person or body acting on its instructions, provided that it is not incompatible with the rules applicable to them'. The figure of an independent intermediary is unknown to the Spanish system – therefore its regime, how to appoint him, who should be informed about, whether the appointment can be contested... are open questions. However, in 2013[351] a new tool was added in the field of insolvency, in which the skills of a mediator and knowledge of insolvency converge: the 'mediador concursal', bankruptcy mediator. Whereas we would advise against limiting the choice of independent intermediaries in the sense of Article 43 EIR to the *mediadores concursales*, their existence and (presumed) capacities[352] to undertake such function should not be forgotten: in this sense an explicit reference to them as suitable persons in the Ley Concursal (or/and in the Ley 5/2012, de 6 de julio, de mediación en asuntos civiles y mercantiles) would be welcome.

An express statement of the consequences of non-compliance with the duties imposed in Article 41 ff EIR (for instance: the liability of the insolvency practitioner could be engaged should he refuse to cooperate with the foreign insolvency practitioner/court, or to ask them for cooperation) would effectively help to raise awareness about their existence.

The national lawmaker may be willing to engage in an advisory role. Such mission may be fulfilled via the preambles to the articulated texts – see for instance Ley 29/2015, Preamble, n° II, *in fine*, where an explicit

---

350 See nevertheless Art 73, in the framework of groups of companies, on the language for the communication of the coordinator and the insolvency practitioner (a common one may be agreed upon), and the coordinator and the court (the official language of the court).

351 Ley 14/2013, de 27 de septiembre, de apoyo a los emprendedores y su internacionalización.

352 Whereas proper functions of mediation are probably not needed in the context of Art 42, the capacity to communicate, the (presumed) knowledge of techniques and skills to act as an intermediary make of mediators appropriate for the task.

mention is made to the *Principios Generales para las comunicaciones judiciales* (sic) drafted by The Hague Conference.[353]

3.3 To the national interpreter and authorities applying the law

*Interpretation/application of the existing rules in the light of the obligations imposed by the regulation and the underlying principles.* The implementation of the rules of the regulation does not necessarily require new ones at the national level. Sometimes an appropriated, object-oriented interpretation and application of already existing national provisions will be enough; in-force rules may be given a further utility and serve the purposes of cross-border communication and cooperation.

In Spain the principles underlying the insolvency regime in force since 2003 set a background favorable to interpretations pro-coordination and cooperation. The Preamble of the LC refers in several occasions to the flexibility of the insolvency proceedings; it also recalls that the system 'concede al juez del concurso una amplia discrecionalidad en el ejercicio de sus competencias, lo que contribuye a facilitar la flexibilidad del procedimiento y su adecuación a las circunstancias de cada caso'.[354] Besides, the Preamble recognizes the inspiration drawn from the UNCITRAL Model Law, and explains the objective pursued by the rules on cross-border situations as follows: 'establecer la mejor coordinación entre ellos, en beneficio de la seguridad jurídica y de la eficiencia económica en el tratamiento de estos fenómenos, lo que constituye una de las materias en las que con mayor relieve se pone de manifiesto la modernización intro-

---

353 What the value of the mention is, in particular whether it has any beyond that of exemplifying the topicality of the subject-matter, may be disputed.
354 Interesting examples of flexibility can be found in the case law: see for instance *Juzgado de lo Mercantil núm. 3 de Barcelona*, Auto de 9 enero 2012, JUR 2014\176918, on the appointment of an administrator for the purposes of 'tutelar interinamente las actuaciones de la deudora durante el plazo de vigencia de las diligencias preliminares, así como familiarizarse con los datos y circunstancias de la compañía para garantizar con ello la agilidad que permita en su caso y en su día tramitar un procedimiento abreviado en los términos que prevé el artículo 190 y 191 de la Ley Concursal'. The court continues: 'Ciertamente no hay en la Ley concursal ningún precepto que permita directamente el nombramiento de un órgano interino de administración concursal –tampoco hay una prohibición expresa- de ahí que se acuda a un expediente de jurisdicción voluntaria para articular esa solicitud'.

ducida por la reforma concursal'. In the light of it it's legitimate to conclude that support is given to the courts to apply already existing national provisions with a view to facilitate the aim of the EIR.

Examples:

- Article 190 LC enables the judge to switch between the so called 'common procedure' to the 'abbreviate procedure'. Such faculty could be used in cross-border cases when useful for a better coordination with the foreign insolvency proceedings.[355]
- The *Auto* opening the insolvency proceedings sets as well the competences of the appointed insolvency practitioner (Article 21(2) LC). Specific mention to the duties and faculties to cooperate, communicate, etc., with a foreign court are advisable:[356] ad ex., an indication whereby the insolvency practitioner shall cooperate with the foreign court, and the extension/precautions to be taken into account when doing it.
- Foreign insolvency practitioners are vested with different functions or roles in the regulation, which make their classification a difficult endeavor.[357] Courts should be flexible in their approach and try not to

---

355  See by way of example a domestic case of related proceedings (which according to Spanish insolvency law are to be managed separately but in a coordinated form): 'a fin de garantizar la tramitación coordinada de los concursos, procede la tramitación de todos ellos por los mismos trámites [del procedimiento ordinario] al amparo del Art 190(1) LC, el cual faculta al juez a escoger el tipo de procedimiento, sin perjuicio de la posibilidad de modificarlo en cualquier momento en atención a las circunstancias concurrentes conforme al apartado 4', *Juzgado de lo Mercantil núm. 9 de Barcelona,* Auto de 27 marzo 2013, AC 2013\1619. Some flexibility is also given to the German courts: see ad ex. Section 5 of the Insolvency Statute.
356  Instructions in this regard can be made later as well. A French example is the initiative of the *Tribunal de Lons-le-Saunier* in a case of French (main) proceedings of *redressement judiciaire,* and Spanish (secondary) proceedings for liquidation. The French court empowered the French insolvency practitioner to present the sales plan approved in France to both the Spanish court and the insolvency practitioner. See *Martínez Casado,* Anuario de Derecho Concursal, 21/2010.
357  For purposes such as appearance before the court: ad ex., are legal counsel and representation compulsory for them? As a matter of fact it is unlikely that one single category fits all: the foreign insolvency practitioner equates sometimes the national insolvency practitioner while in other cases his position is similar to that of a creditor, or of a third party holding nevertheless a legitimate interest (in the

stick to pre-determined national categories which may not suit the European regulation's frame.

- Following the general rule set in Article 131 Ley 1/2000, de 7 de enero, de enjuciamiento civil, Article 187 LC empowers the insolvency judge to enable working days and hours for the practice of urgent measures for the sake of a good administration of the insolvency proceedings. The provision could be useful for the coordination of the conduct of hearings referred to in Article 42(3) EIR.

- Rules enacted with a view to the managing of related insolvency proceedings of several debtors should be explored to ascertain their application (by analogy) to parallel proceedings against one single debtor in a cross-border situation. Examples are provided by Article 27(8) LC on the appointment of insolvency practitioners for related insolvency proceedings affecting several debtors.[358]

- A similar initiative should be undertaken in regard to the rules applying to complex proceedings, such as Article 31 LC, on the appointment of 'auxiliares delegados' Under Article 31 the appointment of 'auxiliares delegados' aims to alleviate the burden of the insolvency practitioner, or to complement his skills – the 'auxiliar delegado' holding the professional knowledge the insolvency practitioner lacks himself. The provision is meant to ensure both the economic and the legal capacities of the insolvency practitioner: it could therefore be useful in the case of parallel proceedings, where the insolvency practitioner appointed for all of them is not familiar with the Spanish insolvency law.

- Article 23(2) LC enables the insolvency court to agree on giving additional publicity to the Auto opening the proceedings as well as to further procedural acts, upon request or ex officio, for their effective diffusion. In a broad interpretation the provision could be used for sup-

---

sense, for instance, of Art 234(1) LOPJ, 'Los Letrados de la Administración de Justicia y funcionarios competentes de la Oficina judicial facilitarán a los interesados cuanta información soliciten sobre el estado de las actuaciones judiciales, que podrán examinar y conocer, salvo que sean o hubieren sido declaradas secretas o reservadas conforme a la ley').

358 The underlying logic is the same; as the *Juzgado de lo Mercantil núm. 9 de Barcelona*, Auto de 27 marzo 2013. AC 2013\1619 said in a case of related insolvency proceedings, 'no hay razón alguna para designar a dos administradores concursales y encarecer innecesariamente los gastos del concurso en perjuicio de la masa activa y pasiva'.

porting cooperation among the main actors (insolvency practitioners and courts) in cross-border proceedings.[359]

## 3.4 To the academia

*Gloss of the legal provisions with useful examples. Analysis of compatibility with national systems.* Academia and legal literature should engage in an effort to understand the new rules correctly. They should promote awareness about them, and support their proper implementation and application in the context of each Member State's legal system. An example in this regard is the well-known study of *P. Busch, A. Remmert, S. Rüntz, H. Vallender*, 'Kommunikation zwischen Gerichten in grenzüberschreitenden Insolvenzen – Was geht und was nicht geht',[360] studying the correspondence between the ALI Principles and the German Insolvency Act (as of 2010).

---

359 It should nevertheless be recalled that the provision addresses the publicity procedural acts require for producing the effect which is consubstantial with them (*publicidad procesal*) – as opposed to simply informing about them (see STS Sala de lo Contencioso-Administrativo, Sección 6ª, Sentencia de 28 marzo 2007, RJ\2007\2142). Accordingly it might not be the more suitable basis for the purpose indicated in the text.

360 *Busch/Remmert/Rüntz/Vallender*, NZI 2010, 417-430. Admitedly, in the light of the position of the authors the pure 'academic' nature of this contribution may be disputed.

## III. Protocols[*]

### Articles 41 f EIR

## 1. Introduction

The EIR explicitly refers to insolvency 'agreements or protocols' for the first time in EU insolvency law.[361] The use of protocols to coordinate different, but connected, insolvency proceedings was of course not unknown to the legal practice, as it goes back to the insolvency practice of common law systems.[362] For this reason, the majority of EU Member States have little experience in the conclusion of insolvency protocols in cross-border cases. Under the EIR 2000 protocols have nonetheless been used in several but major insolvency cases, including *Sendo*[363] and *Nortel Networks*.[364]

Article 41(1) EIR states that the cooperation between insolvency practitioners 'may take any form, including the conclusion of agreements or protocols'. Moreover, Article 42(3) lit. e) EIR provides for the 'coordination in the approval of protocols, where necessary' as a form of cooperation between insolvency courts.

However, the EIR neither defines the notion of 'agreements or protocols' nor it contains any clear-cut rules on their content, conclusion, approval and legal effects. Except for Member States that have implemented

---

[*] Dr. *Matteo Gargantini*, former Senior Research Fellow Max Planck Institute Luxembourg, Commissione Nazionale per le Societa e la Borsa (Consob), and LUISS University, Rome; *Georgia Koutsoukou*, LL.M., former Research Fellow Max Planck Institute Luxembourg. Although the contribution is the result of a joint effort, parts 1, 2.1, 2.4, 2.5, 3 and 3.1-3.6 are to be attributed to Dr. *Matteo Gargantini* and parts 2.2, 2.3, and 3.7-3.11 to *Georgia Koutsoukou*. The opinions expressed are exclusively the authors' and do not reflect those of the institutions they belong to.

361 *Eidenmüller*, MJ 2013, 133, 147; *McCormack*, JPIL 2014, 41, 57.

362 As to the origins of insolvency protocols see *Omar*, ICCLR 2006, 120, 121 ff.; *Flaschen/Silverman*, Tex. Int'l L. J. 1998, 587.

363 Protocol Agreement for the Coordination of a Main Insolvency Proceeding with Secondary Insolvency Proceeding Filed In Conformity With European Regulation N° 1346-2000 Of 29 May 2000, available at: www.iiiglobal.org.

364 Not published, see *Braun/Tashiro*, Cross-border Insolvency Protocol Agreements between Insolvency Practitioners and their Effect on the Rights of Creditors, p 12 ff, available at: https://www.iiiglobal.org/sites/default/files/BraunTashiroand-BraunCBProtocols.pdf.

the 1997 UNCITRAL Model Law on Cross-border Insolvency,[365] Member States often lack rules on insolvency protocols. Lately, bar associations and insolvency practitioner's associations have concluded bilateral agreements, in order to facilitate the conclusion of protocols across jurisdictions. In that context, relevant are the French-German Protocol between the German *Deutscher Anwaltsverein* (DAV) and the French *Conseil National des Administrateurs Judiciaires et des Mandataires Judiciaries* (CNAJMJ) or the French-Italian Protocol between the Italian *Consiglio Nazionale dei Dottori Commercialisti e degli Esperti Contabili* (CNDCEC) and the French CNAJMJ.

## 2. Legal and economic framework

### 2.1 'Agreements or protocols': scope of the analysis

The EIR does not contain any definition of the term 'agreements or protocols'. It seems that the terminology used is broad enough to accommodate any form of insolvency agreement, both binding and non-binding, so as to include similar national tools regardless of their label under local laws or practices.[366] Recital 49 EIR explicitly recognizes that agreements or protocols may vary in form, in that they may be written or oral, and in scope, in that they may range from generic to specific, and may be entered into by different parties. Simple generic agreements may emphasise the need for close cooperation between the parties, without addressing specific issues, while more detailed, specific agreements may establish a framework of principles to govern multiple insolvency proceedings and may be approved by the courts involved, where the national law so requires. They may reflect an agreement between the parties to take, or to refrain from taking, certain steps or actions.

Although the EIR seems to use the term 'agreements' for binding arrangements, and the term 'protocols' for non-binding arrangements, i.e. gentlemen's agreements,[367] this report, for the sake of simplicity, will not distinguish between 'agreements' and 'protocols', unless otherwise specified.

---

365  Greece, Poland, Romania, Slovenia and UK.
366  Recital 49 EIR.
367  Under EIR 2000: *Hess,* Europäisches Zivilprozessrecht (2010), § 9 paras 61 ff.

This analysis deals mainly with protocols adopted in the context of single debtor insolvencies and focuses exclusively on the relationship between main and secondary insolvency proceedings. Nonetheless, some conclusions may easily apply to group insolvencies as well, not only because protocols may help reduce coordination problems between different main proceedings, but also because secondary proceedings may be opened in group insolvencies, too. This may happen for instance because one of the group entities has an establishment with no legal personality (such as a branch) in another Member State, or because the COMI of a group entity is identified at the registered office of the controlling company.

### 2.2 Cooperation 'not incompatible with the rules applicable to each of the proceedings' – legal basis for the conclusion of agreements or protocols

There is an ongoing dispute whether the EIR provides for an autonomous, direct legal basis for the conclusion or approval of insolvency agreements or protocols.[368] If so, insolvency practitioners would be empowered to conclude an insolvency agreement or protocol even in the absence of a legal basis in their national laws. If not, they would have to rely on their national framework relating to such arrangements.

The EIR requires the conclusion of insolvency agreements and protocols, as a form of cooperation, not to be 'incompatible with the rules applicable to each of the proceedings' (Article 41(1) EIR). Courts may cooperate in their approval, 'where necessary' (Article 42(3) lit. e) EIR). It follows therefrom that the EIR relies on the premise that insolvency agreements or protocols are insolvency-related arrangements[369] and, as such, subject to the cumulative application of the insolvency laws (*lex fori con-*

---

368  See *Hess/Koutsoukou*, in: Kronke/Melis/Kuhn (eds), Handbuch Internationales Wirtschaftsrecht, 2nd edn (2017), para 85; under the EIR 2000 *Geroldinger*, in: Clavora/Garber (eds), Grenzüberschreitende Insolvenzen im europäischen Binnenmarkt – die EuInsVO (2011), p 133, 135; contra: *Mangano*, in: Bork/Mangano (eds), European Cross-Border Insolvency Law (2016), para 6.41; *Wessels*, in: Faber et al. (eds), Overeenkomsten en insolventie (2012), p 359, 376.

369  Contra: *Wessels*, in: Faber et al. (eds), Overeenkomsten en insolventie (2012), p 359, 377: insolvency agreements or protocols should be considered as 'contracts' within the sense of Art 1(1) Rome I Regulation and, therefore, should be subject to its conflict of laws rules.

*cursus*) of the parties involved. Consequently, it is a matter of the *lex fori concursus* of each of the parties involved[370] to determine whether parties are authorized to conclude an insolvency agreement or protocol and, if so, the persons entitled to conclude them; the legal nature and the effects of insolvency agreements or protocols; the conditions for judicial approval; and the content and scope of the participation rights of the creditors' committee.[371] This is also aligned with the overall conflict of laws regime of the EIR. In fact, insolvency agreements and protocols cover issues related to the conduct and closure of insolvency proceedings, which are subject to the *lex fori concursus* (Article 7 EIR).[372]

The aforementioned interpretation has the drawback that the cumulative application of two or more insolvency laws may hamper the conclusion of insolvency protocols.[373] Where Member States have not implemented the 1997 UNCITRAL Model Law on cross-border insolvency, which explicitly allows for the 'approval or implementation by courts of agreements concerning the coordination of insolvency proceedings', insolvency practitioners may have difficulties in concluding insolvency protocols or agreements. In order to promote the use of these instruments, Member States are encouraged not to apply restrictive insolvency rules or introduce rules on insolvency agreements or protocols, providing an explicit legal

---

However, it is doubtful whether insolvency agreements or protocols fall within the definition of 'contractual obligations in civil and commercial matters' under Art 1(1) Rome Regulation. First, at the procedural level, the Brussels I[bis] Regulation and the EIR clearly distinguish between 'civil and commercial matters' and insolvency matters; insolvency protocols cover, in most instances, questions related to the conduct and closing of insolvency proceedings. Second, it can be questioned whether and, if so, under which circumstances insolvency agreements or protocols gives rise to 'contractual obligations' within the sense of Art 1(1) Rome I Regulation, given the uncertain legal nature of such arrangements.

370 See also *Reumers*, ECFR 2013, 554, 584. In any case, it should be noted that the application of the *lex fori concursus principalis* would disregard the relationship between main and secondary insolvency proceedings under the EIR, since secondary proceedings are not subordinated to the main proceedings.

371 As to the requirements of the German insolvency law see *Braun/Tashiro*, Cross-border Insolvency Protocol Agreements between Insolvency Practitioners and their Effect on the Rights of Creditors, p 5 ff, available at: https://www.iiiglobal.org/sites/default/files/BraunTashiroandBraunCBProtocols.pdf; *Busch/ Remmert/Rüntz/Vallender*, NZI 2010, 417 ff.

372 *Eidenmüller*, ZZP 2001, 3, 5.

373 Under the EIR 2000: *Hass/Herweg*, in: Geimer/Schütze, Europäisches Zivilverfahrensrecht, Art 3 EuInsVO a.F., paras 65 ff.

basis for their conclusion. This could prevent complicated questions relating to the validity of protocols or insolvency agreements, or even to the liability of the contracting parties. To exploit the full potential of protocols as a coordination tool, this legal basis should expressly allow direct transfers from one proceeding to another (see *infra* para 3.6).

## 2.3 Content of an insolvency protocol: derogation from the coordination rules of the EIR?

Insolvency agreements or protocols, just like any other consensual arrangement, inevitably reflect the legal framework within which they operate. In third countries that lack a comprehensive legal framework on the coordination of cross-border insolvency proceedings, insolvency agreements or protocols usually address, *inter alia*, issues that are covered at European level by the EIR. By way of illustration, U.S. or Canadian insolvency agreements or protocols[374] usually include clauses relating to jurisdictional issues, the determination of the insolvency estate of each of the parallel proceedings, the insolvency practitioners' right to appear or be heard in parallel proceedings, the recognition of judicial decisions etc.[375]

At the European level, most of the agreements or protocols concluded under the EIR 2000 dealt with issues that were not explicitly regulated by the EIR 2000 or merely intended to specify the coordination and cooperation rules of the EIR 2000.[376] For instance, the *Sendo* protocol focused on the following aspects: the practical means of treating the liabilities of the insolvent debtor and the notification of the creditors; the verification of the lodged claims; the treatment of the insolvent debtor's assets (including the disposal of assets and the distribution of proceeds); and treatment of legal costs related to the opening of secondary insolvency proceedings, where the debtor's assets are not sufficient to cover the costs and expenses of such proceedings.

The EIR coordination rules have increased legal certainty for insolvency practitioners and other stakeholders. However, this may come at a cost of reduced flexibility, if and to the extent that parties are not allowed to

---

374  *Canuel*, J. Int'l Bus. & L. 4 2005, 8, 14.
375  As to the typical content of protocols *Zumbro*, Bus. L. Int'l 11 2010, 157, 161 f.
376  As to the need to specify the duty to cooperate under the EIR 2000, see *Omar*, ICCLR 2006, 120, 130.

deviate from the EIR coordination regime. Given that most of the protocols concluded under the EIR 2000 merely specify the existing rules, it is worth examining whether and to what extent a derogation from the coordination rules of the EIR is possible. As a matter of principle, the EIR aims to establish a uniform cooperation and coordination framework in order to enable efficient administration of cross-border insolvencies. However, this neither means that each and every provision of the EIR in the field of coordination of cross-border insolvency proceedings follows the maximum harmonisation principle nor automatically excludes that the involved parties may, under specific circumstances, establish alternative forms of coordination that better suit their individual needs. Where the EIR does not address a specific issue, parties may establish appropriate coordination mechanisms, subject only to any national insolvency law constraints.[377] However, the situation is more complicated where the EIR provides for specific coordination rules. In such a case, the possibility to derogate from the EIR is ultimately a matter of interpretation of the relevant provisions of the EIR.[378] In order to determine whether the provision at stake is mandatory or not, parties may take into account public policy considerations or the need to protect third parties' rights. Due to the inherent uncertainty with regard to the possibility to derogate from the coordination rules of the EIR, it may be advisable to seek (formal or informal) approval by the creditors' committee or the competent court, in order to prevent liability claims. In any event, deviations from the coordination system provided for in the EIR through an insolvency agreement or protocol should not be possible unless (at least) the following conditions are met: the derogation is in the interest of maximization of the estate's value or the organisation of the debtor's business; adequate safeguards for the affected estate are foreseen; and the *pari passu* principle, as established in the EIR, is not affected.

---

377 On the distinction between maximum and comprehensive harmonization see *Enriques/Gatti*, Stan. J.L. Bus. & Fin. 2008, 43, 49-51.

378 Similarly, agreements and protocols adopted in the context of group insolvencies may deviate from the default rule on the allocation of costs among different proceedings set forth by Art 41 EIR, see *infra* Part 3, III. 3.1

2.4 Insolvency protocols and protection of local creditors' interests

National insolvency laws typically provide for some duties of insolvency practitioners towards creditors. Whether these duties qualify as fiduciary (or quasi-fiduciary) under the applicable law or not, value maximization to the benefit of creditors – and of shareholders, as they remain residual claimants – normally underlies these obligations.[379] When multiple proceedings are opened simultaneously, each of the involved insolvency practitioners will therefore exercise his/her powers to increase returns on the insolvency estate he/she is competent for (Article 38(2) EIR refers to the 'general interest of local creditors'). In this scenario, interactions among the multiple actors involved – or the lack thereof – may lead to different outcomes in terms of efficiency, and the ensuing equilibria lie at the heart of the legal uncertainty that surrounds protocols as a way to maximise creditors' returns.

While protocols may increase the overall result of multiple insolvency proceedings taken as a whole, this cannot go to the detriment of local groups of creditors or otherwise be incompatible with the rules applicable to the respective proceedings – otherwise (according to Article 41(1) EIR) cooperation is no longer due. For instance, sharing sensitive information with the main insolvency proceeding will likely ease the management of the common enterprise, but it might also come at the risk of harming the interests of the creditors whose claims arose in connection with the operations of a specific establishment. For this reason, generic pleas in favour of transparency and of the need to give full disclosure of all relevant information may trigger refusals by local insolvency courts and practitioners, if not accompanied by some qualifications (see *infra*). This holds true also for other more pervasive commitments such as waiving the right to start an avoidance action. The fact that a company goes bankrupt does not remove the creditors' (and minority shareholders') need of protection from tunnelling perpetrated through related party transactions.[380] As insolvency practitioners still owe their duties towards the creditors of 'their' respective insolvency proceeding, they should and will normally refrain from entering a protocol that may hamper local creditors, even when a refusal may reduce the total welfare of the creditors involved in all the relevant pro-

---

379  *Tabb*, Law of Bankruptcy (2016), p 475.
380  See generally *Atanasov/Black/Ciccotello*, JCL 2011, 1, 13, 16.

ceedings. In the absence of specific remedies, in fact, the overall increase of the debtor's asset value may not be Pareto-optimal.[381] On the contrary, nothing in the EIR seems to allow forms of cooperation that are detrimental to local creditors, even when all the creditors involved either in the main or in the secondary proceedings would be better off on average (*Kaldor-Hicks* criterion). This has a legal correspondent in the abovementioned limitation under Article 41(1) EIR, which allows cooperation only to the extent that it is 'not incompatible with the rules applicable to each of the proceedings'.

As the economic theory suggests, compensation (including direct transfers) from one group to another may address these potential sources of inefficiency, thus leading to a more satisfactory result for all the parties involved. The intuitive underlying reasoning is that sharing the surplus coordination would produce can facilitate a cooperative game among the interested parties. Once a protocol provides for a redistribution mechanism, an insolvency practitioner's unwillingness to enter it may not be in line with his/her (quasi-)fiduciary duties, as that would prevent local creditors from taking part in the surplus the protocol would lead to.

## 2.5 Protocols and Article 36 undertakings: comparative advantages and disadvantages

No space is of course left to protocols in single debtor insolvencies when synthetic proceedings prevent secondary proceedings (Article 36 EIR).[382] However, secondary proceedings will inevitably retain some practical application even after the EIR has introduced synthetic proceedings, especially because they no longer have to aim at winding-up the relevant establishment.[383] From a procedural perspective, Article 36 undertakings require known local creditors' approval (Article 36(5) EIR). Furthermore, even when undertakings are approved by the known local creditors, secondary proceedings may still be opened if local creditors so require within 30 days of having received notice of the approval of that undertaking (Article 37(2) EIR) and the local court considers that the undertaking does not

---

381  *Eidenmüller*, MJ 2013, 133, 147.
382  See *supra* Part 2, I. 1.2.6.2.
383  See for instance *Reumers*, ECFR 2013, 554, 573.

adequately protect the general interests of local creditors (Article 38(2) EIR).[384]

From a more substantive point of view, in assessing whether the interests of local creditors are better protected by way of secondary proceedings, creditors themselves, insolvency practitioners, and local courts alike should also consider the potentials and the limits of protocols *vis-à-vis* synthetic proceedings.[385] One of the core features of secondary proceedings is the applicability of *lex fori concursus secundarii* to both substantive and procedural rules. Synthetic proceedings, instead, split the applicable rules because they submit to the law of the main proceedings all matters other than those mentioned in Article 36 EIR.[386] Hence, while synthetic proceedings avoid the direct costs, which can be substantial, of opening and running a secondary proceeding, appropriate coordination of main and secondary proceedings through protocols might increase legal certainty in the identification of the applicable law in borderline matters,[387] and ensures that substantive rules on distribution and ranking find a proper match in the corresponding procedural rules.

Directly stemming from the Article 36(2) EIR conflict-of-laws rule is the different governance of insolvency proceedings. Article 36 undertakings tend to settle possibly divergent interests *ex ante*, which is undoubtedly a commendable approach as it can lead to considerable cost savings. However, undertakings are inevitably subject to contractual incompleteness,[388] so that the gap-filling function of contractual governance does not

---

384  If the local courts uphold the request, the insolvency practitioners in the main proceedings shall transfer any assets (or their proceeds, in case of early realization) pertaining to the secondary proceedings back to the competent insolvency practitioners (Art 36(6) EIR).

385  For an analysis of the variables to be considered see *supra* Part 2, I. 3.3.

386  In particular, the distribution of proceeds from the realisation of assets pertaining to secondary proceedings, the ranking of creditors' claims, and the rights of creditors in relation to such assets (Art 36(2) EIR) are subject to the *lex fori concursus secundarii*, as are the rules on creditor approval of the undertakings (Art 36(5) EIR): see *supra*, Part 2, I. 1.2.4 and 2.1.3.

387  This is all the more so because local rules on creditor approval are applicable 'as appropriate' (recital 44, 1st s. EIR, see *supra* Part 2, I. 1.2.4), a wording that is likely to lead to conflicting interpretations. See also *Mucciarelli*, ECFR 2016, 1, 27 (Art 36 undertakings cannot replicate all effects of real secondary proceedings and can only mimic their distributional rules).

388  *Grossman/Hart*, JPE 1986, 691.

lose its importance.[389] Synthetic proceedings entrust this function to the insolvency practitioner of the main (and only) proceeding, subject to an *ex ante* and *ex post* judicial control where the courts of the (potential) secondary proceeding can only intervene by means of provisional or protective measures (Articles 36(8) and (9) EIR).[390] Curbing governance rights of local creditors may reduce their confidence that they will partake in future surpluses, which by definition cannot be taken into account at the beginning of the proceeding.[391]

From a policy perspective, recourse to secondary proceedings – and therefore to protocols and agreements to coordinate main and secondary proceedings – may maintain its relevance as a tool to protect local creditors from excessive legal uncertainty when courts rebut the presumption that the COMI coincides (in the case of companies) with the registered office (Article 3(1), para 2 EIR).[392] The EIR requires that the COMI be located in the place where the debtor conducts the administration of his/her interests on a regular basis and be ascertainable by third parties on the basis of objective criteria. This provides some protection against unpredictable judicial determination of the applicable law and of jurisdiction.[393] However, the fact remains that the EIR, just like its predecessor, relinquishes the only element voluntary creditors can easily ascertain – i.e., the registered office[394] – for a criterion that is with no doubt more difficult to

---

389  *Hart*, EJ 1995, 678.
390  Liability towards local creditors of secondary proceedings may also contribute to reduce agency problems, but it is unclear whether a general duty of care toward those creditors – as opposed to the specific duties set forth by Art 36 as provided by Art 36(10) EIR – may be invoked and enforced.
391  The analysis performed in sec 2.4 with regard to conflicts of interests among creditors taking part in different proceedings equally applies here. While synthetic proceedings are likely to reduce the total costs of the proceeding, and may more easily avoid fragmented management of the insolvency estate, there can be no certainty, *ex ante*, that they will also be Pareto-efficient.
392  See CJEU, 4 September 2014, Case C-327/13, *Burgo Group*, ECLI:EU:C:2014:2158.
393  See for instance CJEU, 2 May 2006, Case C-341/04, *Eurofood IFSC Ltd*, ECLI:EU:C:2006:281, para 37 (excluding that a subsidiary's COMI should be located at the parent company's seat for mere existence of the control relationship).
394  Companies have to mention the registered office in their letters and order forms (Art 5 Directive 2009/101/EC), while no similar requirement applies to the real seat. The fact that under EU insolvency law the *lex fori concursus* depends on the

find out.[395] To be sure, an analysis of the appropriateness of the COMI as a connecting factor falls beyond the scope of this chapter. Suffice it to say that the COMI was originally intended as a way to reduce forum shopping, especially in the vicinity of insolvency, as it is based on factual elements that may be more difficult to move than mere registration.[396] Whatever its merits in the post-*Centros* era,[397] there is no doubt that identifying the CO-MI in a place other than the registered office may easily wrong-foot creditors.[398] Irrespective of general preferences between universality and territoriality,[399] concentration of proceedings is often beneficial, but it should be predictable.[400] Therefore, claiming that synthetic proceedings should always be preferred over secondary proceedings coordinated with protocols because they reduce the costs of having multiple venues would only look at one part, albeit pertinent, of the picture.[401] In a context where the

---

COMI even when this is contrast with what EU company law itself requires to disclose gives, in retrospect, a nuance of deception to the focus Directive 2009/101/EC put on communicating the location of the registered office.

395 The very concept of COMI, if applied to corporate groups, also seems to be quite old-fashioned. For each member of the corporate group, there might be more than one 'place where the debtor conducts the administration of its interests on a regular basis', and none of them may be at the company's registered office. While companies belonging to radial groups normally have a single COMI, in pyramidal groups each layer of the controlling chain may be responsible for coordinating a different aspect of the entrepreneurial activity for the whole group (finance, procurement, marketing, etc.), and this may get even more complicated in circular groups or where the different models are combined.

396 As long as its recognizability is properly enforced, the COMI can also protect (typically: small) creditors that are not likely to verify the registered office their counterparty declares in its correspondence.

397 For an analysis see *Mucciarelli*, EBOR 2013, 175, 190-1 (after *Centros*, COMI does not produce the effects originally envisaged and does not grant legal certainty and predictability); *Gerner-Beuerle/Schuster*, JCLS 2014, 287, 331 (same).

398 Cf *Armour*, CLP 2005, 369, 408; *Ringe*, EBOR 2008, 579, 612-3; *Eidenmüller*, MJ 2013, 133, 143, 145; *Gerner-Beuerle/Schuster*, JCLS 2014, 287, 330; *Gerner-Beuerle et al.*, Study on the Law Applicable to Companies. Final Report (2016), Luxembourg, p 294, 314-315.

399 See *Gopalan/Guihot*, The Geo. Wash. Int'l L. Rev. 2016, 549, 582 ff.

400 See the proposal fleshed out in Part 3, *supra* II. 1.2.1.

401 See also *Mucciarelli*, ECFR 2016, 1, 30 (for group insolvency, coordination of different proceedings is probably more effective and is likely to be preferred over synthetic secondary proceedings).

COMI drives the determination of jurisdiction and applicable law[402] alike, the risk of *ex post* variations inevitably reduce *ex ante* incentives to invest.[403] Lawmakers and academics should not therefore overlook the costs of missed investment opportunities when assessing the relative advantages of coordination through protocols *vis-à-vis* undertakings for synthetic proceedings.

Of course, the need to reduce the costs of *ex post* (and not fully predictable) concentration of proceedings is less pressing – and the relative advantages of protocols as a coordination tool decrease – when the (potential) secondary proceeding only depends on the presence, within a State's territory, of an establishment with no legal personality. When this is the case, there is little or no justification to protect expectations that would not be grounded on any express indication in the official company documents, and a fully-fledged universalistic approach could be pursued.

When creditors trigger secondary proceedings because of legitimate concerns about the ability of the main proceedings to cater to their needs, protocols might outperform undertakings in the capacity to enforce local creditors' rights, which may require different governance tools for the insolvency proceedings. This will crucially depend on the ability of the involved insolvency practitioners to enter protocols, on the breadth of those protocols, and on the binding effect these may have.[404]

### 3. Recommendations and guidelines

As shown in sec 2, there might be certain legal and practical difficulties in concluding or adopting a cross-border insolvency agreement or protocol, since interested parties may be concerned that the protocol will not be regarded, perhaps in hindsight, to be in the best interests of their creditors or will not be compatible with the applicable insolvency laws.[405] Therefore, the conclusion of cross-border insolvency protocols could benefit from specific national rules or practice guidelines. As measures of this kind are

---

402 'Applicable law' includes substantive and procedural law for main proceedings, and procedural law for synthetic secondary proceedings.
403 Unpredictability of insolvency rules increases the cost of debt (and equity) capital: *Valiante*, Study prepared for the EU Parliament (2016), p 15.
404 See *infra* Part 2, II. 3.3 for recommendations.
405 See the threats to the *Lehman* Protocol, *Altman*, San Diego Int'l L.J. 2011, 463, 493.

country-specific, the following analysis merely aims at providing general guidelines to insolvency practitioners and courts for the conclusion and approval of cross-border insolvency agreements and protocols under the EIR, in the light of the relevant past and current practice and considering the coordination regime of the EIR. For ease of understanding, the following analysis broadly follows, and draws from, the 2009 UNCITRAL Practice Guide on Cross-Border Insolvency Cooperation (Part III).[406] This is due to the relevance of the Guide under recital 48 EIR. In drafting protocols, interested parties are advised to make use of this and other relevant soft law instruments,[407] such as the 2007 European Communication and Cooperation Guidelines for Cross-Border Insolvency ('CoCo Guidelines'),[408] as well as the 2014 Cross-Border Insolvency Court-to-Court Cooperation Principles and Guidelines ('EU JudgeCo Principles') and the 2014 Draft INSOL Europe Statement of Principles and Guidelines for Insolvency Office Holders in Europe.[409] Furthermore, several insolvency agreements or protocols incorporate the 2000 ALI Guidelines for Court-to-Court Communications in Cross-Border Cases in their text, usually as an annex.[410]

---

406 Available at: http://www.uncitral.org/pdf/english/texts/insolven/Practice_Guide_english.pdf. The Practice Guide is based upon Art. 27 UNCITRAL Model Law On Cross-Border Insolvency (see ibid, § 223). A detailed analysis of the topics normally dealt with in protocols can be found in *Espiniella*, 10 Anuario de Derecho Concursal (2007), 165.

407 As to the relevance of soft law instruments, see *Wessels,* Insolv.Int. 2014, 100, 103.

408 Available at: www.insol.org/INSOLfaculty/pdfs/BasicReading/Session%205/European%20Communication%20and%20Cooperation%20Guidelines%20for%20Cross-border%20Insolvency%20.pdf. The Protocol in *Nortel Networks* was based upon the CoCo Guidelines, see http://bobwessels.nl/2015/05/2015-05-doc5-coco-guidelines-apply-to-nortel-networks-coordination-protocol.

409 Both available at: www.tri-leiden.eu/publications/.

410 See *Systech* Protocol, *Androscoggin Energy* Protocol, *Nortel* Protocol (Nortel Networks Inc., Case No. 09-10138 (Bankr. D.Del. 2009)); *Madoff Securities* Protocol Order Pursuant to Sections 1526, 1527 and 105(a) of the Bankrutpcy Code Approving Protocols By And Between the Trustee and the Joint Provisional Liquidators of the Madoff Securities International Limited, Securities Investor Protection Corporation v. Bernard L. Madoff Investment Securities Ltd., Adv. Pro. No. 08-1789 (Bankr. S.D.N.Y June 9, 2009)); *Lehman* Protocol, Exhibit C. According to the survey conducted in the preparation of this Study (Q 21), scholars, lawyers and other practitioners are often familiar with one or more of these guidelines, and generally (Q 22: 80%) consider these tools as a valuable aid in

## 3.1 Circumstances supporting the use of insolvency agreements or protocols

Protocols or insolvency agreements are a tool increasingly used in cross-border proceedings. They are intended to create tailored solutions[411] in accordance with the applicable *lex fori concursus*. In particular, protocols or insolvency agreements can facilitate the administration of the proceedings, prevent disputes or conflicts between the insolvency practitioners, reduce administration costs and contribute to maximizing the value of the insolvency estate.[412] For instance, in the *Everfresh* case, the conclusion of an insolvency protocol reportedly contributed to an estimate aggregate value maximization of 40%.[413]

As the conclusion of a protocol or insolvency agreement is costly and requires significant efforts and timely negotiations, insolvency practitioners should contemplate their use when this is worthwhile, taking into account several factors. Protocols or insolvency agreements might be of particular importance when the debtor's assets spread across many different jurisdictions or the insolvency estate is particular complex.[414] In addition, protocols or insolvency agreements are to be considered where the debtor's assets are intermingled (e.g. where a common cash management system has been put in place at the group level).[415] The conclusion of insolvency protocols might not be the appropriate solution where the debtor's assets total value and complexity are limited.[416]

---

providing assistance in the preparation and interpretation of protocols. Some respondents also suggested adding a protocol template as an Annex to the EIR, as this would increase protocols' legitimacy and might increase their use.

411 Insolvency agreements or protocols are better placed to provide case specific solutions than model laws or guidelines, cf *Kamalnath*, IJLSR 2013, 172, 173, 186.

412 *Wessels*, in: Faber et al. (eds), Overeenkomsten en insolventie (2012), p 359, 370.

413 Cf 2009 UNCITRAL Practice Guide on Cross-Border Insolvency Cooperation, § III.7.

414 See for instance the *Madoff Securities* Protocol (and the *Lehman* Protocol (Notice of Debtors' Motion Pursuant to Sections 105 and 363 of the Bankruptcy Code for Approval of a Cross-Border Insolvency Treaty, Lehman Brothers Holdings Inc. et al., Case No. 08-13555 (Bankr. S.D.N.Y., May 26, 2009)).

415 See 2009 UNCITRAL Practice Guide on Cross-Border Insolvency Cooperation, § III. 10.

416 *Berends*, Insolventie in het internationaal privaatrecht (2005), 53. In any case, the debtor's assets must be sufficient to cover the expenses of the conclusion or im-

In the European context, protocols may be especially valuable as an alternative to synthetic proceedings when – in line with the analysis above[417] – it is preferable to apply local (not only substantive, but also) procedural rules. This might be the case in some instances where the debtor's registered office was in the country of the secondary proceeding, but jurisdiction is established in another country where the COMI is identified.

In practice, the parties involved usually explain in the introductory part of protocols the case background as well as the reasons that led to the conclusion of the agreement. For instance, the *Lehman* protocol[418] refers to the 'Need for a Cross-Border Insolvency Protocol', i.e. the 'global and integrated nature' of the *Lehman* business, which extended across several jurisdictions. Including such an explanatory part in an insolvency agreement or protocol could increase the chances of its judicial approval, where necessary, or prevent creditors' objections before courts.[419]

## 3.2 Negotiations

Insolvency practitioners are encouraged to engage in negotiations for the conclusion of protocols at an early stage of the proceedings, whenever possible, so as to avoid disputes or unnecessary litigation.[420] Protocols can be concluded even prior to the formal opening of insolvency proceedings in a Member State,[421] for instance when a provisional liquidator has been appointed or the initiation of insolvency proceedings can be anticipated. At the same time, however, early negotiations may result in non-flexible solutions or solutions that do not correspond to the future needs of the in-

---

plementation of the protocol, see 2009 UNCITRAL Practice Guide on Cross-Border Insolvency Cooperation, § III. 10, lett. (d).

417  See *supra* Part 2, II. 2.5.
418  *Lehman* Protocol, p 3 f.
419  In the *Nakash* case, it was the insolvent debtor that opposed to the insolvency protocol before Israeli courts: see 2009 UNCITRAL Practice Guide on Cross-Border Insolvency Cooperation, § III. 42 and Annex I, sec 26.
420  2009 UNCITRAL Practice Guide on Cross-Border Insolvency Cooperation, § III.11.
421  *Raykin/Wouters*, Emory Bankr. Dev. J. 2013, 387, 419 ff.

solvency administration.[422] As a way out, insolvency practitioners may initially agree on general principles of cooperation, and subsequently add further more specific provisions as long as they gradually address new emerging needs. Appropriate provisions on future amendments, to be immediately included in the protocol, may facilitate this progressive fine-tuning exercise.[423]

All in all, the timing of negotiations is dependent on the circumstances and needs of each case. Interested parties may take into account all relevant aspects before deciding to enter into negotiations for the conclusion of an insolvency agreement or protocol. Depending on the complexity of a case, negotiations may last from several days to several months. For instance, in the *Lehman* case, which is universally regarded as highly complex, the protocol negotiations were concluded in more than seven months.[424]

### 3.3 Authorization and parties to an insolvency agreement or protocol

Insolvency agreements and protocols should contain an introductory section on the parties to the agreement or protocol. Since it is highly uncertain that the EIR provides a direct legal basis for the conclusion of protocols or insolvency agreements[425], contracting parties should also determine the legal basis for the conclusion of an insolvency agreement or protocol under the applicable national law. In addition, the parties should state whether the proposal should be approved by the competent court or the creditors' committee or other formal requirements are necessary.[426]

Broadly speaking, the successful conclusion of a cross-border insolvency protocol depends on how parties and courts involved deal with restrictive national rules – or with the lack of any rules – on the authorization to

---

422  *Hess,* Europäisches Zivilprozessrecht (2010), § 9 para 62; *Ehricke,* WM 2005, 397, 401.
423  See *infra* Part 2, II. 3.9.
424  2009 UNCITRAL Practice Guide on Cross-Border Insolvency Cooperation, § III. 12.
425  See *supra* Part 2, II. 2.2.
426  See for instance the *Madoff Securities* Protocol, p 7.

conclude or approve such an arrangement.[427] For instance, in *Nakash*[428] and *Sendo*,[429] the involved insolvency practitioners concluded a protocol, which was subsequently approved – despite the lack of a direct legal basis for the conclusion and authorisation of a cross-border insolvency protocol – by Israeli and French Courts respectively.

The survey conducted in the preparation of the Study highlighted that, in the respondents' opinion, the lack of a clear legal basis for the validity of protocols (Q 23: 53% of respondents), or for their approval (Q 23: 47% of respondents), is the most mentioned legal obstacle to the conclusion of protocols, together with the uncertain legal nature[430] of these agreements (Q 23: 47%). Given that most of the national statutory insolvency provisions of the EU Member States fail to ensure legal certainty as to which parties are entitled (insolvency practitioners, courts etc.) to conclude insolvency agreements or protocols, interested parties are advised to consult with the creditors' committee before entering into such an arrangement.[431] It is noteworthy that in the *Lehman* case, the signatories felt the need to secure the consent of the creditors' committee to a non-binding insolvency arrangement (protocol).[432]

## 3.4 Language of the insolvency agreement or protocol

Insolvency agreements or protocols should be drafted in a language determined by the contracting parties at their convenience or in a language shared by all contracting parties.[433] The use of the English language should also be encouraged, in order to spare unnecessary translation costs.

---

427 *Ibid*, p 29.
428 Order Approving Cross-border Protocol, Granting Comity to Jerusalem District Court letter for Request, Setting Damages for Initial Stay Violation and Granting Nuc Pro Tunc Stay Relief in Respect of Alleged Further Stay Violations, *in Re: Nakash*, Ch. 11 Case No. 94-B-44840 (BRL) (Bankr. S.D.N.Y. May 23, 1996).
429 Insolvency proceedings before the High Court of Justice, Chancery Division of London, and before the Commercial Court of Nanterre (2006).
430 In the same survey (Q 27), 40% of respondent believe protocols have a contractual nature, while 35% consider them as gentlemen's agreements.
431 Involvement of creditors is recommended by 2009 UNCITRAL Practice Guide on Cross-Border Insolvency Cooperation, § III.17 (mentioning *in Re: The Singer Company N.V.*, No. 99-10578 (Bankr. S.D.N.Y., filed 13 September 1999).
432 *Lehman* protocol, para 19.
433 Cf CoCo Guideline 10.1.

However, an insolvency agreement or protocol might be drafted in more than one language (e.g. *Sendo* and *Pioneer* Protocol, both in English and French).[434]


3.5 Terminology and interpretative rules

As the 2009 UNCITRAL Practice Guide warns,[435] the legal terminology of Member States differ significantly. As a result, the legal terms used in a protocol may be read differently by the contracting parties or the competent courts in the relevant jurisdictions. To prevent disputes on the interpretation of insolvency protocols, insolvency practitioners should include definitions of the terms used. The Glossary in the Appendix of the ALI III Global Principles for the Cooperation in International Insolvency Cases could provide useful assistance. In practice, several insolvency protocols make use of the Glossary of the 1995 IBA Cross-Border Insolvency Concordat (e.g. *Everfresh*).[436] Others contain a case-specific glossary – usually in an Appendix – defining the terms used in the protocol.[437]

In addition, contracting parties should introduce interpretive rules to eliminate divergent interpretation and possible disputes.[438] Insolvency protocols incorporating model laws or guidelines usually provide that the guidelines prevail, should a discrepancy between the protocol and the guidelines arise.[439] Several protocols set out consultative procedures for the prevention of interpretative disputes. By way of illustration, the *Nortel* protocol[440] states that 'the U.S. and Canadian Court may in their sole, respective discretion, provide advice or guidance to each other with respect to legal issues in accordance with the following procedures [...]'.

---

434 2009 UNCITRAL Practice Guide on Cross-Border Insolvency Cooperation, § III. 51.
435 2009 UNCITRAL Practice Guide on Cross-Border Insolvency Cooperation, § III. 52.
436 *Everfresh* protocol, p 3.
437 See *360NETWORKS* protocol, Appendix A (360Networks Inc., Case No. 01-13721, (Bankr. S.D.N.Y. 2001) (New York – British Columbia)).
438 2009 UNCITRAL Practice Guide on Cross-Border Insolvency Cooperation, § III. 54.
439 *Madoff Securities* protocol, p 5.
440 *Nortel* protocol, p 12.

## 3.6 Determining the purpose of the insolvency agreement or protocol

Contracting parties should determine the objective of the protocol, with a view to promoting the coordination of the insolvency proceedings.[441] A common understanding of the goals of the proceedings could help maximise the value of the insolvency estate and prevent disputes among different proceedings running in parallel.

An insolvency agreement or protocol may recall, when declaring its purpose, the coordination of parallel proceedings and the efficient administration to the benefit of all involved parties, but also more specific goals. For instance the *360NETWORKS* protocol states that the contracting parties intend to: '*(a)* harmonize and coordinate activities in the Insolvency Proceedings [...]; *(b)* promote the orderly and efficient administration of the Insolvency Proceedings to, among other things, maximize the efficiency of the Insolvency Proceedings, reduce the costs associated therewith and avoid duplication of effort; *(c)* honour the independence and integrity of the Courts [...]; *(d)* promote international cooperation and respect for comity among the Courts, the 360 Group, the Committees, the Estate Representatives and other creditors and interested parties in the Insolvency Proceedings; *(e)* facilitate the fair, open and efficient administration of the Insolvency Proceedings for the benefit of all of the creditors of the 360 Group and other interested parties, wherever located; and *(f)* implement a framework of general principles to address basic administrative issues arising out of the cross-border and international nature of the Insolvency Proceedings'.[442]

Insolvency protocols may also provide for specific coordination measures or determine the goal of the parallel proceedings (e.g. restructuring of the insolvent debtor's business or its liquidation).[443] The *Madoff Securities* protocol, for instance, aims at coordination, efficiency, communication among representatives, information and data sharing as well as at the identification, preservation and realisation of assets.[444] The *Everfresh* protocol

---

441 *Zumbro*, Bus. L. Int'l 2010, 157, 168.
442 *360NETWORKS* protocol, p 1 ff. Similar provisions can be found in several protocols, see for instance *Systech* protocol, p 2; *Nortel* protocol, p 3; *AIOC* protocol, p 3.
443 2009 UNCITRAL Practice Guide on Cross-Border Insolvency Cooperation, § 47 ff.
444 *Madoff Securities* protocol, para 1.2.

provides that '[t]o the extent permitted by the laws of the respective jurisdictions and to the extent practicable, the Interim Receiver and the
Debtors shall endeavour to submit a proposal in Canada and a plan of reorganization in the United States substantially similar to each other and
the Debtors, the Interim Receiver and the Trustee shall endeavour to coordinate all procedures in connection therewith [...]'.[445]

As long as the maximisation of the value of the insolvency estate can
take advantage of centralised or coordinated management of assets pertaining to one of the proceedings,[446] protocols may profitably provide,
where this is compatible with national laws, compensation mechanisms.[447]
These mechanisms should allow indemnifications for any damages suf-
fered by local insolvency estates that are needed to increase the total value
of the debtor's assets.

### 3.7 Issues to be addressed in insolvency agreements or protocols under the EIR

The EIR establishes a comprehensive legal framework for the coordination of cross-border insolvency proceedings. However, it does not address
exhaustively all relevant aspects. Against this backdrop, insolvency practitioners may wish to specify their duty to cooperate under the EIR or address issues left open by the Regulation in an insolvency agreement or
protocol. It is noteworthy that under the EIR 2000, the contracting parties
in the *Sendo* protocol 'ha[d] come to understand that the (EC) regulation
establishes very general operating principles' and, therefore, 'a practical
means of functioning which would allow for the efficient coordination of
the two insolvency proceedings' was necessary.[448] In addition, insolvency
agreements or protocols may establish tools in order to prevent future litigation between insolvency practitioners.

---

445 *Everfresh* protocol, para 13.
446 See the analysis *supra* in sec 2.4 and 2.5 of this part.
447 Cf Principle 6, Guideline 6.2, Draft INSOL Europe Statement of Principles and
Guidelines for Insolvency Office Holders in Europe; *Santen*, Communication and
cooperation in international insolvency: on best practices for insolvency office
holders and cross-border communication between courts, ERA Forum 16 (2015),
229, 236-7.
448 *Sendo* protocol, p 2.

The following analysis relies on a closer examination of the issues addressed in agreements or protocols concluded in the context of major cross-border insolvency, considering also the current coordination regime of the EIR.

### 3.7.1 Communication

Agreements or protocols typically address the information sharing and communication between the parties involved, in particular the means of communication and the language of communication, which are subject to possible limitations under the applicable laws.

As regards the communication between Courts, the current practice varies. Several arrangements refer to the 2000 ALI Court-to-Court Communications in Cross-Border Cases.[449] Others provide for case specific means of communication. For instance, the *Nakash* protocol[450] requires courts to cooperate to the maximum extent possible in order to avoid conflicting rulings through the insolvency practitioners and/or via telephonic conference. In the *Matlack* case,[451] the contracting parties appointed an intermediary, an 'information officer' that was, inter alia, entrusted with the task of delivering information/reports to the courts involved. The *360NET-WORKS* protocol[452] allows for joint hearings between the insolvency courts.

As to the communication between the insolvency practitioners, agreements or protocols usually determine the formal aspects of that communication. In fact, some of the protocols contain detailed provisions on the language, the means (e-mail, telephone, meetings in person) and the frequency of the communication.[453]

In practice, insolvency agreements or protocols adopt diverging approaches as to the confidentiality of communication. Depending on the ap-

---

449  Cf *Madoff Securities* protocol, para 5.
450  *Nakash* protocol, para 4.
451  *Matlack Systems*, Inc., Case No. 01-01114 (Bankr. D. Del. 2001).
452  *360NETWORKS* protocol, p 3.
453  See for instance the detailed provisions of the *Manhattan Investment Fund* protocol, paras 2-12 (United States Bankruptcy Court for the Southern District of New York, Case Nos. 00-10922(BRL) and 00-10921(BRL)).

plicable law, confidentiality clauses may affect the position of the creditors' committee.[454]

### 3.7.2  Preservation of the debtor's assets

Contracting parties should agree on information exchange in order to identify the insolvent debtor's assets or coordinate their efforts in order to protect the insolvency estate. The *Lehman* protocol[455] contains a lengthy list of measures aiming at preserving the debtor's assets. In addition, that protocol provides for the insolvency practitioners' obligation to cooperate in order to maximize the value of assets, for which multiple debtors (members of the same group of companies) have an interest.

### 3.7.3  Notification of the debtor's creditors

The EIR aims at enabling creditors to lodge their claims in parallel insolvency proceedings (Articles 45(1), 53 and 55 EIR), *inter alia* through a standardized form on the 'lodgement of claims'. Interested parties should be notified individually of the opening of insolvency proceedings by the insolvency court or appointed insolvency practitioner, so that they will be able to lodge their claims (Article 54(1) EIR). In order to meet that obligation, insolvency practitioners may specify in insolvency agreements or protocols the modalities of that notification: the time limits for lodging a claim under the applicable laws; the penalties related to those time limits; the bodies empowered to accept the lodgement of claims; and whether creditors should indicate whether their claim has a privileged status or not.

### 3.7.4  Lodgement of the creditors' claims by insolvency practitioners

Insolvency practitioners are equally allowed, under specific circumstances, to lodge claims – already lodged in their proceedings – in concurrent insolvency proceedings (Article 45(2) EIR). Insolvency agreements or

---

454  See 2009 UNCITRAL Practice Guide on Cross-Border Insolvency Cooperation, §§ 178 ff with further reference to the diverging practice.
455  *Lehman* protocol, p 6 ff.

protocols may contain specific provisions, in order to enable the practitioners of parallel proceedings to lodge the claim lodged in their procedure in the concurrent insolvency procedures. For instance, insolvency practitioners may assume the obligation to notify the other insolvency practitioners of the time limits for the lodgement of the creditors' claims under Article 45(2) EIR. Insolvency practitioners may also list the creditors' claims that are already lodged in their respective procedure and specify the amount of the claim as well as the status of the lodged claims, i.e. whether the claims proven by judicial decision or documents with evidentiary value.

### 3.7.5 Verification of the debtor's liabilities

In addition, insolvency agreements or protocols should contain rules on the verification of the debtor's liabilities, given the possibility of multiple lodgments of the same claim (by the creditor or the insolvency practitioner, Article 45(1) and (2) EIR). For instance, the *Sendo* protocol[456] provides for the independent verification of the debtor's liabilities in accordance with the applicable law in each proceeding. However, in order to avoid multiple payments to the same creditor in one proceeding, the protocol requires that both insolvency practitioners double-check whether a claim lodged by the insolvency practitioner in the parallel proceeding has already been lodged by the creditor of that claim.

### 3.7.6 Administration of the insolvency estate

Protocols or insolvency agreements usually contain provisions on the administration of the insolvency estate. As a first step, insolvency practitioners may commit themselves to provide a list of the assets that are covered by their respective proceedings within a certain time limit. In addition, they might agree to submit informally within a certain time limit their proposal for the realisation of the assets or the restructuring of the business company. In that context, the insolvency practitioner may address several issues such as the treatment of executory contracts, the possible liquida-

---

456 *Sendo* protocol, p 5.

tion of assets or the post commencement financing and the restructuring of the debtor's business.[457]

The *Sendo* protocol provides again an example of cooperation on the liquidation of assets under the EIR 2000. In particular, the insolvency practitioners of the main proceedings had committed not to request the 3-month stay of the liquidation in the secondary proceedings. In exchange, the French liquidator committed not to liquidate the assets covered by the secondary proceedings during the 3-month period. This agreement aimed at enabling, at a later stage, the global transfer and sale of the debtor's assets in the main insolvency proceedings. The global transfer of the assets covered by the secondary proceedings was made contingent upon the French insolvency court's approval. This mutual commitment by insolvency practitioners is a good example of the theoretical framework sketched out at the beginning of sec 3, as it shows that a partial waiver of rights or powers may result in a better management of the insolvency estate, and that all involved stakeholders can benefit from the ensuing surplus.

### 3.7.7 Preventing conflict of powers among insolvency practitioners

With a view to preventing overlapping or conflicting actions of the insolvency practitioners, contracting parties should also insert provisions on the delineation of the insolvency practitioners' powers, e.g. with regard to avoidance actions or allocation of certain assets to a particular insolvency estate. Such provisions could mitigate the risk of parallel litigation or irreconcilable judgments as to the allocation of an asset to a certain insolvency estate, given that according to the CJEU ruling in *Nortel*[458] the courts in both states where main and secondary insolvency proceedings were opened have concurrent jurisdiction on this matter.

### 3.7.8 Distribution of the proceeds

Article 23(2) EIR purports to ensure the equal treatment of creditors. According to that provision, a creditor which has obtained a dividend on its

---

457 2009 UNCITRAL Practice Guide on Cross-Border Insolvency Cooperation, §§ 106 ff.
458 CJEU, 11 June 2015, C-649/13, *Nortel Networks,* ECLI:EU:C:2015:384.

claim shall share in distributions made in other proceedings 'only where creditors of the same ranking or category have, in those other proceedings, obtained an equivalent dividend'. To that aim, insolvency agreements or protocols may specify how proceeds are to be distributed to creditors. For instance, insolvency practitioners may commit themselves to submit a draft distribution plan within a certain time limit to the insolvency practitioners of the parallel proceedings, in order to safeguard the principle of equal treatment of the creditors. Should other involved insolvency practitioners not object to the distribution plan, the insolvency practitioner concerned should be allowed to proceed with his distribution plan. After the distribution of the proceeds, insolvency practitioners should provide each other with a complete list of the creditors that have received a share of the proceeds, specifying also the exact amount distributed to each creditor.[459]

### 3.7.9 Conflict-of-laws issues

Articles 7 ff EIR provide for a comprehensive set of conflict-of-laws rules for cross-border insolvency cases in the EU. However, contracting parties may wish to determine the law applicable to certain transactions, where the conflict-of-laws rules of the EIR fail to provide sufficient clarity. The same applies to (protected) transactions/assets which are subject to the law of third countries, where insolvency proceedings have been initiated, given the limited scope of the conflict-of-laws rules of the EIR.[460]

---

459 *Sendo* protocol, p 8 f.
460 A choice-of-law clause in favor of the laws of the involved parties has been made, in different contexts, in several insolvency protocols concluded outside the EU. See, for instance, *Everfresh* Protocol (Ontario Court of Justice, Toronto, Case No. 32-077978 (20 December 1995), and the United States Bankruptcy Court for the Southern District of New York, Case No. 95 B 45405 (20 December 1995)): 'The proceeds of all Transactions shall be distributed in accordance with the laws of the jurisdiction approving such Transactions'; further III.1.b of the *AIOC Corporation and AIOC Resources AG* Protocol (United States Bankruptcy Court for Southern District Court of New York (Chief Judge Tina L. Brozman), Case Nos. 96 B 41895 and 96 B 41896, (April 3, 1998)): 'The claims reconciliation process shall be administered in accordance with the procedural and substantive laws (both bankruptcy and non-bankruptcy) governing the respective case in which the Party is appointed unless considerations of comity otherwise require'.

### 3.7.10  Costs of the proceedings

Contracting parties may also reach an agreement as to the allocation of the costs of the insolvency proceedings, in particular the costs incurred by the insolvency practitioners during the implementation of the protocol and/or the remuneration of the insolvency practitioners. In allocating the costs, contracting parties should take into account the circumstances of each case and in particular, the debtor's assets in each of the parallel proceedings.

The CoCo Guidelines state that '[o]bligations incurred by the liquidator during proceedings and the liquidator's fees are funded from the assets within those proceedings in which the liquidator is appointed'.[461] This principle has been followed in the past by the *Manhattan Investment Fund* protocol,[462] which allocated the costs incurred by each insolvency practitioner to the proceedings in which the practitioner had been appointed. In addition, under the CoCo Guidelines the costs incurred by the main insolvency practitioner prior to the opening of secondary insolvency proceedings, which are related to the assets that will be covered by the future secondary proceedings, will be funded, in principle, by the estate of the secondary proceedings.[463]

However, the CoCo Guidelines do not address the issue of the cost allocation when the assets of the secondary insolvency proceedings are not sufficient to cover the costs of those proceedings. In such cases, it would be appropriate to allocate these costs to the assets of the main insolvency proceedings, if the opening of secondary insolvency proceedings was requested by the main insolvency practitioner. For instance, the *Sendo* protocol under the EIR 2000, stated that, in the absent of sufficient assets in France, the costs of the French secondary insolvency proceedings initiated by the English insolvency practitioners, should be paid by *Sendo* assets, 'as an expense of the administration in England'.[464]

---

461  CoCo Guideline 11.1.
462  *Manhattan Investment Fund* protocol, para 14.
463  CoCo Guideline 11.2.
464  *Sendo* protocol, p 6.

## 3.8 Legal effects and effectiveness of insolvency agreements or protocols

For the sake of clarity, contracting parties should determine whether the insolvency protocols or agreements have a binding effect upon the parties (usually insolvency practitioners),[465] or merely establish a non-binding framework for cooperation (gentlemen's agreement),[466] taking into account possible limitations and liability concerns under the applicable insolvency law. Contracting parties should also determine the conditions precedent to the effectiveness of the protocol or insolvency agreement (court approval, approval of the creditors' committee).[467]

Insolvency practitioners are advised to seek (formally or informally) the insolvency court's approval and, possibly, the approval of the creditors' committee under national law, even in case where the agreement or protocol has a non-binding effect, so as to avoid possible liability claims.[468]

## 3.9 Flexibility of insolvency agreements or protocols

Contracting parties should safeguard flexibility of protocols or insolvency agreements, by stipulating that they could be modified in order to accommodate unforeseen events or changing circumstances. This is of particular importance, since protocols or insolvency agreements are usually concluded at an early stage, when contracting parties have no insight in the insol-

---

465  Cf *Madoff Securities* protocol, para 12.1 ('This protocol shall be binding on, and inure to the benefit of the representatives' respective successors and assigns, including any liquidator subsequently appointed over MSIL') and para 12.3 ('Each Representative represents and warrants to the other that its execution, delivery and performance of this Protocol is within its power and authority, except to the extent that Tribunal approval is required').

466  See for instance *Sendo* protocol, p 2: 'It is not intended to create a binding precedent'; further *Lehman* protocol, p 2: 'In recognition of the substantive differences among the Proceedings in each jurisdiction, this Protocol should not be legally enforceable nor impose on Official Representatives any duties or obligations [...] *(i)* that may be inconsistent with or that might conflict the duties or obligations to which the Official Representative is subject under the applicable law or *(ii)* that are not in the interest of the debtor's estate'.

467  Cf *Nortel* Protocol, p 11: 'This Protocol shall become effective only upon its approval by both the U.S. Court and the Canadian Court'.

468  2009 UNCITRAL Practice Guide on Cross-Border Insolvency Cooperation, §§ 31 ff.

vent debtor's financial situation, and cannot anticipate the progress of the proceedings.

Amendments are possibly subject to constraints under the applicable insolvency law or to additional requirements laid down in the protocol or insolvency agreement (e.g. court approval, approval of the creditors' committee etc.). For instance, the *Lehman* protocol states that '[t]his Protocol may not be amended, waived, or modified orally [...] except by a writing signed by a party to be bound, and where applicable, approved by the Tribunal with jurisdiction over that party'.[469]

## 3.10 Safeguards

Protocols or insolvency agreements must contain a caveat in favour of court' authority/public policy[470] and non-signatories' substantive rights under the applicable law. Such clauses usually serve only clarification purposes.

## 3.11 Dispute resolution clauses

Contracting parties should include dispute resolution clauses for disputes arising under protocols or insolvency agreements. A survey of protocols or insolvency agreements concluded in major cases reveals that dispute resolution clauses vary considerably.

Several arrangements require that the contracting parties take all possible steps in order to reach an out-of-court settlement, before bringing a dispute to the court(s) having jurisdiction under the agreement. Should all efforts fail, contracting parties may bring the dispute to the court(s) having jurisdiction under the agreement.[471]

---

469 *Lehman* protocol, p 10, para 12.1.
470 *Wessels*, in: Faber et al. (eds), Overeenkomsten en insolventie (2012), p 359, 366. See for instance, the public policy exception in the *AIOC* Protocol, II.I: 'Nothing in this agreement shall prevent the Bankruptcy court and the Swiss court from refusing to approve or take an action required by this agreement, if such action would be manifestly contrary to public policy'.
471 2009 UNCITRAL Practice Guide on Cross-Border Insolvency Cooperation, §§ 69 ff, 46 with further references.

Other protocols or insolvency agreements allow contracting parties to refer all disputes directly to the court designated under the agreement. The court seized of the dispute might then be required to consult or seek a joint hearing with another court. For instance the *360NETWORKS* protocol states: 'Disputes relating to the terms, intent or application of this Protocol may be addressed by interested parties to either the U.S. Court, the Canadian Court or both Courts upon notice as set forth above. Where an issue is addressed to only one Court, in rendering a determination in any such dispute, such Court: *(a)* shall consult with the other Court; and *(b)* may, in its sole discretion, either: *(i)* render a binding decision after such consultation; *(ii)* defer to the determination of the other Court by transferring the matter, in whole or in part, to the other Court; or *(iii)* seek a joint hearing of both Courts'.[472]

---

472 *360 NETWORKS* protocol, p 9.

# Part 3: Insolvencies of groups of companies*

University of Vienna
Articles 56 ff EIR

## I. Introduction

After the original EIR came into force in May 2002, it was frequently pointed out that the Regulation failed to provide express rules on insolvencies of groups of companies.[473] This is indeed true. However, one must not ignore the impact the EIR 2000 had on group scenarios even without containing such express rules.

The European legislator considered the EIR 2000's lack of specific rules dealing with groups of companies an obstacle to the efficient administration of the insolvency of members of a multinational group and to the successful restructuring of the group as a whole.[474] The reform is based on a 'procedural coordination' approach which respects each group member's separate legal identity.[475] Moreover, the legislator adopted an approach

---

\* Univ.-Prof. Dr. Dr. h.c. *Paul Oberhammer*; Univ.-Prof. Dr. *Christian Koller*; Mag. *Katharina Auernig*; Mag. *Lukas Planitzer*, Universität Wien.

473 See *Ehricke*, EWS 2002, 101 ff; *Hirte*, ECFR 2008, 213, 214; *Mankowski*, NZI 2004, 450, 452; *Mevorach*, Norton J. Bank. L. & Prac. 2006, 455; *Oberhammer*, in: Hess/Oberhammer/Pfeiffer (eds), Heidelberg-Luxembourg-Vienna Report (2014), para 584; *Pannen*, in: Pannen (ed), European Insolvency Regulation (2007), Art 1, para 132 f; *Pannen/Riedemann*, NZI 2004, 646, 647; *Paulus*, ZIP 2005, 1948, 1950; *Paulus*, RabelsZ 2006, 458, 459; *Paulus*, Europäische Insolvenzverordnung, 4^th edn (2013), Einleitung, para 43; *Stadler*, , in: Stürner/ Kawano (eds), Cross Border Insolvency, Intellectual Property Litigation, Arbitration and Ordre Public (2011), p 13, 25.

474 Cf Commission Staff Working Document – Impact Assessment accompanying the document Revision of Regulation (EC) No. 1346/2000 on insolvency proceedings SWD(2012) 416 final, p 15 f; Council of the European Union, Note from the French and German delegations to the Working Party on Civil Law Matters (Insolvency), Document 8108/13 (3 April 2013), p 4 f.

475 Cf recital 54. Consequently, a 'substantive consolidation' approach was not considered a viable option for obvious reasons. See also Art 72(3) EIR providing that the group coordination plan shall not include recommendations as to any consolidation of proceedings or insolvency estates.

which can be described as both cautious and, unfortunately, very bureaucratic. One might say that the reform mainly succeeded in creating additional Articles containing express wording on group cases and, therefore, accomplished a symbolical and political rather than a practical goal.[476]

The following sections will focus on key reform issues having an impact on the insolvency of groups of companies: the jurisdiction with respect to insolvencies of groups of companies (I.), the coordination between insolvency proceedings relating to individual group members (II.) and the provisions specifically introducing so-called 'group coordination proceedings' (III.). Additionally, conflict of laws issues relating to corporate insolvencies will be touched upon briefly, although they are not specifically affected by the reform (IV.).

---

476 See e.g. the critical comments by *Bewick,* Int. Insolv. Rev. 2015, 172, 188; *Cohen/Dammann/Sax,* IILR 2015, 117, 120; *Fehrenbach,* GPR 2017, 38, 49; *McCormack,* MLR 2016, 121, 143 and *infra* Part 3, IV. 3.1.

## II. Jurisdiction with respect to insolvencies of groups of companies

One of the main objectives of the reform was the implementation of new rules regarding the clarification of the COMI concept and the prevention of forum shopping in cases where this was deemed abusive. These provisions are of particular importance with respect to the coordination of group insolvencies and will therefore be discussed in the following subsections on the determination of the COMI of a member of a group of companies (1.) and on COMI-migration (2.). Another innovation introduced in the framework of the reform is the definition of 'group of companies' in Article 2(13) and (14) EIR, which will be dealt with at the end of this section (3.).

### 1. Determining the COMI of a member of a group of companies

#### 1.1 Legal framework

The question whether Article 3 of the original EIR allowed for the coordination of insolvencies of groups of companies by concentrating all (main) insolvency proceedings relating to different members of the group in one jurisdiction, thereby creating a sort of 'group COMI', had raised significant practical issues.[477]

The revision of the Regulation aimed at refining the COMI concept by including a definition in Article 3 EIR which, in essence, corresponds to the old recital 13. According to Article 3(1) EIR, the debtor's centre of main interest 'shall be the place where the debtor conducts the administration of its interests on a regular basis and which is ascertainable by third parties'.[478]

---

477 For an overview of the debate on the so-called 'head office' or 'mind of management' approach, cf e.g. *Reuß*, „Forum Shopping" in der Insolvenz (2011), 123 ff; cf also *Mangano*, in: Bork/Mangano (eds), European Cross-Border Insolvency Law (2016), paras 8.24 ff; *Moss*, Brook. J. Int'l. L. 2007, 1005; *Moss*, Brook. J. Corp. Fi. & Com. L. 2014, 250; *Oberhammer*, in: Hess/Oberhammer/Pfeiffer (eds), Heidelberg-Luxembourg-Vienna Report (2014), paras 609 ff; *Ringe*, in: Bork/van Zwieten (eds), Commentary on the European Insolvency Regulation (2016), Art 3, paras 3.105 ff; *Wessels/Markell/Kilborn*, International Cooperation in Bankruptcy and Insolvency Matters (2009), 122 ff.

478 Recital 28 highlights that special consideration should be given to the creditors and to their perception as to where a debtor conducts the administration of its in-

In addition, the new provision curtails the presumption enshrined in Article 3(1) subpara 2 EIR according to which the debtor's COMI is located at the place of the company's registered office. According to recital 30, it should, conversely, be possible to rebut the presumption 'where the company's central administration is located in a Member State other than that of its registered office, and where a comprehensive assessment of all the relevant factors establishes, in a manner that is ascertainable by third parties, that the company's actual centre of management and supervision and of the management of its interests is located in that other Member State'.

Furthermore, the presumption shall only apply if the registered office has not been moved to another Member State within the three-month period prior to the request for the opening of insolvency proceedings.[479] Ostensibly, the purpose of this provision is to prevent 'fraudulent or abusive forum shopping'.[480] As we will show below, this understanding is, however, problematic.[481]

## 1.2 Recommendations and guidelines

### 1.2.1 Recommendations

The concept of COMI is an obvious and effective tool for the improvement of coordination in groups of companies' insolvencies in situations where it leads to a centralization of main insolvency proceedings in a single jurisdiction.[482] The European legislator refrained from creating a real 'group COMI'. It did, however, incorporate major elements of the CJEU's

---

terests when determining whether the debtor's COMI is ascertainable by third parties.

479 See Art 3(1) subpara 2, 2nd s. EIR.

480 Cf recital 31; Council of the European Union, Statement of the Council's Reasons, Document 16636/5/14 (17 March 2015), p 5.

481 See *infra* II. 2.3.1. of this part.

482 See e.g. *Wolf*, Der europäische Gerichtsstand bei Konzerninsolvenzen (2012), 64 ff; cf also *Braun*, NZI 2004, Editorial, V, VI; *Bufford*, Nw. J. Int'l L. & Bus. 2007, 351, 407 f; *Bufford*, IILR 2012, 341, 363; *Eidenmüller*, ECFR 2009, 1, 14 f; *Mevorach*, Insolvency within Multinational Enterprise Groups (2009), 175 ff; *Oberhammer*, in: Hess/Oberhammer/Pfeiffer (eds), Heidelberg-Luxembourg-Vienna Report (2014), para 615; *Pannen*, in: Pannen (ed), European Insolvency Regulation (2007), Art 3, para 46; *Ringe*, in: Bork/van Zwieten (eds), Commentary on the European Insolvency Regulation (2016), Art 3, para 3.107.

findings in *Interedil*[483] in the EIR.[484] Thereby, the reform provides a sufficient basis for a flexible approach taking into account group COMI considerations in order to improve the coordination of insolvencies related to different members of a corporate group.[485] In that sense, it allows a further development of the court practice which emerged after the EIR 2000 came into force[486] in order to obtain an even better coordination of group cases.

The new recital 30 highlights the significance of the company's '*central administration*' and of the '*management of its interests*'. It therefore, albeit cautiously, opens the door for a more 'head office' or 'mind of management' oriented approach, which, in turn, renders it possible to locate the COMI of a subsidiary company at the COMI of its parent company (or

---

483 CJEU, 20 October 2011, Case C-396/09, *Interedil*, ECLI:EU:C:2011:671, paras 50 ff; see also CJEU, 15 December 2011, Case C-191/10, *Rastelli*, ECLI:EU:C:2011:838, paras 34 ff.

484 Cf recitals 28 and 30. Moreover, recital 13 of Regulation No 1346/2000, which is included in Art 3 EIR, already formed the basis for the CJEU's interpretation of Art 3 EIR 2000 in the *Interedil* case. In *Interedil*, the CJEU departed from its earlier approach expressed in C-341/04, 2 May 2006, *Eurofood*, ECLI:EU:C:2006:281, paras 36 f; cf also *Biermeyer*, MJ 2011, 581; *Honorati/ Corno*, IILR 2013, 18; *Moss*, Brook. J. Corp. Fi. & Com. L. 2014, 250, 251.

485 This seems to be acknowledged by recital 53; cf also Commission Proposal COM(2012) 744, p 10. For a more critical assessment see *Mangano*, in: Bork/ Mangano (eds), European Cross-Border Insolvency Law (2016), paras 8.28 f; *Mevorach*, Brook. J. Corp. Fi. & Com. L. 2014, 226, 245.

486 See e.g. *High Court of Justice Leeds*, 16 May 2003, *Re Daisytek-ISA Ltd* [2003] BCC 562, NZI 2004, 219; see also *Amtsgericht München*, 4 May 2004, 1501 IE 1276/04 *(Hettlage)*, NZI 2004, 450 annotated by *Mankowski*; *Amtsgericht Siegen*, 1 July 2004, 25 IN 154/04 *(Zenith)*, NZI 2004, 673, EWiR 2005, 175 annotated by *Mankowski*; *High Court of Justice Birmingham*, 18 April 2005, *MG Rover I* [2005] EWHC 874 (Ch), NZI 2005, 467 annotated by *Penzlin/Riedemann*; *Tribunal de Commerce Nanterre*, 15 February 2006, PCL 2006J00174 *(EMTEC)*, EWiR 2006, 207, annotated by *Penzlin*; *Cour de cassation*, 27 June 2006, *French Republic v Klempka (administrator Daisytek SAS)*, [2006] BCC 841; *Amtsgericht Köln*, 19 February 2008, 73 IE 1/08 *(PIN II)*, NZI 2008, 257; *Oberlandesgericht Wien*, 29 October 2013, 28 R 370/13g, ZIK 2014, 29, see also *Haidmayer*, ZIK 2014, 4; *High Court of Justice London*, 26 January 2015, *Re Northsea Base Investment Ltd & Ors* [2015] EWHC 121 (Ch), NZI 2015, 338, annotated by *Schulz*; *High Court of Justice London*, 17 January 2017, *Thomas & Anor v Frogmore Real Estate Partners GP1 Ltd & Ors* [2017] EWHC 25 (Ch), see also *Schulz*, NZI 2017, 142, and many others.

another group company).[487] We believe that future revisions of the EIR should make additional steps in this direction, e.g. by including such wording into the actual text of the EIR and by providing a broad definition of the term '*a company's central administration*' clarifying that the main aspect of this concept lies in the location where major decisions of the insolvent company are taken (and not decisions merely relating to the day-to-day business administration).[488] The future development not only of CJEU's, but also of national case law should be closely examined in order to identify other aspects which might play a role in this respect.

In order to safeguard the interests of the subsidiary company's creditors, Article 3(1) EIR requires the place where the debtor conducts the administration of its interests to be ascertainable by third parties. In other words, it must be ascertainable by creditors where essential management decisions, e.g. relating to operational strategy or the financing of the company, are implemented. Note that '*ascertainable*' does not mean that the creditors must have actual knowledge of such facts, but must only be in a position to obtain the relevant information by reasonable inquiries.[489] Such understanding of the term '*administration of interests*' should not be undermined by the wording of (new) recital 28 which states that in the event of a COMI-shift, it may be required to inform the creditors of 'the new location from which the debtor is carrying out its activities (…), for example by drawing attention to the change of address in commercial cor-

---

487 Cf CJEU, 20 October 2011, Case C-396/09, *Interedil*, ECLI:EU:C:2011:671, para 53; cf also *Martins Costa/Richter/Gerber-Lemaire/Marchand*, Droit bancaire et financier au Luxembourg (VI) 2014, 3281, 3343 ff; *McCormack*, J. Priv. Int. L. 2014, 41, 49; *Oberhammer*, in: Hess/Oberhammer/Pfeiffer (eds), Heidelberg-Luxembourg-Vienna Report (2014), paras 615 ff.

488 As was already suggested by *Brünkmans*, KSzW 2012, 319, 325 f.

489 See *Konecny*, ZIK 2005, 2, 4; *Mankowski*, in: Mankowski/Müller/Schmidt, Eu-InsVO 2015 (2016), Art 3, para 22; *Steffek*, in: Münchener Handbuch des Gesellschaftsrechts, Band 6, 4th edn (2013), § 37 para 39; see also *Poertzgen/Adam*, ZinsO 2006, 505, 507. The mere possibility of obtaining all relevant information on the basis of reasonable inquiries should be deemed sufficient to qualify facts as ascertainable. For an overly strict approach in this respect, see *High Court of Justice in Northern Ireland*, 20 January 2012, *Irish Bank Resolution Corporation Ltd v Quinn* [2012] NICh 1 para 28 and *High Court of Justice London*, 3 July 2009, *In re Stanford International Bank Limited* [2009] EWHC 1441 (Ch) paras 62 and 70: 'What is ascertainable by third parties is what is in the public domain, and what they would learn in the ordinary course of business with the company'.

respondence, or by making the new location public through other appropriate means'.

Furthermore, it has, in principle, to be accepted that the drafters of the EIR were of the opinion that preventing abusive forum shopping is an important policy objective.[490] According to recital 29, the Regulation 'should contain a number of safeguards aimed at preventing fraudulent or abusive forum shopping'. It is, however, unclear which '*safeguards*' are exactly meant here, and under what circumstances forum shopping is considered '*fraudulent*' and/or '*abusive*' and whether these terms are used interchangeably or whether forum shopping is '*abusive*' as such according to the opinion of the drafters of the recitals. Recital 5 suggests that a transfer of assets or judicial proceedings from one Member State to another in order 'to obtain a more favourable legal position to the detriment of the general body of creditors (forum shopping)' should be avoided. All this, however, is of little help as moving a business to another Member State will usually be caused by the objective of gaining advantages and, of course, will always affect the position of its creditors to some extent. Moreover, we believe that on the one hand, the dangers and detriments of such COMI shifting were overestimated in the legislative process. On the other hand, one must bear in mind that restricting businesses from mobility within the Union always touches upon the freedoms guaranteed under primary law.[491] All in all, we believe that the actual provisions of the EIR should

---

490  Cf recitals 29-34; Commission Staff Working Document – Impact Assessment accompanying the document Revision of Regulation (EC) No. 1346/2000 on insolvency proceedings SWD(2012) 416 final, p 19 ff. For the discussion on forum shopping under the regime of the EIR 2000 in general see e.g. *Hess*, in: Hess/Oberhammer/Pfeiffer (eds), Heidelberg-Luxembourg-Vienna Report (2014), paras 300 ff; *Eidenmüller*, ECFR 2009, 1; *Ringe*, EBOR 2008, 579; *Wright/Fenwick*, IILR 2012, 45.

491  Cf e.g. *Mankowski*, NILR 2017, 95, 99; *Mucciarelli*, EBOR 2013, 175, 185 ff; *Paulus*, NZI 2008, 1, 2.
The European Commission even explicitly acknowledged that COMI relocations of companies 'have been accepted by the Court of Justice as a legitimate exercise of the freedom of establishment' and that in several cases 'relocation to the UK allowed the successful restructuring of a company because of the flexibility which English insolvency law grants companies in this respect', see Commission Staff Working Document – Impact Assessment accompanying the document Revision of Regulation (EC) No. 1346/2000 on insolvency proceedings SWD(2012) 416 final, p 20. For the problematic distinction the Commission draws between

be the basis for dealing with this aspect, and not the vague representations made in the recitals.


### 1.2.2 Guidelines

*Guideline 1: Determining the COMI of a member of a group of companies*

A court examining *ex officio* (according to Article 4 EIR) whether it has jurisdiction to open insolvency proceedings with regard to a member of a group of companies will have to determine the respective group member's COMI. We recommend that the court should take into account whether the group member's '*central administration*' is located in a Member State other than that of its registered office. In such case, the presumption enshrined in Article 3(1) subpara 2 EIR, according to which the debtor's COMI is located at the place of the company's registered office, may be rebutted if (I) a comprehensive assessment of all relevant factors shows that the company's 'actual centre of management and supervision and of the management of its interests' is located in that other Member State and (II) such centre (of management and supervision) is ascertainable by third parties (see recital 30). Such assessment heavily depends on the facts of the individual case.[492] Relevant factors may include:

– where the bodies responsible for the management and supervision of a company are located;[493]
– where the management decisions of the company are taken,[494] in particular, if important decisions going beyond the day-to-day business of the company are generally taken at the level of a parent (or other group) company;

---

COMI shifting with respect to companies and 'bankruptcy tourism' of natural persons cf *Eidenmüller*, MJ 2013, 133, 143 f.

492  By way of illustration, see the exemplary application of the COMI concept in *High Court of Justice London*, 17 January 2017, *Thomas & Anor v Frogmore Real Estate Partners GP1 Ltd & Ors* [2017] EWHC 25 (Ch) paras 34 ff, see also *Schulz*, NZI 2017, 142.

493  See judgment in CJEU, 20 October 2011, Case C-396/09, *Interedil*, ECLI:EU:C:2011:671, para 50.

494  See CJEU, 20 October 2011, Case C-396/09, *Interedil*, ECLI:EU:C:2011:671, para 50.

- the place where decisions relating to contracts crucial for the debtor's business are taken;
- the location where financing was organized or authorized, or from where the cash management system was run;
- the places from which (and in which) the debtor is carrying out its activities and the location of the primary assets,[495] both, however, only in connection with other factors;
- information regarding the factors set forth above that was communicated to creditors by way of commercial correspondence or could have been obtained by the creditors otherwise on the basis of reasonable inquiries.[496]

## 2. COMI migration

### 2.1 Legal framework

In the wake of the reform process an extensive debate on whether the EIR should contain provisions preventing 'abusive' COMI transfers took place.[497] The decision of the European legislator to provide an exemption from the presumption that the debtor's COMI is located at the place of the company's registered office that has been added to Article 3 EIR can be understood in that context. Pursuant to the new Article 3(1) subpara 2 EIR, the presumption shall not apply if the company's registered office has been moved to another Member State in the three months preceding the request for the opening of insolvency proceedings. As we will show below, this provision, however, does not at all prevent 'abusive' or 'fraudulent' COMI shifting, but only becomes relevant in situations where the

---

495 See recital 28 EIR; CJEU, 20 October 2011, Case C-396/09, *Interedil*, ECLI:EU:C:2011:671, para 52.

496 See recital 28 EIR.

497 See e.g. *Eidenmüller*, ECFR 2009, 1, 24; for a response to *Eidenmüller*, see *Armour*, in: de la Feria/Vogenauer (eds), Prohibition of Abuse of Law (2011), 157; see also *McCormack*, CLJ 2009, 169, 196 f; *McCormack*, LS 2010, 126 ff; *Mevorach*, ECFR 2013, 523, 552 f; *Reuß*, "Forum Shopping" in der Insolvenz (2011), 342 ff; *Ringe*, EBOR 2008, 579, 614 ff; *Szydlo*, EBOR 2010, 253, 269; *Vallens*, Rev. proc. coll. May/June 2010, 25, 27; *de Weijs/Breeman*, ECFR 2014, 479, 503 ff.

COMI was not (yet) moved to another Member State. It is not about 'abusive' COMI shifting, but rather only about COMI simulation.[498]

## 2.2 Evaluation

In the light of the foregoing, Questions 34 and 35 were included in the study's questionnaire.[499] Summarizing the results for both, it can be said that the vast majority (Q 34: 80%, 16 pers; Q 35: 90%, 18 pers) of participants was not concerned about problems that could in practice arise as a result of the exemption from the COMI presumption under these specific circumstances.

In their individual comments, the participants specified, *inter alia,* that

- the question of coordination proceedings is not related to the COMI notion;
- these rules are more procedural than substantive and that, if the new seat is the 'real COMI', this should be easy to demonstrate, since it is only an exemption from a 'presumption';
- the exemption does not necessarily want to prevent relocations of the registered offices but aims to protect creditors and third parties; where a shift is made without any harm to these groups of stakeholders, there should be no problem;
- the actual underlying problem is that there is no group COMI as such.
- several participants commented that this is a workable solution and will be dealt with appropriately in practice.

---

498  Cf in this context *Eidenmüller*, ECFR 2009, 1, 9; cf also *Reuß*, "Forum Shopping" in der Insolvenz (2011), 255 ff.
499  Q 34: Do the provisions characterized as 'safeguards aimed at preventing fraudulent or abusive forum shopping' (cf recital 5 and recitals 28 to 31 EIR), in particular the exemption from the presumption in favour of the place of the registered office included in Art 3 EIR, in your view, raise practical problems with regard to insolvencies of groups of companies?; Q 35: Does the exemption from the presumption in favour of the place of the registered office included in Art 3 EIR, in your view, raise practical problems with regard to insolvencies of groups of companies?

## 2.3 Recommendations and guidelines

### 2.3.1 Recommendations

In its Article 3(1) subpara 2, the revised EIR seeks to prevent abusive 'COMI shopping' by providing for a new three-month suspension period. As already pointed out above, however, this provision prevents COMI simulation rather than about abusive COMI migration or 'shopping'. The relocation of a company's registered office does not automatically transfer its COMI.[500] By the same token, the transfer of a company's COMI does not necessarily require relocating the company's registered office. The amendment to Article 3(1) EIR merely prevents the court from relying on the presumption under Article 3(1) EIR when examining its jurisdiction (*ex officio* according to Article 4 EIR) and determining the debtor's CO-MI.[501] A debtor applying for insolvency within said time limit has to prove to the court that it has actually moved its COMI to the respective Member State. Therefore, this provision cannot at all be understood as an indication or presumption that the debtor 'abusively' relocated its registered office when a request to open insolvency proceedings is filed within three months after such relocation.[502] On the contrary, it is completely irrelevant in this context whether the shifting of the COMI was 'abusive'

---

500   See *Brinkmann*, in: K. Schmidt (ed), Insolvenzordnung: InsO mit EuInsVO, 19th edn (2016), Art 3 EuInsVO, para 16; *Ringe*, EBOR 2008, 579, 588; *Steffek*, in: Münchener Handbuch des Gesellschaftsrechts, Band 6, 4th edn (2013), § 37, para 29; *High Court of Justice London*, 15 August 2006, *Hans Brochier Holdings Ltd. v. Exner* [2006] EWHC 2594 (Ch), [2007] BCC 127, NZI 2007, 187, see also *Andres/Grund*, NZI 2007, 137.
      In addition, a change in a company's registered office is generally considered less problematic from the perspective of creditor protection because it can only be undertaken on the basis of the rules adopted by the Member States to implement the tenth company law directive on cross-border mergers; cf *Eidenmüller*, MJ 2013, 133, 145.

501   See *Garcimartín*, ZEuP 2015, 694, 711; *Henry*, Recueil Dalloz 2015, 979, 982; *Leandro*, Il Diritto dell'Unione Europea, 2016, 215, 223; *Mankowski*, in: Mankowski/Müller/Schmidt, EuInsVO 2015 (2016), Art 3, para 37; *Mankowski*, NILR 2017, 95, 102; *McCormack*, MLR 2016, 121, 131; *Moss/Smith*, in: Moss/ Fletcher/Isaacs (eds), The EU Regulation on Insolvency Proceedings, 3rd edn (2016), para 8.562; *Ringe* in: Bork/van Zwieten (eds), Commentary on the European Insolvency Regulation (2016), Art 3, para 3.90.

502   Contra *Commandeur/Römer*, NZG 2015, 988, 989; *Lienau*, in: Wimmer/Bornemann/Lienau, Die Neufassung der EuInsVO (2016), para 235 f; *Wimmer*, ju-

according to whatever standard. If the creditor can prove that it actually moved its COMI to another Member State, this is the basis for this State's jurisdiction to open main proceedings irrespective of allegations of 'abuse'. As a consequence, this provision does not at all prevent any kind of 'abusive' COMI shifting whatsoever, but only helps creditors in cases where a recent COMI shifting alleged by the creditor did not actually take place – irrespective of whether the incorrect representation that the COMI was shifted is based on abusive or fraudulent behaviour or not. Accordingly, the only 'abuse' this provision might prevent is a situation where the debtor, under the old law, relied on the presumption under Article 3(1) EIR within three months after the relocation of the company's registered office although the COMI was not (yet) actually migrated to this place. On balance, the amendment should therefore not have a significant impact on COMI transfers undertaken with regard to insolvencies of groups of companies, e.g. in order to benefit from a certain restructuring regime.[503]

We believe that one cannot exclude that this provision will cause practical problems such as: delays in a company's filing for insolvency; problems with respect to legal certainty and procedural delay based on the complicated situation arising from the necessary establishment of the relevant facts; frustration of the expectations of new creditors.[504] However, such concerns are only expressed by some (20%) of the answers which indicates that the impact of this new rule is (correctly) not overestimated already today. All in all, it might turn out to be just a harmless piece of symbolic legislation. Nevertheless, we suggest to closely evaluate the effects of this new provision in practice after the coming into force of the revised EIR for a period of about two or three years, because the misleading language about 'abusive COMI shopping' voiced in the political process

---

risPR-InsR 7/2015 Anm. 1, II 3; who claim that all COMI shifts which fall within the three months suspension period are in turn presumed to be abusive.

503 For criticism that the suspension period will not have any appreciable impact at all, cf *Fritz*, DB 2015, 1882, 1885; *McCormack*, MLR 2016, 121, 132; *Ringe* in: Bork/van Zwieten (eds), Commentary on the European Insolvency Regulation (2016), Art 3, para 3.88.

504 The European Commission had already voiced similar concerns in its initial impact assessment, see Commission Staff Working Document – Impact Assessment accompanying the document Revision of Regulation (EC) No. 1346/2000 on insolvency proceedings SWD(2012) 416 final, p 35. For a critical assessment of the amendment, cf also *Ringe* in: Bork/van Zwieten (eds), Commentary on the European Insolvency Regulation (2016), Art 3, para 3.85 ff.

might create the impression that national courts are now entitled or obliged to examine whether an actual COMI relocation took place on the basis of 'abusive' motives (applying whatever standard); such an approach might even be abused to veil protectionist motives in determining the jurisdiction of courts in countries from which the COMI has been relocated more or less recently.

### 2.3.2 Guideline

*Guideline 2: Interpretation of the exemption from the presumption in favour of the place of the registered office in Article 3(1) subpara 2 EIR in a group context*

When confronted with an application for insolvency within three months after the registered office of the debtor was moved to another Member State, courts are obliged to examine *ex officio* whether the COMI was also shifted to this State. However, Article 3(1) subpara 2 EIR provides no basis whatsoever for the court to examine whether an actual shifting of the COMI was '*abusive*' or '*fraudulent*'. If the COMI is located in the respective Member State, main proceedings have to be opened irrespective of such factors.

### 3. The definition of 'group of companies' in Article 2 EIR

### 3.1 Legal framework

Accompanying the new provisions on coordination with respect to insolvency proceedings of different members of groups of companies, the EIR Recast has introduced a definition of 'group of companies' and its respective group members in Article 2(13) and (14) EIR. Pursuant to Article 2(13), '*group of company*' encompasses a parent undertaking and all its subsidiary undertakings. Article 2(14) seeks to define the two mentioned types of group members, determining that a '*parent undertaking*' is an entity exercising direct or indirect control over one or more '*subsidiary undertakings*'. In addition, an undertaking that prepares consolidated financial statements in accordance with Directive 2013/34/EU (EU Accounting

Directive)[505] shall be deemed a parent undertaking. In particular, this reference to the EU Accounting Directive, which contains a number of Member State options, might lead to some difficulties with regard to the interpretation and application of the new provisions on insolvencies of international groups of companies.[506]

Moreover, the new provisions do not address the uncertainties regarding the legal nature of the entities mentioned in Article 2 EIR. The recast Regulation contains no express delineation between the definition of a '*subsidiary undertaking*' (Article 2(13) EIR) and an '*establishment*' (Article 2(10) EIR). In *Burgo Group*[507], the CJEU held that secondary proceedings can be opened when the establishment has a distinct legal personality.[508] The CJEU did, thereby, not qualify the subsidiary undertaking as an establishment of its parent undertaking. In this context it is, however, relevant whether the COMI of the subsidiary undertaking can be located at the place of business of the parent company. Where main insolvency proceedings concerning a subsidiary company have been opened in a Member State other than that of its registered office, secondary proceedings might be opened at the subsidiary company's registered place of business, pro-

---

505  Directive 2013/34/EU of the European Parliament and of the Council of 26 June 2013 on the annual financial statements, consolidated financial statements and related reports of certain types of undertakings, amending Directive 2006/43/EC of the European Parliament and of the Council and repealing Council Directives 78/660/EEC and 83/349/EEC, OJ 2013, L 182/19.

506  Cf *Mangano*, in: Bork/Mangano (eds), European Cross-Border Insolvency Law (2016), para 8.20 f; *Eble*, NZI 2016, 115, 121; *Eble*, in: Ebke/Seagon/Blatz (eds), Unternehmensrestrukturierung und Unternehmensinsolvenz (2015), 131, 170.

507  CJEU, 4 September 2014, Case C-327/13, *Burgo Group*, ECLI:EU:C:2014:2158, NZI 2014, 964 annotated by *Mankowski*; see also, *Amey*, International Corporate Rescue – Special Issue, South Square Articles 2015, 8; *Anzenberger*, ZIK 2015, 5.

508  See CJEU, 4 September 2014, Case C-327/13, *Burgo Group*, ECLI:EU:C:2014:2158, para 32. Despite its broad wording the Burgo Group decision does, however, not change the fact that a legally independent subsidiary itself can never be considered an establishment of its parent company (contra: *Baumert*, LMK 2014, 362606; cf also *Paulus*, NZI 2001, 505, 509 f; *Paulus*, Europäische Insolvenzverordnung, 4th edn (2013), Art 2, para 34) Such an interpretation would be irreconcilable with the 'procedural coordination' approach which respects each group member's separate legal identity; cf also *Anzenberger*, ZIK 2015, 5, 6; *Bork*, in: Bork/Mangano (eds), European Cross-Border Insolvency Law (2016), para 7.24 f; *Riedemann*, in: Pannen (ed), European Insolvency Regulation (2007), Art 2, paras 60 ff.

vided that the debtor is carrying out an economic activity with human means and assets which can be qualified as an *'establishment'* in accordance with Article 2(10) EIR.[509]


3.2 Evaluation

In the light of the foregoing, Questions 32 and 33 were included in the study's questionnaire.[510]

The answers to Q 32 bear evidence to significant uncertainty when it comes to the determination and delimitation of the terms 'establishment' (Article 2(10) EIR) and 'subsidiary undertaking' (Article 2(13) EIR). We received some individual comments that can be summarised as follows:

- *'subsidiary undertaking'* is a separate legal entity, while *'establishment'* is not;
- *'subsidiary undertaking'* can be considered as an *'establishment'* for the purpose of secondary proceedings;
- *'subsidiary undertaking'* may itself have an *'establishment'* in the State where its registered office is situated.

The responses to Q 33, on whether the new coordination proceedings for group of companies exclude the application of main and secondary proceedings within a group of companies, suggest that the question of the parallel or non-parallel existence of these two concepts with respect to groups of companies does not seem to be clear either.

---

509  Cf recital 24. The practice of opening secondary proceedings at the actual registered office of the subsidiary company was already well established in some Member States long before the *Burgo Group* judgment; see, e.g. *Landesgericht Innsbruck*, 11 May 2004, 9 S 15/04m (*Hettlage Österreich*), ZIK 2004, 107; *Landesgericht Klagenfurt*, 2 July 2004, 41 S 75/04h (*Zenith Österreich*), NZI 2004, 677; *Fővárosi Bíróság, Budapest*, 17 September 2008, 9. Fpk. 01-08-001806/9, INSOL EIR-case register No 56 and others.
510  Q 32: How would you distinguish the concept of 'establishment' (Art 2(10) EIR) from the concept of 'subsidiary undertaking' (Art 2(13) EIR)? Q 33: Do the new coordination proceedings for groups of companies exclude the application of main and secondary proceedings within a group of companies?

## 3.3 Recommendations and guidelines

### 3.3.1 Recommendations

According to more than 50% of the answers to the questionnaire, the concepts of establishment (Article 2(10) EIR) and of subsidiary undertaking (Article 2(13) EIR) are exclusive in the sense that secondary proceedings are not possible with regard to a '*subsidiary undertaking*'. Moreover, approximately 45% of the stakeholders answered that the new coordination proceedings for groups of companies would exclude the application of main and secondary proceedings within a group of companies. They concluded that the CJEU's decision in *Burgo Group* does no longer apply to the definition of the term '*establishment*' in Article 2(10) EIR.

In light of these answers, it seems necessary to clarify that the newly introduced provisions on groups of companies only aim to provide an additional set of tools.[511] They do not exclude the possibility to open secondary proceedings in respect of a subsidiary company at its place of registration where main insolvency proceedings against said subsidiary company have been opened at the COMI in the Member State of its parent company (or another group company). The CJEU's decision in *Burgo Group* has clearly not been overruled by the revised Insolvency Regulation.[512] This view is also supported by recital 53 EIR, which explicitly acknowledges that the introduction of rules on the insolvency proceedings of groups of companies should not limit the possibility of a court to open insolvency proceedings for several companies belonging to the same group in a single jurisdiction if the court finds that the COMI of those companies is located in a single Member State.

With regard to Article 2(14) EIR, it should be noted that because of this reference to the EU Accounting Directive, the concept of '*group of companies*' can take different forms, depending on how Member States exercised the options provided for by the Accounting Directive. Evidently, the

---

511 Cf Commission Proposal COM(2012) 744, p 10; cf also *Bornemann*, in: Wimmer/Bornemann/Lienau (eds), Die Neufassung der EuInsVO (2016), para 521; *Fehrenbach*, GPR 2017, 38, 45; *McCormack*, MLR 2016, 121, 142; *Moss/Smith*, in: Moss/Fletcher/Isaacs (eds), The EU Regulation on Insolvency Proceedings, 3rd edn (2016), para 8.749; *Reumers*, Int. Insolv. Rev 2016, 225, 240; *Thole/Dueñas*, Int. Insolv. Rev. 2015, 214, 227.

512 See recital 24 which adopts the essence of the *Burgo Group* decision.

European legislator's intention was to base the EIR's definition of groups of companies at least also on the group concept of the EU Accounting Directive in order to achieve a higher degree of consistency in European business law.[513] Therefore, the definitions given in Article 2(13) and (14) EIR should as far as possible be interpreted in conformity with the group concept enshrined in the Accounting Directive. However, the phrase '*shall be deemed*' in Article 2(14) EIR indicates that the definition of '*parent undertaking*' is not limited to companies affected by Directive 2013/34/EU. An undertaking which controls, either directly or indirectly, one or more subsidiary undertakings may still be considered a '*parent undertaking*' even if it is not required to prepare consolidated financial statements in accordance with the Accounting Directive.[514] The second sentence of Article 2(14) EIR establishes a presumption that all undertakings that have to prepare consolidated financial statements in accordance with the Accounting Directive do constitute '*parent undertakings*' within the meaning of the EIR. It is, however, disputed in legal doctrine whether this presumption is rebuttable or not.[515] In our view, the better arguments speak in favour of a rebuttable presumption: the European legislator did not only refer to the concept of control enshrined in the Accounting Directive but rather adopt-

---

513  Cf *Eble*, NZI 2016, 115, 118; *J. Schmidt*, Eurofenix Autumn 2015, 17, 17; *J. Schmidt*, KTS 2015, 19, 36; *van Zwieten*, in: Bork/van Zwieten (eds), Commentary on the European Insolvency Regulation (2016), Art 2, para 2.38; critical towards this approach: *Mock*, GPR 2013, 156, 164. Other European legislative acts which refer to the EU Accounting Directive's Group Concept include e.g. Directive 2014/65/EU (Markets in Financial Instruments Directive II – MiFID II), cf Art 4(1), (32) and (33).

514  Cf *Thole*, in: MüKoInsO, 3rd edn (2016), Art 2 EIR, para 22; *van Zwieten*, in: Bork/van Zwieten (eds), Commentary on the European Insolvency Regulation (2016), Art 2, para 2.38; *Mangano*, in: Bork/Mangano (eds), European Cross-Border Insolvency Law (2016), para 8.20; *Prager/Keller*, WM 2015, 805, 809; *Eble*, NZI 2016, 115, 118.

515  Cf for an irrebuttable presumption, *Esser*, Am. Bankr. Inst. J., March 2015, 38, 39; *Fehrenbach*, GPR 2017, 38, 45; *J. Schmidt*, in: Mankowski/Müller/Schmidt, EuInsVO 2015 (2016), Art 2, para 79; *Thole*, in: MüKoInsO, 3rd edn (2016), Art 2 EIR, para 22; *van Zwieten*, in: Bork/van Zwieten (eds), Commentary on the European Insolvency Regulation (2016), Art 2, para 2.38; contra *Bornemann*, in: Wimmer/Bornemann/Lienau, Die Neufassung der EuInsVO (2016), para 544; *Eble*, NZI 2016, 115, 119; *Eble*, in: *Ebke/Seagon/Blatz* (eds), Unternehmensrestrukturierung und Unternehmensinsolvenz (2015), 131, 152 f who takes the view that the second sentence of Article 2 no 14 EIR establishes a rebuttable presumption; accordingly *Tashiro*, in: Braun, InsO, 7th edn (2017), Art 2, para 83.

ed an abstract definition. It should, therefore, be possible to take into account insolvency-specific objectives when interpreting the definition of *'parent undertaking'*, and as a corollary, the definition of *'group of companies'* in general. Such interpretation requires flexibility which supports the view that Article 2(14), 2nd s. EIR only constitutes a rebuttable presumption. Admittedly, however, the reading of Article 2(14) EIR as establishing an irrebuttable presumption is, for instance, supported by the wording of the provision, viewed in its systematic context. Unlike Articles 3, 2(14), 2nd s. EIR states 'shall be deemed' and not 'shall be presumed'. In addition, an irrebutable presumption would create legal certainty regarding the applicability of Chapter V.

While the definition of *'parent undertaking'* in Article 2(1) lit. j) of the original Commission proposal only seemed to refer to subordination groups, comprising a parent undertaking and at least one subsidiary, the wording of Article 2(14) EIR seems to allow for a broader interpretation. According to Article 22 no 7 of the EU Accounting Directive, Member States may require undertakings that are managed on a unified basis or have a common administrative, managerial or supervisory body, to draw up consolidated financial statements. Groups consisting of companies that operate on the same level and are subject to common direction (such as the so-called *'Gleichordnungskonzerne'* in German law[516]) could therefore fall into the scope of the presumption of the second sentence of Article 2(14) EIR. In contrast, the wording of the actual definition of *'group of companies'* in Article 2(13) EIR[517] suggests that the new provisions on group insolvencies are still only applicable to subordination groups. However, none of the legal consequences provided for under Articles 56 ff and 61 ff EIR require a narrow understanding of the terms *'group of companies'* or *'parent undertaking'*. Rather, a broad understanding of these notions might help to flexibly cope with specific situations in order to give at least some effect to these provisions.

All in all, the attempt to define these terms did not bring about much progress. This is not problematic, as the EIR as a whole and in particular Articles 56 ff and 61 ff EIR did not bring much progress with respect to

---

516  See sec 18(2) dAktG (German Stock Corporation Act): 'If legally separate enterprises are subject to common direction, although none of such enterprises controls the other, such enterprises shall constitute a group and the individual enterprises shall constitute members of such group'.

517  See Art 2(13) EIR: 'a parent undertaking and all its subsidiary undertakings'.

group issues anyway. One should, however, bear in mind with respect to both the development of case law and future legislative steps that these definitions are not the fruits of in-depth reflections of all possible implications of international group companies and should therefore not be regarded as the *ratio scripta* in this field. Rather, they are only an empty frame for future objective-based decisions on specific group issues.

### 3.3.2 Guidelines

*Guideline 3: Interpretation of the definitions of 'group of companies' and 'parent undertaking' in Article 2(13) and (14) EIR*

1. The definition of *'group of companies'* in Article 2(13) EIR should be interpreted broadly and applied also in accordance with Directive 2013/34/EU.
2. An undertaking that controls, either directly or indirectly, one or more subsidiary undertakings may still be considered a *'parent undertaking'* within the meaning of Article 2(14) EIR, even if it is not required to prepare consolidated financial statements in accordance with Directive 2013/34/EU.
3. All in all, one should not overestimate the wisdom of these definitions. As long as they are only the basis for rather weak mechanisms under Articles 56 ff and 61 ff EIR, they should not be construed narrowly.

*Guideline 4: Clarifying the relation between 'subsidiary undertaking' (Article 2(13) EIR) and 'establishment' (Article 2(10) EIR)*

The concepts of *'subsidiary undertaking'* (Article 2(13) EIR) and *'establishment'* (Article 2(10) EIR) operate independently of each other. If the COMI of the subsidiary undertaking is, in application of the criteria set out in Guideline 1, to be located at the seat of the parent company, the courts of this Member State shall have jurisdiction to open insolvency proceedings for the respective group members. Secondary proceedings may be opened in any other Member State where the subsidiary company has an establishment.

*Guideline 5: Relation between the application of main/secondary proceedings and the newly introduced measures to facilitate coordination in the context of groups of companies*

The new provisions introduced for a better coordination of insolvencies concerning members of a group of companies *do not exclude* the possibility of opening secondary proceedings in a group context. Both the group-specific provisions on cooperation and communication (Articles 56–60 EIR) as well as the new group coordination proceedings (Articles 61-77 EIR) have to be regarded as additional tools which do not restrict the already available means of coordinating the insolvency proceedings of members of a group of companies.

## III. Coordination between insolvency proceedings relating to group members

### 1. Legal framework

The reform aims to ensure the efficient administration of insolvency proceedings relating to different companies forming part of a corporate group (cf recital 51). As a consequence of the introduction of new provisions for groups of companies, three scenarios have to be distinguished: the coordination between main and secondary insolvency proceedings in group settings *(a)*, the coordination between main insolvency proceedings opened against different group members *(b)*, and finally the new group coordination proceedings (which will be discussed in a separate section *infra* IV.).

*a) Coordination between main and secondary insolvency proceedings.* The rules for coordination between main and secondary proceedings (in particular Articles 41 ff EIR) apply to groups of companies in cases in which main insolvency proceedings are opened against a subsidiary company at the COMI of the parent company (or another group company) while secondary proceedings are opened at the registered office of the subsidiary company.[518] The main insolvency practitioner may, therefore, exercise the following powers: to give an undertaking to local creditors according to Article 36 EIR in order to prevent the opening of secondary proceedings, to request the opening of secondary proceedings to be stayed (cf Article 38(3) EIR),[519] and to request the conversion of secondary proceedings into another, more appropriate type of proceedings than initially requested or already opened (cf Article 51(1) EIR). The main insolvency practitioner's ability to apply for a suspension of the realisation of assets in the secondary proceedings (cf Article 46 EIR) and to propose a restructuring plan or composition (cf Article 47 EIR) has not been subject to major changes.[520]

*b) Coordination between main insolvency proceedings opened against two or more group members.* The coordination between these proceedings

---

518  This is only possible if the requirements of an establishment (according to Art 2(10) EIR) are met; cf recitals 24 and 53. See on this question also *supra* Part 3, II. 3.1.

519  For the question of coordination between main and secondary proceedings in general, see *supra* Part 2, II.

520  Cf recital 48.

is, on the one hand, governed by the Section 1 of the newly introduced Chapter V on Insolvency Proceedings of Members of a Group of Companies (Articles 56 ff EIR)[521] and, on the other hand, by the new group coordination proceedings.[522] Apart from the provisions on communication and cooperation and the usage of agreements and protocols as coordination tools,[523] the rules dealing with the powers of the insolvency practitioner in proceedings concerning (other) group members need to be mentioned. The European legislator decided against establishing a hierarchy between insolvency proceedings opened against members of a group of companies similar to the relation between main and secondary proceedings. In this regard and outside the scope of group coordination proceedings, the reform rather follows a 'market economy oriented approach'[524] according to which all relevant insolvency practitioners should, in principle, have the right to be heard and to request a stay of any measure related to the realisation of assets in (all) proceedings concerning other group members (cf Article 60(1) EIR).[525] Therefore, the legislation correctly refrained from attempts (which were originally suggested e.g. by the German government)[526] to (abstractly) denominate a 'main main practitioner' for group cases in the regulation; this would indeed have been an impossible task, as groups of companies differ strongly from each other.[527] The insolvency practitioner may, however, only exercise his/her powers 'to the

---

521  According to recital 62, '[t]he rules on cooperation, communication and coordination in the framework of the insolvency of members of a group of companies provided for in this Regulation should only apply to the extent that proceedings relating to different members of the same group of companies have been opened in more than one Member State.'

522  See *infra* Part 3, IV. Pursuant to recital 60 particularly the insolvency practitioner's powers under Art 60 EIR should provide for an '*alternative mechanism*' to achieve a coordinated restructuring of the group for members of the group *not* participating in group coordination proceedings.

523  See *supra* Part 2, III.

524  *Oberhammer*, in: Hess/Oberhammer/Pfeiffer (eds), Heidelberg-Luxembourg-Vienna Report (2014), para 610.

525  With regard to the powers of the group coordinator see *infra* Part 3, IV. 1.

526  Cf also Revision of the European Insolvency Regulation – Proposal by INSOL Europe (2012), 93 ff.

527  Cf UNCITRAL Legislative Guide, Part Three: Treatment of Enterprise Groups in Insolvency (2012), paras 6 ff; *Mevorach*, Insolvency within Multinational Enterprise Groups (2009), 127 ff; *Oberhammer*, in: Hess/Oberhammer/Pfeiffer (eds), Heidelberg-Luxembourg-Vienna Report (2014), paras 587 ff.

extent appropriate to facilitate the effective administration of the proceedings'. In addition, the insolvency practitioner's right to request a stay – which is, or rather could be, the most powerful tool of coordination – is subject to (no less than) four conditions, most notably the existence of a coordinated restructuring plan (according to Article 56(2) lit. c) EIR) that presents a 'reasonable chance of success' (Article 60(1) lit. b) [i] EIR) and the requirement that the insolvency proceedings that should be stayed are not subject to group coordination proceedings.[528]

2. Evaluation

In the light of the foregoing, Q 36 was included in the study's questionnaire.[529] The question aimed at individual answers. Those were indeed not uniform; the overall view expressed was, however, rather positive towards the new powers of insolvency practitioners with regard to insolvency proceedings concerning another member of the group.

The participants, *inter alia,* stressed that

- it could be a useful tool to isolate spoilsports in the group (while admitting that it can also help spoilsports to intervene in other proceedings);
- the possibility to exercise these powers could urge the involved bodies towards a more voluntary cooperation;
- it could be useful for coordinating the realization of assets and rights;

---

528  For a stay to be granted, Art 60(1) lit. b) EIR additionally requires that: *(i)* such a stay is necessary in order to ensure the proper implementation of the restructuring plan; *(ii)* the restructuring plan would be to the benefit of the creditors in the proceedings for which the stay is requested; and *(iii)* neither the insolvency proceedings in which the insolvency practitioner referred to in paragraph 1 of this Article has been appointed nor the proceedings in respect of which the stay is requested are subject to coordination under Section 2 of this Chapter. With regard to the latter proceedings only the group coordinator may request a stay (cf Art 72 (2) lit. e) EIR).

529  Q 36: Does the implementation of Section 1 of the newly introduced Chapter V, in particular the powers of the insolvency practitioner in proceedings concerning members of a group of companies under Art 60 EIR, in your view, have an impact in practice on the coordination of insolvency proceedings related to group members and, if so, in what respect?

– by means of joint agreements and protocols, the insolvency practitioners could determine some sort of hierarchy amongst them and the 'most powerful' insolvency practitioner according to this hierarchy would then make use of all the measures listed in Article 60 EIR (e.g. request the stay); in the absence of an agreed hierarchy, however, the powers enshrined in Article 60 EIR would, according to this view, be of little use since it would be too likely for a request to stay the proceedings (for instance) to be rejected;

– it will depend heavily on the interpretation of the relevant provisions by national courts, in particular the provision according to which a restructuring plan must have a *'reasonable chance of success'*.

## 3. Recommendations and guidelines

### 3.1 Recommendations

The provisions on cooperation and communication in group insolvency proceedings (Articles 56 ff EIR) are to a large extent congruent with the corresponding rules on coordination between main and secondary proceedings (Articles 41 ff EIR).[530] Although it is true that the group-specific rules differ in some aspects from those only concerning main and secondary proceedings,[531] the essential objective of the EIR's rules on cooperation and communication, namely to ensure the efficient administration of the insolvency estate,[532] remains the same. It seems, therefore, only reasonable that the concepts of communication, coordination, and cooperation should be interpreted and applied in a consistent manner.[533]

---

530 This has been a deliberate decision of the European legislator; cf recital 52, 2nd s..

531 Cf *Mangano*, in: Bork/Mangano (eds), European Cross-Border Insolvency Law (2016), para 8.35.

532 Cf recitals 48, 51 and 52, 1st s..

533 See *supra* Part 2, II. 3., Art 41 ff EIR. Moreover, recital 48 points out that 'best practices for cooperation in cross-border insolvency cases, as set out in principles and guidelines on communication and cooperation' should be taken into account by insolvency practitioners and courts. In this regard, mention must be made of the *'European Communication and Cooperation Guidelines for Cross-Border Insolvency'* of 2007 (often referred to as 'CoCo Guidelines'); of the *'Cross-Border Insolvency Court-to-Court Cooperation Principles and Guidelines'* of 2014 ('EU JudgeCo Principles') and of the *'Draft INSOL Europe Statement of Principles and Guidelines for Insolvency Office Holders in Europe'* of 2014, available at: www.tri-leiden.eu/publications/; cf also *supra* n 334.

One of the particular characteristics of the group-specific provisions in sec 1 of the new Chapter V (Articles 56 ff EIR) is that the duties of cooperation and communication within the group context are subject to a number of rather strict limits, most notably that the cooperation must be appropriate to facilitate the effective administration of the proceedings, that it has to be compatible with the rules applicable to the insolvency proceedings and may not entail any conflict of interest (cf Articles 56(1) and 57(1) EIR). These limits must be respected, but should in no way serve as an excuse for courts and insolvency practitioners which are reluctant to cooperate; therefore, these limits should be interpreted in a restrictive fashion. In particular, the requirement of compatibility with the applicable rules does not change the fact that, in principle, national insolvency law may not be construed as incompatible with the duties of cooperation and communication laid down in the EIR.[534]

Another intricate issue which might hamper efficient cooperation and communication in group insolvencies is the allocation of costs. Pursuant to Article 59 EIR, costs of cooperation and communication pursuant to Articles 56-60 EIR shall be regarded as costs and expenses incurred in the respective proceedings. In other words, each insolvency estate must bear its own costs resulting from the cooperation without being indemnified. This may lead to unfair results and is particularly problematic in cases where an individual group company incurs disproportionately high costs because it has to provide the information on most of the group's assets.[535] Article 59 EIR should, therefore, not be interpreted as a mandatory provision, but only as a default rule which can be overridden by agreements or protocols between the insolvency practitioners.[536] Such an interpretation is further supported by Article 56(2) EIR, which allows insolvency practi-

---

534  Cf *Hess/Koutsoukou*, in: Kronke/Melis/Kuhn (eds), Handbuch Internationales Wirtschaftsrecht, 2nd edn (2017), para 102; *Mangano*, in: Bork/Mangano (eds), European Cross-Border Insolvency Law (2016), para 8.49.

535  Cf e.g. *Madaus*, IILR 2015, 235, 240 who mentions the case of *Lehman Brothers Inc.* in which the Lehman Brothers UK subsidiary was in particular affected by information requests.

536  See *Hess/Koutsoukou*, in: Kronke/Melis/Kuhn (eds), Handbuch Internationales Wirtschaftsrecht, 2nd edn (2017), para 101; *Madaus*, IILR 2015, 235, 240; *Mangano*, in: Bork/Mangano (eds), European Cross-Border Insolvency Law (2016), para 8.51; *Tschentscher*, in: Braun, InsO, 7th edn (2017), Art 59, para 6; reluctant *J. Schmidt*, in: Bork/van Zwieten (eds), Commentary on the European Insolvency Regulation (2016), Art 59, para 59.05; *J. Schmidt*, in: Mankowski/

tioners to grant additional powers to a practitioner appointed in an insolvency proceeding of another member of the group and to allocate certain tasks amongst them, because such agreements would only be possible if insolvency practitioners are allowed to deviate from the strict cost allocation of Article 59 EIR.[537]

Outside the scope of group coordination proceedings, Article 60 EIR is the key provision for the coordination between main insolvency proceedings opened against two or more members of a corporate group. The interpretation of this provision will, therefore, be crucial for the efficient coordination of insolvencies relating to different group companies. Article 60 EIR subjects the rights and powers of the insolvency practitioner in proceedings concerning members of a group of companies to certain requirements. A rigid interpretation of these requirements might leave practically no room for the application of this provision. Consequently, the requirements laid down in Article 60 EIR should be interpreted in conformity with its purpose, i.e. to enable efficient coordination by establishing a non-hierarchical network in which a level playing field exists among the insolvency practitioners which should in turn yield the best solution for the whole group.[538]

It should generally be accepted that the reform does not stipulate a strict hierarchy between proceedings relating to different companies of a corporate group.[539] In a non-hierarchical network, it is more likely that the best solution for the whole group prevails.[540] However, the effectiveness of this approach seems to be significantly reduced by the fact that the insolvency practitioner of one group member is only granted very little influence in

---

Müller/Schmidt, EuInsVO 2015 (2016), Art 59, para 6; see also *Reinhart*, in: MüKoInsO, 3rd edn (2016), Art 59 EIR, para 2.

537 Similarly *Mangano*, in: Bork/Mangano (eds), European Cross-Border Insolvency Law (2016), para 8.51.

538 This applies in particular to the conditions that the plan must have a 'reasonable chance of success' and that it must be 'to the benefit of the creditors'. Cf *Hess/Koutsoukou*, in: Kronke/Melis/Kuhn (eds), Handbuch Internationales Wirtschaftsrecht, 2nd edn (2017), para 105; *Reinhart*, in: MüKoInsO, 3rd edn (2016), Art 60 EIR, paras 4 f; *Tschentscher*, in: Braun, InsO, 7th edn (2017), Art 60, paras 16 f.

539 Cf *Leandro*, Il Diritto dell'Unione Europea 2016, 215, 246.

540 See *Oberhammer*, in: Hess/Oberhammer/Pfeiffer (eds), Heidelberg-Luxembourg-Vienna Report (2014), paras 606 ff. *Bornemann* calls this assumption 'questionable', and argues in favour of coordination proceedings under the supervision of one coordinatior see, *Bornemann*, in: Wimmer/Bornemann/Lienau, Die Neufassung der EuInsVO (2016), paras 583 and 592 ff.

the proceedings concerning other group members.[541] In this context, the legislator failed to appreciate the full potential of this tool which could contribute much more to the efficient handling of international insolvencies of groups of companies. This becomes particularly evident when comparing the powers the main insolvency practitioner has in secondary proceedings with those the insolvency practitioner of one group member has in main proceedings concerning another group member. Such insolvency practitioners may, for instance, not propose a restructuring plan in the respective other proceedings or request their conversion into a more appropriate type of proceeding. Considering the requirements for a stay of the realisation of assets in insolvency proceedings concerning a group member (under Article 60(1) lit. b) EIR), it seems unlikely that the insolvency practitioner's power to request such a stay will provide an effective tool for coordination.[542]

Against this background, there will be a strong incentive for corporate groups to follow the practice that has already been applied under the old regime.[543] In these cases, main proceedings against the parent company (or another group company) and against all (or at least some) subsidiary companies are opened at the COMI of the parent company and, if necessary, secondary proceedings at the registered office of the respective subsidiary company. This group COMI approach[544] does, of course, require that the COMI of the parent and the subsidiary company coincide. Recital 53 explicitly acknowledges that the introduction of rules on the insolvency proceedings of groups of companies should not limit the possibility for a court to open insolvency proceedings for several companies belonging to the same group in a single jurisdiction if the court finds that the COMI of those companies is located in a single Member State. In such a scenario, it will also be easier to appoint a single insolvency practitioner for members

---

541 The original Commission proposal provided insolvency practitioners with significantly more extensive rights in proceedings concerning other members of the same group (cf Art 42d Commission proposal COM(2012) 744). For the critical discussion on this point following the proposal, cf *J. Schmidt*, in: Bork/van Zwieten (eds), Commentary on the European Insolvency Regulation (2016), Art 62, paras 61.01. Cf also *infra* n 568.
542 Cf *Esser*, Am. Bankr. Inst. J. March 2015, 38, 78; *Fehrenbach*, GPR 2017, 38, 49.
543 See *supra* n 488.
544 See *supra* Part 3, II. 1.2.1.

of the group, provided that a conflict of interests can be avoided.[545] Consequently, this approach, which was developed by practice under the EIR 2000, goes far beyond the group coordination tools under Articles 56 ff and 61 ff EIR.

## 3.2 Guidelines

*Guideline 6: National provisions on cooperation and communication*

Member States are advised to adopt rules on cooperation and communication with regard to domestic group insolvency proceedings corresponding to Articles 56-60 EIR. These rules should be interpreted in accordance with the provisions of the EIR.

*Guideline 7: Limits on cooperation and communication*

The limits on cooperation and communication, such as the requirement of compatibility with 'the rules applicable to such proceedings' included in Article 56 EIR, are to be interpreted in a very restrictive manner. In particular, national provisions may not be construed as incompatible with the duties of cooperation and communication, as these uniform law obligations generally override such national rules. Conflicts between said obligations and national provisions should always be resolved on the basis of an objective-oriented interpretation. In this context, national insolvency law can only prevent the application of cooperation obligations under the EIR where such cooperation is incompatible with achieving main objectives of these national proceedings.

*Guideline 8: Costs of cooperation and communication in proceedings concerning members of a group of companies*

Article 59 EIR should not be interpreted as a mandatory provision on the apportionment of costs. Insolvency practitioners should be allowed to deviate from this rule in insolvency protocols or agreements.

---

545 Cf recital 50; cf also *Bewick*, Int. Insolv. Rev 2015, 172, 184; *Reumers*, Int. Insolv. Rev. 2016, 225, 234 f.

*Guideline 9: Interpretation of Article 60 EIR*

9.1 Courts are advised to interpret powers and rights conferred on insolvency practitioners by Article 60 EIR in a broad fashion, consistent with the purpose of facilitating the efficient administration of group insolvency proceedings. In particular, there should be no disproportionate requirements as to the four conditions which must be fulfilled pursuant to Article 60(1) lit. b) EIR for the exercise of the right to request a stay of any measure related to the realisation of the assets.

9.2. When exercising their discretionary powers under Article 60(2), the courts should be guided by the objective of achieving the restructuring or an efficient sale of the group business as a whole. In particular, they should consider:

– the chance of success for the implementation of the restructuring plan;
– the chance of selling the group business as a whole;
– the interests of the creditors in the proceedings;
– the costs resulting from their decisions;
– the positions of the insolvency practitioners involved.

## IV. The new group coordination proceedings

### 1. Legal framework

The purpose of the new group coordination proceedings is supposedly to improve the coordination of (parallel) insolvency proceedings relating to different group members, to allow for a coordinated restructuring of the group, and, more generally, to ensure the efficiency of the coordination.[546] In achieving these goals, the impartial[547] group coordinator (cf Article 71 EIR) plays a key role. The procedure[548] consists of four parts: first, the opening stage following a request for the opening of group coordination proceedings filed by an insolvency practitioner appointed in insolvency proceedings related to a group member;[549] second, the decision opening group coordination proceedings which entails the appointment of a group coordinator (Article 68 EIR); third, coordination activities taken by the group coordinator, in particular the proposal of a group coordination plan setting out an integrated approach to the resolution of the group members' insolvencies (cf Article 72(1) lit. b) EIR); and fourth, the confirmation of (or decision on) the group coordinator's remuneration (Article 77 EIR).

Any court having jurisdiction over the insolvency of a member of the group has jurisdiction to decide on a request to open group coordination proceedings (Article 61(1) EIR).[550] In case of parallel requests, Article 62 EIR provides for a priority rule in favour of the court first seized. The court will then have to inform the insolvency practitioners of the group companies on the request and the proposed coordinator, but only if it is

---

546 Cf recital 54. The group coordination procedure should always strive to have a generally positive impact for the creditors (see recital 57).

547 Pursuant to Art 72(5) EIR, the group coordinator shall perform his/her duties impartially and with due care; for a thorough discussion see *Eble*, ZIP 2016, 1619, 1621.

548 Chapter V sec 2, on the one hand, contains uniform procedural rules, and on the other, refers to the *lex fori concursus* of the court before which a request to open group coordination proceedings is brought (see e.g. Arts 61(2); 69(1), (2) lit. b), and (4); 71(1); 72(2) lit. c); 74(1); and 77(5) EIR).

549 Such request shall, *inter alia*, propose a person to be nominated as group coordinator and an outline of the proposed group coordination (cf Art 61(3) EIR).

550 Until group coordination proceedings have been opened, two-thirds of all insolvency practitioners appointed in insolvency proceedings concerning a group member can, however, agree on a court that shall have exclusive jurisdiction (see Art 66 EIR).

satisfied that the conditions of Article 63(1) EIR are met. Article 63(1) EIR requires the court to be satisfied that *(a)* the opening of such proceedings is appropriate to facilitate the effective administration of the insolvency proceedings relating to the different group members, and *(b)* no creditor of any group member expected to participate in the proceedings is likely to be financially disadvantaged by the inclusion of that member in such proceedings.

The insolvency practitioners may, within thirty days after receipt of the court's notice, opt out of the group coordination proceedings (i.e. object to the inclusion of the respective proceedings) or object (only) to the person proposed as a coordinator (Article 64 EIR). If the insolvency practitioner of a group company opts out, the insolvency proceedings relating to that group member shall not be affected by the court's decision to open group coordination proceedings or by the group coordinator's powers (cf Article 65(2) EIR). This does, however, not exclude the possibility to opt in at a later point (pursuant to Article 69(1) lit. b) EIR). The group coordinator has the power to decide on the admissibility of such request to opt in. He/she has to consult all insolvency practitioners of group companies involved (cf Article 69(2) EIR) and grant the request if the criteria in Article 63(1) lit. a) and b) EIR mentioned above are fulfilled[551] or if all insolvency practitioners agree.[552]

The participating insolvency practitioners of group companies shall consider the group coordinator's recommendations and the group coordination plan. However, they are not obliged to follow them. If they decide against following them, they shall give reasons for their refusal to the group coordinator and, if applicable, to the competent body under the applicable *lex fori concursus* (cf Article 70(2) EIR).

The group coordinator has to be qualified to act as an insolvency practitioner '*under the law of a Member State*' and must not be one of the insolvency practitioners of a group company (Article 71 EIR). It is the group coordinator's duty to identify and outline recommendations for the coordinated conduct of the insolvency proceedings and to propose a group coor-

---

551  The coordinator's decision may be challenged before the court which has opened group coordination proceedings, Art 69(4) and recital 56 EIR.
552  For more details see *J. Schmidt*, in: Parry/Omar (eds), Banking and financial insolvencies: the EU regulatory framework (2016), 87 ff; *J. Schmidt*, ZVglRWiss 2017, 93 ff.

dination plan (Article 72(1) EIR).[553] Additionally, Article 72(2) EIR lists the group coordinator's powers. These powers, however, only extend to group members participating in the group coordination proceedings. The group coordinator's powers and rights under Article 72(2) EIR include: *(a)* the right to be heard and participate, in particular by attending creditors' meetings, in any of the proceedings in respect of any group member, *(d)* request information from any insolvency practitioner in respect of any member of the group,[554] and *(e)* the right to request a stay for a period of up to six months of the proceedings opened in respect of any member of the group.

Note that the group coordinator may not only request a suspension of the realisation of assets but a stay of the proceedings for up to six months. (Such request may, however, only be granted if a stay is 'necessary in order to ensure the proper implementation of the plan and would be to the benefit of the creditors in the proceedings for which the stay is requested'). Additionally, the group coordinator may mediate any dispute arising between two or more insolvency practitioners of group members (Article 72(2) lit. b) EIR).

There is an obvious risk that the advantages that group coordination proceedings could have in theory might not only be frustrated by the bureaucratic approach of the provisions outlined above, but also by the costs of those proceedings. The EIR contains provisions aiming at lowering that risk.[555] According to recital 58, the costs of the coordination and the share of those costs that each group member will bear are determined in accor-

---

553 Art 72(1) lit. b) EIR provides a list of what a coordination plan might contain, e.g. a proposal for *(i)* the measures to be taken in order to re-establish the economic performance and the financial soundness of the group or any part of it; *(ii)* the settlement of intra-group disputes as regards intra-group transactions and avoidance actions; *(iii)* agreements between the insolvency practitioners of the insolvent group members.

554 Provided that information is or might be of use when identifying and outlining strategies and measures in order to coordinate the proceedings. In this regard, it is important to note that the respective insolvency practitioner does not have to provide information if it is incompatible with the applicable *lex fori concursus* (cf Art 74(1) EIR).

555 See Art 61(3) lit. d) EIR requiring the requesting party to submit an outline of the estimated costs; Art 72(6) EIR according to which the group coordinator has to inform all participating insolvency practitioners and seek approval of the court opening coordination proceedings where the costs exceed 10% of the estimated costs; cf also recital 58.

dance with the law of the Member State in which group proceedings have been opened. A decision on costs by the court is only required if one of the participating insolvency practitioners objects to the final statement of costs and the share to be paid established by the group coordinator (Article 77(2) EIR). In addition, Article 77(3) EIR requires a request for a decision on costs by the objecting insolvency practitioner or the group coordinator. Article 77(5) EIR only refers to the following criteria for the court's cost decision: the share of costs each group member will bear should be '*adequate, proportionate and reasonable*'.[556] The cost decision may be challenged in accordance with the procedure set out under the law of the Member State where group coordination proceedings have been opened.

All this, however, does not change the fact that the new group coordination proceedings will actually cost time and money without having convincing advantages.[557] They obviously have been created for political reasons rather than on the basis of a thorough analysis of what could work in practice: the legislator rather wanted to create something 'new and great' with respect to groups of companies, and this was done on the basis of a very bureaucratic mindset. One can, however, not exclude that there will be future cases where clever lawyers will be able to use or abuse this new legal monstrosity in ways which are not foreseeable today.

## 2. Evaluation

In the light of the foregoing, Question 37 was included in the study's questionnaire.[558] Its last point, which referred to the newly introduced group coordination proceedings, also provided for a possibility to express individual thoughts and comments. The general impression appears to be rather sceptical towards the new coordination procedure. In summary, the concerns brought forward by the participants were that

---

556  Cf recital 58 and Art 77(4) EIR which refers to these criteria set out in Art 77(1) EIR.
557  Cf for our own critical assessment *infra* Part 3, IV. 3.1. and n 567 for further references.
558  Q 37: Does the adoption of group coordination proceedings, in your view, improve the coordination of (parallel) insolvency proceedings relating to different group members and the restructuring of corporate groups and, if so, why or why not?

- it was too complex and time-consuming;
- it was too formalistic and over-regulated;
- it was too expensive to be attractive;
- there were too many different conflicting interests, laws, judges, and practitioners involved;
- the mere voluntary basis of the proceedings on the one hand but also the opt-out procedure on the other hand might lead to the participation of a very passive insolvency practitioner that has no incentive to contribute;
- due to the considerably low level of actual powers of the group coordinator, the effectiveness of the new group coordination system could be questioned.

Several responses expressed the view that

- the proceedings, if used, would only be suitable for big groups of companies, where actual coordination is needed;
- it would depend to a large extent on the capacity and professionalism of the stakeholders involved;
- it will be decisive how it will be dealt with in practice.

## 3. Recommendations and guidelines

### 3.1 Recommendations

The reform adds group coordination proceedings as an additional instrument to the EIR's tool box for coordinating insolvency proceedings relating to different members of a corporate group.[559] However, these group coordination proceedings create a need for (additional) coordination, e.g. between group coordination proceedings and coordination measures taken by insolvency practitioners of group members not participating in group coordination proceedings. There is an obvious risk that group coordination proceedings will rather complicate than facilitate the coordination of (parallel) insolvency proceedings relating to different group members and re-

---

559 Cf recital 60; *Moss/Smith*, in: Moss/Fletcher/Isaacs (eds), The EU Regulation on Insolvency Proceedings, 3rd edn (2016), para 8.749; *J. Schmidt*, in: Bork/van Zwieten (eds), Commentary on the European Insolvency Regulation (2016), Art 61, para 61.08; *J. Schmidt*, in: Mankowski/Müller/Schmidt, EuInsVO 2015 (2016), Art 61, para 11; *Thole/Dueñas*, Int. Insolv. Rev. 2015, 214, 227.

structuring efforts. The coordinator's recommendations are not binding;[560] they merely have to be considered by the insolvency practitioners of group companies. Consequently, coordination and restructuring efforts proposed by the group coordinator can easily be blocked by insolvency practitioners of group companies. The right to request a stay according to Article 72(2) lit. e) EIR is the group coordinator's most powerful tool vis-à-vis the insolvency practitioners of group companies taking part in the coordination process. The success of such requests, however, depends on whether the court finds that the respective insolvency proceeding's creditors would benefit from a stay. If local creditors and stakeholders oppose the stay of the proceedings, the court might be inclined to dismiss the request. Nevertheless, this right might turn out to be advantageous for coordination purposes at least where courts, insolvency practitioners, and stakeholders respect the authority of the group coordinator.

In order to open group coordination proceedings, the court has to be satisfied that no creditor of any group member expected to participate in the proceedings is likely to be financially disadvantaged by the inclusion (Article 63(1) lit. b) EIR).[561] This threshold seems rather high. In addition, it is questionable on the basis of which comparison it has to be evaluated whether a creditor is likely to be financially disadvantaged. The fact that the value of the respective insolvency estate is reduced by the costs necessary for the coordination proceedings will, arguably, not as such suffice to deny the opening of group coordination proceedings. A different result might follow where the costs outweigh the advantages of group coordination proceedings. In general, the rule on costs and the question on how these costs are shared by the participating group members are likely to give rise to controversies in practice.[562]

The reform does not explicitly deal with the recognition of decisions rendered in group coordination proceedings. This may raise intricate ques-

---

560 Cf *Bornemann*, in: Wimmer/Bornemann/Lienau, Die Neufassung der EuInsVO (2016), para 525; *McCormack*, MLR 2016, 121, 144; *Thole/Dueñas*, Int. Insolv. Rev. 2015, 214, 227; *Vallender*, ZIP 2015, 1513, 1521.
561 Cf *Moss/Smith*, in: Moss/Fletcher/Isaacs (eds), The EU Regulation on Insolvency Proceedings, 3rd edn (2016), Art 63, para 8.777.
562 See Art 77 EIR; cf *Bornemann*, in: Wimmer/Bornemann/Lienau, Die Neufassung der EuInsVO (2016), para 645; *Cülter*, in: Braun, InsO, 7th edn (2017), Art 77, paras 6 f and 21; *Madaus*, IILR 2015, 235, 243; *McCormack*, MLR 2016, 121, 144; *Thole/Dueñas*, Int. Insolv. Rev. 2015, 214, 225; *Wimmer*, jurisPR-InsR 7/2015 Anm. 1, II 9 g) dd).

tions in case parallel requests for opening group coordination proceedings are filed before courts of different Member States and one of them opens group coordination proceedings in violation of the priority rule laid down in Article 62 EIR.[563] Arguably, Article 19 EIR applies by analogy.[564] This question is also relevant for determining the effects a decision dismissing a request for opening group coordination proceedings might have on requests before courts of other Member States.

We are not at all convinced that the new group coordination proceedings will turn out to be a significant success. This view is shared by many academics and practitioners who have already expressed concerns in this respect.[565] Moreover, such concerns have been echoed by the majority of the responses to the questionnaire of the project, highlighting that the group coordination proceedings only trigger additional costs, provide for complex bureaucratic procedures, and will most likely not be successful due to their non-binding nature.

We therefore suggest that future legislation should provide for additional measures in order to strengthen the coordination between insolvencies of group companies by improving tools of coordination between the insolvency practitioners in charge of the respective group companies. In this context, we refer to the initial proposal of the European Commission on the subject which already included much more far-reaching tools in this respect. We suggest that future amendments of the EIR should return to this concept. On this basis, measures such as the ones already drafted by the European Commission in the course of the revision of the EIR should be contemplated. Most importantly, the approach according to which all

---

563  A particular problem in this respect is that neither the notice pursuant to Article 63 EIR nor the actual opening of group coordination proceedings are explicitly qualified as 'mandatory information' that has to be made publicly available according to Article 24 EIR; cf *J. Schmidt*, in: Mankowski/Müller/Schmidt, EuInsVO 2015 (2016), Art 62, paras 8 ff; *J. Schmidt*, in: Bork/van Zwieten (eds), Commentary on the European Insolvency Regulation (2016), Art 62, para 62.06.

564  Contra: *Thole/Dueñas*, Int. Insolv. Rev. 2015, 214, 226.

565  See, *inter alia, Bewick*, Int. Insolv. Rev. 2015, 172, 187; *Cohen/Dammann/Sax*, IILR 2015, 117, 120 f; *Epeoglou*, UCL Journal of Law and Jurisprudence 2017, 31, 50 ff; *Hess/Koutsoukou*, in: Kronke/Melis/Kuhn (eds), Handbuch Internationales Wirtschaftsrecht, 2nd edn (2017), para 109; *Fehrenbach*, GPR 2017, 38, 49; *Kindler/Sakka*, EuZW 2015, 460, 466; *McCormack*, MLR 2016, 121, 143 f; *Thole/Dueñas*, Int. Insolv. Rev. 2015, 214, 218 ff; *Van Galen*, ERA Forum 2015, 251 ff; *Weiss*, Int. Insolv. Rev. 2015, 192, 212.

relevant insolvency practitioners should, in principle, have the right to be heard, to request a stay of any measure related to the realisation of assets in proceedings concerning other group members, and to propose a reorganisation plan in a way which would enable the respective creditors' committee or court to take a decision on it.[566] Accordingly, future legislation in this field should aim at developing the rules laid down in Articles 56 ff EIR, while the group coordination proceedings under Article 61 ff EIR are probably simply a legislative dead end.

In addition, we believe that the effects of the very narrow prerequisites for '*undertakings*' according to Article 36 EIR and their effects in practice should be closely examined after the coming into force of the revised EIR. If it turns out that these requirements are too strict and the new mechanism has, therefore, no sufficient actual effect in practice, the wording of said provision should be reconsidered.

Finally, the expectation that the new group coordination proceedings might turn out to be a failure in practice leads us to the conclusion that courts and practitioners should engage in the further development of other coordination mechanisms including, but not limited to, the ones outlined above.[567]

## 3.2 Guidelines

*Guideline 10: Recommendation of ex ante arrangements between insolvency practitioners*

In light of the voluntary nature of group coordination proceedings, the insolvency practitioners involved are advised to seek agreement on the general course of the proceedings, the allocation of the proposed costs, and, most importantly, on the question who the coordinator should be before initiating coordination proceedings. They should treat the coordination

---

566  Cf Art 42d of the original Commission proposal, COM(2012) 744. See also, for the initial approach, the explanatory memorandum attached to the Commission proposal, COM(2012) 744, p 9: 'These procedural tools enable the liquidator which has the biggest interest in the successful restructuring of all companies concerned to officially submit his reorganisation plan in the proceedings concerning a group member, even if the liquidator in these proceedings is unwilling to cooperate or is opposed to the plan'.

567  See *supra* Part 3, III 3.1.

proceedings as just one option of cooperation, they should reflect whether the costs of the coordination proceedings are justified in the light of their limited advantages, and they should examine whether cooperation without such proceedings is more appropriate in the specific case.

*Guideline 11: Eligibility requirements for the coordinator*

Courts should only appoint very well-respected insolvency practitioners with broad international experience who, in particular, enjoy the trust of all practitioners involved.

## V. Conflict of laws

### 1. Legal framework

Insolvencies of groups of companies can also raise intricate conflict of laws issues regarding the scope of application of the *lex fori concursus* and the *lex societatis*.[568] The question becomes, for instance, relevant where the presumption under Article 3 EIR is rebutted and, therefore, the COMI of a (group) company is not located at the respective company's registered office. This can lead to a divergence between the applicable company law and the applicable insolvency law (under Article 7 EIR). In insolvency proceedings relating to members of a group of companies, the relationship between company and insolvency law is, for example, relevant for the following issues: the liability of managing directors[569] or shareholders[570] of a (group) company, the subordination of shareholder loans, the piercing of the corporate veil, the automatic extension of the company's insolvency to its shareholders (as provided in some legal systems), and the effects a restructuring (or reorganisation) plan might have on the legal regime of the entity, e.g. by modifying its organisational, financial, or capital structure.

The reform does not specifically address the *lex fori concursus/lex societatis*-delineation issue. However, from a jurisdictional perspective Article 6(2) EIR aims to safeguard procedural economy by avoiding split-jurisdic-

---

568  For the difficult demarcation between the applicable insolvency and company law see generally, e.g., *Eckert*, Internationales Gesellschaftsrecht (2010), 219 ff; *Eidenmüller*, RabelsZ 2006, 474; *Gerner-Beuerle/Schuster*, JCLS 2014, 287, 305 ff; *Haas/Vogel*, NZG 2011, 457; *Kolmann/Keller*, in: Gottwald (ed), Insolvenzrechtshandbuch, 5th edn (2015), § 133 paras 112 ff; *Pannen/Riedemann*, in: Pannen (ed), European Insolvency Regulation (2007), Art 4, paras 15 ff; *Thole*, Gläubigerschutz durch Insolvenzrecht (2010), 819 f; *Virgós/Garcimartín*, The European Insolvency Regulation: Law and practice (2004), paras 129 ff, all with many further references.

569  See, e.g., *Oberlandesgericht Wien*, 18 April 2008, 4 R 20/08b, ZIK 2009, 67 regarding actions for damages under Austrian law (§§ 25, 81 ff Austrian GmbHG) against the managing directors; cf also *infra* Part 3, V. 2.1. for CJEU, 10 December 2015, Case C-594/14, *Kornhaas*, ECLI:EU:C:2015:806.

570  For instance in veil-piercing cases or with respect to claims for the reimbursement of payments made on shareholders' loans.

tion caused by the jurisdictional characterisation of actions at the 'intersection' of company, insolvency, and general civil law.[571]

## 2. Recommendations and guidelines

### 2.1 Recommendations

Both corporate law relating to insolvencies and insolvency law relating to corporations are diverse to a very large extent in Europe today.[572] Therefore, it seems almost impossible to achieve an approximation of laws or even uniform law in the near future.[573] Presently, the EIR does not even contain provisions on conflicts of law issues relating to claims under corporate law. It would be very helpful if future legislation were to create such uniform rules.

We do, however, believe that such rules should not be drafted 'out of the blue'. Since the enactment of the original EIR, the CJEU has rendered a wealth of case-law relating to the delineation between the Brussels Regulation and the EIR. Since the CJEU's judgment in the *Seagon/Deko Marty Belgium* case, this case-law does not only serve as the basis for said delineation, but is also the basis for cases where the courts of the Member State within the territory of which insolvency proceedings have been opened have exclusive jurisdiction for insolvency-related matters according to Article 6 EIR.[574] We have reviewed the case-law relating to said delineation, that is, the definition of the wording 'action which derived directly from the insolvency proceedings and is closely linked with them' (see Article 6(1) and Article 32(1) subpara 2 EIR). We believe that the

---

571 For a detailed discussion see *Laukemann,* in: Hess/Oberhammer/Pfeiffer (eds), Heidelberg-Luxembourg-Vienna Report (2014), paras 542 ff and para 564.

572 For a comparative analysis of substantive insolvency law in the EU countries cf *McCormack/Keay/Brown,* European Insolvency Law: Reform and Harmonization (2017).

573 However, the recent 'Proposal for a Directive of the European Parliament and of the Council on preventive restructuring frameworks, second chance and measures to increase the efficiency of restructuring, insolvency and discharge procedures and amending Directive 2012/30/EU' (COM/2016/0723 final – 2016/0359 [COD]) can be seen as a first step towards greater harmonization.

574 For a critical evaluation of this novelty cf *Albrecht,* ZInsO 2015, 1077, 1080; *Mankowski,* in: Mankowski/Müller/Schmidt, EuInsVO 2015 (2016), Art 6, paras 3 ff; *Thole,* ZEuP 2014, 39, 59; *Wimmer,* jurisPR-InsR 7/2015 Anm. 1 II 5.

principles developed by the CJEU in all these cases (with the exception of the infamous *SCT Industri* case[575]) could also serve as the basis of a conflict of laws rule.

In its much-discussed *Kornhaas* decision,[576] the CJEU has adopted a similar approach. The court referred to its earlier judgment in *H.*[577] where it had held that a national provision, such as the first sentence of sec 64(2) of the German Law on limited liability companies ('GmbHG'), under which the managing director of an insolvent company must reimburse the payments which he/she made on behalf of that company after it had become insolvent, derogates from the common rules of civil and commercial law because of the insolvency of that company. From this, the Court inferred that an action based on this provision and brought in the context of insolvency proceedings is an action deriving directly from insolvency proceedings and closely connected with them. Following up on this characterisation of sec 64(2) of the GmbHG as being covered by insolvency law, the Court held in the *Kornhaas* decision that sec 64(2) of the GmbHG must be regarded as being covered by the law applicable to insolvency proceedings and their effects within the meaning of Article 4(1) of Regulation No 1346/2000. In other words, the CJEU applied a test to delineate the scope of application of the *lex fori concursus* and *the lex societatis* which resembles the *Gourdain/Nadler* formula (now incorporated in Article 6(1) EIR). This is reinforced by the Court's argument that sec 64(2) of the GmbHG falls within the scope of Article 4 of Regulation No 1346/2000 because it 'contributes to the attainment of an objective which is intrinsically linked, mutatis mutandis, to all insolvency proceedings, namely the prevention of any reduction of the assets of the insolvent estate before the insolvency proceedings are opened, so that the claims of all the

---

575 See judgment in CJEU, 2 July 2009, Case C-111/08, *SCT Industri*, ECLI:EU:C:2009:419; for critical comments see *Mankowski*, NZI 2009, 571; *Oberhammer*, IPRax 2010, 317.

576 See judgment in CJEU, 10 December 2015, Case C-594/14, *Kornhaas*, ECLI:EU:C:2015:806; see also *Böcker*, DZWIR 2016, 180; *Kindler*, EuZW 2016, 136; *Mankowski*, NZG 2016, 281; *Schall*, ZIP 2016, 289; *Ringe*, JZ 2016, 573; *Wessels*, ECL 2016, 82.

577 See judgment in CJEU, 4 December 2014, Case C-295/13, *H*, EU:C:2014:2410, para 23, EuZW 2015, 141 annotated by *Kindler*; see also *Magnus*, LMK 2015, 366550; *Trenker*, ZIK 2015, 8.

company's creditors may be satisfied on equal terms'.[578] We believe that this approach to this conflicts of law issue would not only dramatically clarify the legal situation, but could also improve coordination of insolvency proceedings of groups of companies.

## 2.2 Guideline

*Guideline 12: Applicable law*

Courts are advised to apply the *lex fori concursus* to all claims which derive directly from the insolvency proceedings and are closely linked with them. In this context, the interpretation of this notion should be based on the CJEU's case law with respect to the '*Gourdain/Nadler*-formula'.

---

578 CJEU, 10 December 2015, Case C-594/14, *Kornhaas*, ECLI:EU:C:2015:806, para 20.

# Annex: Expert Contributions

Annex I: Interpreting and amending Annex A to Regulation 848/2015

Avv. Giorgio Corno[*]

1. Insolvency proceedings which fall within the scope Annex A of Regulation 848/2015

Regulation 848/2015 (hereinafter: 'EIR') applies to insolvency proceedings relating to debtors who perform activities different from those mentioned in Article 1(2) EIR, and whose COMI or establishment is located in Member States (apart from Denmark).

Given a great variety of different existing procedures in the Member States, the European Commission provides universal recognition to insolvency proceedings listed in Annex A,[1] whereas no recognition is granted to insolvency proceedings not listed in Annex A, even if they fall within the scope of the Regulation, as defined by Article 1(1) EIR.

When a new insolvency proceeding approved by a Member State meets the scope of the said Regulation, as defined in Article 1(1) EIR, an amendment to Annex A may be adopted by the European Parliament and the Council according to the ordinary legislative proceeding set forth in Article 294 TFEU, reacting to the initiative of a Member State notifying a substantial reform of its domestic law. Specifically, it has to be clarified if proceedings proposed for inclusion are full or interim proceedings;[2] are collective;[3] public;[4] based on laws on insolvency;[5] fall under Article 1(1) lit. a), b) and c) EIR; may be commenced, in situations where there is only a likelihood of insolvency, for the purpose to avoid the debtor's insolvency or the cessation of the debtor's business activities;[6] or in situations where

---

[*] The author sincerely thanks *Stefania Bariatti* and *Antonio Leandro* for their constructive comments on this paper. Any errors are its own.
1 As expressed within Regulation 848/2015 by Art 1(1), last paragraph; Art 2(1) and recital 9 EIR.
2 As defined in recital 15 EIR.
3 As defined in Art 2(1) EIR.
4 As defined in recital 12 EIR.
5 As defined in recital 16 EIR.
6 Art 1(1), subpara 2 EIR.

there is insolvency, for the purpose of rescue, adjustment of debt, reorganization or liquidation.[7]

Regulation 848/2015 does not clarify if an amendment to Annex A is admissible if only some of the now mentioned conditions are met.[8]No amendment of the said Annex A appears to be required for insolvency proceedings of a Member State which are not listed but may be qualified – according to the laws of the interested Member State – as a sub-category of proceedings that are already listed within the said Annex A.

The scope of this contribution is to show the problems which may arise in the interpretation of Annex A as well as in the amendment process of Annex A, having regard to Italian law.[9]

## 2. Italian insolvency proceedings which fall within the scope of Regulation 848/2015

Annex A of Regulation 848/2015 lists the following Italian insolvency proceedings: *fallimento, concordato preventivo, liquidazione coatta amministrativa, amministrazione straordinaria, accordi di ristrutturazione, procedure di composizione della crisi da sovra indebitamento del consumatore (accordo o piano)*, and *liquidazione dei beni*.

Other proceedings related to those now mentioned are provided for by certain provisions of Royal Decree 267/1942 and subsequent amendments (hereinafter: 'Italian Insolvency Act'): *(i)* Article 161(VI) co. of the Italian Insolvency Act (so-called *concordato in bianco*);[10] *(ii)* Article 182[bis](VI)

---

7 Art 1(1) EIR.
8 As we will see in this article with regard to *convenzione di moratoria* under Article 182[septies](V) – (VII) of the Italian Insolvency Act.
9 This contribution refers only to certain Italian insolvency proceedings. Specifically, it does not refer to the following inoslvency proceedings: *liquidazione coatta amministrativa, amministrazione straordinaria, accordi di ristrutturazione, procedure di composizione della crisi da sovra indebitamento del consumatore (accordo o piano), e liquidazione dei beni*; as well as to any related sub proceedings.
10 In order to anticipate the effects of filing of the application for *concordato preventivo*, Art 161(VI) co. LF allows a debtor facing a financial crisis to submit to the court an application to open the *concordato preventivo* proceeding together with (only) just the financial statements of the past three years and a detailed list of his creditors, reserving to himself the right to submit, within the term set out by the court: *(i)* a *concordato preventivo* proposal together with the aforementioned documents and the plan which grounds the proposal; and *(ii)* a request for certification of a restructuring agreement according to Art 182[bis] of the Italian Bankruptcy Act.

co. of the Italian Insolvency Act (so-called *procedura di moratoria preventiva*);[11] *(iii)* Article 186[bis] of the Italian Insolvency Act (so-called *concordato preventivo con continuità aziendale*);[12] *(iv)* Articles 182 and 185 of the Italian Insolvency Act (*esecuzione del concordato preventivo*, ie. esecuzione del *concordato preventivo*[13]); *(v)* Article 182[septies] of the Italian Insolvency Act (so-called *accordi di ristrutturazione con banche e inter-*

---

Upon such an application, the court assigns the debtor the required term or a shorter one in order to submit the applications. The court may appoint a judicial commissioner
and must impose on the debtor a duty to file detailed information, on a monthly basis, on the financial status and management of the enterprise, to be filed by the court's clerk in the registry of the enterprises. If the debtor fails to meet this information obligation, the court may close the procedure. If the report shows that the debtor's activity is not adequately directed to the future submission of the proposal, the court may reduce the term. Filing of a *concordato preventivo* produces the procedural effects as well as the substantive effects of a full application of a *concordato preventivo* proceeding, among which as a *stay* of enforcement claims and a limitation of debtor's powers with regard to acts exceeding the ordinary course of business.

11  According to Art 182[bis](VI)-(VII) co. LF, the debtor may apply to the court for a prohibition regarding the commencement or continuation of precautionary or enforcement actions prior to the filing of a request for rectification of an *accordo di ristrutturazione* according to Art 182[bis] LF. To that extent, the debtor needs to file, together with the application: *(i)* the documentation described by Art 161, first paragraph, letters a, b, c, d, regarding his detailed economic and financial situation; *(ii)* a self-certification that an agreement is being negotiated with creditors representing at least 60 percent of the entrepreneur's debt (usually represented by financial institutions or large suppliers); and *(iii)* a report from a professional regarding the agreement's suitability to ensure full payment of creditors who do not take part in negotiations. In this case, the court sets a hearing within 30 days from filing of the request and verifies that all the aforementioned requirements are met. If so, it gives the debtor another 60 days to file the restructuring agreement.

12  According to Art 186[bis] LF, a debtor facing a financial crisis (stato di crisi) may propose a preventive agreement (*concordato preventivo*) to its creditors based on a plan which provides for the continuation of the business by the debtor himself or through sale or division of the company. Should this be the case, the debtor needs to attach to the plan an analytical indication of the costs and revenues expected from the continuation of the business, the necessary financial resources and how to cover the aforementioned costs; as well as a report from an expert as described in Art 161, third paragraph of Italian Bankruptcy Act, who states that the proposal is functional to the best satisfaction of creditors.

13  As soon as the *concordato preventivo* proposed by the debtor, approved by any affected creditors, is verified by the court, the plan which grounds the agreement needs to be performed, in order to satisfy the obligations towards creditors con-

*mediari finanziari*).[14] Proceedings listed under *(i)* and *(ii)* above may be qualified as interim insolvency proceedings;[15] proceeding mentioned under *(iii)* above may be qualified as pre-insolvency proceedings; proceedings listed under *(iv)* above may be qualified as full proceedings; and proceeding mentioned under *(v)* may be qualified as hybrid proceedings.

Furthermore, Article 182septies(VI)–(VIII) co. of the Italian Insolvency Act (so-called *convenzione di moratoria con banche e intermediari finanziari*) rules on a provisional moratorium agreement between the debtor and banks or financial institutions holding of at least 75 percent of debts to banks and financial institutions, which is effective also against non-assenting banks and financial institutions. As this effect overcomes non assenting creditors legitimate expectations with respect to the dispute resolution forum and applicable law, Article 182septies of Italian Insolvency Act entitles them to file an opposition against the said *convenzione di moratoria* based on specific grounds.[16]

The said proceedings and agreements are not listed in Annex A, but meet all or some of the requirements mentioned in Article 1(1) EIR. Specifically they: *(i)* are all based on Italian Insolvency Law, which provides rules for *fallimento* (bankruptcy), *concordato preventive* (agreement with creditors), and *liquidazione coatta amministrativa* (mandatory administrative liquidation). Italian Insolvency Law relates to insolvency and

---

tained therein within the time frames of the plan. The debtor performs any required action unless the plan offered the assignment of the debtor's assets, where the insolvency court, upon verification of the *concordato preventive*, appoints a *liquidatore giudiziale* (judicial liquidator) which disposes of the debtor's assets, sells them and collects claims and distributes the proceeds among creditors under the supervision of the judicial commissioner. Both the debtor and the *liquidatore giudiziale* operate according to the instructions issued by the court within the verification decree and, when required, subject to the previous authorization of the appointed creditors' committee. The deputy judge plays a very limited role during the performance of a *concordato preventivo*.

14 According to Art 182septies LF, the debtor may agree with banks and financial institutions owning at least half of the overall debt aimed for its restructuring. If such agreement is approved by banks and financial institutions representing at least of 75% of the overall debt against them, dissenting banks and financial institutions are bound to the agreement, if certain conditions have been met. These proceedings have been inspired by English Schemes of Arrangements and meet with the latter certain conditions.

15 In line with recital 15.

16 The content of this proceeding is described in chapter 4 of this article.

has been designed exclusively for insolvency situations (in accordance with recital 16); *(ii)* take place in situations where the debtor faces insolvency or likelihood of insolvency;[17] and, specifically, aim at debtor's rescue, adjustment of debt, reorganisation and liquidation of its assets, in case of insolvency; or at avoiding the debtor's insolvency or the cessation of the debtor's business activities, in case of likelihood of insolvency; *(iii)* are 'collective' according to the meaning of Article 2(1) EIR. Specifically, *concordato in bianco, procedura di moratoria preventivo, concordato preventivo con continuità aziendale* and *esecuzione del concordato preventivo* include all debtor's creditors; whereas *convenzioni di moratoria* and *accordi di ristrutturazione con banche e intermediari finanziari* require the consent of a significant part of a debtor's creditors[18] and do not affect the claims of creditors which are not involved in them; *(iv)* proceedings regulated by *(a)* Article 161(VI) co. of the Italian Insolvency Act (so-called *concordato in bianco*); *(b)* Article 182^bis(VI) co. of the Italian Insolvency Act (so-called *procedura di moratoria preventiva*); *(c)* Article 186^bis of the Italian Insolvency Act (so-called *concordato preventivo con continuità aziendale*); *(d)* Article 182^septies of the Italian Insolvency Act (so-called *accordi di ristrutturazione con banche e intermediari finanziari*) and (e) Articles 182 and 185 of the Italian Insolvency Act (*esecuzione del concordato preventivo*) are subject to publicity and, therefore, 'public' in order to allow creditors to become aware of them and to lodge their claims; and to give creditors the opportunity to challenge the jurisdiction of the court which has opened the proceedings, in accordance with recital 12.[19]

A temporary stay of individual enforcement proceedings may be granted by a court (*procedura di moratoria preventiva*) in order to allow for negotiations between the debtor and its creditors. The proceedings in which such stay is granted provide for suitable measures to protect the general body of creditors, and, where no agreement is reached, these proceedings are preliminary to one of the proceedings referred to in point (a) or (b) of Article 1(1) EIR and, specifically, to a *fallimento*, a *concordato preventivo* or to an *accordi di ristrutturazione* proceeding.

---

17  The so-called a stato di crisi, which, according to Art 161 of the Italian Insolvency Act, includes stato di insolvenza.

18  Equal to at least 75% of the claims of banks and financial creditors.

19  The application of this requirement to *Convenzioni di moratoria* is discussed in chapter 4 of this article.

Some of the said proceedings (*concordato in bianco*; *concordato preventivo con continuità aziendale; esecuzione del concordato preventivo*) meet either the conditions of Article 1(1) lit. a) EIR – as they partially divest debtor of its assets, leaving him partially in possession of the said assets, as defined by Article 2(3) EIR; and provide for the appointment an insolvency practitioner, as defined by Article 2(5) EIR and listed in Annex B – or of Article 1(1) lit. b) EIR, as they make the assets and affairs of a debtor subject to control or supervision by a court, as defined by Article 2(6) lit. i) EIR.

Others (*concordato in bianco* and *procedura di moratoria preventiva*) meet the conditions of Article 1(1) lit. c) EIR, as they are opened and conducted for a certain period of time on an interim or provisional basis, before a court issues an order confirming the continuation of the proceedings on a non-interim basis (in accordance with *recital 15*).

This said Italian non-listed insolvency proceedings fall, either wholly or partially, within the scope of Regulation 848/2015, as described in Article 1 EIR;[20] and may, therefore, be qualified as 'insolvency proceedings', for the purpose of the said Regulation. Some concerns will be later expressed only for *convenzioni di moratoria*.

3. Italian proceedings which may be included or qualified as a sub-category of insolvency proceedings listed in Annex A

Given the EIR's relevance for the inclusion of a Member State's insolvency proceeding within Annex A, it needs to be considered whether the above mentioned Italian non-listed insolvency proceedings may be included in those already listed or need to be listed in Annex A, following the above mentioned legislative proceeding.

---

20 This conclusion does not apply to the proceeding mentioned in Art 15(8) of the Italian Insolvency Act, which allows the court, upon request of an interested party, to order precautionary or protective measures to safeguard the assets or the business subject to the order. Among these measures, the bankruptcy court could appoint a provisional liquidator who could act in accordance with what provided by recital 36 and of Art 52 EIR. However, I do not think that the proceeding under Art 15(8) of the Italian Insolvency Act could be qualified as an insolvency proceeding for the purposes of Regulation 848/2015 as it is neither collective, nor public, nor it meets the conditions under Art 1(1) EIR and, among them, the one under Art 1(1) lit. c) EIR.

Such listing is not required if the said proceedings are or may be qualified as sub-proceedings of the ones already listed in Annex A of EIR. Such scrutiny needs to be made based on Italian law, applicable to them according to Articles 7 and 35 EIR.

Based on this scrutiny, I think that the majority of the above mentioned Italian non-listed proceedings do not need an amendment of Annex A. Specifically, based on Italian court precedents and literature: *(i)* proceedings under Article 161(VI) co. of the Italian Insolvency Act (c.d. *procedura di concordato in bianco*),[21] Article 186[bis] of the Italian Insolvency Act (*concordato preventivo in continuità aziendale*)[22] and Articles 182 and 185 of the Italian Insolvency Act (*esecuzione del concordato preventivo*[23]) may be qualified as *concordato preventivo* proceedings; *(ii)* provisional proceedings under Article 182[bis](VI) co. of the Italian Insolvency Act (c.d. *procedura di moratoria preventiva*)[24] and under Article 182[septies] of the Italian Insolvency Act (*accordi di ristrutturazione con banche e intermediari finanziari*)[25] may be considered as sub-proceedings of *accordi di ristrutturazione dei debiti* proceedings.

This explains why the above mentioned proceedings have not been listed in Annex A by the Italian government during the preparation of Regulation 848/2015.

Therefore, I think that no amendment of Annex A of Regulation 848/2015 is required for Italian insolvency proceedings which fall under Article 161(VI) co. of the Italian Insolvency Act (c.d. *procedura di concordato in bianco*); under Article 186[bis] of the Italian Insolvency Act (*concordato preventivo in continuità aziendale*); under Article 182[bis](VI) co. of the Italian Insolvency Act (c.d. *procedura di moratoria preventiva*); under

---

21  *Corte Suprema di Cassazione*, 31 March 2016, n 6277; *Corte Suprema di Cassazione*, 14 March 2016, n 4977; *Corte Suprema di Cassazione*, 14 January 2015, n 495. Such interpretation conforms to the one of *Tribunale di Reggio Emilia*, 6 March 2013, confirmed by *Corte di Appello di Bologna*, 25 June 2013, both available at: www.ilcaso.it. Against such interpretation see *Corte di Appello di Firenze*, 27 June 2016.

22  *Corte di Appello di Firenze*, 31 August 2015, available at: www.ilcaso.it.

23  *Fabiani*, Fallimento e concordato preventivo, Bologna, 2014, p 646.

24  *Corte di Appello di Milano*, 17 January 2013, available at: www.ilcaso.it. On this topic see, as well, among others *Fabiani*, Fall. 2010, 904 ff; *Didone*, Il dir. fallim. 2011, 23 ff.

25  Art 182[septies]1 LF expressly confirms that the rules therein complete the rules of *accordi di ristrutturazione del debito* under Art 182[bis] LF.

Articles 182 and 185 (*esecuzione del concordato preventivo*) and under Article 182septies of the Italian Insolvency Act (*accordi di ristrutturazione con banche e intermediari finanziari*).[26]

4. Does 'convenzione di moratoria' fall within the scope of insolvency proceedings as defined in Article 1(1) Regulation 848/2015?

Different issues raises the so-called *convenzioni di moratoria* governed by Article 182septies(V) co. ff of the Italian Insolvency Act, according to which the debtor and banks or financial institutions holding of at least 75 percent of debts to banks and financial institutions may agree on a provisional moratorium. Where a professional who meets the conditions of competence and independence set by Article 67(3) lit. d) of the Italian Insolvency Act certifies that the legal positions and economic interests among agreeing creditors are the same, such moratorium agreement (so-called *convenzione di moratoria*) is binding for assenting as well as for non-assenting banks and financial creditors, subject to information about negotiations to non-assenting creditors and their allowance to take part in *bona fide* to negotiations.

Article 182septies of the Italian Insolvency Act has been approved with Law Decree on 27th June 2015, no 83, converted into law on 6th August 2015, no 132, and, therefore, following publication of Regulation 848/2015 on the Official Journal of the European Union. Therefore, it has to be considered whether it may be qualified as an insolvency proceeding which falls within the scope of Article 1 EIR; and, if affirmative, whether it is eligible for the inclusion in Annex A.

*Convenzione di moratoria* meets only certain conditions set by Article 1 EIR. Specifically, it is: *(i)* effective – also for non-assenting banks and financial institutions, by operation of law – for a duration agreed between the parties, which makes it provisional; *(ii)* functional to negotiations with banks and financial institutions only[27] – who usually represent a significant part of creditors and are involved in negotiations and impaired by

---

26  *De Cesari*, Il Fall. 2015, 1033 ff agrees on this interpretation.

27  A Parliamentary committee, (so-called *Commissione Rordorf*), established with ministerial decree of the Italian ministry of justice on 28th January 2015, submitted to the Italian Parliament, in March 2016, a reform project of the insolvency procedures regulations. Among the proposed reforms, the (not yet in force) project provides for the extension of *convenzioni di moratoria to creditors*, even different

them (according to Article 2(1) EIR) – whereas it does not affect claims of other creditors not involved in negotiations. This allows to consider the negotiation proceeding for a *convenzione di moratoria* collective, according to Article 2(1) EIR; *(iii)* based on laws relating to insolvency, in accordance with Article 1(1) EIR; *(iv)* usually negotiated and executed in a situation where there is only a likelihood of insolvency, for the purpose of avoiding debtor's insolvency or the cessation of the debtor's business activities and rescuing the debtor, in line with Article 1(1), subpara 2 EIR. Such *convenzione di moratoria* grants a moratorium – inclusive of a temporary stay of individual enforcement proceedings – on claims by non-assenting creditors by operation of law, in order to facilitate negotiations between the debtor and its (financial) creditors, in the interest of debtor and protects the general body of creditors, in line with Article 1(1) lit. c) EIR. Non-assenting banks and financial institutions, based in the Member State where the *convenzione di moratoria* is negotiated and abroad, are bound by the moratoria as soon as they receive the notice of its execution. Non-assenting banks and financial institutions are granted suitable measures for the protection of their interests, and, specifically, may file an appeal to the competent court in order to make the *convenzione di moratoria* ineffective vis-à-vis themselves. It is not clear whether foreign non-assenting banks and financial institutions are bound by the said *convenzione di moratoria* irrespective of the law governing their claims and irrespective of the 'regular' (agreed) forum for an adversarial dispute resolution.

From a different perspective, however: *(i)* banks and financial institution – inclusive of those who will oppose to it – are made aware about commencement of negotiations for a *convenzione di moratoria* and are allowed to take part in negotiations *in bona fide*. However, negotiations are

---

from banks and financial intermediaries, representing at least seventy-five percent of debts belonging to one or more categories, whose legal positions and economic interests are the same, if they are part of negotiations and reserved their right to oppose to their verification in case of fraud, non-truthfulness of the data, non-performability of the agreement or possibility of more satisfying alternative solutions. Such provision has also been included in the proposal of law for the empowerment of the Italian government to reform existing insolvency regulations (*Delegation to the Italian Government for the reform of the rules on distressed enterprises and insolvency as resulting from removal of articole 15 from the law proposal no 3671, resolved by the assembly on 18th May 2016*), recently (February 2017) approved by the Italian *Camera dei Deputati* and currently (July 2017) under exam of the Italian *Senato della Republica*.

conducted on a confidential basis, without a court order, so as to minimize publicity, that may adversely impact on business continuity and decrease the business value; *(ii)* a *convenzione di moratoria* does not provide for a judgment opening an insolvency proceeding or a confirmation of such opening; as well as the appointment of an insolvency practitioner. Therefore, no judgment opening the proceeding according to Article 2(7) EIR may be published in accordance with Article 24 EIR; *(iii)* a *convenzione di moratoria* does not preclude an out of court agreement based on a certified plan (so-called *piano attestato*) according to Article 67 of the Italian Insolvency Act;[28] as well a restructuring agreement under Article 182septies of the Italian Insolvency Act with banks and financial institutions (so-called *accordo di ristrutturazione con banche e intermediari finanziari*) and, in general, under Article 182bis of the Italian Insolvency Act to be verified within an insolvency proceeding (so-called *accordi di ristrutturazione dei debiti*); as well as an agreement reached within a *concordato preventivo* proceeding; and, finally, any other Italian insolvency proceedings listed in Annex A of the EIR.

### 5. Effects of a 'convenzione di moratoria' on foreign dissenting banks and financial institutions

Based on the above arguments, it may be questioned whether *convenzioni di moratoria* are insolvency proceedings according to the said Article 1(1) EIR and, therefore, whether they are eligible for the inclusion in Annex A of Regulation 848/2015.

As above mentioned, Article 182septies(V) co. and ff of the Italian Insolvency Act, if certain conditions are met, makes the moratorium agreement effective for dissenting banks and financial institutions.

It has, however, to be considered if such rule of law should prevail on the applicable law which was contractually agreed between the debtor and dissenting banks and financial institutions with a legal seat in a Member State different from the one of the Italian debtor, and whose claim is grounded on a contract governed by a law different from Italian law[29] or

---

28 Which cannot be considered as an insolvency agreement according to the EIR, unless certain conditions are met, as confirmed by *De Cesari*, Il Fall. 2015, 1033 ff.

29 *Tribunale di Napoli*, 22 September 2016, 1264/16 (*unpublished order*) recently accepted an opposition filed by a bank (Unicredit Luxembourg SA) with registered

would be available under the non-insolvency rules of the applicable international law regime.[30]

Article 20 EIR would apply to the latter if the *convenzione di moratoria* could be qualified as an insolvency proceeding under EIR and a judgment opening such proceeding had been issued.

However, this is not the case. The *convenzione di moratoria*, in fact, may be qualified as an agreement aimed at provisionally regulating the effects of a financial crisis through a temporary moratorium.[31] Therefore, it should be considered if and on which grounds such *convenzione di moratoria* may be considered binding, according to Article 182septies LF, for dissenting banks and financial institutions with a legal seat in a Member State different from the one of the Italian debtor, and whose claim is grounded on a contract governed by a law different from Italian law.

Article 182septies(V) co. ff of the Italian Insolvency Act belongs to those recent Italian provisions in favor of an amicable composition of a financial crisis and according to which the interest of a qualified majority should prevail over those of dissenting minority creditors, avoiding, therefore, the latter opportunistic dissent or lack of interested in the proposed amicable composition. Based on this argument, Article 182septies(V) co. ff of the Italian Insolvency Act could be considered crucial for the safeguard of public interests of the State and, specifically, for its economic organization; and, therefore, overcome any law chosen by the interested parties,[32] and, specifically by the debtor and the dissenting bank or financial institution.

If so, Article 182septies(V) co. ff LF may be qualified as a mandatory provision under Article 9 of Regulation (EC) no 593/2008 on the law applicable to contractual obligations; and, therefore should prevail on the foreign law applicable to the agreement entered between the said banks and financial institutions and the debtor.

Consequently, dissenting banks and financial institutions with a legal seat in a Member State different from the one of the Italian debtor, and whose claim is grounded on a contract governed by a law different from Italian law shall be bound to the *convenzione di moratoria* by operation of Italian law as well as other dissenting banks and financial institutions.

---

office in Luxembourg to a *convenzione di moratoria* signed and executed by an Italian debtor.

30 *Eidenmüller*, ECGI Law Working Paper N° 335/2016, December 2016.
31 *Fabiani*, Il Fall. 2015, 1269 ff.
32 CJEU, 17 October 2013, Case C-184/12, *Unamar*, ECLI:EU:C:2013:663.

Annex II: The system of insolvency registration in the EU Insolvency
Regulation (Recast)

Professor Dr. Bob Wessels[*]

## 1. Introduction

In the last edition of one of my books[1] I criticized the quality of the system to provide information to the 'known creditors' (Article 40(1) EIR
2000) and the absence of any rules for providing information to 'unknown' creditors. Also, the fact that it was hardly possible for a court in
one Member State to assess whether in another Member State already
main insolvency proceedings had been opened resulted in several casual-
ties. Moreover, for creditors the situation was rather rough. In practice it
proved to be a lengthy, complex and costly exercise to get information
about the commencement of insolvency proceedings in another Member
State, the consequences that such opening would have for such a creditor
(e.g. time limits to file a claim or asserting a right to separation), and more
generally in finding reliable information on the contents of other Member
States' insolvency laws and (possible) differences with the laws about
which this creditor, i.e. its judicial advisor, would be knowledgeable.[2]

The latter problem is addressed by Article 86 EIR ('Information on national and Union insolvency law'), which provides that Member States
shall provide and update regularly a short description of their national legislation and procedures relating to insolvency, in particular relating to the
matters listed in Article 7(2) EIR. The Commission shall make the information available to the public.[3]

Article 92 EIR ('Entry into force') provides that the EIR applies from
26 June 2017, with the exception of Article 86 EIR, which shall already
apply from 26 June 2016. In spring 2016, *Andrea Csőke*, member of the
Supreme Court in Hungary, confesses[4], that not everybody will be able to

---

[*] Professor Dr. *Bob Wessels* is Professor emeritus for International Insolvency Law at
the University of Leiden, The Netherlands.

[1] *Wessels*, International Insolvency Law, 3rd edn (2012), para 10915.

[2] Other authors expressed similar concerns, see e.g. *Koller/Slonina*, in: Hess/Ober-
hammer/Pfeiffer (eds), Heidelberg-Luxembourg-Vienna Report (2014), paras
939 ff.

[3] See: https://e-justice.europa.eu/content_insolvency-447-en.do?clang=en.

[4] *Csőke*, eurofenix Spring 2016, 29.

perform these obligations on time. Nearly a year later (June 2017) it can be observed that indeed many Member States lag behind.

Article 92 EIR provides two other different dates for the entry into force, being Article 24(1) EIR, which shall apply from 26 June 2018, and Article 25 EIR, which shall apply from 26 June 2019. The articles mentioned form a part of Articles 24-27 EIR, relating to insolvency registers. The EIR provides for the establishment and the interconnection of insolvency registers (Articles 24 and 25 EIR) and determines who will bear the costs of establishing and interconnecting these registers (Article 26 EIR). The EIR also provides rules for access to the information via the system of interconnection (Article 27 EIR).

The establishment of these registers is an obligation for the Member States (Article 24(1) EIR). This duty is limited to insolvency proceedings that fall within the scope of the EU Insolvency Regulation. According to *Thole*, these Articles 24-27 EIR represent the quintessence (*Herzstück*) of the 2015 reform of the Insolvency Regulation.[5] Indeed, the recast of the EU Insolvency Regulation was based on the European Commission's identification of five main shortcomings in the original regulation, which has been in place since 2002. One of the shortcomings was the ragged registration system.

The Articles mentioned create rules of European uniform substantive law.[6] Bork rightly submits that having an eye for the costs of registration – lowering the pay-out to creditors – and delays the process of registration may cause to the progress in insolvency proceedings, justifies these rules for insolvency registers: enforcing the principles of transparency, procedural justice and equal treatment of creditors.[7] Articles 24-27 EIR form the core of my contribution, not so much an enticing subject and also containing non-insolvency law elements, but in insolvency practice a dire necessity.

---

5  *Thole*, in: Münchener Kommentar InsO, 3rd edn (2016), Art 102 und 102a EGInsO, Länderberichte EuInsVO 2015. On these Articles see *Szirányi*, in: Parry/Omar (eds), Reimagining Rescue, (2016), p 27-38; *Veder*, in: Bork/van Zwieten (eds), Commentary on the European Insolvency Regulation (2016), paras 24.01 ff; *Dugue/Becker*, in: Insolvency and Restructuring in Germany, Yearbook (2017), 2016, p 30 ff.

6  Thus *Mangano*, in: Bork/Mangano (eds), European Cross-border Insolvency Law (2016), para 1.53.

7  See *Bork*, Principles of Cross-border Insolvency Law (2017), para 6.136.

2. Aim of interconnected insolvency registers

Recital 76 provides: 'In order to improve the provision of information to relevant creditors and courts and to prevent the opening of parallel insolvency proceedings, Member States should be required to publish relevant information *in cross-border insolvency cases* in a publicly accessible electronic register. In order to facilitate access to that information for creditors and courts domiciled or located in other Member States, this Regulation should provide for the interconnection of such insolvency registers via the European e-Justice Portal. Member States should be free to publish relevant information in several registers and it should be possible to interconnect more than one register per Member State.'[8]

A first question is which 'information' is addressed?

Article 4(1) EIR leads to a decision of which it is required that it is published (Article 28(1) EIR) and it must be contained in the insolvency registers (Article 24(2) lit. d) EIR). The chosen wording regarding the information to be published ('... to publish relevant information *in cross-border insolvency cases*'[9] in a publicly accessible electronic register, in recital 76), and what this information specifically needs to contain (e.g. Article 24(2) lit. d) EIR '... whether jurisdiction for opening proceedings is based on Article 3(1), 3(2) or 3(4) EIR'), as well as the goal of providing this information (in recital 76: 'In order to facilitate access to that information for creditors and courts domiciled or located in other Member States, this Regulation should provide for the interconnection of such insolvency registers via the European e-Justice Portal') seems to indicate that only those proceedings mentioned in Annex A (compare Article 24(2) lit. c) EIR) will be taken into the register that indeed have extra-territorial effect.

This reading would necessitate making a selection between 'cross-border' cases and pure domestic cases. If this would be possible at all – cross-border effects may only come to the surface some time after the opening of proceedings – and if it would be clear who has to make this selection (the 'Member State', or an agency on its behalf, the court, the insolvency practitioner, 'if any' (see Article 24(2) lit. g) EIR), such a limitation is difficult to align with the general goal of enhancing the effectiveness on collective insolvency proceedings and the *effet utile* of EU law. See in this

---

8  Italics made by the author.
9  Italics made by the author.

way too *Dugué*.[10] This author submits that national legislators should oblige 'courts' to supply the register with information (unless it is clearly a domestic case). I wonder whether the better solution should not be a technology driven one: all cases in the register, which is, if I am correct, the present practice in the system of the European e-Justice Portal.

A second question is: who is to provide such information? Recital 76 (cited *supra*) says that Member States should be required to publish relevant information. In the system of the Regulation this seems to refer to the duty to establish the facilities of having (interconnected) registers available. On providing information, in general, the Regulation is ambivalent. Article 54(1) EIR prescribes – its text is nearly similar as its predecessor Article 40 EIR – that '… the court of that State having jurisdiction or the insolvency practitioner appointed by that court, must inform known foreign creditors, i.e. those creditors who have their habitual residence, domicile or registered office in the other Member States' (see Article 2(5) EIR). It is a rule of substantive law, which applies to both main and secondary proceedings, having being opened. The provision does not specify who is required to provide the information: the court or the insolvency practitioner? Literature, however, reflects standard practice: information is to be provided by the insolvency practitioners, which also seems to be the obvious person to bring Article 24 EIR to life.[11] In relevant cases under the recasted Regulation this person also could be the debtor in possession.

3. Part of existing effort in building EU-wide interconnection of national insolvency registers

The system provided in Articles 24-27 EIR builds on ongoing initiatives in the area of electronic access to judicial documentation. On 7 July 2014, the European Commission launched an EU-wide interconnection of national insolvency registers by linking up databases from seven Member States: the Czech Republic, Germany, Estonia, Netherlands, Austria, Romania and Slovenia.[12] More countries are expected to join at a later stage.

---

10  *Dugué*, in: Braun (ed), Insolvenzordnung, 7th edn (2017), Art 24 EIR, para 20.
11  See *Wessels*, International Insolvency Law, 3rd edn (2012), paras 10951 ff.
12  See     https://e-justice.europa.eu/content_interconnected_insolvency_registers_search-246-en.do?clang=en. The present insolvency register in the Netherlands contains a list with insolvency proceedings, insofar as those procedures have been opened pursuant to Art 3(1) and (2) EIR 2000 regarding debtors who have an

As of 1 April 2017 Belgium opened its central Solvency Register, but I could not detect a form of interlinking.[13] The aim the Commission's initiative is to serve as a one-stop shop for businesses, so creditors, entrepreneurs or investors can carry out the same checks as they would when they are investing in their home country. The connection will also support creditors looking for following up actions or data on insolvency cases taking place in another EU Member State – thanks to information being available at one web address: the European e-Justice Portal. Access to EU-wide insolvency registers is believed to improve the efficiency and effectiveness of cross-border insolvency proceedings. The press release of July 2014 mentions as benefits: *(i)* quicker, real-time access to insolvency information crucial for business decisions through a single point of access; *(ii)* key insolvency information will be available free of charge, in the languages of the European Union, and *(iii)* clear explanations on the insolvency terminology and systems of the participating Member States will help users to better understand the content.[14]

4. Establishment of insolvency registers

Article 24 EIR is a rather lengthy provision regarding the establishment of insolvency registers. Article 24(1) EIR creates – for the first time under the EU Insolvency Regulation – a specific obligation for a Member State

---

establishment in the Netherlands. It can be found at https://www.rechtspraak.nl/ SiteCollectionDocuments/EU-registratie.pdf. For use by a non-Dutch court of creditor the list is rather useless. It is in Dutch. The date of listing is not provided. Based on my practical experience, I know of non-Dutch main insolvency proceedings for debtors having an establishment in the Netherlands, which have not been listed. The register uses uncommon Dutch words for 'establishment'. It lists a Spanish (probably main) proceeding, regarding three Dutch BV's referring to 'concurso voluntario', which is not included in Annex A.

13 See www.regsol.be. The Belgian legislation does not anticipate the EIR. In accordance with the Act of 1 December 2016, the existing Belgian bankruptcy legislation was amended, and the settlement of the bankruptcy file is now being organized electronically. Due to the establishment of the Central Register Solvency and the REGSOL application, from 1 April 2017 onwards all creditors of a bankrupt company must submit their claims electronically. The insolvency practitioner ('curator') then processes them.

14 See for related documents www.bobwessels.nl, blog 2014-07-doc6, and see for background: *Mangano*, in: Bork/Mangano (eds), European Cross-Border Insolvency Law (2016), paras 6.76 ff.

itself. It shall establish and it shall maintain in its territory 'one or several registers in which information concerning insolvency proceedings is published (insolvency registers)'. The definition for 'insolvency registers' could just as well have been taken into the list of definitions in Article 2 EIR.

The provision is not specific to the nature of 'one or several' of these registers, but the following articles certainly presuppose these being registers available via internet (see e.g. 'interconnection' and 'European e-Justice Portal' in Article 25(1) EIR). The 'information concerning insolvency proceedings' in the meaning of Article 24(1) EIR seems to be rather wider than the information referred to in recital 76, being 'relevant information in cross-border insolvency cases'.

The information as referred to in Article 24(1) EIR relates both to main insolvency proceedings as well as to secondary insolvency proceedings. The information shall be published as soon as possible after the opening of such proceedings, see Article 24(1) EIR, last line.

Under the EIR in some cases secondary proceedings are not opened. The main insolvency practitioner has been given the right to give an undertaking in order to avoid secondary insolvency proceedings, see Article 36 EIR. Although the provision is rather vague in this regard, the undertaking is given to the local creditors in the other Member State. Article 36(5) EIR presupposes that 'known local creditors' in another Member State will know about the undertaking given (and therefore will be notified by the main insolvency practitioner), it would certainly assist the effectiveness of the instrument of an 'undertaking' that the undertaking given would be published in the registers. In such a case the publication of information in the registers under the EIR can, however, not be limited to the legal effects '… other than those set out in national law and in Article 55(6) EIR.' See Article 24(5) EIR. Article 55(6) EIR is relevant for determining the minimum time limit for foreign creditors to lodge their claims in the insolvency proceedings.

## 5. Mandatory information

Article 24(2) EIR provides that, subject to the conditions laid down in Article 27 EIR ('Conditions of access to information via the system of interconnection'), the information in the meaning of Article 24(1) EIR shall include ten categories of information. This latter information is defined as 'mandatory information' and will, therefore, result in a minimum amount of standardised information, see recital 77, first line. However, Member States are not precluded to include '... documents or additional information', see Article 24(3) EIR. The term 'mandatory information' could have been set up as a definition that could have been taken into the list of definitions in Article 2 EIR.

In Article 24(2) EIR the following mandatory information is referred to:

(a) the date of the opening of insolvency proceedings. This is the date in the meaning of Article 2(8) EIR ('the time of the opening of proceedings').[15]

(b) the court opening insolvency proceedings and the case reference number, if any;

(c) the type of insolvency proceedings referred to in Annex A that were opened and, where applicable, any relevant subtype of such proceedings opened in accordance with national law;

(d) whether jurisdiction for opening proceedings is based on Article 3(1), 3(2) or 3(4) EIR;

Indeed, Article 3(1) EIR leads to a decision of which it is required that it is published (Article 28(1) EIR) and it must be contained in the insolvency registers (Article 24(2) lit. d) EIR).

(e) if the debtor is a company or a legal person, the debtor's name, registration number, registered office or, if different, postal address;

(f) if the debtor is an individual whether or not exercising an independent business or professional activity, the debtor's name, registration number, if any, and postal address or, where the address is protected, the debtor's place and date of birth;

(g) the name, postal address or e-mail address of the insolvency practitioner, if any, appointed in the proceedings;

(h) the time limit for lodging claims, if any, or a reference to the criteria for calculating that time limit;

(i) the date of closing main insolvency proceedings, if any;

---

15 *Thole*, in: Münchener Kommentar InsO, 3rd edn (2016), Art 27 EIR 2015, para 7, mistakenly, refers to Art 2(7) EIR, which provides a definition for 'judgment opening insolvency proceedings' (making a distinction between two types of decisions).

(j) the court before which and, where applicable, the time limit within which a challenge of the decision opening insolvency proceedings is to be lodged in accordance with Article 5, or a reference to the criteria for calculating that time limit.

Regarding this set of minimum information I limit myself to a few remarks.

Neither the filing of a request for opening group proceedings nor the notice by the court seized pursuant to Article 63 EIR nor the opening of group coordination proceedings is explicitly included in the 'mandatory information' to be published in the insolvency registers pursuant to Article 24(2) EIR. This is a serious flaw in the registration system. As the wording stands now, one might bring the opening of group coordination proceedings and the appointment of a coordinator under Article 24(2) lit. a) and g) EIR, respectively, however this comes not without problems in light of the legal definitions of 'insolvency proceedings' and 'insolvency practitioner' in Article 2(4) and (5) EIR. Even if the opening of group coordination proceedings and the appointment of a coordinator has to be published in the insolvency register, there remains the problem of knowledge in the interim period between the filing of the request and the publication of the opening. Yet, the duties of communication and cooperation laid down in Articles 56-58 EIR presumably also require the insolvency practitioners and the courts involved to inform one another of pending requests at least after a notice pursuant to Article 63 EIR has been issued.

A second remark relates to a distinction to be made with regard of the information to be provided between a natural person exercising an independent business or professional activity, or a natural person without such a business/activity. I refer to the latter person as consumer. Recital 77, second line, says: 'Where the debtor is an individual, the insolvency registers should only have to indicate a registration number if the debtor is exercising an independent business or professional activity. That registration number should be understood to be the unique registration number of the debtor's independent business or professional activity published in the trade register, if any.' For consumers, see Article 24(4) EIR and the text below.

As to the information to be provided, it seems that the role of a Member State is passive regarding creditors, that is to say: just providing information, not more (but not less either). As to time limits in the meaning of Article 24(2) lit. h), j) EIR, recital 78 is saying: 'Information on certain aspects of insolvency proceedings is essential for creditors, such as time lim-its for lodging claims or for challenging decisions. This Regulation should, however, not require Member States to calculate those time-limits on a case-by-case basis. Member States should be able to fulfil their obli-gations by adding hyperlinks to the European e-Justice Portal, where self-explanatory information on the criteria for calculating those time-limits is to be provided.'

Article 24(3) EIR determines that Article 24(2) EIR shall not preclude Member States from including documents or additional information in their national insolvency registers. The paragraph provides as an example directors' disqualifications related to insolvency.[16] In literature for this cat-egory of data the term optional information has been suggested.[17]

## 6. Consumers

Article 24(4) EIR provides an exclusion to the duty for a Member State to publish mandatory information. A Member State is not obliged to include in the insolvency registers said information 'in relation to individuals not exercising an independent business or professional activity, or to make such information publicly available through the system of interconnection of those registers, provided that'. The EIR safeguards to protect a zone of privacy around any consumer. Article 27(3) and (4) EIR allows Member States to include additional search criteria or set additional conditions for such individuals and authorizes Member States not to include information regarding consumers in the insolvency registration.

Article 24(4) EIR, allowing information regarding consumers not to be published in the registers, at the end reads '... provided that known for-eign creditors are informed, pursuant to Article 54 EIR, of the elements re-ferred to under lit. j) of paragraph 2 of this Article.' Article 54 EIR con-tains a duty to inform known foreign creditors. It is a duty for the insol-vency practitioner, so it should inform about the court before which and, where applicable, the time limit within which a challenge of the decision opening insolvency proceedings is to be lodged in accordance with Article

---

16  See *Muzsalyi*, Directors' Liability: What Should Be the Minimum Degree of Har-monisation in the EU? (October 2016), available at: https://ssrn.com/ abstract=2914600.
17  See *Müller*, in: Mankowski/Müller/Schmidt, EuInsVO 2015 (2016), Art 24, para 20.

5 EIR ('Judicial review of the decision to open main insolvency proceedings'), or a reference to the criteria for calculating that time limit. See Article 24(2) lit. j) EIR. The provision functions as a safety valve for the benefit of a creditor who has not been informed by the insolvency practitioner.[18]

If a Member State makes use of the possibility of exclusion (in the meaning of Article 24(4) EIR first paragraph), the insolvency proceedings shall not affect the claims of foreign creditors who have not received this information.[19]

Here, a reference to Article 83 EIR ('Access to personal data via the European e-Justice Portal') seems appropriate. It provides: 'Personal data stored in the national insolvency registers referred to in Article 24 EIR shall be accessible via the European e-Justice Portal for as long as they remain accessible under national law.' Interestingly, *Tajti* submits that the goals of insolvency laws and data protection laws are antagonistic: while the interest of the former is designed to facilitate access to information by creditors and courts so as to stimulate free movement of services and goods, data-protection rules aim rather to restrict access.[20] As these two ends are not irreconcilable, the EIR should find, according to this author: '... the proper balance by ensuring access to no more information than what is necessary for the efficient and effective conduct of cross-border insolvency proceedings'.[21]

7. Legal effect of information in the registers

I already noted that the publication of 'information in the registers under this Regulation shall not have any legal effects other than those set out in national law and in Article 55(6) EIR.' See Article 24(5) EIR. Article

---

18  See *Mangano*, in: Bork/Mangano (eds), European Cross-Border Insolvency Law (2016), para 6.83. For the historical background of Art 24(4), see *Müller*, in: Mankowski/Müller/Schmidt, EuInsVO 2015 (2016), Art 24, para 14.

19  See *Dugué*, in: Braun (ed), Insolvenzordnung, 7th edn (2017), Art 24 EIR, para 15.

20  See *Tajti*, in: Bork/van Zwieten (eds), Commentary on the European Insolvency Regulation (2016), para 78.09.

21  He provides an in-depth comment to Art 78–83 EIR (regarding data protection), with references to specialised literature on privacy and data protection laws. See also the overview by *Becker*, in: Braun (ed), Insolvenzordnung 7th edn (2017), Vorbemerkung vor Art 78-83, paras 1 ff.

55(6) EIR is relevant for determining the minimum time limit for foreign creditors to lodge their claims in the insolvency proceedings.

The term 'information in the Registers under this Regulation' in Article 24(5) EIR may cast doubt. *Müller* submits that it only relates to the mandatory information in the meaning of Article 24(1) EIR.[22] The wording, however, is wide enough to have the optional information in the meaning of Article 24(3) EIR included.

Another legal effect than signaled in Article 55(6) EIR has been noted by *Veder*. He submits that publication of the opening of insolvency proceedings in the insolvency registers, once interconnected on the basis of Article 25 EIR, has no bearing on Article 31 EIR ('Honoring of an obligation to a debtor'). *Veder* signals as the most preferable approach to stipulate in Article 31 EIR that if performance took place after the opening of insolvency proceedings in another Member State and which was ascertainable through the interconnected insolvency registers, the third party debtor is presumed to have been aware of the opening of the insolvency proceedings. He rightly submits that this should also have been reflected in Article 24(5) EIR.[23]

8. Interconnection of insolvency registers

Article 25 EIR concerns a topic which is not directly related to insolvency, i.e. the interconnectedness of insolvency registers. Article 25(1) EIR creates a specific duty for the European Commission. The Commission shall establish a decentralized system for the interconnection of insolvency registers by means of implementing acts.[24]

It has been common knowledge that the way national insolvency registers were organized (if at all) to include all information necessary for foreign courts (to decide whether, and if so, which type of proceeding should be opened, see recital 76: 'to prevent the opening of parallel insolvency

---

22  *Müller*, in: Mankowski/Müller/Schmidt, EuInsVO 2015 (2016), Art 24, para 21.

23  *Veder*, in: Bork/van Zwieten (eds), Commentary on the European Insolvency Regulation (2016), para 24.10.

24  Art 87 EIR ('Establishment of the interconnection of registers') provides that the Commission shall adopt implementing acts establishing the interconnection of insolvency registers as referred to in Art 25 EIR. Those implementing acts shall be adopted in accordance with the examination procedure referred to in Art 89(3) EIR.

proceedings'), was not in line with an effective use of the Regulation. Apart from the (near to) absence of any system of inter-relationship between these registers, other obstacles for a full functional system to share all information necessary are issues such as finding access to such a register, lack of standardization of information and of course language in which such information could be available. As indicated *supra*, in 2014, the European Commission presented a first step towards an EU-wide interconnection of national insolvency registers by linking up databases from seven Member States. A next step is reflected in Article 25 EIR.

Article 25(1) EIR will result in 'a decentralized system for the interconnection of insolvency registers by means of implementing acts'. In Article 25(2) EIR reference is made to the procedure of working with a 'delegated' act. The Commission shall adopt the six topics mentioned in Article 25(2) EIR by 26 June 2019. That date is repeated in Article 92 lit. c) EIR.

Article 26 EIR provides a system for who is bearing the costs for establishment, maintenance and development of the system of interconnection of insolvency registers and the cost of establishing and adjusting national registers to make these compatible and operationable within the European e-Justice Portal. It provides that the EU itself will bear the costs for establishment, maintenance and development of the system of interconnected insolvency registers. The cost of establishing and adjusting national registers to make these compatible and interoperable within the European e-Justice Portal will be borne by the respective member states.

9. Conditions of access to information via the system of interconnection

Article 27 EIR addresses the conditions for access to the information in the insolvency registers via the European e-Justice Portal. There are two categories: *(i)* information free of charge, and information for which a reasonable fee may be requested, see Article 27(2) EIR. Access to the mandatory information referred to in lit. a) to j) of Article 24(2) EIR is available free of charge, via the system of interconnection of insolvency registers. Member States may, however, charge '… a reasonable fee for access to documents or additional information' that they choose to include in the insolvency registers (so: the optional information).

Restrictions or conditions to access information can be included in as far as it concerns information relating to consumers, i.e. individuals not exercising an independent business or professional activity and where the insolvency proceedings are not related to an independent business or professional activity, see Article 27(3) and (4) EIR.

Article 27(3) EIR allows to set additional conditions or '… supplementary search criteria' for access in as far it concerns information relating to individuals not exercising an independent business or professional activity, '… in addition to the minimum criteria referred to in lit. c) of Article 25(2) EIR', i.e. the minimum criteria for the search service by the European e-Justice Portal. Recital 79 is clear: 'In order to grant sufficient protection to information relating to individuals not exercising an independent business or professional activity, Member States should be able to make access to that information subject to supplementary search criteria such as the debtor's personal identification number, address, date of birth or the district of the competent court, or to make access conditional upon a request to a competent authority or upon the verification of a legitimate interest.' Supplementary search criteria should protect these individual debtors against unauthorized parties being able to access their data by simply typing in a debtor's name in the interconnected register. Article 27(3) EIR provides the Member States with discretion ('may'), and Article 27(4) EIR does the same. Member States may require that access to the information referred to in Article 27(3) EIR be made conditional 'upon a request to the competent authority.' Member States may also make access conditional 'upon the verification of the existence of a legitimate interest for accessing such information'.

The provision does not set criteria to define 'legitimate interest'.

In the latter case, Article 27(4) EIR continues, the requesting person shall be able to submit the request for information electronically by means of a standard form via the European e-Justice Portal. Where a legitimate interest is required, it shall be permissible for the requesting person to justify his request by electronic copies of relevant documents. For a creditor it is logical to submit its own name, address and identification number, a copy of a contract or the proof of any outstanding debt. One can envisage that the management of the European e-Justice Portal provides some guidelines for certain categories of creditors. The Commission expects an efficient system, as Article 27(4), 5th s. EIR prescribes that the requesting person shall be provided with an answer by the competent authority within 3 working days, in the 6th s. adding that the requesting person shall not be obliged to provide translations of the documents justifying his request, or to bear any costs of translation which the competent authority may incur.

Although the protection of a debtor's privacy is an interest of main importance, it should be weighed against the interest of a creditor of having easy access to the interconnected register. For instance if a Member State would require to fill in the debtor's address as a condition for having access, this can be easily disrupted by the creditor by changing his address.

Also here it is suggested that the management of the e-Justice Portal system provides guidelines to assist Member States in their weighing the balance. It may be needed that Member States' laws regarding data protection must be amended or should include some additions, for instance also how long information has to stay within the interconnected insolvency registers, after proceedings have ended. Also the insolvent debtor has a right to be forgotten.

## 10. Conclusion

The recasted EU Insolvency Regulation will make it easier to access insolvency-specific information, especially in cross-border situations. For foreign creditors it will become easier (read: less problematic) to obtain information about insolvency proceedings opened or pending in other Member States. The system of obtaining information concerning insolvency proceedings involving companies or individuals who exercise a business activity is designed as a simple set-up in which core information can be accessed. The obtained information with respect to consumers is more troublesome. Exemptions from the publication duty and restrictions on access to information as designed are the result of a balance between ensuring access to information than what is necessary for the efficient and effective conduct of cross-border insolvency proceedings against the interest of a consumer-debtor to have its data protected for reasons of privacy.

## Annex III: Opening statement on the coordination and cooperation of main and secondary proceedings

### Professor Dr. Christoph Thole*

I have been asked to open the discussion on the cooperation and coordination of main and secondary proceedings, to present some 'appetizers' for the discussion and to come up with some preliminary thoughts on potential problems of the new law. The issues that need to be addressed are the following: A first look goes to the general approach of the recast, then I will discuss one of the central new features of the recast being the undertaking ('synthetic secondary proceedings'), and finally some remarks will be made with respect to the law on the cooperation and communication of insolvency practitioners and courts.

### 1. Key features of the new law

The recast sticks to the principle of modified universality. Secondary proceedings remain possible. That has been a matter of debate, and there a few scholars who argue this might be too conservative and a full swing to full and comprehensive universality would have been better.[1] In substance, what we possibly see is a concession to political reality. However, from a doctrinal, scientific point of view, the question remains whether we need secondary proceedings at all. Some argue the new law is a second-best approach only; the complete abolition of secondary proceedings would have been better.[2]

A second core feature is a further restriction to secondary proceedings, i.e. the 'synthetic proceedings' on the one hand and the abolition of the requirement that the secondary proceeding needs to be a liquidation procedure on the other hand.

---

* Original opening statement presented at the conference in Luxembourg in October 2016 by Prof. Dr. *Christoph Thole*, Institute of International and European Insolvency Law, University of Cologne.
1 *Arts*, Norton J. Bankr. L. & Prac.= download, available at: https://www.iiiglobal.org/sites/default/files/media/Arts%20-%20Main%20and%20Secondary%20Proceedings.pdf, p 12 ff.
2 *Eidenmüller*, MJ 2013, 133 ff = ECGI – Law Working Paper No. 199/203, available at: http://ssrn.com/abstract=2230690, p 18.

Thirdly, the recast tries to further promote and enhance communication and cooperation duties. However, the new provisions are largely soft law. They are designed as duties, but, as a matter of fact, more or less have an appellative character only (see *infra* III).

2. Are secondary proceedings useful?

Let me discuss this general approach more closely. As mentioned earlier, some scholars argue that secondary proceedings are more or less useless and should have been abolished altogether. They are perceived as costly and said to have a disrupting effect on the main proceedings. The right to apply for a secondary proceeding can sometimes be used in a strategic way, for instance by 'blackmailing' the insolvency administrator into concessions or by more or less blackmailing those creditors who would be worse off if the law of the state of the secondary proceeding applied. Some argue that the protection of local creditors could be achieved by other instruments such as specific protection schemes for employees.[3] One of the main arguments against a necessity for secondary proceedings is that the local creditors of the establishment often know quite well or can at least predict where the COMI is located and that they can adjust to this.[4]

However, in my opinion, secondary proceedings are at least not too bad. We need to be realistic. If secondary proceedings would have been abolished completely, this would have facilitated COMI-Shopping and abusive strategies even more. And too be fair, depending on the structure and business of the debtor, the acceptance of insolvency proceedings could at least in some cases be impaired if local creditors would have to participate in a foreign and far-away proceeding. Thus, secondary proceedings can be useful in some situations. The restructuring option is often over-estimated. We should not forget that in most cases companies end up in liquidation. This might be less so in international cases but still secondary proceedings can be useful in order to pursue a liquidation strategy in the state of the establishment on a rather clear and well-defined basis.

Thus, it might well be good political realism that instead of completely abolishing secondary proceedings the lawmaker opted for 'synthetic proceedings' instead.

---

3 *Arts* (n 1), p 14.
4 *Arts* (n 1), p 14.

## 3. The undertaking (Articles 36 ff EIR)

This leads to a few remarks on the undertaking, which allows a court seized with an application for a secondary proceeding to dismiss the application if the undertaking adequately protects the general interests of the creditors (Article 38(2) EIR).

– First, the new rules form a complex set. A few problems of the new law can easily be identified. Pursuant to Article 36(5) EIR, the undertaking shall be approved by local creditors. The rules on qualified majority and voting that apply to the adoption of restructuring plans apply to such approval. This is quite complicated.

– Furthermore, the right to challenge the distribution pursuant to the undertaking could potentially delay proceedings for years.

– The binding effect of the undertaking is a matter of some doubt.[5] The undertaking shall specify the value of the assets. This can hardly be done or at least it is hardly feasible for the undertaking to be binding in this respect because the secondary estate is a moving target; for instance, avoidance claims with respect to assets associated with the establishment might still be pending at the time of the undertaking. The problem is that the amount of the estate can best be determined at a later stage in the course of the proceeding, but the later the undertaking, the higher the risk of the initiation of real secondary proceedings.

– There will also be some potential for a shifting of assets prior to the granting of the undertaking. Recital 46 exclusively deals with a removal of assets after the undertaking has been given.

– Furthermore, we might see some problems with several undertakings, because an undertaking can be made in each state in which the debtor has an establishment. As the time of the granting of the undertaking may differ from establishment to establishment, we could potentially have several undertakings at different points in times, but the problem then is that parts of the estate and property that once belonged to the state of the first undertaking may have been shifted to the state of the now second undertaking in the meantime. This will inevitably lead to the problem how to properly determine the amount of the estate in the respective synthetic secondary proceeding. Potentially, it would also be possible for the administrator to transfer some or even all of the assets

---

5 See *Skauradzun*, ZIP 2016, 1563 ff.

to the state of the main proceedings prior to giving the undertaking, thus depriving local creditors of the economic perspective of an undertaking. This asset shifting by the insolvency practitioner is not abusive per se as it may well follow the necessities of running an insolvency proceeding in an international enterprise. Still, this will certainly be a matter of debate between influential local creditors and the insolvency practitioner.

– The alignment with the main proceeding seems unclear. Generally speaking, problems may arise because creditors including the non-local creditors will participate in the distribution in both the main proceeding and the synthetic proceeding. This is generally dealt within Article 23 EIR (former Article 20 EIR 2000). However, this provision has not been adjusted to the undertaking.

– In Article 37(2) EIR, it reads that an application for a secondary proceeding shall be lodged within 30 days of having received notice of the approval of the undertaking. It remains to be seen how this 'having received notice' is to be interpreted in a given and individual situation.[6]

– What is more important is that it is unclear whether the adequate protection test in Article 38 EIR when deciding on whether or not a secondary proceeding may be opened relates to economic interests only or whether other interests such as political or atmospheric issues may be taken into account.[7] Recital 42 does not give any ultimate guidance; it requires the court to take into account that the undertaking has been approved by a qualified majority of local creditors.

– Furthermore, once secondary proceeding have been opened, they cannot be terminated as a whole even if the undertaking is granted at a later point in time;[8] so time might be crucial because creditors interested in a secondary proceeding could file their application before the undertaking has been given or approved by the local creditors.

As can be derived from the issues mentioned above, the undertaking is far from being easy to handle.[9] New legal issues will inevitably come up, and the practice will have to deal with them in some or the other way. I have

---

6  See Study *infra* Part 2, I. 2.2.2.
7  *Arts* (n 1), p 18; cf *Pluta/Keller*, in: Festschrift Heinz Vallender (2015), p 437, 447; *Prager/Keller*, WM 2015, 805, 808.
8  *Brinkmann*, KTS 2014, 381, 397.
9  *Brinkmann*, KTS 2014, 381, 395.

some doubts as to whether the undertaking will be used as a common and standard operation in international insolvency cases.

4. The new law on cooperation and communication (Articles 41 ff EIR)

The third issue to be looked at is the cooperation and communication between main and secondary proceedings. The new law can be outlined as follows:

– There is still no power of the insolvency practitioner of the main proceeding to interfere directly with the secondary proceeding. He is confined to an application for a stay of process of realisation of assets (Article 46 EIR); furthermore, he may exercise the rights a creditor would have in the secondary proceeding (Article 45 EIR).
– The new rules on the cooperation and communication between the practitioners are flexible. This is to be welcomed.
– Communication can take any form (Article 41(1), 2nd s. EIR). This includes delivery of documents and is dependent on the needs specified by the requesting insolvency practitioner. Some specific duties are stipulated in Article 41(2) EIR. However, there is a decisive safeguard and caveat. The cooperation must not be incompatible with the rules applicable to the respective proceedings. However, this caveat may be interpreted, at least cooperation must not be detrimental to the own proceeding. Thus, the insolvency practitioner of the secondary proceeding remains obliged to increase and preserve the estate of the secondary proceeding. He has no general duties towards the general estate of the main proceeding; the recast of the EIR does not oblige the secondary insolvency practitioner to generally take the interests of the main proceeding into account. It follows that, to be realistic, cooperation is less a question of a hard, enforceable duty but more or less left to the parties' willingness to cooperate and to share information. These duties are real duties as mandated by the EIR, but the safeguards are high and the recast does not stipulate hard consequences in a case of violation of the duty to cooperate. I believe this rather tentative approach is a sensible one. It remains to be seen how cooperation works in practice. But it would have been too early to impose hard duties on the practitioners under European law. Admittedly, I miss some provisions regarding disputes between the insolvency practitioners on the cooperation duties. There are no express rules on jurisdiction and the applicable law in this

cross-border context. Thus, should a dispute arise, it remains unclear which court enjoys the competence to decide on that matter; the respective insolvency practitioner will try to keep such a dispute in his respective Member State.

– The cooperation and communication between courts (Article 42 EIR) will probably be a matter of practice rather than of law. I do not think the recast will lead to hard legal questions in this respect. The question is rather how these duties fit into the respective national culture. For instance, German judges are probably rather reluctant to enter into a flexible communication with courts of other Member States; thus, the problem is not the law but the willingness to deal with the law in a pragmatic way as required in an international proceeding.

– The rules on the cross-cooperation between courts and insolvency practitioner might even be slightly too flexible. The provision speaks of cooperation 'by any appropriate means'. There is a caveat 'to the extent that such cooperation and communication are not incompatible with the rules applicable to each of the proceedings and do not entail any conflict of interests'. This could mean anything or nothing. The interpretation of this caveat will be largely left to the insolvency practitioner and courts themselves and left to finding a mutual agreement. Parties will be reluctant to bring a lawsuit in order to enforce the cross-cooperation duty. Once again, it is unclear which court would be competent to decide on the scope of such duties. But: as said before, it is probably good to pursue a rather soft and pragmatic approach, and this is why the new rules are to be welcomed, despite and partly because of their flexibility.

Annex IV: From 'prisoner's dilemma' to reluctance to use judicial discretion: the enemies of cooperation in European cross-border cases – the situation of Italy, and beyond

Professor Dr. Renato Mangano[*]

## 1. Introduction

The people that drew up Regulation 2015/848 increased the duties of co-operation and communication imposed on courts and insolvency practitioners appointed in main and secondary proceedings. While Regulation 1346/2000 provided a single Article imposing a duty of cooperation and communication on liquidators only (Article 31 EIR 2000), Regulation 2015/848 contains many Articles imposing duties of cooperation and communication on both courts and insolvency practitioners (Articles 41-44 EIR). These duties refer both to those cases where insolvency proceedings are already opened, and to those where a request to open insolvency proceedings is still pending. These duties are cross-direction ones in the sense that a court of a Member State A dealing with a cross-border case X not only is obliged to cooperate and communicate with that court of that Member State B dealing with the same case X, but it has also to cooperate and communicate with that insolvency practitioner who is appointed there, as well as that insolvency practitioner who is appointed in Member State A for the case X is obliged to cooperate and communicate with that court of Member State B dealing with the same case X. Further, Regulation 2015/848 employs duties of cooperation and communication as a regulatory device to regulate insolvencies within groups of companies (Articles 56-77 EIR).[1] However, these duties fall outside of the scope of this paper.

---

[*] *Renato Mangano* is a Professor of Commercial Law at the University of Palermo (Italy). This paper reproduces with some changes the text of a lecture given at a Conference titled 'The Implementation of the New Insolvency Regulation – Improving Cooperation and Mutual Trust'. This conference was held at the Max Planck Institute Luxembourg for Procedural Law on 7th October 2016.

[1] Actually, concerning group insolvencies, Regulation 2015/848 distinguishes between two distinct regulatory devices, which are called 'Cooperation and communication' (Arts 56-60) and 'Coordination' (Arts 61-77). Nevertheless, coordination is a form of cooperation too, where 'contract' is supplemented by 'hierarchy', to use *Oliver Williamson's* terminology.

The choice of policy consisting in increasing the duties of cooperation and communication between main and secondary proceedings complies with an established tradition of common law courts and practitioners dealing with cross-border cases — these courts have always cooperated with each other to a great extent;[2] this choice also corresponds to a commonly shared idea that private international law is based on cooperation.[3] Moreover, the idea of thoroughly regulating the duties of cooperation and communication by means of a EU-Regulation is expected to remove some cultural and legal (national) constraints which prevent civil law courts from cooperating to the same extent as those of common law jurisdictions and, especially, to make cooperation in cross-border insolvency cases smoother. However, cooperation – which hereinafter includes communication, unless otherwise provided – is an open issue. This explains why, in some EU Member States, courts and insolvency practitioners needed time to start to smoothly cooperate; and this explains why, outside the scope of European law, the UNIDROIT 'Convention on international interests in mobile equipment' (Cape Town Convention) does not establish a duty to cooperate in insolvency issues and why the Protocols attached to this Convention consign the only prescription devoted to this subject to the class of opt-in prescriptions, with the result that a state signing that Convention which also intends to be subject to the duty of cooperation (insolvency assistance) is required to make an express relevant declaration.[4]

---

2 *Wessels/Markell/Kilborn*, International Cooperation in Bankruptcy and Insolvency Matters (2009), *passim* and p 174.

3 See, *inter alia*, *Slaughter*, Harv. Int'l L.J. 2003, p 191 ff, and European Parliament – DG for Internal Policies, Study on A European Framework for Private International Law: Current Gaps and Future Perspectives, 2012, available at: www.europarl.europa.eu/document/activities/cont/201212/20121219ATT58300/20121219ATT58300EN.pdf.

4 UNIDROIT Convention on International Interests in Mobile Equipment (2001). This is available to download at: http://www.unidroit.org/instruments/security-interests/cape-town-convention. This regulation is supplemented by three protocols which refer to 'aircraft equipment', 'railway rolling stocks' and 'space assets', respectively. The opt-in prescriptions concerning cooperation (Insolvency assistance) are laid down by Art XII of the 'Protocol on Aircraft equipment'; Art X of the 'Protocol on Railway rolling stocks'; and Art XXII of the 'Protocol on space assets'. These Protocols are available at the following addresses respectively: www.unidroit.org/instruments/security-interests/aircraft-protocol; www.unidroit.org/instruments/security-interests/rail-protocol; www.unidroit.org/instruments/security-interests/space-protocol.

But why is cooperation an open issue? Are these difficulties due to an endemic bad attitude of courts and insolvency practitioners of some jurisdictions regarding cooperating with each other? Are they due to a lack of trust, or difficulties in communicating in a foreign language? Probably they are, at least partially. Nevertheless, these conjectures remain on the surface of the problem and do not get to the root of it. Moreover, in this respect the literature dealing with cooperation does not provide a great help. In fact scholars either focus on the *input* to cooperation – for instance, in European cross-border cases they concentrate on the legal basis for cooperation, i.e. on Article 4(3) TEU and Article 81(2) lit. a) and c) TFEU;[5] or they focus on the *output* from cooperation – for instance, a distinguished author wrote that 'a new concept of 'judicial comity' is evolving and that it is providing a framework of ground-rules for establishing and developing judicial dialogue.'[6] By contrast, to our knowledge no writers have paid sufficient attention to the *process* of cooperation and, accordingly, to its logic and limits.

This paper will directly focus on the process of cooperation, in order to facilitate the application of Regulation 2015/848. The central idea is that prescriptions imposing duties of cooperation and communication have no specific contents, since they have an intrinsic open texture; this characteristic requires courts and insolvency practitioners to make choices between different rulings and activities; it might also produce 'prisoner's dilemmas', and may even challenge those who have to interpret and apply them. Arguably, awareness of this characteristic might prove helpful to apply them and, if necessary, to pave the way for proposals for a better regulation. These includes the idea of setting up at European level an ombudsman in order to mediate any conflicts between courts and insolvency practitioners belonging to different jurisdictions and prevent them from litigating before courts.

2. Article 31 EIR 2000, and its application in Italy

Regulation 1346/2000 only devotes one Article to cooperation. This is indexed 'Duty to cooperate and communicate information' (Article 31 EIR 2000). Put simply, this Article imposes on liquidators appointed in main

---

5  *Wessels*, International Insolvency law, 3rd edn (2012), para 10853.
6  *Wessels*, Insolv. Int. 2014, 5.

and secondary proceedings a duty 'to communicate information to each other' and a duty 'to cooperate with each other', provided that these duties are not incompatible with the rules applicable to each of the proceedings. This regulation contains a short exemplification of the duty of information by providing that the liquidators '[should] immediately communicate any information which may be relevant to the other proceedings, in particular the progress made in lodging and verifying claims and all measures aimed at terminating the proceedings'. This regulation provides a specification of the duty of cooperation as well, in the sense that the liquidator appointed in the secondary proceedings '[should] give the liquidator in the main proceedings an early opportunity of submitting proposals on the liquidation or use of the assets in the secondary proceedings.' Finally, the Explanatory Report to Regulation 1346/2000 contains both additional exemplifications and the statement that '[w]here appropriate, the applicable national law will determine the liquidator's liability when the latter has not respected the duties arising from Article 31 EIR 2000.'[7]

Article 31 EIR 2000 is unanimously considered unsatisfactory for many reasons. *Inter alia*, these consist both in the fact that this Article only refers to cooperation between liquidators, and in the fact that this Article contains – at least expressly – no prescriptions allowing liquidators to conclude agreements and protocols. This explains why, especially in the early years of its application, in civil law jurisdictions there was no evidence of cooperation between courts, and why liquidators appeared reluctant to conclude agreements and protocols. Nevertheless, this situation slowly changed, at least in some countries. For example, as long ago as 2004 the Vienna Higher Regional Court ruled that the 'prevailing opinion' and the United Nations Commission on International Trade Law (UNCITRAL) Model law were found to reflect the existence of a wider obligation of cooperation also involving courts,[8] just as in the last few years there has been increasingly signing of agreements and protocols in proceedings involving France and Germany.[9] Moreover, in 2012 the CJEU conclusively ruled that 'the principle of sincere cooperation laid down in Article 4(3) TEU requires the court having jurisdiction to open secondary proceedings, in applying those provisions, to have regard to the objectives of the main

---

7 *Virgós-Schmit*, Report on the Convention of Insolvency Proceedings (1996), para 234.

8 *Oberlandesgericht Wien*, 9 November 2004, 28 R 225/04w—[2004] EIRCR(A) 72.

9 *Wessels*, International Insolvency law, 3rd edn (2012), para 10855.

proceedings and to take account of the scheme of the Regulation, which, as observed in paragraphs 45 and 60 of this judgment, aims to ensure efficient and effective cross-border insolvency proceedings through mandatory coordination of the main and secondary proceedings guaranteeing the priority of the main proceedings'.[10]

Italy features a modest number of cases where Italian courts and insolvency practitioners have cooperated with their foreign colleagues. In this respect, the *Cirio del Monte*, *Illochroma Italia* and *Parmalat* issues are the most relevant cases in point. First, consider the *Cirio del Monte* case, which – actually – refers to a case where only main proceedings were opened, but the court and insolvency practitioners needed assistance in enforcement abroad. These proceedings were administrative in nature, but a court which was territorially competent had to ascertain that the debtor was insolvent and to issue an order opening the insolvency proceeding.

On 7th August 2003, the Court of Rome declared the insolvency of *Cirio Del Monte Italia SpA*, *Cirio Finanziaria SpA* and *Cirio Holding SpA*, on the ground that their registered offices were in Italy, while the Italian Minister of Productive Activities opened one set of extraordinary administration proceedings only, on the ground that these three companies belonged to the same group.[11] On 14th August 2003, the Court of Rome also declared the insolvency of *Cirio Del Monte NV*, whose registered office was in The Netherlands, on the ground that this company was a wholly owned subsidiary of the group and that its operational and executive centre was in Italy.[12] The extraordinary administration proceedings, which had been previously opened, involved this company too, and the insolvency practitioners appointed there smoothly cooperated with Dutch authorities in order to enforce Italian decisions in The Netherlands.

Secondly, consider the *Illochroma Italia* case. This company belonged to a group of five companies. They were *Illochroma Group NV*, the parent company, which entirely owned *Illochroma France SA*, *Illochroma Belgium NV*, *Illochroma Italia SrL* and *Illochroma Central Europe Sp. z o.o.* These five companies had their registered offices in Belgium, France, Italy and Poland, respectively. On 21st April 2008, the Court of Roubaix-Tourcoing, in France, opened one set of main insolvency proceedings against

---

10 CJEU, 22 November 2012, Case C-116/11, *Bank Handlowy and Adamiak*, ECLI:EU:C:2012:739.
11 *Tribunale Ordinario di Roma*, 7 August 2003, Il dir. fallim. 2003, p 1000.
12 *Tribunale Ordinario di Roma*, 14 August 2003, Il dir. fallim. 2003, p 999.

all the five companies, on the ground that the executive centre of every company was situated in France.[13] An Italian creditor of *Illochroma Italia SrL, Burgo Group SpA*, tried to lodge its claim in the French proceedings. However, this lodging was unsuccessful, since this request was out of time. Accordingly, on the 20th October 2008, *Burgo Group SpA* applied to the Court of Ivrea, in Italy, for the opening in Italy of secondary proceedings concerning *Illochroma Italia SrL*. This application was successful and the Court of Ivrea opened secondary insolvency proceedings against *Illochroma Italia SrL*.[14] The French practitioner challenged the Italian decision before the Court of Appeal of Turin, on the ground that in such a case the opening of secondary proceedings was not appropriate because the Italian creditor had no – *in iure* – interest in opening secondary proceedings in Italy — the Italian creditor had a right to lodge his claim in the French proceedings which also involved the assets of *Illochroma Italia SrL*. However, the Court of Appeal of Turin stated that the main insolvency proceedings opened in one Member State must be recognised by the courts of the other Member States, but that Regulation 1346/2000 granted the Italian creditor a right to apply for the opening of secondary proceedings in Italy.[15] This litigation resulted in a request to the CJEU for a preliminary ruling; the CJEU inter alia ruled that 'when establishing the conditions for the opening of secondary proceedings, Member States must comply with EU law and, in particular, its general principles, as well as the provisions of that regulation [*i.e.* of Regulation 1346/2000].'[16]

Thirdly, consider the *Parmalat* case, which offers both an example of smooth cooperation and an example of bitter clashes between courts and insolvency practitioners belonging to different jurisdictions. In 2003, the Parmalat group collapsed in deep financial crisis. On 24th December 2003, the parent company *Parmalat SpA* filed its request for opening extraordinary administration proceedings. Immediately afterwards, the Minister granted this request, and appointed Mr Enrico Bondi as the extraordinary

---

13 *Greffe du Tribunal de Commerce de Roubaix-Tourcoing*, 21 April 2008, RG n° 2008-1062 – [2008] EIRCR(A) 342 RG n°2008-1062.

14 *Tribunale di Ivrea*, 20 October 2008. This case is unreported.

15 *Corte di appello di Torino*, 10 March 2009, Il Fall. 2009, p 1293 – [2009] EIRCR(A) 249.

16 CJEU, 4 September 2014, Case C-327/13, *Burgo Group*, ECLI:EU:C:2014:2158, statement No 3. The ruling of the Court of Appeal of Turin was also confirmed by the Italian Supreme Court (Cass., Sez. Un., 29 October 2015, n 22093, Il Fall. 2016, p 829).

administrator for the whole group. Again, these proceedings were administrative in nature, but a court which was territorially competent had to ascertain that the debtor was insolvent and to issue an order opening insolvency proceedings. Therefore, on 27th December 2003, the Court of Parma stated that *Parmalat SpA* was insolvent and opened insolvency proceedings in Parma.[17] Since *Parmalat SpA* had many subsidiaries abroad, which were insolvent too, Mr Bondi intended to apply the 'one group – one COMI' doctrine and extent the Parma proceedings to some foreign subsidiaries, on the ground that they were wholly owned by *Parmalat SpA* and that their activities were entirely decided in Parma. For example, this happened smoothly as regards *Parmalat Netherlands BV,* which was a subsidiary located in The Netherland.[18]

As said, the *Parmalat* case also showed an example of non-cooperation, which resulted in distrust between courts and insolvency proceedings belonging to different jurisdictions, in opportunistic behaviours and in a conclusive request to the CJEU for a preliminary ruling. This happened as regards *Eurofood IFSC, Ltd* (which will be hereinafter called '*Eurofood*'), which was a wholly owned subsidiary of *Parmalat SpA*, located in the Republic of Ireland. This was the 'plot'. On 27th January 2004, the Bank of America, which had been informed that Mr Bondi intended to 'move' the COMI of *Eurofood* to Italy, applied to the High Court in Dublin in order to file an involuntary winding up case for *Eurofood* under Irish law and requested the appointment of a temporary administrator; on the same day, the High Court of Dublin appointed Mr Pearse Farrell as a provisional liquidator for *Eurofood*;[19] on 29th January 2004, Mr Farrell gave notice of his appointment to Mr Bondi. On 5th February, Mr Bondi applied to the Italian Minister for admission of *Eurofood* to Italian insolvency proceedings and, on 10th February, the Italian Minister extended the Italian proceedings to *Eurofood*, although he was aware that this company had already been submitted to insolvency proceedings in Ireland. On 10th February 2004, Mr

---

17  *Tribunale di Parma*, 27 December 2003, available at: www.parmalatinamminis-trazionestraordinaria.it/it/PRcomstampa/sentenza%20Parmalat.pdf.
18  *Tribunale di Parma*, 4 February 2004, Riv.dir.int.priv. e proc. 2004, p 693.
19  To our knowledge, the 27 March 2004 decision is unreported. However, on 23rd March 2004 the High Court of Dublin confirmed it, and stated that the opening of insolvency proceedings at that time, and the consequent appointment of Mr Farrell, operated retrospectively, with the result that both acts had to be considered as dated on 27.3.2004. In this respect, see *Pannen*, in: Pannen (ed), European Insolvency Regulation, 2007, p 142.

Bondi applied to the Court of Parma for declaring the *Eurofood* insolvency. The court set a hearing and ordered Mr Bondi to give notice of the hearing to 'interested parties'. On 12th February 2004, Mr Bondi filed a report with the Court of Parma on *Eurofood* case, but he neither provided a copy to Mr Farrell nor informed him about the hearing. On 20th February, the Court of Parma declared the insolvency of *Eurofood*.[20] The case resulted in a request to CJEU for a preliminary ruling, while the Court of Parma was accused of having violated Article 31 EIR 2000 and the principles of fair trial and, especially, of having failed to give the Irish provisional liquidator an opportunity of hearing so he did not have sufficient time to prepare a defence.[21]

Finally, none of the cases above mentioned showed the use of agreements and protocols. Indeed, scholars and practitioners report that, in Italy, there is no evidence either of signing of agreements and protocols, or of a debate concerning their nature and practicability.[22]

3. Taking lessons from the Illochroma and Eurofood cases: legal uncertainty produces 'prisoner's dilemmas'

The *Eurofood* case, and in certain respect the *Illochroma* one as well, contain an important lesson for lawmakers and interpreters. Here, an endeavour will be made to make this concept more explicit.

Judicial cooperation is based on the principles of sincere cooperation and mutual trust. Within the European Union, these principles are based

---

20  *Tribunale di Parma*, 20 February 2004, Foro it. 2004, 1567.
21  CJEU, 2 May 2006, Case C-341/04, *Eurofood IFSC*, ECLI:EU:C:2006:281.
22  *Lener-Rosato*, in: Leonard (ed), Restructuring & Insolvency 2015, p 240, this statement is also available at: https://gettingthedealthrough.com/area/35/jurisdiction/15/restructuring-insolvency-2016-italy, para 50. By contrast, in June 2015 the Italian 'Consiglio Nazionale dei Dottori Commercialisti e degli Esperti Contabili' (CNDCEC) concluded with the French 'Conseil National des Administrateurs Judiciaires et des Mandataires Judiciaires' (CNAJMJ) a French-Italian Protocol on cooperation in cross-border insolvency issues involving the jurisdictions of France and Italy. After the presentation of this paper a German lawyer maintained that this Protocol would be extended to a non-specified Association of German lawyers. On 16th November 2016, Dr Francesca Maione, director of the Italian 'Consiglio Nazionale dei Dottori Commercialisti e degli Esperti Contabili' (CNDCEC), who had been expressly asked about this extension, officially denied it. In any cases, these Protocols are something different from those referred to in this paper and, now, in Art 41 EIR.

on Article 4(3) TEU, Art. 67(1) and (4) TFEU and Article 81(2) lit. a) and c) TFEU. However, sincere cooperation and mutual trust also require legal certainty and foreseeability in legal situations with cross-border implications. In fact, if each court and insolvency practitioner can individually establish which law should apply to and which court should be competent in each cross-border legal relationship and which judgments of which other Member States are to be recognised, each court and each insolvency practitioner have an incentive to act opportunistically and to pursue the interest of those parties that are located in their own jurisdiction, *i.e.* to overprotect local debtors, local creditors, local employees, local company directors, etc.

In the *Eurofood* case, the 'acquis communautaire' of that time – *i.e.* Regulation 1346/2000 without the successive CJEU clarifications – contained many gaps and was not totally clear about many points involved. For example, Regulation 1346/2000 contained no prescriptions about group insolvencies; it was not clear about the COMI determination, especially if a company was a letter-box company; it did not clarify whether the 'prior in time' principle laid down by Article 3(3) also applied where the proceedings which had been opened first were temporary proceedings only. This case demonstrates that, although in the long run both courts and insolvency practitioners would have had better outcomes by cooperating, each of them preferred not to cooperate, with the result of lengthening the time of the proceedings, increasing their costs and, accordingly, poorly satisfying the interests of the parties involved, no matter if they were local or not.

The development of the *Eurofood* case reproduces the dynamic of the so-called iterated game of 'prisoner's dilemma' where two completely 'rational' individuals who have the dilemma of whether to cooperate or not intentionally decide not to cooperate even if it appears that it is in their best interests to do so. The following matrix depicts the application of this game to court behaviours.

|  | COOPERATE | NON-COOPERATE |
|---|---|---|
| **COOPERATE** | $Court_A = 3$<br>$Court_B = 3$ | $Court_A = 0$<br>$Court_B = 5$ |
| **NON-COOPERATE** | $Court_A = 5$<br>$Court_B = 0$ | $Court_A = 1$<br>$Court_B = 1$ |

For the sake of simplicity, consider a cross-border case where $Court_A$ and $Court_B$ are required to cooperate. Both $Court_A$ and $Court_B$ have two choices, namely either to cooperate or not to cooperate. Each court must make a choice depending on the other court's possible choice, but without knowing what the other court will really do. This is the dilemma. The matrix above illustrates this dynamic. $Court_A$ chooses a row, in order to decide whether to cooperate or not. $Court_B$ chooses a column, in order to decide whether to cooperate or not. The outcomes of the game are expressed in term of payoffs. They range from 1 to 5 points. These points conventionally quantify how court behaviours are individually efficient, in terms both of quickness of local proceedings and protection of local interests. The sum of those payoffs referred to in a single cell expresses how court behaviours are efficient for the cross-border case as whole.

Suppose that $Court_A$ thinks that $Court_B$ will cooperate. $Court_A$ has two choices, namely either to cooperate or not to cooperate. Here, the first column of figure 1 features the two possible outcomes. If $Court_A$ cooperates, it will receive a payoff of 3 points — here, $Court_B$ will receive 3 points too. By contrast, if $Court_A$ does not cooperate, it will receive a payoff of 5 points, while $Court_B$ will receive 0 points. Now, suppose that $Court_A$ thinks that $Court_B$ will not cooperate. Again $Court_A$ has two choices, namely either to cooperate or not to cooperate. Here, the second column of the matrix features the two possible outcomes. If $Court_A$ cooperates, it receives a payoff of 0 points, while $Court_B$ will receive 5 points. By contrast, if $Court_A$ does not cooperate, it will receive a payoff of 1 point — here, $Court_B$ will receive 1 point too.

This means that, no matter what $Court_B$ does, $Court_A$ will receive higher payoffs by not cooperating than by cooperating — 5 points are more than 3 points, and even more than 1 or 0 points. But this also means that, if neither $Court_A$ or $Court_B$ cooperate, both do worse than if both had cooperated (1 point is less than 3 points). Similarly, this logic holds for $Court_B$. Further, this modelling of strategic interaction between courts means that, if $Court_A$ continues to interact with $Court_B$ – as happens in a real cross-border insolvency case – $Court_A$ will certainly assume that $Court_B$ will not cooperate and $Court_A$ will therefore insist in its strategy of non-cooperation. Similarly, this logic will hold for $Court_B$.

The lesson is the following: if a legal framework is lacking on legal certainty and foreseeability, courts and/or insolvency practitioners dealing with the same case but belonging to different jurisdictions tend not to cooperate. This is because no matter what the other court and/or insolvency practitioner do/does, in the short term it pays for each court and/or insolvency practitioner not to cooperate.

4. Taking lessons from reluctance to conclude agreements and protocols: accepting that these forms of cooperation require courts and insolvency practitioners to make a choice between alternative rulings and activities

Italian case law provides for another opportunity to study cooperation more in depth. As said, in Italy cooperation refers to cases where courts and insolvency practitioners mainly need assistance abroad. The *Cirio del Monte* and *Parmalat Netherlands BV* issues are cases in point. By contrast, there is no notice either of agreements and protocols or of those other forms of cooperation which, like agreements and protocols, require courts and insolvency practitioners to make a choice between alternative possible rulings or activities. This means that, in Italy, there is no notice of those forms of cooperation concerning how to sell assets, whether restructuring by means of an asset deal or by an insolvency plan, how to exercise voting rights, and so on.

In the past, this situation existed in other civil law jurisdictions even featuring a larger number of cross-border insolvency cases, such as in Germany and France. Why? We will try to explain this within legal reasoning. First, consider a prescription which is specific in contents, such as that provided by the first sentence of Article 3(1) EIR 2000. This lays down: '[t]he courts of the Member State within the territory of which the centre of the debtor's main interests is situated shall have jurisdiction to open insolvency proceedings.' This prescription could arouse problems of textual interpretation (*e.g.,* what does 'centre of main interests' mean? What do insolvency proceedings mean?, etc.). The requests for preliminary ruling in the *Eurofood* and *Interedil* cases are cases in point.[23] However, after the interpreter has solved these problems of interpretation, this prescription proves to be easy to apply to a specific case. In effect, this prescription requires courts and insolvency practitioners to make an easy deduction which could be written as follows:

- in any case, '[t]he courts of the Member State within the territory of which the centre of the debtor's main interests is situated shall have jurisdiction to open insolvency proceedings' – major premise;
- in the specific case, a debtor ALFA has its centre of the debtor's main interests in Italy – minor premise;

---

23 CJEU, 2 May 2006, Case C-341/04, *Eurofood IFSC*, ECLI:EU:C:2006:281; CJEU, 10 March 2011, Case C-396/09, *Interedil* ECLI:EU:C:2011:132.

– in the specific case, Italian courts have jurisdiction to open insolvency proceedings in Italy – conclusion.

This form of application is a syllogism, which requires no choices between alternative possible rulings or activities. This concerns most prescriptions, and there are a plenty of examples of them in Regulation 1346/2000 as well as in Regulation 2015/848.

Now consider a prescription imposing a duty of cooperation, such as that provided by the first sentence of Article 31 EIR 2000. This lays down the following: "the liquidator in the main proceedings and the liquidators in the secondary proceedings shall be duty bound to cooperate with each other." This prescription too could arouse problems of textual interpretation (*e.g.*, what form is required to cooperate?, etc.). However, this prescription also arouses problems of choice. In fact, if one tries to apply the prescription involved to a specific case, one achieves the following result:

– in any case, 'the liquidator in the main proceedings and the liquidators in the secondary proceedings shall be duty bound to cooperate with each other' – major premise;
– in the specific case, the liquidator ALFA is appointed in the main insolvency proceedings X and the liquidator BETA is appointed in the secondary insolvency proceedings Y, and both proceedings concern the same debtor Z – minor premise;
– in the specific case, 'the liquidator ALFA appointed in the main proceedings X and the liquidators BETA appointed in the secondary proceedings Y shall be duty bound to cooperate with each other' – conclusion.

Here, the form of reasoning is the same as in the previous case. However, the conclusion contains nothing more than what the insolvency practitioner ALFA and the insolvency proceedings BETA already knew. In fact, while – in the abstract (*in any case*) – they know that thy have to cooperate with each other – in the concrete (*in the specific case*) – they have no idea what they have to do.

Legal theorists are absolutely aware of these shortcomings and, in this respect, they point out that these prescriptions, such as those imposing duties of cooperation and information, are problematic since they involve choices between rival possible forms of application.[24] To come back to Article 31 EIR 2000, this implies that the sentence laying down 'the liquidator in the main proceedings and the liquidators in the secondary proceedings shall be duty bound to cooperate with each other' may command *either* that insolvency practitioners have to conclude a binding protocol regulating the proceedings *ex ante*, *or* that they have to agree upon what is to be done step-by-step. Moreover, these choices may be referred *either* to every step of each set of proceedings, *or* to some specific steps of them, *either* to the decision concerning rescuing or liquidating *or* to the execution of these decisions, and so on – one could say *ad infinitum*.[25]

Traditionally, common-law courts and insolvency practitioners are familiar with these choices and accept that interpreting and applying open textured prescriptions could imply subjective evaluations and consequentialist arguments. In this respect, a passage by Roscoe Pound is illuminating. 'Behind the characteristic doctrines and ideas and technique of the common-law lawyer there is a significant frame of mind. It is a frame of mind which habitually looks at things in the concrete, not in the abstract; which puts its faith in experience rather than in abstractions. It is a frame of mind which prefers to go forward cautiously on the basis of experience from this case or that case to next case, as justice in each case seems to require, instead of seeking to refer everything back to supposed universals. It is a frame of mind which is not ambitious to deduce decision from the case in hand from a proposition formulated universally...It is the frame of mind behind the sure-footed Anglo-Saxon habit of dealing with things as they arise instead of anticipating them by abstract universal formulas.' [26] By contrast, civil-law courts and insolvency practitioners encounter more

---

24 *MacCormick*, Legal Reasoning and Legal Theory (2003), p 100 ff, and *Canaris/ Larenz* (eds), Methodenlehre der Rechtswissenschaft, 3rd edn (1995), p 98. In this respect, these authors express more or less the same concept. However, while *Neil MacCormick* refers to the UK and the common-law tradition, the book by *Claus-Wilhelm Canaris and Karl Larenz* refer to the German tradition. This might be considered quite representative of legal reasoning in civil-law jurisdictions, and it strongly influenced Italian legal thinking.

25 Moreover, while Regulation 1346/2000 restricted secondary proceedings to liquidation proceedings only (Art 27), Regulation 2015/848 does not contain this restriction any longer (Art 34).

26 *Pound*, The future of the Common law (1937), p 18. This passage is quoted by *Zweigert/Kötz*, Einführung in die Rechtsvergleichung: Auf dem Gebiete des Privatrechts, 3rd edn (1996), p 253.

difficulties in interpreting and applying open textured prescriptions. Certainly, civil-law courts are also aware that, sometimes, the application of a prescription implies more efforts than an activity of mechanical deduction and that in these cases judges have to make choices between several rival rulings, or – to use a German expression – that they have discretion in judgement (*Beurteilungsspielraum*).[27] However, traditionally civil-law legal theorists consider this discretion as a danger to justice. This explains why, in this respect, two distinguished German authors compare administrative authorities (*Behörde*) and judges; state that both have discretion; but point out that, while administrative authorities may focus on facts and make their choices by means of consequentialist evaluations comparing means and goals (*Zweckmäßigkeitserwägungen*), judges have mainly to focus on the normative contents of prescriptions.[28]

The lesson is the following: cooperation requires courts and insolvency practitioners to make choices between alternative rulings and activities. If courts and insolvency practitioners belong to a jurisdiction which has a restricted culture of judicial discretion, they tend to minimize efforts in cooperation.

## 5. Explaining Articles 41-44 EIR within legal reasoning

Fortunately, not every civil law court is so reluctant to apply insolvency law prescriptions requiring choices between alternative rulings — for instance, after a period of hesitation, both German and French courts and insolvency practitioners started cooperating in rescue proceedings and concluding agreements and protocols which incorporate choices between al-

---

27 *Canaris/Larenz*, Methodenlehre der Rechtswissenschaft, 3rd edn (1995), p 117. This point needs specification, even if within the restricted room of a footnote. Germany has a long tradition of standards-based regulation, which certainly requires courts to make choices or – to use a German expression – to make standards concrete. § 157 of the German Civil Code (*Bürgerliches Gesetzbuch; BGB*) is a case in point — this paragraph employs the standard of 'good faith' (*Treu und Glauben*). However, traditionally the use of this form of regulation by those who drew up the German Civil Code was considered as a problematic exception to the use of rules-based regulation — the title and contents of a monograph by *Hedemann*, Die Flucht in die Generalklauseln (1933) are very representative in this respect. The title of this book might be translated into English: 'Escape into standards'.

28 *Canaris/Larenz*, Methodenlehre der Rechtswissenschaft, 3rd edn (1995), p 117.

ternative rulings and activities.[29] Moreover, compared with Regulation 1346/2000, Regulation 2015/848 contains many improvements in this respect. These are of various kinds, as will be explained hereinafter.

First, the people that drew up Regulation 2015/848 improved the legal framework where courts and insolvency practitioners have to cooperate, filled in gaps of Regulation 1346/2000 and clarified many points which were ambiguous. For example, concerning the framework which was relevant for the *Eurofood* case, the people that drew up Regulation 2015/848 introduced a regulation on group insolvencies (Articles 56-77 EIR; recital 53 EIR); made COMI determination easier and more precise (Articles 3-6 EIR, and recitals 30-32 EIR); and specified that for the purpose of this regulation the term 'insolvency practitioner' also includes those who are appointed on an interim basis only (Article 2(5) EIR). Moreover, many other actions were taken, which hopefully will be able to reduce 'prisoner's dilemmas' and the inclination not to cooperate.

Second, the people that drew up Regulation 2015/848 increased the quantity of the duties of cooperation and communication. *Inter alia*, this increase consists in devoting to this topic four Articles, which refer to 'Cooperation and communication between insolvency practitioners' (Article 41 EIR), 'Cooperation and communication between courts' (Article 42 EIR), 'Cooperation and communication between insolvency practitioners and courts' (Article 43 EIR) and 'Costs of cooperation and communication' (Article 44 EIR), respectively; listing some topics where insolvency practitioners and/or courts have to communicate information and cooperate with each other; expressly allowing conclusion of agreements and protocols. Moreover, as regards 'Cooperation and communication between courts' and 'Cooperation and communication between insolvency practitioners and courts', Regulation 2015/848 anticipated the duties involved at the time where main proceedings have been opened and the request to open secondary proceedings is still pending or, *vice versa*, where territorial proceedings have been opened and the request to open main proceedings is still pending. By contrast, as regards 'Cooperation and communication between courts' Regulation 2015/848 established that, 'where appro-

---

29  *Wessels/Markell/Kilborn*, International Cooperation in Bankruptcy and Insolvency Matters, *passim*. By contrast, Italian scholars are increasingly aware of the limits of Italian legal practice, with the result that they consider a more pragmatic approach to regulation as highly desirable. In this respect, see *Terranova*, Elogio dell'approssimazione. Il diritto come esperienza comunicativa, 2015, p 313 ff.

priate, courts may appoint an independent person or body acting on its instructions.'

This second group of improvements, which manifestly enjoys the experience of most common model laws and codes of best practices,[30] follows two regulatory trajectories. Accordingly, these improvements could be sorted as follows:

## 5.1 Improvements aimed at specifying the logic of the duty of cooperation and information

These elements contain a teleological element which – in the abstract – expresses the purpose of cooperation, in order to require courts and insolvency practitioners to determine the means and the activities which – in the concrete – appear most appropriate. For example, in Regulation 2015/848 these elements are:

Recital 40 EIR (Secondary insolvency proceedings can serve different purposes, besides the protection of local interests. Cases may arise in which the insolvency estate of the debtor is too complex to administer as a unit, or the differences in the legal systems concerned are so great that difficulties may arise from the extension of effects deriving from the law of the State of the opening of proceedings to the other Member States where the assets are located. For that reason, the insolvency practitioner in the main insolvency proceedings may request the opening of secondary insolvency proceedings where the efficient administration of the insolvency estate so requires);

Recital 48 EIR (Main insolvency proceedings and secondary insolvency proceedings can contribute to the efficient administration of the debtor's insolvency estate or to the effective realisation of the total assets if there is proper cooperation between the actors involved in all the concurrent proceedings. Proper cooperation implies the various insolvency practitioners

---

30 In this respect, see: The UNCITRAL Model Law on Cross-Border Insolvency (1997), its Guide to Enactment and Interpretation (2013) and the UNCITRAL Practice Guide on Cross-Border Insolvency Cooperation (2009) – all available at: www.uncitral.org/uncitral/en/uncitral_texts/insolvency/1997Model.html; The III/ALI Transnational Insolvency: Global Principles for the Cooperation in International Insolvency Cases (2009); The European Communication and Cooperation Guidelines for Cross- border Insolvency (2007) ('CoCo Guidelines'); Cross-Border Insolvency Court-to-Court Cooperation Principles and Guidelines (2014).

and the courts involved cooperating closely, in particular by exchanging a sufficient amount of information. In order to ensure the dominant role of the main insolvency proceedings, the insolvency practitioner in such proceedings should be given several possibilities for intervening in secondary insolvency proceedings which are pending at the same time. In particular, the insolvency practitioner should be able to propose a restructuring plan or composition or apply for a suspension of the realisation of the assets in the secondary insolvency proceedings);

Recital 49 EIR (In light of such cooperation, insolvency practitioners and courts should be able to enter into agreements and protocols for the purpose of facilitating cross-border cooperation of multiple insolvency proceedings in different Member States concerning the same debtor or members of the same group of companies, where this is compatible with the rules applicable to each of the proceedings. Such agreements and protocols may vary in form, in that they may be written or oral, and in scope, in that they may range from generic to specific, and may be entered into by different parties. Simple generic agreements may emphasise the need for close cooperation between the parties, without addressing specific issues, while more detailed, specific agreements may establish a framework of principles to govern multiple insolvency proceedings and may be approved by the courts involved, where the national law so requires. They may reflect an agreement between the parties to take, or to refrain from taking, certain steps or actions);

Article 41(2) lit. a) EIR (In implementing the cooperation set out in paragraph 1, the insolvency practitioners shall: [...] as soon as possible communicate to each other any information which may be relevant to the other proceedings, in particular any progress made in lodging and verifying claims and all measures aimed at rescuing or restructuring the debtor, or at terminating the proceedings);

Article 42(3) EIR (The cooperation referred to in paragraph 1 may be implemented by any means that the court considers appropriate. It may, in particular, concern: *(a)* coordination in the appointment of the insolvency practitioners; *(b)* communication of information by any means considered appropriate by the court; *(c)* coordination of the administration and supervision of the debtor's assets and affairs; *(d)* coordination of the conduct of hearings; *(e)* coordination in the approval of protocols, where necessary.

## 5.2 Improvements aimed at specifying the limits of the duty of cooperation and information in terms of consistency with the system as a whole

These elements contain systematic references which – in the abstract – feature a framework within which – in the concrete – courts and insolvency practitioners have to interpret and apply those prescriptions imposing the duty of cooperation and communication. Sometimes these elements require courts and insolvency practitioners to balance conflicting duties, such as the duty of communication which is imposed by Regulation 2015/848 and the duty to protect confidential information which is imposed by other sources of law. For example, in Regulation 2015/848 these elements are:

Article 41(1) EIR: The insolvency practitioner in the main insolvency proceedings and the insolvency practitioner or practitioners in secondary insolvency proceedings concerning the same debtor shall cooperate with each other to the extent such cooperation is not incompatible with the rules applicable to the respective proceedings.

Article 41(2) lit. a) EIR: (…) provided appropriate arrangements are made to protect confidential information;

Article 42(1) EIR: (…) to the extent that such cooperation is not incompatible with the rules applicable to each of the proceedings. For that purpose, the courts may, where appropriate, appoint an independent person or body acting on its instructions, provided that it is not incompatible with the rules applicable to them.

Article 42(2) EIR: (…) provided that such communication respects the procedural rights of the parties to the proceedings and the confidentiality of information.

Article 44 EIR: The requirements laid down in Articles 42 and 43 EIR shall not result in courts charging costs to each other for cooperation and communication.

## 6. Concluding remarks: from cooperating 'in the shadow of soft-law' to cooperating 'in the shadow of hard-law'. Corollaries

Probably, the evolution of cooperation in European cross-border cases is going to go much further.

Originally, cooperation in international insolvency cases – which here includes cooperation across Europe – was a mere habit of common law courts and insolvency practitioners. They had no duties, even imposed by soft-law instruments, but created case by case an environment of mutual assistance making application of international private law prescriptions smoother. Later, some international bodies such as the UNCITRAL, the American Law Institute (ALI), the International Insolvency Institute (III), drew up codes of best practices, which provided courts and insolvency practitioners around the world with soft-law guidance and assistance. Outside Europe, cooperation in cross-border cases still works in this manner.

The people that drew up Article 31 EIR 2000 marked an important step forward since it established a duty of cooperation by means of an instrument of hard law. This Regulation was passed in 2000; however, it exactly reproduced the contents of 1995 Convention on Insolvency proceedings, which – it is worth noting – was conceived before the 1999 Treaty of Amsterdam had developed 'judicial cooperation in civil matters' as an independent and separate field of European law. Probably, this early origin explains why Article 31 EIR 2000 lays down only a few 'commands', and why it has been appreciated by courts and practitioners more as a source of principles – *i.e.* of the principles of cooperation and communication – than as a source of rules which thoroughly regulate cooperation and communication. This is because Article 31 EIR 2000 has rarely considered as operating in a free-standing manner — in 2004 the Vienna Higher Regional Court ruled that the 'prevailing opinion' and the United Nations Commission on International Trade Law (UNCITRAL) Model law were found to reflect the existence of a wider obligation of cooperation also involving courts,[31] while in the early years European bodies maintained that new codes of best practices were necessary to correctly apply Article 31 EIR 2000 and, for this purpose, they drew up the 'INSOL-Europe European Communication and Cooperation Guidelines for Cross-border Insolvency (2007)' ('CoCo Guidelines') and 'The EU Cross-Border Insolvency Court-to-Court Cooperation Principles and Guidelines (2014)'. To use and adapt a successful metaphor, this means that within Regulation 1346/2000 courts and insolvency practitioners cooperate 'in the shadow of soft-law'.[32]

---

31  *Oberlandesgericht Wien*, 9 November 2004, 28 R 225/04w [2004] EIRCR(A) 72.

32  The metaphor at stake is that of 'bargaining in the shadow of the law'. Actually, this refers to that situation where the parties seek to achieve an agreement by reference to what will happen if they fail to achieve agreement and they are forced to go to court. See *Mnookin/Kornhauser*, Yale L.J. 1979, p 950-997.

Regulation 2015/848 recast Regulation 1346/2000, and enlarged the regulation on cooperation and communication. Above, we said that this change greatly improved that regulation; now, we might also add that, for the first time, the spirit of the Treaty of Amsterdam produced and legitimated a set of prescriptions which thoroughly regulate cooperation and communication in European cross-border cases. Of course, this statement does not mean that additional improvements are not possible and even desirable.[33] By contrast, it means that the people that drew up Regulation 2015/848 changed their regulatory pace; took into account that Article 81 TFEU expressly provides 'judicial cooperation in civil matters'; and conceived Articles 41-44 of Regulation 2015/848 as a true form of rules-based regulation which lays down who, how and when has to cooperate. To continue to use the abovementioned metaphor, this means that within Regulation 2015/848 courts and insolvency practitioners will cooperate 'in the shadow of hard-law'.

Slowly, the latter development might additionally detach the class of cooperation in European cross-border cases from the class of cooperation in international non-European cases. Courts and insolvency practitioners across Europe might decide to cooperate not only because they are conscious that their actions affect each other in a form of mutualistic exchange, but also because they get the feeling that law and authority requires them to cooperate. They might start to concretely appreciate that passage of the Explanatory Report which suggests that '[w]here appropriate, the applicable national law will determine the liquidator's liability when the latter has not respected the duties arising from Article 31 EIR'; [34] and they might become more sympathetic to considering some non-observance of the duties involved as an infringement of Article 47 of the Charter of Fundamental Rights of the European Union and of Article 6 of Convention of Human Rights and Fundamental Freedoms.[35]

---

33 For instance, in this respect the EU Commission ought also to establish that, if there are more than one set of secondary insolvency proceedings, the duties imposed on courts and insolvency practitioners also have a horizontal extension, binding the courts and the insolvency practitioners in the many secondary proceedings to each other. Moreover, concerning those additional improvements which would be desirable see the Annotated Guidelines by this Study.

34 *Virgós-Schmit*, Report on the Convention of Insolvency Proceedings (1996), para 234.

35 In this respect, see the Opinion of Advocate General concerning the Case CJEU, 27 September 2005, Case C-341/04, *Eurofood IFSC*, ECLI:EU:C:2005:579. How-

Certainly, this trend could disappoint common-law lawyers, who always look with suspicion on any transformation from light-touch regulation to authoritative regulation.[36] Certainly, this trend will prove to be useful for civil lawyers, such as Italian courts and insolvency practitioners, who always appreciate the strength of hard law and the threat of sanctions. Probably, a lawmaker who intends to additionally improve Articles 41-44 EIR and reconcile the common-lawyers view with the civil-lawyers view might introduce at European level an ombudsman who will mediate between the parties and, possibly, provide advice and assistance to courts. He ought to have the power to investigate, recommend corrective action and promote friendly solutions between the parties, but he ought to have no power to issue binding decisions, as courts do.

7. Coda: Spontaneous comments on the relevant sections of the 'Annotated Guidelines'

The thoughts expressed *supra* allow me to make some comments on the sections concerning 'Instruments to avoid or postpone secondary proceedings', 'Cooperation between main and secondary proceedings', and 'Protocols' of Annotated Guidelines on Regulation 2015/848. These comments, which express a *prima facie* assessment, will be featured in an apodictic way.

7.1 Article 36 EIR

I agree that the introduction of the 'undertaking in order to avoid secondary insolvency proceedings' (Article 36 EIR) is worthy of appreciation.

This regulation allows the interpreter to consider the 'undertaking' either as a *contract* (even if subject to the approval of creditors and court) where the insolvency practitioner in the main proceedings swaps the local

---

ever, in the *Eurofood* case the infringement of these rights was evaluated as a possible ground of non-recognition of the Italian decision in accordance with Art 26 EIR 2000 (public policy).

36 *Ferran*, JCLS 2001, 381 ff, available to download at: <ssrn.com/ abstract=294462>. Actually, this paper refers to the fields of company law and financial markets law.

creditor's agreement not to request the opening of secondary proceedings with the practitioner's promise that the distribution of the debtor's local assets should be distributed in accordance with local national law, or as a form of *segregation* (or *ring-fencing*) of the debtor's assets. Probably, the idea of contract appears more compliant with the 'improvised nature' of the undertaking performed by the English courts, especially in the *MG Rover* and *Collins & Aikmann* cases, while the idea of segregation appears more compliant with the contents of recital 43 EIR. This states '[f]or the purposes of giving an undertaking to local creditors, the assets and rights located in the Member State where the debtor has an establishment should form a sub-category of the insolvency estate, and, when distributing them or the proceeds resulting from their realisation, the insolvency practitioner in the main insolvency proceedings should respect the priority rights that creditors would have had if secondary insolvency proceedings had been opened in that Member State.'

The Annotated Guidelines clearly opt for the thesis of segregation. Therefore, they state that '[t]hose assets situated in the Member State in which secondary proceedings could be opened (including the proceeds received from their realization) shall form a sub-category of the insolvency estate (cf recital 43 EIR) liable for both local and other creditors, which otherwise would be entitled to lodge their claims in secondary proceedings according to Article 45 EIR.' [37]

The thesis of segregation seems to have many implications. On this point, the Annotated Guidelines state that '[t]he scope of an undertaking, *i.e.* the distribution and priority rights under the law of the Member State where secondary proceedings could be initiated, should apply to all creditors, including non-local creditors.'[38] But, probably, the thesis of segregation has many other corollaries. For example, the above-mentioned cross-filing might make a decision to rescue the firm more complex. Moreover, the thesis of segregation might also imply that the insolvency practitioner might transfer assets from the 'sub-category' of the insolvency estate to the insolvency estate as a whole, and *vice versa*.

However, I wonder whether the EU Commission really intended to go beyond the English courts' idea and wanted to transform 'contract' into 'segregation'; whether recital 43 EIR, which – it is worth noting – is non-

---

37  See *supra* Part 2, I. 3.1.1.
38  See *supra* Part 2, I. 3.1.2., and 1.2.2.

binding, employs the so-called 'Inversionsmethode' (doctrine of inversion) which, according to the advocates of the German *Interessenjurisprudenz*, is a pathological way of interpreting and applying a legal instrument or a single prescription – here, the doctrine of inversion would overrate the rationale of the regulatory intervention, which – it was said – only consists in avoiding secondary proceedings, and it would consider Article 36 EIR as introducing secondary proceedings, even if virtual in nature.[39] And, finally, I wonder whether there will be the risk that the thesis of segregation would reintroduce the shortcomings and costs of opening secondary proceedings, except that there will be no additional insolvency practitioners and fees to pay for them.

I agree that more legal certainty about the start of the time limit to request the opening of secondary proceedings would be desirable; that the parties involved being informed is crucial, and that it might be increased and improved; and that national courts when requested to open secondary proceedings might be inclined to conclude that an undertaking will not adequately protect the general interests of local creditors. I am moreover convinced that the insolvency practitioner in the main proceedings might also have opportunistic behaviour, which – this time – would consist in under-protecting local interests.[40] I agree that, before an undertaking becomes binding through approval, a court might open secondary proceedings although the process of approving the undertaking is underway, and that this shortcoming might threaten the rationale of Article 36 EIR. I agree that the special regulation on security rights *in rem* (Articles 8-10 EIR) prevent courts and insolvency practitioners from employing the mechanism of 'undertaking', but I would add that this shortcoming should suggest revising the regulation on security rights *in rem*.[41] Again, I agree that some prescriptions should be devoted to the relation between Article 36 EIR and the regulation on group insolvencies, but I maintain that this point might be better dealt with within the Chapter of Regulation

---

39  *Canaris/Larenz*, Methodenlehre der Rechtswissenschaft, 3rd edn 1995, p 283.
40  *Mangano*, in: Bork/van Zwieten (eds), Commentary on the European Insolvency Regulation (2016), para 38.14.
41  *McCormack/Bork* (eds), Security rights and the European Insolvency Regulation (2017), section 4.4. Since this book mainly refers to security rights *in rem* in Regulation 1346/2000, it does not deal with the fact that the special regulation on security rights *in rem* is considered as incompatible with the 'undertaking'.

2015/848 which is devoted to group insolvencies – this Chapter is commonly considered as being worthy of an all-round revision.

## 7.2 Articles 41-44 EIR

I agree that the EU has an educational role within Member States, and that it has to help Member States to perform a change management. Moreover, I would add that one has to bear in mind that this change management necessarily needs time, and that this time could vary country-by-country.

The Annotated Guidelines state that, although Regulation 2015/848 is of direct application in the Member States 'sometimes an active intervention of the national lawmaker is required' and, immediately afterwards, that '[t]o assess whether intervention is needed a task of assessment of the existing legal framework in each Member State must be performed to determine where the system stands, and to what extent it already allows for a swift implementation of the regulation – or, conversely, it hinders it.'[42]

This statement might make sense, especially where a jurisdiction, such as the Italian one, has no set of private international law prescriptions which are devoted to cross-border insolvency cases – Article 9 of the Italian Insolvency Statute (R.D. 16.3.1942 No 267, commonly called 'Legge fallimentare') hardly regulates some minor aspects of international jurisdiction. However, this negative feature also has the advantage that there will be no conflicts between the prescriptions of Regulation 2015/848 and some putative prescriptions concerning cooperation and communication in insolvency cases which already existed.

I agree that '[t]he national lawmakers may be willing to engage in an advisory role' and that [s]ometimes an appropriated, object-oriented interpretation and application of already existing national provisions will be enough;[43] I further approve the idea that '[a]cademia and legal literature should engage in an effort to understand the new rules correctly. They should promote awareness about them, and support their proper implementation and application in the context of each Member State's legal system academia.'[44] However, in the previous pages I have tried to demonstrate that some shortcomings in cooperation are intrinsic to the nature of

---

42 See *supra* Part 2, II. 3.1.
43 See *supra* Part 2, II. 3.1.3.
44 See *supra* Part 2, II. 3.1.4.

prescriptions imposing cooperation,[45] and now I would be willing to add that additional insights might produce information overload – less is more.


## 7.3 Protocols

I am absolutely aware that neither the Regulation 2015/848 nor national laws provides any guidance concerning agreements and protocols, and that Italian jurisdiction has no experience with them. Therefore, I suggest that, in Italy, insolvency practitioners should apply to courts to have them officially approved. Further, proceedings-by-proceedings, a formal approval by the creditors' committee appears to be required by law.

I agree that Regulation 2015/848 'is based on a minimum harmonization approach in the field of coordination of cross-border insolvency proceedings. Therefore, involved parties may derogate from the coordination system provided for in the EIR through an insolvency agreement or protocol. This should be possible, under the following conditions: it is in the interest of maximization of the estate's value or the organisation of the debtor's business; adequate safeguards for the affected estate are foreseen; and the *pari passu* principle, as established in the EIR, is not affected.'[46]

I agree that '[t]o promote the use of insolvency protocols or agreements, Member States are encouraged not to apply restrictive insolvency rules or introduce rules on the protocols or insolvency agreements. This could prevent complicated questions in relation to the validity of protocols or insolvency arrangements or even to the liability of the contracting parties'.[47] However, again it is important to bear in mind, on the one hand, that Regulation 2015/848, as a higher ranked source of law, necessarily prevails over national law restrictions and, on the other hand, that any action taken by Member States to encourage non-application of restrictive insolvency rules will never be able to overcome those shortcomings, which are intrinsic to the nature of prescriptions imposing cooperation, with the result that courts and insolvency practitioners should always face dilemmas and choices — to use and adapt an old Latin expression, this means: *dura natura legis, sed natura*.[48]

---

45  *Supra*, para 4.
46  See *supra* Part 2, III. 2.3.
47  See *supra* Part 2, III. 2.2.
48  The original expression is: 'dura lex, sed lex'.

Annex V: Opening statement on the new rules for the insolvency of
groups of companies

Professor Dr. Reinhard Bork[*]

Our first session will deal with Chapter V EIR, which regulates the insolvency proceedings of members of a group of companies. These provisions
are completely new and the European legislator deserves praise for having
presented the first set of rules on this subject in cross-border insolvency
law worldwide. The goal of Chapter V is to ensure the efficient administration and coordination of various insolvency proceedings while at the
same time respecting each group member's separate legal personality; it is
the outcome of a long and controversial debate as to how European insolvency law on groups of companies should be regulated, and even whether
it should be regulated at all. Ultimately, three key decisions have been
made:

- first, the proceedings should not be substantively consolidated in the
  vein of the U.S. Bankruptcy Code but should instead simply follow the
  tenet 'one company, one estate, one insolvency procedure', meaning
  that there are as many insolvency proceedings as there are insolvent
  group members and that no proceedings for the group as such exist;
- second, the new rules are confined to a procedural level by regulating
  cooperation and communication between courts and practitioners in
  Articles 56 – 60 EIR;
- third, these provisions are supplemented with innovative rules on
  group coordination proceedings in Articles 61 – 77 EIR.

There has been much support of, yet also much criticism of, the new
regime on group insolvencies and I will turn your attention to a few select
points which may be of specific interest for practitioners and may influence the acceptability of Chapter V.

1) My first observation regards the definition of group of companies in
Article 2(13) and (14) EIR. According to Article 2(13), 'group of companies' means a parent undertaking and all of its subsidiary undertakings.
This wording encompasses vertical groups only and omits horizontal
groups. This has been the subject of severe criticism, and the European

---

[*] Original opening statement presented at the conference in Luxembourg in October
2016 by Prof. Dr. *Reinhard Bork*, University of Hamburg.

legislator has responded by adding (14), which states that 'parent under-taking' means an undertaking which controls, either directly or indirectly, one or more subsidiary undertakings. Of great significance is Article 2(14), 2nd s., according to which an undertaking that prepares consolidated financial statements in accordance with the Financial Statement Directive shall be deemed as a parent undertaking. According to the prevailing opin-ion, this includes horizontal groups. But leaves certainly room for further questions. First of all, the relevant provisions of the Directive, especially in Article 22, are rather lengthy and complicated, and thus they are only of assistance for specialised accountants. It is therefore dubious whether the reference to the Directive ensures legal certainty. Another important ob-jection regards Article 22 of the Directive, which, especially in its para 2, is content with the *possibility* of controlling other undertakings, while the EIR requires *actual* control. It is debatable whether this problem can be solved by understanding the reference to the Directive as a rebuttable pre-sumption.

2) The norms on cooperation and communication are borrowed from similar regulations for the official bodies of main and secondary proceed-ings, and mirror internationally accepted best practice. I restrict myself to mentioning only Part 3 of the UNCITRAL Legislative Guide on Insolven-cy Law, which was published in 2010. It deals with the treatment of enter-prise groups in insolvency, recommending intensive cooperation and com-munication. However, two short remarks are necessary.

First, Article 56 EIR makes the cooperation duty for insolvency practi-tioners conditional on ascertaining that cooperation is compatible with the rules applicable to the national proceedings and does not produce any con-flict of interest. It should be stressed that *every* insolvency practitioner in-volved in group insolvencies is eager to achieve the best possible outcome for the estate and their creditors. Hence, a conflict of interests is unavoid-able to a certain extent. The wording of Article 56 EIR must therefore be construed narrowly in the sense that it only covers conflicts arising from cooperation measures which reduce or jeopardise the estate, for example if cooperation entails transmission of valuable know-how, patents or busi-ness secrets, making assets available to other group members which could have been disposed of with a large profit for the individual group member, or provides information which enables other insolvency practitioners to file for transactions avoidance. Otherwise, the limitations would weaken the obligation to cooperate considerably.

My second remark concerns Article 60 EIR. Although the new EIR does not provide an enforceable right to the provision of information by foreign insolvency practitioners or courts, or to their assistance, or to coordinated action, this norm enables each insolvency practitioner involved to intrude upon the insolvency proceedings of any other group member. They may especially request a stay of any measure related to the realisation of assets, provided that (1) a restructuring plan for all or some members of the group has been proposed and presents a reasonable chance of success, (2) such a stay is necessary in order to ensure the proper implementation of the restructuring plan, (3) the restructuring plan would be to the benefit of the creditors in the proceedings for which the stay is requested, and (4) neither the insolvency proceedings in which the insolvency practitioner has been appointed nor the proceedings in respect of which the stay is requested are subject to coordination proceedings. The court may order a stay of up to three months, which may be extended to a maximum period of six months. Any quick or pre-packaged sale of assets could thus be delayed by a maximum of six months, if a feasible plan proposes more value for creditors. Thus, only a proper test of a plan's feasibility will prevent 'procedural chaos'. Another problem may be that the implementation of the stay order is not the task of the insolvency practitioner who requested the stay but of the insolvency practitioner of the proceedings for which the stay was requested. Finally, several requests for stays can be made, which may lead to significant costs, delay and uncertainty.

3) The most controversial part of Chapter V concerns group coordination proceedings. Articles 61–77 EIR provide for the appointment of a group coordinator on the application of any insolvency practitioner appointed in insolvency proceedings opened in relation to a member of the group. The coordinator can be appointed by any national court that has jurisdiction over insolvency proceedings of a member of the group. His task is to identify and outline recommendations for the coordinated conduct of the insolvency proceedings, which are not binding on the national insolvency practitioners, and to propose a group coordination plan that identifies, describes and recommends a comprehensive set of measures appropriate to an integrated approach towards the resolution of the group members' insolvencies. The coordinator has no power to make binding decisions and operates as a mediator rather than an insolvency practitioner. In a nutshell, the group coordination proceedings feature three key elements: (1) a coordination court, (2) a coordinator, and (3) a group coordination plan. Ultimately, this constitutes a deliberate compromise between the

need to centralise the coordination process in order to achieve as much co-ordination as possible and the need to preserve the autonomy of the individual proceedings. However, this poses some questions which must be answered.

First, is it reasonable to authorise all national courts administering insolvency proceedings regarding a group member to appoint a coordinator? The European legislator wisely did not adopt the idea of connecting jurisdiction through a group COMI (although this does not exclude the possibility that all group members may have their COMI in the same state). The price of not using a group COMI is the competing jurisdiction of all courts involved in the group members' insolvencies and an incentive for forum shopping, as far as coordination proceedings are concerned. Admittedly, the priority rule in Article 62 EIR tries to ensure that only one court decides, but this court may be far away from the thick of the action and may be the target of forum shopping in being tasked with making a decision which should instead fall to a more appropriate court. If an English company has headquarters in Luxembourg, the main production company in Germany and a small distribution subsidiary in Romania, is it really appropriate to give the courts in Romania jurisdiction to appoint the coordinator? Article 66 EIR addresses this problem by stating that where at least two-thirds of all insolvency practitioners appointed in insolvency proceedings of the members of the group have agreed that a court of another Member State having jurisdiction is the most appropriate court for the opening of group coordination proceedings, that court shall have exclusive jurisdiction. However, given that this is a long, expensive and complicated procedure and that a two-thirds majority may be hard to reach, this is not very likely to be used by the insolvency practitioners.

Second, is the appointment procedure adequately designed? In my view, this must be doubted as well. If the court which has received the request for appointing a coordinator, after having checked the conditions for opening coordination proceedings, must then inform all insolvency practitioners involved in the court's national language (in my example given above this would be Romanian, which the insolvency practitioners in England, Germany and Luxemburg probably would not understand, leading to more delays through the necessity of appointing translators), wait for 30 days to receive objections or even an agreement from at least two thirds of the insolvency practitioners that another court should have jurisdiction, this does not strike me as being a smooth procedure.

Third, is the professional quality of the coordinator guaranteed? According to Article 71 EIR, the coordinator must be independent (which needs no further comment) and eligible to act as an insolvency practitioner under the laws of one of the Member States. This means that in my example given above, the Romanian court may appoint a person who is eligible not under Romanian law, but under Lithuanian law, which the Romanian court is hopefully familiar with. One must therefore hope that all parties involved behave reasonably and suggest an experienced person whose competence and integrity is beyond any doubt. It would be better if there were a single set of requirements to act as a coordinator contained within the EIR itself. After all, Article 75 EIR provides for the revocation of an inept coordinator. However, the efficiency of this provision must also be questioned, since the liability of the coordinator in the event of any problems is not directly addressed, which, by the way, may deter qualified persons from accepting the position of group coordinator.

Fourth, is the coordinator sufficiently equipped, i.e. do coordinators have the necessary tools? In my view, they have no tools other than the power of their professional and moral authority. They are not authorised to make binding decisions: despite Article 74 EIR, which establishes a duty to cooperate for all insolvency practitioners involved, the national insolvency practitioners are not bound to even speak with the coordinator, since they may opt out of the coordination proceedings at will – a weapon which may be abused in the sense of holding up proceedings to push through inappropriate demands. Insolvency practitioners may also refuse to comply with the coordinator's plans and proposals, although they would have to explain their non-compliance to their national authorities. Against this background, it may be of general interest that the German legislature has recently suggested making the relevant decisions of the insolvency practitioner (including opt-out decisions) contingent upon the consent of the creditors' committee. In the end, the rules are to some extent nothing more than mere guidelines of a programmatic, invitational nature.

Fifth, and finally, do we need coordination proceedings? It has skilfully been argued that reasonable insolvency practitioners will use the general rules on cooperation and communication, which even provide for a coordinated restructuring plan, to agree on a reasonable solution for the whole group. Hence, in most cases the complex, overregulated and expensive group coordination proceedings will not be necessary, as the obligations to cooperate and communicate will suffice. Where such an agreement is not possible or where insolvency practitioners do not act reasonably, a coordinator has a challenging task in front of him, given the option of the insolvency practitioners to opt out and the non-binding character of the coordinator's suggestions. It seems questionable whether such a soft coordination procedure would be effective when an earlier attempt at 'uncoordinated' cooperation has already proven unsuccessful. Hence, under the principle of subsidiarity, the question remains whether group coordination proceedings need to be regulated at all or whether cooperation and coordination can be left to the group members' individual insolvency practitioners.

Annex VI:  Insolvency of corporate groups under the recast Insolvency
Regulation: progress or reason for concern?

Professor Irit Mevorach[*]

## 1. Introduction

The recast Insolvency Regulation will enter into force in June 2017.[1] For
the first time, the Regulation will offer specific solutions for international
group insolvencies. Although at this stage, it is largely guesswork to try
and predict what will be the actual outcomes of proceedings concerning
groups pursuant to the new provisions, it is nonetheless timely to attempt
to identify challenges for the implementation of the recast Regulation. To
the extent that there is reason for concern, pointing out to the potential
problems may alleviate at least some of the issues through raising the
awareness of key actors involved in cross-border insolvency proceedings
of groups (e.g. insolvency practitioners and courts) regarding such challenges.

   Although the purpose of this short paper is to consider the potential
progress or else concern going forward under the new regime, method-
ologically the paper will go backwards to the early days of the Regulation
and recount its brief history, highlighting the key stages in the development of the Regulation and practice of group insolvencies in Europe.
Through this brief (and simplified) historical overview, the paper attempts
to highlight the shift that took place in the approach to groups from a focus on centralization of all relevant group member proceedings in a single
jurisdiction to a regime that is primarily based on cooperation and voluntary coordination between multiple proceedings. The paper's key argument is that although the attempt to explicitly address groups is to be ap-
plauded and although some features of the new provisions may be useful
going forward, the concern is that the pragmatic approach developed in
the practice under the original Regulation will be curtailed. It is also the
paper's purpose to highlight the fact that centralizations are still a legitimate and adequate approach for cross-border insolvency of groups under

---

* This paper was presented at the 'Implementation of the New Insolvency Regulation', Luxembourg Conference, Max Planck Institute for Procedural Law, 7 October 2016 by Professor Irit Mevorach, University of Nottingham.
1 Regulation (EU) 2015/848 of the European Parliament and of the Council of 20
May 2015 on insolvency proceedings (recast).

the recast Regulation, and should be pursued, especially in cases of smaller and centrally controlled groups.

2.  The European Insolvency Regulation (2000)[2]: no provisions for groups

The original Insolvency Regulation did not contain specific rules regarding groups. It was an intentional decision not to address groups at that stage of development of the cross-border insolvency regime for Europe. The *Virgós-Schmit* Report, which has been issued to serve as an interpretive guide to the Insolvency Convention that was later transformed into the Regulation, recognized this omission. It stated that:

> '[T]he Convention offers no rule for groups of affiliated companies (parent-subsidiary schemes). The general rule to open or to consolidate insolvency proceedings against any of the related companies as a principal or jointly liable debtor is that jurisdiction must exist according to the Convention for each of the concerned debtors with a separate legal entity. Naturally, the drawing of a European norm on associated companies may affect this answer.'[3]

It seems that it was clear to the negotiators and drafters of the draft Convention and Regulation that enterprise groups present complicated issues. In addition to differences in size, multinational groups use different structures (vertical, horizontal, integrated, centralized, decentralized, etc.), and they require consideration of both the conflict between universalism and territorialism, as methods to resolve cross-border insolvency, and the company law/corporate group dilemma between entity and enterprise law.[4]

3.  The practice since 2002: group centralizations

Notwithstanding the absence of explicit provisions for groups, group proceedings did take place in Europe, and not infrequently. These group cases were addressed under the Regulation after it entered into force in 2002. Even though the Regulation did not provide a specific regime for groups, it did not preclude the application of the Regulation to such cases either.

---

2  Council Regulation (EC) No 1346/2000 of 29 May 2000.
3  *Virgós-Schmit*, Report on the Convention on Insolvency Proceedings (1996) 6500/1/96, REV1, DRS 8 (CFC), [76].
4  See generally *Mevorach*, Insolvency within Multinational Enterprise Groups (2009).

In fact, many of the cross-border insolvency cases addressed under the Regulation have been cases of groups. Often in these cases, Member States' courts and insolvency practitioners have taken what was called at the time 'a pragmatic approach'.[5] Thus, they have attempted to centralize all the proceedings against the (relevant) group members in a single jurisdiction, by identifying a single location where all the group members' COMIs were located, usually at the place of the enterprise group head-office which was thought to coincide with the main head-office of each of the group members. This approach ensured that the enterprise did not lose the synergies and links between the entities during the insolvency process. It also reduced the costs of the process, by avoiding the opening of multiple parallel proceedings against aspects of what were essentially (in economic reality terms) single enterprises.[6]

Thus, although the Regulation seemed to have presumed an 'entity law' approach as explained by the *Virgós-Schmit* approach noted above, courts did not really ignore the group reality when making decisions about jurisdiction. For the purpose of the private international aspect of insolvency (i.e. jurisdiction and the ensuing effects in terms of applicable law and powers of the office holder), group entities were not simply considered as separate and distinct. Courts did take into account that entities were linked and that the group was managed centrally. While this approach in principle did not entail mixing of assets and debts (substantive consolidation), a de facto procedural consolidation did take place.

---

5 See *Moss*, Brook. J. Int'l. L. 2007, 1005.
6 This approach was apparent both before and after the decision of the Court of Justice of the European Union in CJEU, 2 May 2006 Case C-341/04, *Eurofood IFSC*, ECLI:EU:C:2006:281, which expressed a rather conservative approach concerning group centralizations. Examples include: *Re Daisytek-ISA Ltd*, [2003] BCC 562; *Re Energotech SARL*, [2007] BCC 123 (Tribunal de Grande Instance (France)); *Amtsgericht München*, 4 May 2004, 1501 IE 1276/04, Hettlage-Austria, NZI 2004, 450; *Amtsgericht Köln*, 19 February 2008, PIN group SA (Luxembourg), NZI 2008, 257; *Energotech SARL* Tribunal de Grande Instance Lure (France) 29 March 2006, [2007] BCC 123. See also *Mevorach*, J.Priv.Int.L. 2010, 327.

4. The case of Interedil (2011)[7]: adoption of central administration as a
   key connecting factor

The decision of the CJEU in *Interedil* has been a milestone in the understanding and development of the Regulation, particularly regarding the jurisdictional test (under which the main insolvency proceedings against a
debtor under the Regulation should take place at its centre of main interests: COMI, which is regarding companies and legal persons presumed to
be at the registered office; but the presumption can be rebutted). Before
*Interedil,* the determination of the appropriate location for handling the
main insolvency proceedings, based on COMI, was subject to much debate. Thus, the COMI standard has been criticized for being too vague and
unclear. It could refer, it was argued, to a variety of factors such as the location of most assets, or creditors, subsidiaries or branches, location of
management, location of shareholders and so forth. Ascertaining these factors and balancing them could yield different and unpredictable results.
The problem was considered even more pronounced in the context of
groups where the variety of factors would be applied to different group
members that may have different centres of main interests. Generally, it
has been argued that a jurisdictional standard which is based on the
debtor's real seat is prone to manipulations, compared to a standard based
on registered office (place of incorporation).[8]

*Interedil* firmly established, however, the significance of the central ad-
ministration/ head-office functions test, and in that it followed the practice, where notwithstanding the debate, real seat had prevailed and the
head-office functions criterion stood out as the key determinative factor in
circumstances where different factors pointed to different forums.[9] The
CJEU in *Interedil* explained that:

> '[A] debtor company's main centre of interests must be determined by attach-
> ing greater importance to the place of the company's central administration,
> as may be established by objective factors which are ascertainable by third
> parties (...) Where a company's central administration is not in the same
> place as its registered office, the presence of company assets and the existence
> of contracts for the financial exploitation of those assets in a Member State
> other than that in which the registered office is situated cannot be regarded as
> sufficient factors to rebut the presumption unless a comprehensive assessment

---

7  CJEU, 20 October 2011, Case C-396/09, *Interedil,* ECLI:EU:C:2011:671.
8  See e.g. *Eidenmüller,* EBOR 2005, 423; *McCormack,* CLJ 2009, 169.
9  See *Mevorach,* J.Priv.Int.L. 2010, 327, 342-347.

of all the relevant factors makes it possible to establish, in a manner that is ascertainable by third parties, that the company's actual centre of management and supervision and of the management of its interests is located in that other Member State;'[10]

The decision had implications beyond the issue of the treatment of corporate groups, yet its focus on the central administration (actual centre of management and supervision) as a key connecting factor reinforced the practice of group centralizations. Centralization of group members' proceedings is less probable if the jurisdiction test applied to each member is based on the place of the member's registered offices, which in the case of multinational groups tend to be located in different countries, or on factors such as the location of assets or employees which are indicators of the presence of offices or branches. Central administration/ head-office functions, on the other hand, provides a potential single point of entry for the administration of the process.[11] These developments further solidified the pragmatic approach that was developed in the practice whereby proceedings were centralized in the location of the head-office functions of the group that as such coincided with the COMI of each entity.

---

10  CJEU, 20 October 2011, Case C-396/09, *Interedil*, ECLI:EU:C:2011:671, para 59.
11  For a detailed discussion of the way a group home country may be identified in various group structures, see *Mevorach*, ICLQ 2008, 427. On the international level, too, and roughly at the same time, UNCITRAL (Working Group V) took on board to address issues related to COMI by way of a revision of the Guide to Enactment of the UNCITRAL Model Law on Cross-Border Insolvency. Work commenced in 2011 resulting in amendments to the Guide to Enactment published in 2014. The conclusions of the deliberations concerning the meaning of COMI largely followed the *Interedil* approach and noted central administration ascertainable by creditors as the principal factor that will tend to indicate (for the purposes of recognition under the Model Law) whether the location in which the foreign proceeding has commenced is the debtor's COMI (UNCITRAL Model Law on Cross-Border Insolvency with Guide to Enactment and Interpretation, 2014, para 145).

## 5. The parliament proposals (2011)[12]: centralization as the primary solution

Even though the practice evolved in a rather satisfactory manner, there was clearly a gap in the Regulation. The Regulation did not address groups and this was peculiar considering the large number of group cases. Furthermore, the absence of regulation on groups did create some uncertainties. Fundamentally, one could question the legitimacy of the approach that allowed the centralization of proceedings. Even if this approach is acceptable, further questions arise regarding the outcome of such centralizations, namely what can or cannot be done in the main forum where several group proceedings take place. Is it the aim to procedurally consolidate the proceedings in the group main forum, for devising a reorganization plan, or more generally to achieve a group solution, and is it possible in certain circumstances to substantively consolidate the assets and/or debts of the insolvent group members?

The Regulation was also due for revision after ten years in force, and therefore it was timely to consider during this revision process the possibility of addressing group insolvencies explicitly in the recast Regulation. The European Parliament took on board to formulate a possible regime for groups. In 2011, it published its proposals. The Parliament recommended that where the group structure allows it, proceedings should be centralized in the jurisdiction of the group headquarters. Any additional proceedings opened against members of the same group would be ancillary to the main group proceedings. Where the group was decentralized, mandatory cooperation and coordination mechanisms should be imposed. It was also proposed that in cases of intermingled groups, where asset and debts were mixed together in the ordinary course of business, proceedings could be consolidated substantively, namely the assets and debts of the different group members may be pooled together.[13]

---

12 European Parliament, Report with recommendations to the Commission on insolvency proceedings in the context of EU company law (2011/2006(INI)), 17.10.2011.

13 *Ibid*, Part 3: Recommendations on the insolvency of groups of companies.

6. The recast Insolvency Regulation (2015): a shift to cooperation and coordination

After the parliament proposal, negotiations continued between the European bodies and various drafts were considered.[14] The final approach adopted in the recast Regulation was eventually quite different from the Parliament proposal described above, as the focus shifted from centralization to provisions concerning cooperation and coordination of multiple proceedings, and to a coordination process which is largely voluntary.

The recast Regulation includes a separate chapter on groups (Chapter V) with more than twenty provisions. The chapter contains two parts with two schemes (or tools) for addressing the insolvency of corporate groups. The first scheme is based on cooperation. Articles 56-60 EIR require that insolvency office-holders (practitioners) appointed in the insolvency proceedings of members belonging to the same corporate group cooperate and communicate with each other to facilitate the effective administration of the proceedings to the extent that cooperation is not incompatible with the rules applicable to the proceedings and that there is no conflict of interest.

Specifically, the practitioners must communicate relevant information and consider the possibility of coordinating the administration of the group affairs, including the possibility of negotiating a group restructuring. In the course of such cooperation, the practitioners may also agree to grant additional powers to an insolvency practitioner appointed in one of the proceedings or on the allocation of certain tasks among them. The courts presiding over insolvency proceedings, that are pending or that are already opened, concerning members of the same corporate group, must also cooperate and communicate where such cooperation is conducive to an effecting administration of the process. Finally, the cooperation duty is also extended to the interaction between practitioners and courts. The recast Regulation further prescribes that all the practitioners appointed have similar rights to be heard, request a stay if a restructuring plan has been proposed (subject to certain conditions) or apply for the opening of coordination proceedings.

---

14 For more detail see *Mevorach*, in: Sarra/Romaine (eds), Annual Review of Insolvency Law (2013), 285.

Coordination proceedings is the second scheme provided in the recast Regulation, in Articles 61-77 EIR. A request to open such a proceeding may be presented in any of the courts having jurisdiction over the insolvency proceedings of a member of the group, but the court first seized will have jurisdiction (except where two-thirds of the insolvency practitioners agreed which court should be the coordinating court). The request should present the outline of the proposed group coordination. The court should be satisfied that the opening of the proceedings is appropriate to facilitate the effective administration of the proceedings and that no creditor of any of the group members is likely to be financially disadvantaged by the inclusion of the group member in the proceeding. Any of the other practitioners appointed in proceedings of group members may object to the inclusion of the member in the coordinating proceedings and shall in that regard obtain any approval that may be required under the local law (of the state where they were appointed). In case of objection, the member is not included in the group coordination proceedings unless at a later stage the practitioner decides to opt-in and include the group member in the coordination proceedings. The coordinator appointed in the coordination proceedings may recommend a group coordination plan which shall be considered by the other practitioners, yet the practitioners are not obliged to follow in whole or in part the coordinator's recommendations or the group coordination plan, they are only required to give reasons for not following the recommendations.

7. Progress or concern?

In contrast with the original Regulation, the recast Regulation addresses groups directly. Thus, it can no longer be claimed that the Regulation omits a major enterprise structure from its scope and explicit provisions. The separate chapter devoted to groups is also rather comprehensive and detailed.[15] It provides a variety of tools and imposes certain obligations, aimed at encouraging the design of group-wide solutions. Its provisions concerning the duty to cooperate between multiple proceedings concerning members of the same enterprise groups are particularly important. Groups come about in different shapes and structures, and in certain cases

---

15 Indeed, arguably excessively detailed and cumbersome (see also *Thole/Dueñas*, Int.Insolv.Rev. 2015, 214, 227, noting that: 'The new group coordination procedure is designed in an overly formalistic and constitutional manner').

the opening of multiple proceedings is sensible in view of the way the group enterprise was managed in the ordinary course of business.[16] In such cases, it is essential that those presiding over the process cooperate fully to achieve a group solution where such solution would be beneficial for the group stakeholders. The new provisions impose such duty to cooperate, and provide additional guidelines concerning the specific steps that may be taken in the course of such cooperation.

The provisions regarding coordination, in the second part of the new regime, attempt to provide a potentially more centralized scheme for the administration of the group process. However, these provisions give limited powers to the coordinators of group coordination proceedings, as their recommendations are not binding and only require a consideration by the other practitioners. The coordination process is voluntary, whereby insolvency practitioners may decide whether to take part or not in the coordination at any stage. This scheme provides some important guidelines, again especially for large groups in distress, and may work well where all relevant parties are willing to cooperate and take part in the process and see merit in doing so under the coordination of the coordinator. Absent such a cooperative approach, achieving a group solution may be difficult.[17]

Furthermore, the concern is that the focus on cooperation and coordination in the recast Regulation will curtail the pragmatic approach that has been developed in the practice, whereby multiple proceedings were avoided in the first place and a de facto procedural consolidation of the proceedings took place in a single forum. Although cooperation between multiple proceedings and potentially coordination is predictably useful for the large decentralized groups, groups may be smaller in size or in any event, centrally controlled, thus a vertical approach that minimizes multiplicity of processes would be most efficient. Even though it is still possible under the recast Regulation to identify a mutual COMI for all group members, and although mutual COMI is assisted by the new definition of COMI that followed *Interedil* (see above), this approach is noted only in the recitals without further specification.[18] It is also provided in the specific chapter on groups (in Article 72 EIR) that a group plan proposed by a coordinator

---

16  See *Mevorach*, ICLQ 2008, 427.
17  See also *Thole/Dueñas*, Int.Insolv.Rev. 2015, 214, 220; *McCormack*, MLR 2016, 121, 144.
18  Regulation (EU) 2015/848 of the European Parliament and of the Council of 20 May 2015 on insolvency proceedings (recast), recital 53.

shall not include recommendations as to any consolidation of proceedings (procedural consolidation) or insolvency estates (substantive consolidation), without regard to the fact that such approach may be the most efficient in relevant circumstances.[19]

8. Conclusion and a way forward

The Regulation makes some important progress where it acknowledges groups and ensures that the key actors in the process will attempt to cooperate in group cases going forward and consider a group solution that may benefit the group stakeholders as a whole. Yet, where it is possible to avoid multiple proceedings (i.e. centralize the process), it is generally easier to achieve group solutions. Greater awareness of the possibility of centralization may go some way towards addressing the risk that this approach will be curtailed and pursued less frequently. It is possible under the recast Regulation, as explained in recital 53 EIR, to identify a mutual COMI for all group members that should be subject to the joint solution and place the proceedings in one place.

This paper attempted to highlight, however, the fact that centralization is not only a possibility but also often the best approach, especially when centrally controlled groups face financial difficulties. Centralization can avoid costs of multiple proceeding and can smooth the process of devising joint solutions, beneficial for the general body of creditors. Centralizations also do not risk the integrity of the corporate 'veil', as entities are united only for private international law purposes, namely for concentrating the proceedings. In the usual case, the entities remain separate in terms of their assets and liabilities, and the concentration or consolidation is only procedural. Concentration based on COMI also does not circumvent the Regulation's scheme concerning the applicable law, and the recast Regulation also contains mechanisms to address (in the COMI jurisdiction) differences in priority treatment in places where an enterprise has establishments.[20]

---

19  Cf UNCITRAL Legislative Guide on Insolvency Law, Part Three: Treatment of Enterprise Groups in Insolvency (United Nations, New York, 2012). See also *Madaus*, IILR 2015, 235, 237.
20  Regulation (EU) 2015/848 of the European Parliament and of the Council of 20 May 2015 on insolvency proceedings (recast), Art 36. See also *Collins & Aikman Europe SA* [2006] EWHC 1343 (Ch); *Nortel Group* [2009] EWHC 206 (Ch).

Even though the provisions in Chapter V of the recast Regulation exclude procedural consolidation, it can be argued that this limitation only applies in the context of the group coordination proceedings under the second, alternative, scheme. Procedural consolidations should be possible going forward including by identifying a mutual COMI based on the head-office functions factor, and to the extent that the applicable law (the law of the forum) does not prohibit such a solution. Substantive consolidation, where the entities and not only the proceedings are mixed, is certainty a tool to be reserved to the special cases of groups that were very highly integrated (in terms of their assets). It is a mechanism that is not widely available in legal systems, although the international standard for insolvency regimes recommends that this tool is included in domestic insolvency laws concerning groups.[21]

Finally, it is also important that after the entry into force of the recast Regulation, its implementation will be monitored. In that regard, it should be considered whether the Regulation has facilitated or at least did not curtail effective solutions not only for specific type of (mainly large) groups but for the variety of cases involving members of corporate groups.

---

21 UNCITRAL Legislative Guide on Insolvency Law, Part Three: Treatment of Enterprise Groups in Insolvency (United Nations, New York, 2012), recommendation 220.

# Bibliography

## 1. CJEU case-law

CJEU, 17 January 2006, Case C-1/04, *Staubitz-Schreiber*, ECLI:EU:C:2006:39;

CJEU, 2 May 2006, Case C-341/04, *Eurofood IFSC*, ECLI:EU:C:2006:281;

CJEU, 12 February 2009, Case C-339/07, *Seagon*, ECLI:EU:C:2009:83;

CJEU, 2 July 2009, Case C-111/08, *SCT Industri*, ECLI:EU:C:2009:419;

CJEU, 10 September 2009, Case C-292/08, *German Graphics Graphische Maschinen*, ECLI:EU:C:2009:544;

CJEU, 20 October 2011, Case C-396/09, *Interedil*, ECLI:EU:C:2011:671;

CJEU, 15 December 2011, Case C-191/10, *Rastelli Davide e C.*, ECLI:EU:C:2011:838;

CJEU, 19 April 2012, Case C-213/10, *F-Tex*, ECLI:EU:C:2012:215;

CJEU, 8 November 2012, Case C-461/11, *Radziejewski*, ECLI:EU:C:2012:704;

CJEU, 22 November 2012, Case C-116/11, *Bank Handlowy and Adamiak*, ECLI:EU:C:2012:739;

CJEU, 17 October 2013, Case C-184/12, *Unamar*, ECLI:EU:C:2013:663;

CJEU, 16 January 2014, Case C-328/12, *Schmid*, ECLI:EU:C:2014:6;

CJEU, 4 September 2014, Case C-157/13, *Nickel & Goeldner Spedition*, ECLI:EU:C:2014:2145;

CJEU, 4 September 2014, Case C-327/13, *Burgo Group*, ECLI:EU:C:2014:2158;

CJEU, 4 December 2014, Case C-295/13, *H*, ECLI:EU:C:2014:2410;

CJEU, 11 June 2015, Case C-649/13, *Comite d'enterprise de Nortel Networks and Others*, ECLI:EU:C:2015:384;

CJEU, 10 December 2015, Case C-594/14, *Kornhaas*, ECLI:EU:C:2015:806;

CJEU, 16 April 2015, Case C-557/13, *Lutz*, ECLI:EU:C:2015:227;

CJEU, 8 June 2017, Case C-54/16, *Vinyls Italia SpA*, ECLI:EU:C:2017:433.

## 2. National case-law

Amtsgericht Köln, 19 February 2008 – 73 IE 1/08, *PIN group SA*, Neue Zeitschrift für Insolvenz- und Sanierungsrecht (NZI) 4 (2008), p 257 ff;

Amtsgericht München, 4 May 2004 – 1501 IE 1276/04, *Hettlage-Austria*, Neue Zeitschrift für Insolvenz- und Sanierungsrecht (NZI) 8 (2004), p 450 ff;

Amtsgericht Siegen, 1 July 2004, 25 IN 154/04, *Zenith*, Neue Zeitschrift für Insolvenz- und Sanierungsrecht (NZI) 2004, p 673 ff, Entscheidungen zum Wirtschaftsrecht (EWiR) 4 (2005), p 175 ff;

Bundesgerichtshof, Equitable Life, judgment of 15 February 2012, IV ZR 194/09;

High Court of Justice Chancery Division Companies Court, 9 June 2006, *Re Collins & Aikman Europe* SA et al. [2006] EWHC 1343 (Ch);

Corte di Appello di Milano, 17 January 2013, available at: www.ilcaso.it;

Corte di Appello di Firenze, 27 June 2016;

Corte di Appello di Firenze, 31 August 2015, available at: www.ilcaso.it;

Corte di Appello di Torino, 10 March 2009, Il Fallimento e le altre procedure concorsuali (Il Fall.) 2009, p 1293 – [2009] EIRCR(A) 249;

Corte Suprema di Cassazione, 14 January 2015, n 495;

Corte Suprema di Cassazione, 14 March 2016, n 4977;

Corte Suprema di Cassazione, 31 March 2016, n 6277;

Corte Suprema di Cassazione, Sezioni Unite, 29 October 2015, n 22093, Il Fallimento e le altre procedure concorsuali (Il Fall.) 2016, p 829;

Cour de cassation, 27 June 2006, *French Republic v Klempka (administrator Daisytek SAS)*, [2006] BCC 841;

High Court of Justice Chancery Division (Companies Court), 26 September 2005, *Re DAP Holding NV* [2005] EWHC 2092 (Ch);

District Court of Amsterdam, 27 February 2007;

Fővárosi Bíróság, Budapest, 17 September 2008, INSOL EIR-case register No 56;

Greffe du Tribunal de Commerce de Roubaix-Tourcoing, 21 April 2008, RG n° 2008-1062 – [2008] EIRCR(A) 342 RG n° 2008-1062;

High Court of Justice London, 15 August 2006, *Hans Brochier Holdings Ltd. v Exner* [2006] EWHC 2594 (Ch), [2007] BCC 127, Neue Zeitschrift für Insolvenz- und Sanierungsrecht (NZI) 3 (2007), p 187 ff;

High Court of Justice London, 3 July 2009, *In re Stanford International Bank Limited* [2009] EWHC 1441 (Ch);

High Court of Justice in Northern Ireland, 20 January 2012, *Irish Bank Resolution Corporation Ltd v Quinn* [2012] NICh 1;

Juzgado de lo Mercantil núm. 3 de Barcelona, Auto de 9 enero 2012, JUR 2014\176918;

Juzgado de lo Mercantil núm. 9 de Barcelona, Auto de 27 marzo 2013, AC 2013\1619;

Landesgericht Innsbruck, 11 May 2004, 9 S 15/04m, *Hettlage Österreich*, Zeitschrift für Insolvenzrecht und Kreditschutz (ZIK) 2004, 107;

Landesgericht Klagenfurt, 2 July 2004, 41 S 75/04h, *Zenith Österreich*, Neue Zeitschrift für Insolvenz- und Sanierungsrecht (NZI) 12 (2004), 677;

Chancery Division, 30 March 2006, *446 Re MG Rover Belux SA/NV (in admin.)* [2007] BCC 446;

High Court of Justice Birmingham, 18 April 2005, *MG Rover I* [2005] EWHC 874 (Ch), Neue Zeitschrift für Insolvenz- und Sanierungsrecht (NZI) 8 (2005), p 467 ff;

High Court of Justice London, 11 February 2009, *Nortel Group* [2009] EWHC 206 (Ch), Zeitschrift für Wirtschaftsrecht (ZIP) 12 (2009), p 578 ff;

Oberlandesgericht Wien, 9 November 2004, 28 R 225/04w- [2004] EIRCR(A) 72;

Oberlandesgericht Wien, 18 April 2008, 4 R 20/08b, Zeitschrift für Insolvenzrecht und Kreditschutz (ZIK) 2009, p 67 ff;

Oberlandesgericht Wien, 29 October 2013, 28 R 370/13g, Zeitschrift für Insolvenzrecht und Kreditschutz (ZIK) 2014, p 29 ff;

High Court of Justice Chancery Division Companies Court, 7 February 2003, *BRAC Rent-A-Car International Inc* [2003] EWHC 128 (Ch);

High Court of Justice Leeds, 16 May 2003, *Re Daisytek-ISA Ltd,* [2003] BCC 562, Neue Zeitschrift für Insolvenz- und Sanierungsrecht (NZI) 4 (2004), p 219 ff;

High Court of Justice London, 26 January 2015, *Re Northsea Base Investment Ltd & Ors* [2015] EWHC 121 (Ch), Neue Zeitschrift für Insolvenz- und Sanierungsrecht (NZI) 8 (2015), p 338 ff;

High Court of Justice Chancery Division Companies Court, 6 May 2011, *Rodenstock GmbH* [2011] EWHC 1104 (Ch);

*STS Sala de lo Contencioso-Administrativo,* Sección 6ª, Sentencia de 28 marzo 2007, RJ\2007\2142;

High Court of Justice London, 17 January 2017, *Thomas & Anor v Frogmore Real Estate Partners GP1 Ltd & Ors* [2017] EWHC 25 (Ch);

Tribunal de Commerce Nanterre, 15 February 2006, PCL 2006J00174, *EMTEC,* Entscheidungen zum Wirtschaftsrecht (EWiR) 7 (2006), p 207 ff;

Tribunal de Grande Instance Lure (France), 29 March 2006, *Energotech SARL* [2007] BCC 123;

Tribunale di Ivrea, 20 October 2008, this case is unreported;

Tribunale di Napoli, 22 September 2016, 1264/16;

Tribunale di Parma, 20 February 2004, Il Foro italiano (Foro it.) 2004, 1567;

Tribunale di Parma, 4 February 2004, Rivista di diritto internazionale private e processuale (Riv.dir.int.priv. e proc.) 2004, p 693;

Tribunale di Reggio Emilia, 6 March 2013, confirmed by Corte d'Appelo di Bologna, 25 June 2013, both available at: www.ilcaso.it;

Tribunale die Parma, 27 December 2003, available at: http://www.parmalatinamminist razionestraordinaria.it/it/ PRcomstampa/sentenza%20Parmalat.pdf;

Tribunale Ordinario di Roma, 14 August 2003, Il diritto fallimentare (Il dir. fallim.) 2003, p 999;

Tribunale Ordinario di Roma, 7 August 2003, Il diritto fallimentare (Il dir. fallim.) 2003, p 1000.

## 3. Literature

*Albrecht, Achim*, Die Reform der EuInsVO ist abgeschlossen – eine Übersicht, Zeitschrift für das gesamte Insolvenzrecht (ZInsO) 23 (2015), p 1077 ff;

*Altman, Jamie*, A Test Case in International Bankruptcy Protocols: The Lehman Brothers Insolvency, San Diego International Law Journal (San Diego Int'l L.J.) 12 (2011), p 463 ff;

*Amey, Robert*, Case Review – C-327/13 Burgo Group SpA v Illochroma SA (in liquidation), International Corporate Rescue – Special Issue, South Square Articles 2015, p 8 ff;

*Armour, John*, Who Should Make Corporate Law? EC Legislation versus Regulatory Competition, Current Legal Problems (CLP) 58 (2005), p 369 ff;

*Andres, Dirk/Grund, Andreas*, Die Flucht vor deutschen Insolvenzgerichten nach England – Die Entscheidungen in dem Insolvenzverfahren Hans Brochier Holdings Ltd., Neue Zeitschrift für Insolvenz- und Sanierungsrecht (NZI) 3 (2007), p 137 ff;

*Anzenberger, Philipp*, Sekundärinsolvenz auch im Sitzstaat der Schuldnerin, Anmerkungen zu EuGH C-327/13, Burgo Group SpA/Illochroma SA in Liquidation, Zeitschrift für Insolvenzrecht und Kreditschutz (ZIK) 2015, p 5 ff;

*Armour, John*, Abuse of European Insolvency Law? A Discussion, in: de la Feria, Rita/ Vogenauer, Stefan (eds), Prohibition of Abuse of Law, Oxford and Portland, Oregon 2011, p 157 ff;

*Arts, Robert*, Main and Secondary Proceedings in the recast of the European Insolvency Regulation – The only good secondary proceeding is a synthetic secondary proceeding, Norton Journal of Bankruptcy Law and Practice (Norton J. Bankr. L. & Prac.) 24 (2015), p 436 ff, available at: https://www.iiiglobal.org/sites/default/files/ media/Arts%20-%20Main%20and%20Secondary%20Proceedings.pdf;

*Atanasov, Vladimir A./Black, Bernard S./Ciccotello, Conrad S.,* Law and Tunneling, Journal of Corporation Law (JCL) 37 (2011), p 1 ff;

*Bariatti, Stefania/Corno, Giorgio*, Il Regolamento (UE) 2015/848 del Parlamento Europeo e del Consiglio del 20 maggio 2015 relativo alle procedure di insolvenza (rifusione). Una prima lettura, available at: ilfallimentarista.it, 2015;

*Bariatti, Stefania/Corno, Giorgio*, Centro degli interessi principali, available at: ilfallimentarista.it, 2016;

*Baumert, Andreas J.*, EuGH: Eröffnung eines Sekundärinsolvenzverfahrens auch am satzungsmäßigen Sitz der Gesellschaft, Anmerkung zu EuGH, Urteil vom 4.9.2014 – C-327/13 – „Burgo Group SpA./. Illochroma SA in Liquidation", Lindenmaier-Möhring-Kommentierte BGH-Rechtsprechung (LMK) 2014, 362606;

*Berends, André*, Insolventie in het internationaal privaatrecht, Deventer 2005;

*Bewick, Samantha*, The EU Insolvency Regulation, Revisited, International Insolvency Review (Int. Insolv. Rev.) 24 (2015), p 172 ff;

*Biermeyer, Thomas*, Case Note – Case C-396/09 *Interedil Srl*, Judgment of the Court of 20 October 2011, Maastricht Journal of European and Comparative Law (MJ) 18 (2011), p 581 ff;

*Böcker, Philipp*, Gesellschaftsrecht oder Insolvenzrecht? Keine »Einheit der Rechtsordnung« im IPR – Besprechung des EuGH-Urteils vom 10.12.2015 – Rs.C-594/14 – Kornhaas, DZWIR, 2016, 180, Deutsche Zeitschrift für Wirtschafts- und Insolvenzrecht (DZWIR) 26 (2016), p 174 ff;

*Bork, Reinhard/van Zwieten, Kristin* (eds), Commentary on the European Insolvency Regulation, Oxford 2016;

*Bork, Reinhard/Mangano, Renato*, European Cross-Border Insolvency Law, Oxford 2016;

*Bork, Reinhard*, Moratoria (or "stays") under the new European Insolvency Regulation, Insolvency Intelligence (Insolv. Int.) 29 (2016), p 1 ff;

*Bork, Reinhard* (ed), Principles of Cross-border Insolvency Law, Cambridge/Antwerp/Portland 2017;

*Bork, Reinhard/McCormack, Gerard* (eds), Security rights and the European Insolvency Regulation, Cambridge/Antwerp/Portland 2017;

*Bornemann, Alexander/Brinkmann, Moritz /Herchen, Axel* (eds), European Insolvency Regulation – Commentary, Munich 2017;

*Braun, Eberhard/Tashiro, Annerose*, Cross-border Insolvency Protocol Agreements between Insolvency Practitioners and their Effect on the Rights of Creditors, available at: https://www.iiiglobal.org/sites/default/files/BraunTashiroandBraunCBProtocols.pdf;

*Braun, Eberhard*, Der neue Sport in Europa: Forumshopping in Insolvenzverfahren oder: die moderne Form von Britannia rules the waves, Neue Zeitschrift für Insolvenz- und Sanierungsrecht (NZI) 1 (2004), Editorial;

*Braun, Eberhard* (ed), Insolvenzordnung, 7th edn, Munich 2017;

*Brinkmann, Moritz*, Grenzüberschreitende Sanierung und europäisches Insolvenzrecht, Zeitschrift für Insolvenzrecht – Konkurs, Treuhand, Sanierung (KTS) 4 (2014), p 381 ff;

*Brünkmans, Christian*, Die Renaissance der Sitztheorie im europäischen Insolvenzrecht, Kölner Schrift zum Wirtschaftsrecht (KSzW) 3 (2012), p 319 ff;

*Bufford, Samuel L.*, Center of Main Interests, International Insolvency Case Venue, and Equality of Arms: The Eurofood Decision and the European Court of Justice, Northwestern Journal of International Law & Business (Nw. J. Int'l L. & Bus.) 27 (2007), p 351 ff;

*Bufford, Samuel L.*, Revision of the European Union Regulation on Insolvency Proceedings – Recommendations, International Insolvency Law Review (IILR) 3 (2012), p 341 ff;

*Busch, Peter/Remmert, Andreas/Rüntz, Stephanie/Vallender, Heinz*, Kommunikation zwischen Gerichten in Grenzüberschreitenden Insolvenzen: Was geht und was geht nicht, Neue Zeitschrift für Insolvenz- und Sanierungsrecht (NZI) 11 (2010), p 417 ff;

*Canaris, Klaus-Wilhelm/Larenz, Karl*, Methodenlehre der Rechtswissenschaft, 3rd edn, Berlin 1995;

*Canuel, Edward T.*, United States – Canadian Insolvencies: Reviewing Conflicting Legal Mechanisms, Challenges and Opportunities for Cross-Border Cooperation, Journal of International Business and Law (J. Int'l Bus. & L.) 4 (2005), p 8 ff;

*Carballo Piñeiro, Laura*, Vis attractiva concursus in the European Union: its development by the European Court of Justice, Revista para el Análisis del Derecho 2010;

*Carrasco Perera, Angel/Torralba Mendiola, Elisa*, UK "schemes of arrangement" are "outside" the scope of the European Regulation on Insolvency Proceedings. What does "outside" actually mean?, available at: http://www.gomezacebo-pombo.com/media/k2/attachments/uk-schemes-of-arrangement-are-outside-the-scope-of-the-european-regulation-on-insolvency-proceedings-what-does-outside-actually-mean.pdf;

*Castagnola, Angelo*, Regolamento CE 1346/2000 e *vis attractiva concursus*: verso un'universalità meno limitata?, Rivista di diritto processuale (Riv. dir. proc.) 2010, p 925 ff;

*Cohen, Adrian/Dammann, Reinhard/Sax, Stefan*, Final text for the Amended EU Regulation on Insolvency proceedings, International Insolvency Law Review (IILR) 2 (2015), p 117 ff;

*Commandeur, Anja/Römer, Alexander*, Aktuelle Entwicklungen im Insolvenzrecht – Neufassung der Europäischen Insolvenzverordnung, Neue Zeitschrift für Gesellschaftsrecht (NZG) 25 (2015), p 988 ff;

*Csöke, Andrea*, EIR Recast: Some tiny interesting details, eurofenix Spring 2016, p 29 ff;

*Dammann, Reinhard/Müller, Friederike*, Erste Anwendung der Interedil-Rechtsprechung des EuGH zum COMI im Coeur Défense-Urteil der Cour d'appel von Versailles vom 19.1.2012, Neue Zeitschrift für Insolvenz- und Sanierungsrecht (NZI) 16 (2012), p 643 ff;

*Dammann, Reinhard/Rapp, Alexis*, La clarification du rôle joué par la procédure secondaire dans l'architecture du règlement relatif aux procédures d'insolvabilité transfrontalières, Recueil Dalloz 2015, p 45 ff;

*Dammann, Reinhard/Menjucq, Michel/Roussel, Galle*, Le nouveau règlement européen sur les procedures d'insolvabilité, Revue des procédures collectives (Rev. proc. coll.) 2015, p 10 ff;

*Dammann, Reinhard*, Sinn und Zweck von Sekundärverfahren nach der Reform der EuInsVO, in: Exner, Joachim/Paulus, Christoph G. (eds), Festschrift für Siegfried Beck zum 70. Geburtstag, Munich 2016, p 73 ff;

*De Cesari, Patrizia*, Il Regolamento 2015/848e il nuovo approccio europeo alla crisi dell'impresa, Il Fallimento e le altre procedure concorsuali (Il Fall.) 2015, p 1033 ff;

*Didone, Antonio*, Gli accordi di ristrutturazione del debitti (ART. 182-[Bis] L. Fall). Presupposti, procedimento ed effetti della anticipazione delle misure protettive dell'impresa in crisi, Il diritto fallimentare (Il dir. fallim.) 2011, p 23 ff;

*Dugue, Ronan/Becker, Manuela*, The European Insolvency Regulation in theory and practice – The new European insolvency register portal, in: Insolvency and Restructuring in Germany, Yearbook (2017), Achern 2016, p 30 ff;

*Eble, Maximilian J.*, Die Unternehmensgruppe in der Europäischen Insolvenzverordnung 2017, in: Ebke, Werner/Seagon, Christopher/Blatz, Michael (eds), Unternehmensrestrukturierung und Unternehmensinsolvenz, Baden-Baden 2015, p 131 ff;

*Eble, Maximilian J.*, Auf dem Weg zu einem europäischen Konzerninsolvenzrecht – Die "Unternehmensgruppe" in der EuInsVO 2017, Neue Zeitschrift für Insolvenz- und Sanierungsrecht (NZI) 4 (2016), p 115 ff;

*Eble, Maximilian J.*, Der Gruppenkoordinator in der reformierten EuInsVO – Bestellung, Abberufung und Haftung, Zeitschrift für Wirtschaftsrecht (ZIP) 34 (2016), p 1619 ff;

*Eckert, Georg*, Internationales Gesellschaftsrecht. Das internationale Privatrecht grenzüberschreitend tätiger Gesellschaften, Vienna 2010;

*Ehricke, Ulrich*, Die neue Europäische Insolvenzverordnung und grenzüberschreitende Konzerninsolvenzen, Europäisches Wirtschafts- und Steuerrecht (EWS) 3 (2002), p 101 ff;

*Ehricke, Ulrich*, Die Zusammenarbeit der Insolvenzverwalter bei grenzüberschreitenden Insolvenzen nach der EuInsVO, Wertpapier-Mitteilungen (WM) 9 (2005), p 397 ff;

*Eidenmüller, Horst/van Zwieten, Kristin*, Restructuring the European Business Enterprise: The EU Commission Recommendation on a New Approach to Business Failure and Insolvency, available at: papers.ssrn.com;

*Eidenmüller, Horst*, Der nationale und der internationale Insolvenzverwaltungsvertrag, Zeitschrift für Zivilprozess (ZZP) 114 (2001), p 3 ff;

*Eidenmüller, Horst*, Free Choice in International Company Insolvency Law in Europe, European Business Organization Law Review (EBOR) 6 (2005), p 423 ff;

*Eidenmüller, Horst*, Gesellschaftsstatut und Insolvenzstatut, Rabels Zeitschrift für ausländisches und internationales Privatrecht (RabelsZ) 70 (2006), p 474 ff;

*Eidenmüller, Horst*, Abuse of Law in the Context of European Insolvency Law, European Company and Financial Law Review (ECFR) 6 (2009), p 1 ff;

*Eidenmüller, Horst*, A New Framework for Business Restructuring in Europe: The EU Commission's Proposals for a Reform of the European Insolvency Regulation and Beyond, Maastricht Journal of European and Comparative Law (MJ) 20 (2013), p 133 ff, available at: http://ssrn.com/abstract=2230690;

*Eidenmüller, Horst*, What is an insolvency proceeding?, European Corporate Governance Institute (ECGI) – Law Working Paper No. 335/2016;

*Enriques, Luca/Gatti, Matteo*, Is There a Uniform EU Securities Law After the Financial Services Action Plan?, Stanford Journal of Law, Business and Finance (Stan. J.L Bus. & Fin.) 14 (2008), p 43 ff;

*Espiniella Menendez, Angel*, Los protocolos concursales, 10 Anuario de Derecho Concursal (2007), p 165 ff;

*Esser, H. Philipp*, Reform of the EU Regulation: New Framework for Insolvent Company Groups: Part I, American Bankruptcy Institute Journal (Am. Bankr. Inst. J.) 2015, p 38 ff;

*Fabiani, Massimo,* L'ulteriore upgrade degli accordi di ristrutturazione e l'incentivo ai finanziamenti nelle soluzioni concordate, Il Fallimento (Il Fall.) 2010, p 904 ff;

*Fabiani, Massimo,* La convenzione di moratoria diretta a disciplinare in via provvisoria gli effetti della crisi, Il diritto fallimentare (Il dir. fallim.) 2015, p 1269 ff;

*Fehrenbach, Markus,* Die reformierte Europäische Insolvenzverordnung (Teil II), Zeitschrift für das Privatrecht der Europäischen Union (GPR) 1 (2017), p 38 ff;

*Ferran, Eilis,* Corporate Law, Codes and Social Norms-Finding the Right Regulatory Combination and Institutional Structure, Journal of Corporate Law Studies (JCLS) 2 (2001), p 381 ff, available at: <ssrn.com/ abstract=294462>;

*Flaschen, Evan D./Silverman, Ronald J.,* Cross-border Insolvency Cooperation Protocols, Texas International Law Journal (Tex. Int'l L. J.) 33 (1998), p 587 ff;

*Fletcher, Ian,* The European Insolvency Regulation recast: the main features of the new law, Insolvency Intelligence (Insolv. Int.) 28 (2015), p 97 ff;

*Fritz, Daniel,* Die Neufassung der Europäischen Insolvenzverordnung: Erleichterung bei der Restrukturierung in grenzüberschreitenden Fällen? (Teil 1), Der Betrieb (DB) 33 (2015), p 1882 ff;

*Fritz, Daniel,* Besser Sanieren in Deutschland? Wesentliche Aspekte der Einpassung der Europäischen Insolvenzverordnung in das deutsche Recht, Betriebsberater (BB) 2017, p 131 ff;

*Garcimartin, Francisco,* The review of the EU Insolvency Regulation: some proposals for amendment, NVRII Preadviezen/Reports 2011, p 17 ff;

*Garcimartin, Francisco,* The review of the Insolvency Regulation: Hybrid procedures and other issues, International Insolvency Law Review (IILR) 3 (2011), p 321 ff;

*Garcimartin, Francisco,* The EU Insolvency Regulation Recast: Scope, Jurisdiction and Applicable Law, Zeitschrift für Europäisches Privatrecht (ZEuP) 4 (2015), p 694 ff;

*Garcimartin, Francisco,* The EU Insolvency Regulation Recast: Scope and Rules on Jurisdiction, available at: papers.ssrn.com 2016;

*Geimer, Reinhold/ Schütze, Rolf A.,* Europäisches Zivilverfahrensrecht, 3rd edn, Munich 2010;

*Gerner-Beuerle, Carsten/ Schuster, Edmund,* The Costs of Separation: Friction Between Company and Insolvency Law in the Single Market, Journal of Corporate Law Studies (JCLS) 14 (2014), p 287 ff;

*Gerner-Beuerle, Carsten et al.,* Study on the Law Applicable to Companies. Final Report (2016), Luxembourg, p 294 ff;

*Geroldinger, Andreas,* Die Koordinierung von Parallelverfahren nach der EuInsVO, in: Clavora, Selena/Garber, Thomas (eds), Grenzüberschreitende Insolvenzen im europäischen Binnenmarkt – die EuInsVO (2011), p 123 ff;

*Gopalan, Sandeep/Guihot, Michael,* Cross-Border Insolvency Law and Multinational Enterprise Groups: Judicial Innovation as an International Solution, The George Washington International Law Review (The Geo. Wash. Int'l L. Rev.) 48 (2016), p 549 ff;

*Gottwald, Peter* (ed), Insolvenzrechtshandbuch, 5th edn, Munich 2015;

*Grossman, Sanford J./Hart, Oliver D.*, The costs and benefits of ownership: A theory of vertical and lateral integration, 94 Journal of Political Economy (1986), p 691 ff.

*Hart, Oliver D.*, Corporate Governance: Some Theory and Implications, The Economic Journal 105 (1995), p 678 ff;

*Haas, Ulrich/Vogel, Oliver*, Durchsetzung gesellschaftsrechtlicher und insolvenzrechtlicher Haftungsansprüche im internationalen Konzern, Neue Zeitschrift für Gesellschaftsrecht (NZG) 12 (2011), p 457 ff;

*Haidmayer, Barbara*, Zum Interessenmittelpunkt einer Tochtergesellschaft in der Konzerninsolvenz – Anmerkungen zu OLG Wien 28 R 370/13g1, Zeitschrift für Insolvenzrecht und Kreditschutz (ZIK) 2014, p 4 ff;

*Hedemann, Justus Wilhelm*, Die Flucht in die Generalklauseln: eine Gefahr für Recht und Staat, Tübingen 1933;

*Henry, Laurence Caroline*, Le nouveau règlement 'insolvabilité': entre continuité et innovations, Recueil Dalloz 2015, p 979 ff;

*Hess, Burkhard*, Europäisches Zivilprozessrecht (2010), § 9;

*Hess, Burkhard*, Hybride Sanierungsinstrumente zwischen der Europäischen Insolvenzverordnung und der Verordnung Brüssel I, in: Bruns, Alexander et al. (eds), Festschrift für Rolf Stürner zum 70. Geburtstag, Tübingen 2013, p 1253 ff;

*Hess, Burkhard/Oberhammer, Paul/Pfeiffer, Thomas* (eds), European Insolvency Law – Heidelberg-Luxembourg-Vienna Report, Munich 2014;

*Hess, Burkhard/Koutsoukou, Georgia*, in: Kronke, Herbert/Melis, Werner/Kuhn, Hans (eds), Handbuch Internationales Wirtschaftsrecht, 2nd edn, Cologne 2017, Teil O;

*Hirte, Heribert*, Towards a Framework for the Regulation of Corporate Groups' Insolvencies, European Company and Financial Law Review (ECFR) 5 (2008), p 213 ff;

*Honorati, Costanza/Corno, Giorgio*, A double lesson from Interedil: higher courts, lower courts and preliminary ruling and further clarifications on COMI and establishment under EC Insolvency Regulation, International Insolvency Law Review (IILR) 1 (2013), p 18 ff;

*Janger, Edward*, Virtual Territoriality, Columbia Journal of Transnational Law (Colum. J. Transnat'l L.) 48 (2010), p 401 ff;

*Jault-Seseke, Fabienne/Robine, David*, Le règlement 2015/848: le vin nouveau et les vieilles outres, Revue critique de droit international privé 2016, p 21 ff;

*Kamalnath, Akshaya*, Cross-Border Insolvency Protocols: A Success Story?, International Journal of Legal Studies and Research (IJLSR) 2 (2013), p 172 ff;

*Kindler, Peter/Sakka, Sami*, Die Neufassung der europäischen Insolvenzordnung, Europäische Zeitschrift für Wirtschaftsrecht (EuZW) 12 (2015), p 460 ff;

*Kindler, Peter*, Insolvenzrecht: Zuständigkeit nach EuInsVO für Klagen gegen Geschäftsführer nach § 64 GmbHG, Europäische Zeitschrift für Wirtschaftsrecht (EuZW) 4 (2015), p 141 ff;

*Kindler, Peter*, Insolvenzrecht als Tätigkeitsausübungsregel – Die sachliche Reichweite der Niederlassungsfreiheit nach dem Kornhaas-Urteil des EuGH, Europäische Zeitschrift für Wirtschaftsrecht (EuZW) 4 (2016), p 136 ff;

*Kirchhof, Hans-Peter/Stürner, Rolf/Eidenmüller, Horst* (eds), Münchener Kommentar zur Insolvenzordnung, Vol. 4, 3rd edn, Munich 2016;

*Koller, Christian*, Zielkonflikt im Europäischen Insolvenzrecht: Präventive Sanierung versus territoriale Liquidation, Praxis des Internationalen Privat- und Verfahrensrechts (IPRax) 2014, p 490 ff;

*Konecny, Andreas*, Thesen zum Mittelpunkt der hauptsächlichen Schuldnerinteressen gem art 3 Abs 1 EuInsVO, Zeitschrift für Insolvenzrecht und Kreditschutz (ZIK) 2005, p 2 ff;

*Kuipers, Jan-Jaap*, Schemes of arrangement and voluntary collective redress: a gap in the Brussels I Regulation, Journal of Private International Law (J.Priv.Int.L.) 8 (2012), p 225 ff;

*Latella, Dario*, The "COMI" Concept in the Revision of the European Insolvency Regulation, European Company and Financial Law Review (ECFR) 11 (2015), p 479 ff;

*Laukemann, Björn*, Präventive Schutzverfahren im Spannungsfeld von Universalität und Territorialität, ecolex 2013, p 373 ff;

*Laukemann, Björn*, Avoidance actions against third state defendants: jurisdictional justice or curtailment of legal protection? European Court of Justice 16 January 2014, Case C-328/12 – Schmid/Hertel, International Insolvency Law Review (IILR) 2 (2014), p 101 ff;

*Laukemann, Björn*, Regulatory copy and paste: The allocation of assets in cross-border insolvencies – methodological perspectives from the Nortel decision, Journal of Private International Law (J.Priv.Int.L.) 12 (2016), p 379 ff;

*Leandro, Antonio*, Amending the European Insolvency Regulation to strengthen main proceedings, Rivista di diritto internazionale privato e processuale (Riv. dir. intern. priv. e proc.) 2014, p 317 ff;

*Leandro, Antonio*, A First Critical Appraisal of The New European Insolvency Regulation, Il Diritto dell'Unione Europea (dUE) 2 (2016), p 215 ff;

*Legrand, Véronique*, Le nouveau règlement européen relative aux procédures d'insolvabilité transfrontalières: premier aperçu, in: Petites affiches 22 janvier 2015, N° 16, p 8 ff;

*Leible, Stefan/Reichert, Jochem* (eds), Münchener Handbuch des Gesellschaftsrechts, VI, Munich 2013;

*Lener, Raffaele/Rosato, Giovanna*, in: Leonard, Bruce (ed), Restructuring & Insolvency, London 2015, p 226 ff, this statement is also available at: https://gettingthedealthrough.com/area/35/jurisdiction/15/restructuring-insolvency-2016-italy;

*Linna, Tuula*, Cross-Border Debt Adjustment – Open Questions in European Insolvency Proceedings, International Insolvency Review (Int. Insolv. Rev.) 23 (2014), p 20 ff;

*Linna, Tuula*, Actio pauliana and res judicata in EU insolvency proceedings, Journal of Private International Law (J.Priv.Int.L.) 11 (2015), p 568 ff;

*MacCormick, Neil*, Legal Reasoning and Legal Theory, Oxford 2003;

*Madaus, Stephan,* Insolvency proceedings for corporate groups under the new Insolvency Regulation, International Insolvency Law Review (IILR) 3 (2015), p 235 ff;

*Madaus, Stephan,* As simple as it can be? – Anregungen zum Gesetzentwurf der Bundesregierung zur Durchführung der Verordnung (EU) 2015/848 über Insolvenzverfahren (BT-Drs. 18/10823), Neue Zeitschrift für Insolvenz- und Sanierungsrecht (NZI) 2017, p 203 ff;

*Madaus, Stephan,* Die Zusicherung nach Art. 36 EuInsVO – Das Ende virtueller Sekundärinsolvenzverfahren?, in: Kayser, Godehard/Smid, Stefan/Riedemann, Susanne (eds), Festschrift für Klaus Pannen zum 65. Geburtstag, Munich 2017, p 223 ff;

*Magnus, Robert,* Anwendbarkeit der Europäischen Insolvenzverordnung auf die Haftung eines Geschäftsführers für Zahlungen in der Krise – Anmerkung zu EuGH, Urteil vom 04. Dezember 2014, C-295/13 „H/H.K.", Lindenmaier-Möhring-Kommentierte BGH-Rechtsprechung (LMK) 2015, 366550;

*Mankowski, Peter,* Zuständigkeit des Insolvenzgerichts am Sitz der Konzernmutter bei Leitung der Verwaltung der Schuldnerin – Hettlage, Anmerkung zu AG München, Beschluss vom 4. 5. 2004 – 1501 IE 1276/04, Neue Zeitschrift für Insolvenz- und Sanierungsrecht (NZI) 8 (2004), p 450 ff;

*Mankowski, Peter,* Kurzkommentar zu AG Siegen 1.7.2004 – 25 IN 154/04 (NZI) 2004, 673), Entscheidungen zum Wirtschaftsrecht (EWiR) 4 (2005), p 175 ff;

*Mankowski, Peter,* Zulässigkeit von Sonderzahlungen zur Vermeidung eines Sekundärinsolvenzverfahrens – MG Rover – Anmerkung zu High Court of Justice Birmingham, Beschluß vom 30. 3. 2006 – No. 2377/2006, Neue Zeitschrift für Insolvenz- und Sanierungsrecht (NZI) 7 (2006), p 416 ff;

*Mankowski, Peter,* EuGH: „Enger Zusammenhang" zwischen Zivilklage und Konkursverfahren – Anerkennung von Entscheidungen eines anderen Mitgliedstaats, Anmerkung zu EuGH, 2 July 2009 – C-111/08 (SCT Industri AB i likvidation/Alpenblume AB), Neue Zeitschrift für Insolvenz- und Sanierungsrecht (NZI) 10 (2009), p 570 ff;

*Mankowski, Peter,* EuGH: Antragsbefugnis für die Eröffnung eines Sekundärinsolvenzverfahrens, Anmerkung zu EuGH, Urteil vom 4.9.2014 – C-327/13 (Burgo Group SpA/Illochroma SA in Liquidation), Neue Zeitschrift für Insolvenz- und Sanierungsrecht (NZI) 22 (2014), p 964 ff;

*Mankowski, Peter,* Zusicherungen zur Vermeidung von Sekundärinsolvenzen unter Art. 36 EuInsVO – Systhetische Sekundärverfahren, Neue Zeitschrift für das Recht der Insolvenz und Sanierung (NZI) 23 (2015), p 961 ff;

*Mankowski, Peter/Müller, Michael/Schmidt, Jessica,* EuInsVO 2015, Munich 2016;

*Mankowski, Peter,* Insolvenzrecht gegen Gesellschaftsrecht 2:0 im europäischen Spiel um § 64 GmbHG – Anmerkung zu EuGH, NZG 2016, 115 – Kornhaas, Neue Zeitschrift für Gesellschaftsrecht (NZG) 8 (2016), p 281 ff;

*Mankowski, Peter,* The European World of Insolvency Tourism: Renewed, But Still Brave?, Netherlands International Law Review (NILR) 64 (2017), p 95 ff;

*Martínez Casado, Valentin,* El tratamiento de la insolvencia de un grupo de sociedades francés implantado en España, Anuario de Derecho Concursal, 21/2010, p 235 ff;

*Martins Costa, Cintia/Richter, Dirk/Gerber-Lemaire, Martine/Marchand, Aurore,* Regulation No. 1346/2000 on insolvency proceedings: The difficult COMI determination, the treatment of groups of companies and forum shopping in light of the CJEU's and domestic case law, and the modernization of the Regulation, ALJB Droit bancaire et financier au Luxembourg 2014, p 3281 ff;

*McCormack, Gerard,* Jurisdictional Competition and Forum Shopping in Insolvency Proceedings, Cambridge Law Journal (CLJ) 68 (2009), p 169 ff;

*McCormack, Gerard,* Reconstructing European insolvency law – putting in place a new paradigm, Legal Studies (LS) 30 (2010), p 126 ff;

*McCormack, Gerard,* Reforming The European Insolvency Regulation: A Legal And Policy Perspective, Journal of Private International Law (J.Priv.Int.L.) 10 (2014), p 41 ff;

*McCormack, Gerard,* Something Old, Something New: Recasting the European Insolvency Regulation, The Modern Law Review (MLR) 79 (2016), p 121 ff;

*McCormack, Gerard/Keay, Andrew/Brown, Sarah,* European Insolvency Law: Reform and Harmonization, Cheltenham 2017;

*Mendiola, Elisa Torralba,* 'Synthetic' insolvency proceedings, November 2015, available at: http://www.gomezacebo-pombo.com/media/k2/attachments/synthetic-insolvency-proceedings.pdf;

*Mevorach, Irit,* The Road to a Suitable and Comprehensive Global Approach to Insolvencies Within Multinational Corporate Groups, Norton Journal of Bankruptcy Law and Practice (Norton J. Bankr. L. & Prac.) 15 (2006), p 455 ff;

*Mevorach, Irit,* The Home Country of a Multinational Enterprise Group Facing Insolvency, International and Comparative Law Quarterly (ICLQ) 57 (2008), p 427 ff;

*Mevorach, Irit,* Insolvency within Multinational Enterprise Groups, Oxford 2009;

*Mevorach, Irit,* Jurisdiction in Insolvency: A Study of European Courts' Decision, Journal of Private International Law (J.Priv.Int.L.) 6 (2010), p 327 ff;

*Mevorach, Irit,* Enterprise Groups in Insolvency, Recent International Developments, in: Sarra, Janis P./Romaine, Barbara (eds), Annual Review of Insolvency Law, Toronto 2013, p 285 ff;

*Mevorach, Irit,* Forum shopping in times of crisis: a directors' duties perspective, European Company and Financial Law Review (ECFR) 10 (2013), p 523 ff;

*Mevorach, Irit,* Cross-border insolvency of enterprise groups: the choice of law challenge, Brooklyn Journal of Corporate, Financial and Commerical Law (Brook.J.Corp.Fi.&Com.L.) 9 (2014), p 226 ff;

*Mnookin, Robert H./Kornhauser, Lewis,* Bargaining in the Shadow of the Law: The Case of Divorce, The Yale Law Journal (Yale L.J.) 88 (1979), p 950 ff;

*Mock, Sebastian,* Das (geplante) neue europäische Insolvenzrecht nach dem Vorschlag der Kommission zur Reform der EuInsVO, Zeitschrift für das Privatrecht der Europäischen Union (GPR) 3 (2013), p 156 ff;

*Monsèrié-Bon,* Commentaire de l'article 1er, in Règlement (UE) n°2015/848 du 20 mai 2015 relatif aux procédures d'insolvabilité, Commentaire article par article, 2015, p 35 ff;

*Moss, Gabriel/Paulus, Christoph G.*, The European Insolvency Regulation – the case for urgent reform, Insolvency Intelligence (Insolv. Int.) 19 (2006), p 1 ff;

*Moss, Gabriel*, Group Insolvency – Choice of Forum and Law: The European Experience under the Influence of English Pragmatism. (Symposium: Bankruptcy in the Global Village the Second Decade), Brooklyn Journal of International Law (Brook J Int'l L) 32 (2007), p 1005 ff;

*Moss, Gabriel*, Group Insolvency – Forum – EC Regulation and Model Law Under the Influence of English Pragmatism Revisited, Brooklyn Journal of Corporate, Financial and Commercial Law (Brook. J. Corp. Fin. & Com. L.) 9 (2014), p 250 ff;

*Moss, Gabriel*, ECJ takes worldwide jurisdiction, Insolvency Intelligence (Insolv. Int.) 28 (2015), p 6 ff;

*Moss Gabriel/Fletcher, Ian/Isaacs, Stuart* (eds), The EU Regulation on Insolvency Proceedings, 3rd edn, Oxford 2016;

*Mucciarelli, Federico*, Not just efficiency: insolvency law in the EU and its political dimension, European Business Organization Law Review (EBOR) 14 (2013), p 175 ff;

*Mucciarelli, Federico*, Private international law rules in the Insolvency Regulation Recast: a reform or a restatement of the *status quo?*, European Company and Financial Law Review (ECFR) 13 (2016), p 1 ff;

*Mucciarelli, Federico*, Procedure concorsuali secondary, localizzazione dei beni del debitore e protezione di interessi locali, Giurisprudenza commerciale (Giur. comm.) 2016, p 13 ff;

*Muzsalyi, Robert*, Directors' Liability: What Should Be the Minimum Degree of Harmonisation in the EU? (October 2016), available at: https://ssrn.com/abstract=2914600;

*Oberhammer, Paul*, Im Holz sind Wege: EuGH SCT./. Alpenblume und der Insolvenztatbestand des Art. 1 Abs. 2 lit. b) EUGVVO, Praxis des Internationalen Privat- und Verfahrensrechts (IPRax) 4 (2010), p 318 ff;

*Omar, Paul*, Communication and co-operation between insolvency courts and personnel, International Company and Commercial Law Review (ICCLR) 17 (2006), p 120 ff;

*Omar, Paul*, Addressing the reform of the Insolvency Regulation: wishlist or fancies?, Insolvency Intelligence (Insolv. Int.) 20 (2007), p 7 ff;

*Pannen, Klaus/Riedemann, Susanne*, Der Begriff des „centre of main interests" i.S. des Art. 3 I 1 EuInsVO im Spiegel aktueller Fälle aus der Rechtsprechung, Neue Zeitschrift für Insolvenz- und Sanierungsrecht (NZI) 12 (2004), p 646 ff;

*Pannen, Klaus* (ed), European Insolvency Regulation, Berlin 2007;

*Panzani, Luciano,* Scope of application of the Council Regulation 1346/2000, available at: iiiglobal.org;

*Paulus, Christoph G.*, Die europäische Insolvenzverordnung und der deutsche Insolvenzverwalter, Neue Zeitschrift für Insolvenz- und Sanierungsrecht (NZI) 10 (2001), p 505 ff;

*Paulus, Christoph G.*, Überlegungen zu einem modernen Konzerninsolvenzrecht, Zeitschrift für Wirtschaftsrecht (ZIP) 44 (2005), p 1948 ff;

*Paulus, Christoph G.,* Die ersten Jahre mit der Europäischen Insolvenzverordnung, Erfahrungen und Erwartungen, Rabels Zeitschrift für ausländisches und internationales Privatrecht (RabelsZ) 70 (2006), p 458 ff;

*Paulus, Christoph G.,* Die EuInsVO – wo geht die Reise hin?, Neue Zeitschrift für Insolvenz- und Sanierungsrecht (NZI) 1 (2008), p 1 ff;

*Paulus, Christoph G.,* Europäische Insolvenzverordnung, 4rd edn, Frankfurt on the Main 2013;

*Paulus, Christoph G.,* Internationales Restrukturierungsrecht, Recht der Internationalen Wirtschaft (RIW) 9 (2013), p 577 ff;

*Paulus, Christoph G.,* The ECJ's understanding of the universality principle, Insolvency Intelligence (Insolv. Int.) 27 (2014), p 70 ff;

*Payne, Jennifer,* Cross-Border Schemes of Arrangement and Forum Shopping, Oxford Legal Studies Research Paper No. 68/2013;

*Penzlin, Dietmar/ Riedemann, Susanne,* Bestimmung des Mittelpunkts der hauptsächlichen Interessen des Schuldners – MG Rover – Anmerkung zu High Court of Justice Birmingham, Beschluß vom 18. 4. 2005, Neue Zeitschrift für Insolvenz- und Sanierungsrecht (NZI) 8 (2005), p 467 ff;

*Penzlin, Dietmar,* Kurzkommentar zu Tribunal de Commerce de Nanterre, Urt. v. 15.2.2006 – PCL 2006J00174, Entscheidungen zum Wirtschaftsrecht (EWiR) 7 (2006), p 207 ff;

*Piekenbrock, Andreas,* Das Europäische Insolvenzrecht im Umbruch, Kölner Schrift zum Wirtschaftsrecht (KSzW) 3 (2015), p 191 ff;

*Pluta, Michael/Keller, Christoph,* Das virtuelle Sekundärinsolvenzverfahren nach der reformierten Europäischen Insolvenzverordnung, in: Graf-Schlicker, Marie Luise/ Prütting, Hanns/Uhlenbruck, Wilhelm (eds), Festschrift für Heinz Vallender zum 65. Geburtstag, Cologne 2015, p 437 ff;

*Poertzgen, Christoph/Adam, Dietmar,* Die Bestimmung des ›centre of main interests‹ gem. Art. 3 Abs. 1 EuInsVO, Zeitschrift für das gesamte Insolvenzrecht (ZInsO) 10 (2006), p 505 ff;

*Pound, Roscoe,* The future of the Common Law, Harvard 1937;

*Prager, Martin/Keller, Christoph,* Der Entwicklungsstand des Europäischen Insolvenzrechts, Zeitschrift für Wirtschafts- und Bankenrecht, Wertpapier-Mitteilungen (WM) 17 (2015), p 805 ff;

*Raykin, Alla/Wouters, Nora,* Corporate group cross-border between the United States & European Union: Legal & economic developments, Emory Bankruptcy Developments Journal (EBDJ) 29 (2013), p 387 ff;

*Reumers, Michele,* Cooperation between Liquidators and Courts in Insolvency Proceedings of Related Companies under the Proposed Revised EIR, European Company and Financial Law Review (ECFR) 10 (2013), p 554 ff;

*Reumers, Michele,* What is in a Name? Group Coordination or Consolidation Plan — What is Allowed Under the EIR Recast?, International Insolvency Review (Int.Insolv.Rev.) 25 (2016), p 225 ff;

*Reuß, Philipp M.,* „Forum Shopping" in der Insolvenz, Tübingen 2011;

*Ringe, Wolf-Georg*, Forum Shopping Under the EU Insolvency Regulation, European Business Organization Law Review (EBOR) 9 (2008), p 579 ff;

*Ringe, Wolf-Georg*, Haftung des "Director" einer englischen "Limited" gemäß § 64 GmbHG (Anmerkung zu EuGH Urt. vom 10.12.2015 – Rs C-594/14, Kornhaas), Juristen Zeitung (JZ) 71 (2016), p 573 ff;

*Santen, Bernard*, Communication and cooperation in international insolvency: on best practices for insolvency office holders and cross-border communication between courts, 16 ERA Forum (2015), p 229 ff;

*Schall, Alexander*, Das Kornhaas-Urteil gibt grünes Licht für die Anwendung des § 64 GmbHG auf eine Limited mit Sitz in Deutschland – Alles klar dank EuGH! – Zugleich Besprechung EuGH v. 10. 12. 2015 – Rs C-594/14, ZIP 2015, 2468 – Kornhaas, Zeitschrift für Wirtschaftsrecht (ZIP) 7 (2016), p 289 ff;

*Schmidt, Jessica*, Das Prinzip "eine Person, ein Vermögen, eine Insolvenz" und seine Durchbrechungen vor dem Hintergrund der aktuellen Reformen im europäischen und deutschen Recht, Zeitschrift für Insolvenzrecht (KTS) 1 (2015), p 19 ff;

*Schmidt, Jessica*, Group insolvencies under the EIR recast, eurofenix Autumn 2015, p 17 ff;

*Schmidt, Jessica*, The Opt-out and opt-in rules for group coordination proceedings in the EIR: a critical evaluation and focus on large-scale insolvencies, in: Parry, Rebecca/Omar, Paul J. (eds), Banking and financial insolvencies: the European regulatory framework, Nottingham 2016, p 87 ff;

*Schmidt, Jessica*, Opt-out und Opt-in in Gruppen-Koordinationsverfahren nach der EuInsVO 2015, Zeitschrift für Vergleichende Rechtswissenschaft (ZVglRWiss) 116 (2017), p 93 ff;

*Schmidt, Karsten* (ed), Insolvenzordnung: mit EuInsVO, 19th edn, Munich 2016;

*Schulz, Patrick*, Bestimmung des COMI von Gesellschaften eines internationalen Reederei-Konzerns – Anmerkung zu High Court London, Entsch. vom 22.1.2015 – 2015 EWHC 121 (Ch) (Re Northsea Base Investment), Neue Zeitschrift für Insolvenz- und Sanierungsrecht (NZI) 8 (2015), p 338 ff;

*Schulz, Patrick*, Die Bestimmung des COMI nach Art. 3 EuInsVO aF bei Immobilien-SPV – Anmerkung zu High Court London, Entsch. vom 17.1.2017 – 2017 EWHC 25 (CH) (Re Frogmore Real Estate Partners), Neue Zeitschrift für Insolvenz- und Sanierungsrecht (NZI) 5 (2017), p 142 ff;

*Skauradszun, Dominik*, Die 'tatsächlichen Annahmen' der Zusicherung nach Art. 36 Abs. 1 Satz 2 EuInsVO n.F., Zeitschrift für Wirtschaftsrecht (ZIP) 33 (2016), p 1563 ff;

*Skauradszun, Dominik*, Einstweilige Maßnahmen und Sicherungsmaßnahmen nach Art. 36 Abs. 9 EuInsVO n.F., Zeitschrift für Insolvenzrecht (KTS) 2016, p 419 ff;

*Slaughter, Anne-Marie*, A Global Community of Courts, Harvard International Law Journal (Harv. Int'l L.J.) 44 (2003), p 191 ff, available at: http://www.europarl.europa.eu/document/activities/cont/201212/20121219AT-T58300/20121219ATT58300EN.pdf;

*Stadler, Astrid*, International Jurisdiction under the Regulation 1346/2000/EC on Insolvency Proceedings, in: Stürner, Rolf/Kawano, Masanori (eds), Cross Border Insolvency, Intellectual Property Litigation, Arbitration and Ordre Public, Tübingen 2011, p 13 ff;

*Steffek, Felix*, Insolvenz und Sanierung deutscher Unternehmen in England, in: Leible, Stefan/Reichert, Jochem (eds), Münchener Handbuch des Gesellschaftsrechts, Vol. 6, 4th edn, Munich 2013, p 755 ff;

*Szydlo, Marek*, Prevention of Forum Shopping in European Insolvency Law, European Business Organization Law Review (EBOR) 11 (2010), p 253 ff;

*Szirányi, Pal*, EU-wide Interconnection of Insolvency Registers, in: Parry, Rebecca/ Omar, Paul J. (eds), Reimagining Rescue, Nottingham 2016, p 27 ff;

*Tabb, Charles Jordan*, Law of Bankruptcy, 4th edn, St. Paul 2016, p 475;

*Terranova, Giuseppe*, Elogio dell'approssimazione. Il diritto come esperienza comunicativa, Pisa 2015;

*Thole, Christoph*, Gläubigerschutz durch Insolvenzrecht, Tübingen 2010;

*Thole, Christoph*, Vom Totengräber zum Heilsbringer – Insolvenzkultur und Insolvenzrecht im Wandel, Juristenzeitung (JZ) 15/16 (2011), p 765 ff;

*Thole, Christoph/Swierczok, Arthur*, Der Kommissionsvorschlag zur Reform der EuInsVO, Zeitschrift für Wirtschaftsrecht (ZIP) 12 (2013), p 550 ff;

*Thole, Christoph*, Die Reform der Europäischen Insolvenzverordnung – Zentrale Aspekte des Kommissionsvorschlags und offene Fragen, Zeitschrift für Europäisches Privatrecht (ZEuP) 1 (2014), p 39 ff;

*Thole, Christoph/Dueñas, Manuel*, Some Observations on the New Group Coordination Procedure of the Reformed European Insolvency Regulation, International Insolvency Review (Int. Insolv. Rev.) 24 (2015), p 214 ff;

*Trenker, Martin*, Anwendung der EuInsVO auf Organhaftungsansprüche wegen Gläubigerbevorzugung – Anmerkungen zu EuGH C-295/13 H/H.K., Zeitschrift für Insolvenzrecht und Kreditschutz (ZIK) 2015, p 8 ff;

*Undritz, Sven-Holger*; Sekundärinsolvenzverfahren nach der Europäischen Insolvenzverordnung – Eine Geschichte von „loyalen Dienern", „Störenfrieden" und „virtuellen Welten", in: Graf-Schlicker, Marie Luise/Prütting, Hanns/Uhlenbruck, Wilhelm (eds), Festschrift für Heinz Vallender zum 65. Geburtstag, Cologne 2015, p 745 ff;

*Vaccarella, Romano*, Recognition in Italy of an English Order endorsing an agreement between a company and its creditors. Parere *pro veritate*, Corriere trimestrale della litigation internazionale (Int'l Lis) 2014, p 52 ff;

*Valiante, Diego*, Harmonising insolvency laws in the Euro Area: rationale, stock-taking and challenges. What role for the Eurogroup, Study prepared for the EU Parliament (2016), p 15;

*Vallender, Heinz*, Europaparlament gibt den Weg frei für eine neue Europäische Insolvenzverordnung, Zeitschrift für Wirtschaftsrecht (ZIP) 32 (2015), p 1513 ff;

*Vallens, Jean-Luc*, Réviser le règlement communautaire CE 1346/2000 sur les procédures d'insolvabilité, Revue des procédures collectives (Rev. proc. coll.) 2010, p 25 ff;

*Van Calster*, Geert, COMIng, and here to stay. The Review of the European Insolvency Regulation, available at: papers.ssrn.com, 2016;

*Van Galen, Robert*, The Recast Insolvency Regulation and groups of companies, ERA Forum (2015) 16:241;

*Virgós, Miguel/Schmit, Etienne*, Report on the Convention on Insolvency Proceedings (1996), Council of the EU Document, available at: http://aei.pitt.edu/952;

*Virgós, Miguel/Garcimartín, Francisco Javier*, The European Insolvency Regulation: Law and practice, The Hague 2004;

*Wautelet, Patrick R.*, Insolvabilité européenne et procédures secondaires (June 8, 2015), available at SSRN: http://dx.doi.org/10.2139/ssrn.2687625;

*de Weijs, Rolef J./Breeman, Martijn,* Comi-migration: Use or Abuse of European Insolvency Law?, European Company and Financial Law Review (ECFR) 4 (2014), p 495 ff;

*Weiss, Michael,* Bridge over Troubled Water: The Revised Insolvency Regulation, International Insolvency Review (Int. Insolv. Rev.) 24 (2015), p 192 ff;

*Wessels, Bob/Markell, Bruce A./Kilborn, Jason*, International Cooperation in Bankruptcy and Insolvency Matters, Oxford 2009;

*Wessels, Bob*, The role of courts in solving cross-border insolvency cases, Insolvency Intelligence (Insolv. Int.) 24 (2011), p 65 ff;

*Wessels, Bob*, Cross-border insolvency agreements: what are they and are they here to stay?, in: Prof. mr. N.E.D. Faber, Prof. mr. J.J. van Hees, Mr. N.S.G.J. Vermunt, Overeenkomsten en insolventie, Deventer 2012, p 359 ff;

*Wessels, Bob*, International Insolvency Law, 3rd edn, Deventer 2012;

*Wessels, Bob*, Contracting Out of Secondary Insolvency Proceedings: The Main Liquidator's Undertaking in the meaning of Article 18 in the Proposal to Amend the EU Insolvency Regulation, Brooklyn Journal of Corporate Financial and Commercial Law (Brook.J.Corp.Fi.&Com.L.) 9 (2014), p 63 ff;

*Wessels, Bob*, Themes of the future: rescue businesses and cross-border cooperation, Insolvency Intelligence (Insolv. Int.) 27 (2014), p 4 ff;

*Wessels, Bob*, Towards a next step in cross-border judicial cooperation, Insolvency Intelligence (Insolv. Int.) 27 (2014), p 100 ff;

*Wessels, Bob* (ed), EU Cross-Border Insolvency Court-to-Court Cooperation Principles, Hague 2015;

*Wessels, Bob*, CJEU Case Note: CJEU 10 December 2015, C-594/14 (Kornhaas v. Dithmar), European Company Law (ECL) 13 (2016), p 82 ff;

*Wessels, Bob*, The European Union Regulation on Insolvency Proceedings (Recast): The First Commentaries, European Company Law (ECL) 13 (2016), p 129 ff;

*Wimmer, Klaus*, "Übersicht zur Neufassung der EuInsVO", juris-PR InsR 7/2015, Anm. 1, II 7b;

*Wimmer, Klaus /Bornemann, Alexander /Lienau, Marc D.*, Die Neufassung der EuInsVO, Cologne 2016;

*Wimmer, Klaus*, Die Regelungen zu den synthetischen Sekundarinsolvenzverfahren in der Neufassung der EuInsVO, in: Exner, Joachim/Paulus, Christoph G. (eds), Festschrift für Siegfried Beck zum 70. Geburtstag, Munich 2016, p 587 ff;

*Wimmer, Klaus*, Das Gesetz zur Durchführung der Verordnung (EU) 2015/848 über Insolvenzverfahren, jurisPR-InsR 11/2017 Anm. 1;

*Wolf, Ulrich M.,* Der europäische Gerichtsstand bei Konzerninsolvenzen, Tübingen 2012;

*Wright, David /Fenwick, Sam*, Bankruptcy tourism – what it is, how it works and how creditors can fight back, International Insolvency Law Review (IILR) 1 (2012), p 45 ff;

*Zumbro, Paul H.*, Cross-border insolvencies and international protocols, Business Law International (Bus. L. Int'l) 11 (2010), p 157 ff;

*Zweigert, Konrad/Kötz, Hein*, Einführung in die Rechtsvergleichung: Auf dem Gebiet des Privatrechts, 3$^{rd}$ edn, Tübingen 1996;

## 4. Legal texts

Beschlussempfehlung und Bericht des Ausschusses für Recht und Verbraucherschutz (6. Ausschuss) zu dem Gesetzentwurf der Bundesregierung zur Durchführung der Verordnung (EU) 2015/848 über Insolvenzverfahren (26 April 2017), Bundestagsdrucksache 18/12154, available at: http://dip21.bundestag.de/dip21/btd/18/121/181 2154.pdf;

Commission Recommendation of 12 March 2014 on a new approach to business failure and insolvency, COM (2014) 1500;

Commission Staff Working Document – Impact Assessment accompanying the document Revision of Regulation (EC) No. 1346/2000 on insolvency proceedings SWD(2012) 416 final;

Convention on Insolvency Proceedings of 23 November 1995, printed in http://aei.pitt.edu/2840;

Council of the European Union, Proposal for a Regulation of the European Parliament and of the Council amending Council Regulation (EC) No 1346/2000 on insolvency proceedings – Groups of Companies/Note from the French and German delegations, 4 et seq, available at http://data.consilium.europa.eu/doc/document/ ST-8108-2013-INIT/en/pdf;

Council Regulation (EC) No 44/2001 of 22 December 2000 on jurisdiction and the recognition and enforcement of judgments in civil and commercial matters;

Directive 2009/138/EC of the European Parliament and of the Council of 25 November 2009 on the taking-up and pursuit of the business of Insurance and Reinsurance (Solvency II), OJ 2009 L 335/1;

Directive 2013/34/EU of the European Parliament and of the Council of 26 June 2013
on the annual financial statements, consolidated financial statements and related reports of certain types of undertakings, amending Directive 2006/43/EC of the European Parliament and of the Council and repealin g Council Directives 78/660/EEC
and 83/349/EEC, OJ 2013, L 182/19;

Directive 2014/65/EU of the European Parliament and of the Council of 15 May 2014
on markets in financial instruments and amending Directive 2002/92/EC and Directive 2011/61/EU, OJ L173, 12 June 2014;

Draft European Parliament legislative resolution on the proposal for a regulation of the
European Parliament and of the Council replacing the lists of insolvency proceedings and insolvency practitioners in Annexes A and B to Regulation (EU) 2015/848
on insolvency proceedings, COM(2016)0317 – C8-0196/2016 – 2016/0159(COD);

Entwurf eines Gesetzes zur Durchführung der Verordnung (EU) 2015/848 über Insolvenzverfahren (11 January 2017), Bundestagsdrucksache 18/10823), available at:
http://dip21.bundestag.de/dip21/btd/18/108/1810823.pdf. (last visited 24 January
2017);

Impact assessment accompanying the document Commission Recommendation on a
New Approach to Business Failure and Insolvency;

Ley 14/2013, de 27 de septiembre, de apoyo a los emprendedores y su internacionalización;

Ley 17/2014, de 30 de septiembre, por la que se adoptan medidas urgentes en materia
de refinanciación y reestructuración de deuda empresarial;

Ley 22/2003, de 9 de julio, Concursal;

Proposal for a Directive of the European Parliament and of the Council on preventive
restructuring frameworks, second chance and measures to increase the efficiency of
restructuring, insolvency and discharge procedures and amending Directive
2012/30/EU/* COM/2016/0723 final – 2016/0359 (COD);

Proposal for a Regulation of the European Parliament and of the Council amending
Council Regulation (EC) No 1346/2000 on insolvency proceedings /* COM/
2012/0744 final – 2012/0360 (COD);

Proposal for a Regulation of the European Parliament and of the Council amending
Council Regulation (EC) No 1346/2000 on insolvency proceedings /* COM/
2012/0744 final – 2012/0360 (COD)

Regulation (EU) No 1215/2012 of the European Parliament and of the Council of 12
December 2012 on jurisdiction and the recognition and enforcement of judgments
in civil and commercial matters (recast);

## 5. Other

ALI Guidelines for Court-to-Court Communications in Cross-Border Cases (2000);

ALI III Global Principles for the Cooperation in International Insolvency Cases
(2009);

*Bariatti, Stefania,* The Extension of the Scope of the EIR, in EU Project 'Implementation of the New Insolvency Regulation': Kick-off conference' (paper drafted for the conference which took place in Vienna on 17 April 2015)

City of London Law Society (CLLS), Response to Proposed changes to the European Insolvency Regulation: Call for Evidence, https://www.gov.uk/government/uploads/system/uploads/attachment_data/file/279289/insolvency-lawyers-association-evidence.pdf, 25 February 2013;

Cross-Border Insolvency Court-to-Court Cooperation Principles and Guidelines 2014 ("EU JudgeCo Principles");

Draft INSOL Europe Statement of Principles and Guidelines for Insolvency Office Holders in Europe 2014;

European Parliament- DG for Internal Policies, Study on A European Framework for Private International Law: Current Gaps and Future Perspectives, 2012;

European Parliament, Report with recommendations to the Commission on insolvency proceedings in the context of EU company law (2011/2006(INI)), 17.10.2011;

Report from the Commission to the European Parliament, the Council and the European Economic and Social Committee on the application of Council Regulation (EC) No 1346/2000 of 29 May 2000 on insolvency proceedings, COM(2012)0744 – C7-0413/2012 – 2012/0360(COD);

Report on the Convention of 9 October 1978 on the Accession of the Kingdom of Denmark, Ireland and the United Kingdom of Great Britain and Northern Ireland to the Brussels Convention and to the Protocol on its interpretation by the Court of Justice);

Revision of the European Insolvency Regulation – Proposal by INSOL Europe, June 2012;

Study on a new approach to business failure and insolvency – Comparative legal analysis of the Member States' relevant provisions and practices' of 12 May 2014 (TENDER NO. JUST/2012/JCIV/CT/0194/A4);

The European Communication and Cooperation Guidelines for Cross- border Insolvency (2007) (the 'CoCo Guidelines');

The World Bank, Doing Business, Washington 2010, p 77 ff;

UNCITRAL Legislative Guide on Insolvency Law, Part Three: Treatment of Enterprise Groups in Insolvency (United Nations, New York, 2012);

UNCITRAL Model Law on Cross-Border Insolvency with Guide to Enactment and Interpretation, 2014;

UNCITRAL Practice Guide on Cross-Border Insolvency Cooperation (2009);

UNIDROIT Convention on International Interests in Mobile Equipment (2001), available at: http://www.unidroit.org/instruments/security-interests/cape-town-convention, and the protocols are available at: http://www.unidroit.org/instruments/security-interests/aircraft-protocol; http://www.unidroit.org/ instruments/ security-interests/ rail-protocol; http://www.unidroit.org/instruments/security-interests/space-protocol;